Water for Gotham

Water

for Gotham

A History

Gerard T. Koeppel

Princeton University Press
Princeton, New Jersey

Published by Princeton University Press, 41 William Street, Princeton, New Jersey 08540
In the United Kingdom: Princeton University Press, Chichester, West Sussex

Library of Congress Cataloging-in-Publication Data

Koeppel, Gerard T., 1957–
    Water for Gotham : a history / Gerard T. Koeppel.
        p.   cm.
    Includes bibliographical references and index.
    ISBN 0-691-01139-7 (alk. paper)
    1. Water-supply—New York (State)—New York—History.   2. Water-supply
engineering—New York (State)—New York—History.   3. Croton Aqueduct
(N.Y.)—History.   I. Title.
TD225.N5 K64   2000
363.6′1′097471—dc21   99-056626

This book has been composed in Adobe Minion by Princeton Editorial Associates, Inc.,
Roosevelt, New Jersey, and Scottsdale, Arizona

The paper used in this publication meets the requirements of ANSI/NISO Z39.48-1992
(R1997) (*Permanence of Paper*)

www.pup.princeton.edu

Printed in the United States of America

10 9 8 7 6 5 4 3 2 1

Frontispiece: Union Square, circa 1848. In this lithograph featuring the Croton fountain at Union Square, the octagonal 13th Street Reservoir building is shown one block south and east of the square. (I. N. Phelps Stokes Collection. Miriam and Ira D. Wallach Division of Art, Prints and Photographs. The New York Public Library. Astor, Lenox and Tilden Foundations.)

For Diane, Jackson, Harry, and Kate

Contents

Illustrations

Cities, like other living things, need water to survive, and even more water to flourish. As they grow, they grow thirstier, and the thirst must be quenched—usually from rivers far beyond their limits.

New York City, confined to southern Manhattan during its first two centuries, was no exception. But it would take generations of foul wells, epic filth, epidemic disease, devastating fires, confounding politics, the suppression of public interest by private intrigue, and technological uncertainty before the thirst of the narrow, salt-ringed island was slaked.

Water is taken for granted by modern city dwellers, who turn on a tap not knowing or caring how the water got there. I was the same way, until a chance encounter with the plaza fountains of New York's Seagram Building, the bronze and glass icon of modernity on Park Avenue. On a stifling July day, I paused for a moment beside the broad, shallow basins, water jets rising high from the centers and cascading down. A fine, cool mist spread rainbows around me, and the heat and the noise of the city melted away, leaving only the sounds of the upward-rushing waters and their splashing return to the rippling pool. When my reverie was halted by the intrusion of taxi horns and bus exhaust, I decided to find out the origins of the transporting waters.

In my search to discover where New York City's water came from, I became familiar with the city's great research libraries and its Department of Environmental Protection (DEP), which is responsible for the water supply. Early in 1992, the DEP asked me to write a brief monograph on the first two hundred years of water in New York, from the natural supplies available to Dutch trappers in the early 1600s to the opening of the Croton Aqueduct in October 1842. My text was to be part of a 150th anniversary celebration of that great public project, which delivered Croton River water from Westchester County forty miles north of the city. The Croton had changed New York from a place notorious for bad water to one celebrated for good.

Alas, a budgetary crisis nixed the city's Croton commemoration, and my monograph was eventually published as the cover story of an *American Heritage* quarterly, *Invention & Technology*. A book editor saw the piece and asked for a full treatment, which is the volume that follows.

"The present in New York is so powerful that the past is lost," observed essayist John Jay Chapman in 1909. Chapman's insight explains why Croton sesquicentennials get canceled, and why no previous book has been written on how Dutch, English, and American New York suffered for generations without ample fresh water. I hope this book will fill that void, allowing a glimpse at one essential aspect of this powerful city's past.

Modern New Yorkers complain about their dirty, corrupt, impossible city, but the good old days exist only in the imagination. The city's lack of good water was demonstrated dramatically in 1832, when an epidemic disease unknown in America brought death in ratios unimaginable today. New York's destiny changed with that catastrophe. The lack of good water threatened the city's very survival; abundant good water became a necessity for it to flourish.

Acknowledgments

In taking longer to complete this book than anyone thought possible, I have many people and organizations to thank for their help and understanding along the way. Inevitably, I will fail to name some who deserve credit.

First, the public and private institutions, and their incredible librarians and archivists who maintain our links between the past, the present, and the future: the New-York Historical Society, especially Mariam Touba and May N. Stone; the New York Public Library, especially the librarians of the Local History and Genealogy Division; the New York City Municipal Archives, especially Kenneth Cobb; the Chase Manhattan Archives, especially Jean Elliot and Shelly Diamond; the defunct Engineering Societies' Library; the Jervis Public Library, especially Keith Kinna; the Westchester County Archives; the Hudson River Museum of Westchester, especially Old Croton exhibit co-curator Tema Harnik; Brian Goodman of the Old Croton Trailway State Park; the Croton Historical Society; Charlotte Hegyi at the Warren Hunting Smith Library, Hobart and Willam Smith Colleges; Jami Peelle at Kenyon College; the late Seymour Durst and his Old York Library of New York history; the Museum of the City of New York; and the New York University Archives.

Chief among the individuals whose knowledge, guidance, and patience have, I hope, been rewarded: Dan Larkin, Helen Tower Wilson, William Lee Frost, Camilla Calhoun, Richard Colles Johnson, Estelle Fox Kleiger, Edward Winant, Walter Ristow, Cornelia Cotton, Sidney Horenstein, Sally Tannen, Penny and Loren Singer, Ann and Dick Reynolds, Til Connal, the editors at *American Heritage* who accepted an article over the transom, and the engineers and other employees, especially Natalie Millner, of the New York City Department of Environmental Protection, the custodian of the city's vast modern water supply.

A friend once inscribed a book to me: "A writer can't have too many readers." Those who read and commented on the manuscript chapters, or helped in other ways, include Dick Singer, Ben Rosenstadt, Tony Steen, Dennis Powell, Dorothy Carpenter, Carolyn Swartz, Waldemar Korzeniowsky, Elizabeth Harris, Peter Johnson, Patricia Corrigan, and Elyn and Barry Rosenthal.

The book became a reality through the efforts of my thorough agent Russ Galen; my first editor, Jack Repcheck, who wisely saw a book in a magazine piece; and Kristin Gager, my editor, who gamely slashed the bulky manuscript into something readable.

I owe deep gratitude to my parents, Bevin Koeppel and Elinor Koeppel, who urged the book to completion so that they and their friends might finally be able to buy multiple copies.

My wife Diane provided constant support throughout, from the earliest research to publication. Her advice resonates on many of the following pages. Our children, Jackson, Harry, and Kate have earned their reward for patience: more time now for themselves on the family computer.

Water for Gotham

"Give Us Cold Water"

*Cold water, cold water, give us cold water, was the constant
and imploring cry.*

—Remarks on the Cholera

Mary Fitzgerald was "a neat housekeeper," said the doctors, her family
"decent and cleanly people, and their habits temperate."[1] So the fate that
awaited the thirty-five-year-old wife and her two children would seem especially cruel.

The Fitzgeralds had emigrated from Ireland to Quebec in the fall of 1831,
soon making their way south to Albany and eventually on to New York
City. On the third of May they took the first floor of a house at 75 Cherry
Street, a couple of blocks from where George Washington had made his
home as president a half-century earlier. Mr. Fitzgerald—his Christian name
is lost to posterity—was by all accounts a steady man. He was a tailor, well
situated in the dockside neighborhood favored by New York's "slop tai-
lors" who sold ready-made clothes to sailors. Whether these hopeful
Fitzgeralds would have had a future in America is unknown; within a few
weeks most of the family had died.

June 25, 1832, was a hot summer Monday in New York, then a flourishing but filthy port city of just under a quarter-million people. The mercury hit 90° under the noonday sun, the barometer was high and steady,
a faint southwesterly breeze barely stirred the air. There had been no rain

for a week, less than an inch for the month, and none would fall until well into July.[2]

Fitzgerald headed off to Brooklyn that day, taking a ferry across the East River. When he returned late in the evening, he became terribly sick. Early the next day, his children, Jeremiah, age 4, and Margaret, age 7, also took ill. Several doctors came to the house, but nothing could be done: the children both died on Wednesday. Although their father recovered, their mother, Mary Fitzgerald, took ill and died on Friday.

As described in a contemporary medical treatise, the deaths were ugly and agonizing, beginning with evacuation of the bowels, leg cramps, nausea, stomach pain, a debilitated feeling, and a livid appearance. Over a course of hours came violent headaches, giddiness, great languor, increasing tightness in the chest, and severe pains throughout the body. As the pulse weakened, food was vomited undigested, followed by watery phlegm. Urination ceased, excessive thirst took over, and cramping began anew from the toes up the torso. The voice became feeble and hoarse, the eyes dulled and sank in the head, and the victim appeared as a cold, contracted, blue-tinged but still-living corpse. After clammy perspiration and another round of spasms, the faintly beating heart stopped, the patient granted a few moments ease just before the end.[3]

Mary, Margaret, and Jeremiah Fitzgerald were buried in the soon-overwhelmed cemetery of the first St. Patrick's Cathedral. The city Board of Health, for reasons of its own, attributed their deaths to *cholera morbus,* a mild, seasonal feature of New York life.[4] The doctors who had attended them, though, suspected otherwise.

The Fitzgeralds had in fact been the first New Yorkers to die from Asiatic cholera, a strange and hideous disease new to North America. Originating in India in 1826, by early 1832, the cholera had spread by trade routes through much of Asia and Europe with staggering death tolls: twenty thousand of fifty thousand pilgrims at Mecca, 9,400 Moscow and St. Petersburg residents, 7,600 Parisians. The disease swept the British Isles late in 1831; within months, it reached Irish ports and headed west across the Atlantic on miserable packet ships carrying tens of thousands of refugees from Ireland's economic collapse.[5]

In early June 1832, cholera broke out in Canada. Eighteen hundred people died in Montreal, twenty-two hundred in Quebec, which was then a city of only twenty-eight thousand permanent residents.[6]

From Canada, the disease headed west along the St. Lawrence River to Lake Ontario and Detroit, where locals favored polluted wells over the clean Detroit River, and down Lake Champlain to the upper Hudson River, Albany, and points south.[7] Though health officials had stepped up cleaning dirty streets and harbor slips for months, Asiatic cholera would find a most congenial host in New York City, a city judged by sage ex-mayor Philip Hone to be filthier than any in Canada or Europe.[8]

When doctors cautiously reported the first deaths from the disease, politicians, merchants, and newspaper editors equivocated on alerting the public. Fearing the end of business in America's commercial capital, recorder Richard Riker, the city's chief magistrate, conspired to delay an official announcement of the cholera's threat until early July, when it was too late for quarantines or other emergency measures. Nineteen people died on July 7; by the end of the month, two thousand were dead. The toll would have been higher, but over one hundred thousand New Yorkers decided to flee. An "unwanted silence" pervaded the city by midsummer; one could walk the length of Broadway and "scarce meet a soul." The dense cloud of smoke from factory furnaces and domestic hearths that often hung over the city was "scarcely discernible" in August.[9]

By the time the epidemic ended in October, the official death toll had reached 3,516, or just under one in fifty New Yorkers, a much higher rate than in Paris, which had twice the number of deaths but five times the population. And the actual number of deaths was certainly higher: there were sick New Yorkers who died after fleeing, some who stayed and died undiagnosed, and some such as the Fitzgeralds who stayed and died officially misdiagnosed. Among the notable victims were Magdelen Bristed, the oldest and favorite daughter of John Jacob Astor, America's richest man, who had safely removed himself to a recovering Europe; alderman George E. Smith, who was whispered to have brought on his demise with intemperance; the presidents of three fire insurance companies; and dozens of other business leaders, doctors, clergymen, and their families.

By far, though, the greatest number of deaths was among the city's poor, buttressing the belief among the righteous that the filth, intemperance,

debauchery, irreligious behavior, and general moral squalor attributed to
the impoverished were cholera's cause. Others believed diet was the ticket
to deliverance, though the epidemic carried off meat eaters, vegetarians,
and adherents to Sylvester Graham's fashionable diet of fruits and grains
alike. Socially prominent doctors John Rhinelander and James DeKay had
returned from early observations in Canada advising brandy-and-water
and port wine, respectively, as cholera specifics. Despite the uncertain health
benefits, the advice was so highly regarded that "Dr. Rhinelander" and
"Dr. DeKay" became the society bar pours of New York's cholera days and
beyond.

In fact, none of the city's doctors had any idea what caused Asiatic
cholera. The disease, like many others of the time, was generally thought
to be "atmospheric" and conveyed by "miasmic vapors." This led to
unrestricted medical theorizing about causes—dampness, dryness, heat,
cold—and a dizzying array of attempted cures, freely practiced on private patients and at the various cholera hospitals set up around town.
Among the cures tried were bleeding, mustard (given internally and top-
ically), calomel, opium, hot punch and hartshorn, tobacco, heated sand-
bags, and the quite popular "four hours' rubbing from two stout men,"
which seemed to relieve the patient's cramps but also friction-heated
him to collapse.[10]

Copying reported success in Europe, several doctors experimented
with saline solutions; results were inconclusive. Rhinelander fell back on
bleedings as "our sheet anchor." At the height of the epidemic, the
physician-publishers of the *Cholera Bulletin* threw up their hands: "The
cholera is, and that is all we know!"[11]

New York's doctors were not alone. No one in 1832 knew how cholera
killed. It was not until 1849, during the next global cholera epidemic
(1846–63), that British physician (and obstetrician to Queen Victoria) John
Snow theorized that cholera was waterborne and contracted orally. He
demonstrated that a single pump in London's Broad Street, supplied by
polluted Thames River water, spread most of the cholera. Deaths from
cholera stopped when the pump handle was removed, on Snow's advice.
Lingering beliefs in "miasmas" or divine providence were put to rest
during the next London outbreak in 1854. Noting that Lambeth Water
Company, one of the two private water companies serving residents on

the south side of the Thames, had recently moved its intake from a sewage-filled area of the river to a clean one, Snow determined that in a fourteen-week period only 461 Lambeth customers died, while over four thousand of their neighbors taking Southwark and Vauxhall Company water succumbed. It was not until 1883 that German bacteriology pioneer Robert Koch discovered *Vibrio cholerae,* the comma-shaped cholera bacterium.[12]

Cholera (minus the anachronistic "Asiatic") is known today to be an acute bacterial infection of the salty, alkaline surroundings of the small intestine. Not particularly contagious, the disease is generally spread through contact with infected feces, most often via sewage-contaminated water. The rapid, deadly loss of body fluids and salts as cholera takes hold is readily reversed by prompt oral or intravenous rehydration with an alkaline solution of sodium chloride; the 1832 experiments with saline injections likely failed because they were too conservative. In places with bad water and few doctors, cholera still remains a threat, but for most it's a nineteenth-century disease.

Dealing for the first time with epidemic cholera, doctors and other observant New Yorkers in 1832 did note a link to water, if only because the victims all called for it. A trio of visiting physicians from Providence reported "an almost universal demand for drink. Cold water, cold water, give us cold water, was the constant and imploring cry."[13]

New York's parched cholera patients might have fared better if their doctors had had clean water to offer them, but their city was entirely without it. Indeed, as had been noted by visitors for generations, the city's chief disadvantage was the lack of good water.[14]

New York still took most of its drinking water from neighborhood wells, which had grown increasingly impure and polluted. Spring water, carted from upisland, supplied only those who could afford it. The cholera outbreak finally proved that a better system was needed.

One way or another, good water is always obtained by cities. Ancient Rome, the model for Western urbanism, tapped local wells, springs, and the fresh Tiber River for four and a half centuries before building the first of its famous aqueducts. From 312 B.C. to A.D. 226, Roman slaves built eleven gravity-fed masonry channels from distant lakes, rivers, and springs. In its glory days, ancient Rome's million people had access to thirty-eight million gallons of fresh water a day. Four of its original aqueducts still bring water to the modern city.[15]

Los Angeles, on the final frontier of Western civilization, was a dusty Mexican pueblo when cholera decimated New York in 1832. By the turn of the century, Los Angeles had expanded to some three hundred thousand people spread over a hundred square miles, but a lack of water threatened further development. Surrounded by ocean and desert and meagerly watered by rain and the slender Los Angeles River, the city trusted its future to William Mulholland, an Irish immigrant who had risen from ditch digger for the local water company in 1878 to chief of its deficient works, which the city took over in 1902. Convinced by several droughts that no amount of conservation would preserve the city's shallow natural aquifer, Mulholland and other collaborators set their sites on the Owens River, 250 miles away in the Sierra Nevada mountains. Land and water rights were purchased in secret, desperate river valley farmers were pacified or outwitted, and laws were bent or broken. City bonds were issued for $25 million, and an eight-foot round cast iron pipe was laid from the mountains, across the Mohave Desert, to the city. Completed in 1913, the Los Angeles Aqueduct was the first in a series of water conquests that made Greater Los Angeles possible. "A city quickly finds its level," Mulholland asserted in 1905, "and that level is its water supply."[16]

New York did not find its level so readily. Starting with the first Dutch traders, Manhattanites pursued business and went easy on health and comfort, tolerating degenerated natural water sources and devastating fire and disease while encouraging a succession of dreamers and schemers plotting doubtful new water supplies. Even after the 1832 cholera epidemic, another ten years of frustrating politics, economics, and engineering would pass before the completion of the monumental effort to water the island city from the mainland Croton River. Only then did Gotham obtain a level of water equal to its fame.

Manahata Goes Dutch

The place encircled by many swift tides and sparkling waters.
—Walt Whitman, *Good-bye My Fancy*

Nobody really knows what Manhattan means. Scholarly interpretations of Delaware tribal words—from Manahata to Manahachtanienk—range widely: "the island of hills," "the place where timber is procured for bows and arrows," "cluster of islands with channels everywhere," "people of the whirlpool," "the island where we all became intoxicated." The last pre-European inhabitants weren't much help; numbering at best several hundred from two local tribes, they decamped for the mainland soon after the Dutch "white skins" arrived in 1624.[1]

Absent academic consensus, the poets have tried their hand, especially native son Walt Whitman, who mused on "Mannahatta" in poems and prose for decades: "the place around which there are hurried and joyous waters, continually";[2] "a plot of ground, an island, about which the waters flow—keep up a devil of a swirl, whirl, ebullition—have a hell of a time";[3] "a point of land surrounded by rushing, tempestuous, demonic waters."[4] Finally, in 1891, the aging poet settled on "MANNAHATTA, 'the place encircled by many swift tides and sparkling waters.'" "How fit a name," he wrote in *Good-bye My Fancy*, "for America's great democratic island city!"[5]

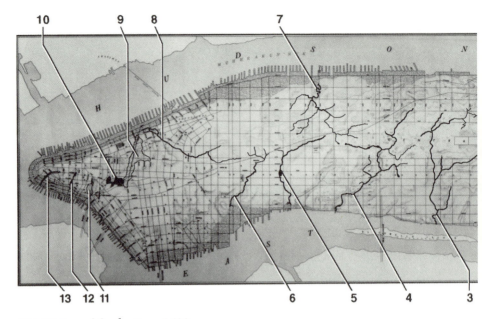

FIGURE 1. *Manhattan, 1609*
Based on surveys from the colonial period though 1867, this 1909 plan by Townsend
MacCoun is the most accurate map of Manhattan's natural water courses. It is still
consulted by builders. Key: 1, Sherman's Creek; 2, Harlem Creek; 3, Saw Kill; 4, streams

Whitman wasn't the first local poet to sing the praises of Manhattan's
surrounding waters. Those honors went back in 1659 to Jacob Steendam,
prosperous Dutch trader and the first poet of New Netherland:

> See: two streams my garden bind,
> From the East and North they wind,—
> Rivers pouring in the sea,
> Rich in fish, beyond degree.[6]

The trouble was that the rivers were salt. This would soon make life difficult for people who needed fresh water to survive.

When European civilization took root in what was to become New York
City, it was a wild and fertile place. According to Dutch planter Daniel Denton, there were forests of white and red oak, maple, cedar, walnut, chest-

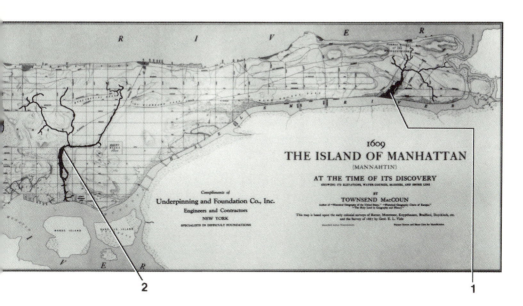

emptying into Turtle Bay; 5, stream featuring Sun Fish Pond; 6, Cedar Creek; 7, Great Kill; 8, Minetta Water; 9, Lispenard Meadows; 10, Fresh Water or Collect Pond; 11, Beekman's Swamp; 12, Smit's Vly; 13, Heere Gracht (Broad Street). (© Collection of The New-York Historical Society; water courses emphasized for clarity.)

nut, beech, birch, sassafras, holly, and hazel. The fields were filled with fruits and berries (mulberries, persimmons, grapes, huckleberries, cranberries, plums, raspberries, strawberries) and herbs (purslaine, white orage, egrimony, violets, penniroyal, alicampane, sarsaparilla).

The land abounded with animal life—bear, cougar, deer, wolf, fox, raccoon, bobcat, skunk, and hare—and the skies were thick with fowl—wild turkey, heath hen, quail, partridge. Especially plentiful were wild pigeon: "the light can hardly be discerned where they fly," observed one colonizer; "they are shot here by the thousand," remarked another of the now extinct passenger pigeon. Of shore birds, there were crane, geese, brant, duck, widgeon, and teal. In the salt waters there were tuna, perch, sturgeon, bass, herring, mackerel, weakfish, stone bream, eel, sheepshead, and sole, as well as whales, porpoise, otter, and seal. Oysters grew so large they had to be cut in three to eat.[7]

No creature was more identified with Manhattan than the beaver, emblazoned on the coat of arms of New Amsterdam in 1630. The town, established as a trading outpost of the Dutch West India Company, made beaver its first business. The island was "bought" from the Indians for sixty guilders in 1626; by 1635, sixty thousand beaver skins worth some four hundred thousand guilders had passed through New Amsterdam traders' hands.[8] Not all of the treasured rodents were Manhattan natives but, especially in the early years, trappers looked no further than the island's countless freshwater ponds, brooks, and streams.

At the island's northern tip, a large stream later named Sherman's Creek drained the highlands into the Muscota, now the Harlem River. Reckewa's Creek (later Haerlem Creek or Montagne's Kill) was so imposing it split the Manhattan holdings of its original occupying tribes; it ran from what is now Morningside Heights all the way to the Harlem near its turbulent intersection with the East River.

The tributaries of the Saw Kill formed in what today are the northern reaches of Central Park, flowing into the East River near today's 74th Street. Another network of streams originating west of what is now Central Park found its East River outlet far down at Deutel (Turtle) Bay, the terrapin-thick inlet now harboring the United Nations. Kip's Bay was the outlet of what came to be known as Sun Fish Pond, where Park Avenue and 31st Street now meet; the pond was fed by streams forming around what is now Times Square. Cedar Creek, originating near today's Madison Square, emptied into an East River marsh at today's 18th Street.

Along the island's rocky upper western shore, numerous nameless rills spilled over ledges into the North (now Hudson) River. In a deep bay at the western foot of today's 42nd Street, the Great Kill emptied three small streams from the Reed Valley, famed for freshwater fish and fowl. Farther south ran the wide, deep, and turbulent brook the natives were said to have called "Mannette." Originating in high ground around today's Union Square, these Minetta waters gained strength as they flowed to the Hudson past Sappockanican, a native settlement later renamed Greenwich. Built-over but unbowed, the Minetta still makes its rainy season way into Greenwich Village basements.

A few hundred yards south of Minetta was Lispenard Meadows, the broad marshy western outlet of Manhattan's greatest natural feature, the

Fresh Water Pond. Also called simply "the kolck" (Dutch for a small body of water), later corrupted into the Collect, the spring-fed pond spread over some seventy acres, surrounded by wooded hills. "To anyone but a Dutchman—who always preferred a ditch to a lake—there was no more beautiful spot on the lower island," wrote George E. Hill and George E. Waring, historians of Manhattan's natural water supplies.[9]

Lying east of Broadway between today's Chambers and Canal Streets, the Fresh Water was the center of lower Manhattan Native life. On its northwest shore sat the Indian village of Werpoes, reputedly named for the abundant hare ("wapoos") there.[10] Like the Native settlements farther north, Werpoes was abandoned soon after the arrival of the Dutch.

The Fresh Water was perhaps seventy feet deep; its numerous underground sources would provide drinking water well into the 1800s. The secret of the Fresh Water's excess lay beneath it. Manhattan's bedrock of mica schist runs above or near ground level in its gradual descent from the island's northern heights to Greenwich Village, where near today's Washington Square it plunges hundreds of feet. The rock rises to a subterranean depth of about one hundred feet at today's Chambers Street, then halves that depth in a modest rise to the island's southern tip. The Fresh Water flourished where the bedrock was deep.

With its marshy outlets stretching to the Hudson and the East River along what became Canal Street, the Fresh Water effectively made two islands of Manhattan: the abundantly watered rocky bulk to the north, and the low-lying tip to the south that looked like home to the Dutch.

The area south of the Fresh Water was covered with a porous, loamy soil, impregnated with briny water and punctuated by swamps. Just several hundred feet south of the swampy ground east of the Fresh Water was Bestevaer's Kripplebush, known later as Beekman's Swamp. Buried today beneath the ramps of the Brooklyn Bridge, the Kripplebush was a large, brier-tangled salt marsh fed by the East River. A few hundred yards farther south was Smit's Vly (Smith's Valley or Fly), a long, broad saltwater meadow, reaching all the way back from the river to today's Broadway. At its higher western end, the Fly's most notable feature was a grassy-banked, pebble-bottomed fresh water streamlet called the Maagde Paetje (Maiden's Path), said to have been the favored open-air laundry of Dutch girls, whose memory remains in today's Maiden Lane.

FIGURE 2. New Amsterdam, 1660
This detail of the "Castello Plan" shows the canals that became Broad and Beaver
Streets, the wall that became Wall Street, and the bucket-and-pole yard wells dug
by Dutch brewers and others. (© Collection of The New-York Historical Society.)

    Just south of the Maagde Paetje was the Dutch town, secured inside an
islandwide timber wall (now Wall Street) built in 1653 as a defense
against an Indian attack that never came. In the twenty-two acre trian-
gle bounded by the wall and the rivers, the Dutch set to work digging their
familiar ditches. They transformed a deep, natural inlet on the east side
of town into a large, timber-lined canal called the Heere Gracht (now Broad
Street). Crossed by three bridges, the Ditch extended nearly to the wall,
allowing unmasted boats to float at high tide "almost through ye towne."
Intersecting the Ditch, the industrious burghers dug out a smaller canal

called the Bevers Gracht (now Beaver Street), draining off a marsh fed by two small streams from which trappers had wiped out their first bounty.[11]

With little fresh water flowing within the town itself, the people of New Amsterdam collected rain water in cisterns and dug shallow wells. By the early 1660s, several of these wells began to figure in the life of the town. Wealthy merchant Jacob Kip, appointed the first city clerk of New Amsterdam in 1653, had a large well in the rear yard of his house at the northern end of the Heere Gracht.[12] But the rest of the private wells of record were tapped for New Amsterdam's preferred beverage, beer.

For the most part during this period, fresh water was used for livestock and cooking. In a town surrounded by salt water and swamp, turning limited fresh water into beer was an essential industry. A tile-roofed brewery, built in 1633, was among New Amsterdam's first substantial buildings.[13] Brewers were among the town's most notable citizens.

"Brew" means "to boil down," and a New Amsterdam brewer needed water from a well of his own to get started. Malt or hops were steeped in water; the mixture was then boiled and fermented in wooden barrels. For serving, the beer usually was heated and drunk warm.[14] Pieter Van Couwenhoven, for several years one of the town's five *schepens* (legislators), drew water from a well behind his brewhouse at the upper reaches of the town.[15] His older brother Jacob had a "great stone brewhouse" in the heart of town, with water supplied by a well on the grounds. After Jacob died (in 1670), his brewery passed to various creditors, among them Oloff Stevensen Van Cortlandt, prosperous founder of one of colonial America's most prominent families and for many years a schepen or *burgomaster* (one of two administrators similar to mayors); during Dutch rule, Van Cortlandt was proprietor of a large brewery with its obligatory well near the Heere Gracht. Out on the eastern end of the Bevers Gracht, Michiel Jansen sank a well and opened a brewhouse in 1656, after his brewery in Pavonia (across the Hudson at today's Jersey City) was burned down in a Native uprising. Across the street was the Red Lion Brewery, with a well in its large yard. Established by Isaac De Forest, first in the line of another prominent American family, the Red Lion flourished in the 1660s under Joannes and Daniel Verveelen.

All of the brewers' primitive wells featured wood buckets suspended from long, counterpoised poles. The wells may have been lined with

FIGURE 3. Smit's Vly, late 17th century
This lithograph, prepared for the 1861 *Manual of the Common Council,* shows the foot of the stream favored by Dutch women doing their laundry, with a well typical for the period. This later became Maiden Lane. (Photo by Barry Rosenthal.)

wood, were likely very shallow, and, given the geological conditions, provided water best drunk after boiling with the requisite ingredients into beer.

The human condition also troubled the groundwater. The neighborhood accumulation of rubbish, ashes, and animal carcasses compelled the burgomasters in 1657 to order residents to sweep in front of their houses and bring their garbage to five designated areas. The order was largely ignored, though, until a fine was imposed for dumping in the Ditch.[16]

Long before underground sewers carried off the waste of New York, "filth" disposal was a private matter. Urban privies flourished in the European Middle Ages but were relatively slow to gain hold in Manhattan where the tide-flushed rivers beckoned. As early as 1658, though, the burgomasters ordered the removal of all privies with street-level outlets, which most of them had, a source of great wallowing for roaming pigs and great stench and foul streets for human inhabitants. The order was apparently ignored for at least three years, when the *schout* (sheriff) was instructed to oversee further privy removals.[17]

Human waste was only part of the problem. An ineffective 1648 order to fence the town's hogs led the burgomasters ten years later to consider a citywide hog ban, a drastic measure thwarted by the substantial hog lobby; hogs were merely ordered ringed through the nose, making them easier to catch but otherwise preserving their run of town. By 1664, the schout was unsure how to dispose of numerous dead hogs "to prevent the stench, which proceeds therefrom."[18]

That July, town administrators came face to face with the issue of water quality for the first time. Daniel Verveelen, proprietor of the Red Lion Brewery, and Willem Abrahamsen Van der Borden, a prominent carpenter, filed a joint complaint that a tannery newly established between their properties on Prinsen Straet (an extension of today's Beaver Street) would spoil the water in their wells. The two upstanding citizens were especially concerned about the effect of an intended tanning pit. Official New Amsterdam was unmoved: "as others have been allowed to make a tannery behind their house and lot," Verveelen and Borden and their wells deserved no special protection.[19] Thus, with government approval, the corruption of the town's natural water supply was permitted to advance.

Greater troubles, though, were brewing for New Amsterdam. On the same day that the burgomasters and schepens discounted the concerns of Borden and Verveelen came word from Boston that an English fleet had recently departed for the west.

As it turned out, the Dutch had dug themselves a hole. Or rather, hadn't. Six years earlier, the burgomasters had resolved to ask their local governor, the famously peevish pegleg Peter Stuyvesant, about having a well sunk at the foot of Broadway.[20] Nothing came of this good intention to build the town's first public well, a costly lapse for Stuyvesant.

In the summer of 1664, the commercial outpost of Dutch progress clung anxiously to Manhattan's narrow toe. In New Amsterdam's final days, 350 buildings lined a dozen dirt and cobbled streets fanning out from Fort Amsterdam, its doors opening at the foot of Broadway. The fort was a short-walled wood, gravel, and sod affair on low ground, habitually trampled by the town's roaming pigs and goats. It contained a church, a storehouse, a prison, barracks, and the governor's house. What the fort didn't have was any water. This would help undo the Dutch.[21] Beyond its wall, New Amsterdam's fifteen hundred people beheld a new land of plenty. Within, they were about to suffer a water shortage.

English warships staking the Crown's claim to all of Dutch America—the same fleet reported from Boston earlier—sailed up the harbor in late August 1664, threatening fire or siege. Dutch courage failed from too little to drink. Hoping to preserve the town's commercial prospects and willing to trade unpopular Governor Stuyvesant for something possibly more benevolent, ninety-three of New Amsterdam's most prominent residents urged him to surrender "in the speediest, best and most reputable manner."[22] At eight in the morning on the 29th, at a mill on the eastern outlet of the Fresh Water, Stuyvesant obliged.

Justifying to his West India Company employers the bloodless capitulation, Stuyvesant explained that his "little fort . . . is situate in an untenable place . . . encompassed only by a slight wall [and] crowded all around about with buildings . . . in many places, higher than the walls." "Besides this," he stressed, "the fort was . . . without either well or cistern." When the English fleet arrived, the fort "was hastily provided with 20 [to] 24 water barrels" procured from ships at dock, a short supply for a garrison in a seiged fort. "Hence then, 'tis to be deduced how easy 'twould be to recover it back; how difficult, nay, impossible for us to defend it."[23]

"The . . . excuse sounds very strange to the Company," his employers later replied.[24] Nonetheless, the English flag went up at the renamed Fort James, and New Amsterdam became New Yorke. Dutch days were done, but the search for enough fresh water was just beginning.

English Well-Being

There is no good water in the town.

—*Peter Kalm's Travels*

That Peter Stuyvesant misjudged how to water his fort-bound troops was made evident in 1666 by new English governor Richard Nicolls. He was very proud of a well he had made in the fort "beyond the Imagination of the Dutch, who would [not] beleeve it till they saw it finisht, which produces very good water." Even thirteen years later, a visitor remarked on its "fine water." Nicolls had beat the Dutch with the city's first public well. For better at first but eventually for worse, public wells would supply the city for the next two centuries.[1]

New York's second public well, the first lined with stone, was built in 1671 in the rear yard of the Stadt Huys, the first City Hall. Facing the East River at the corner of Pearl Street and Coenties Slip, this imposing, two-story brick building had begun its half-century of service in the 1640s as the city's chief watering hole, the Stadt Herbergh or City Tavern. From the 1650s, court was held upstairs, while prisoners were held in the basement. The execution of the well was overseen, fittingly, by the city's first executioner, Benjamin Johnson, who called the hall home. The killing business apparently was slow because six months after his January 1671 appointment Johnson was presenting bills for having the well built and in July was paid some 195 florins to cover his various disbursements.[2] The City Hall well was the high point of Johnson's career in public service. A year and a half later, he was convicted of running a theft ring and sentenced to lashings, severing of an ear, and banishment.[3]

Notwithstanding the loss of Johnson, the town's population increased to twenty-two hundred after nearly a decade of English rule.[4] Demand for accessible fresh water increased accordingly. The first efforts at systematic public well-digging began in 1677.

An English-style Common Council of mayor and aldermen attended to serious fire, sanitary, and water matters. By February 1677, leather buckets owned by the city corporation and used by the citizens at fires, had become scattered and were ordered returned. Having the previous year ordered all butchers to relocate outside the wall, the council now ordered that they be accommodated with a large public slaughterhouse to be built at Smit's Vly just north of the wall. Finally, the council ordered that "Severall Weells bee made ... (for the publiqve good of the Cytie) by the inhabitants of Each Streete" designated to have one.[5]

The council made no pretense of doing the public work itself, ordering that the inhabitants take note of the law and dig the wells "with all possible speede" or face unspecified penalties. Six locations were designated, though the matter of financing was not. This may explain why only one of the six wells appears to have been dug. There's no record of who did the work or paid for it, but the well was sunk in the middle of Broadway just south of Exchange Alley.

The population at the tip of Manhattan grew steadily through the mid-1680s, and institutions grew with it. The ward system was created in 1683, with six wards designated by geography: West, South, Dock, East, North, and the Out Ward beyond the wall. Elections for mayor, aldermen, assistant aldermen (initially called common councilmen), and lesser officials would be conducted by ward until the 1850s.

After the initial false start, the public well system was established in 1686. After a survey of desirable locations by the town constable, the council ordered up eight wells, to be sunk in the middle of several streets and lined with stone. This time the council ordered that building costs be split by the city and the inhabitants. New York's first native-born mayor Stephanus Van Cortlandt (Olaff's son), designated neighborhoods that would each be served by a well. Construction and maintenance costs would be assessed by the "Conveniency" each house had to its neighborhood well. Residents that didn't pay up were threatened with forced sales of their possessions to cover the assessment.[6]

Certain neighborhood residents were named to make sure each of the wells was maintained, and most of the wells came to be known by the names of their caretakers. Thus, "De Riemer's Well" at the head of Bridge Street near Whitehall was overseen by Peter De Riemer, an assessor and former constable. A well near the intersection of Stone Street and Broad Street, created when the Ditch was filled ten years earlier, was known as "Ten Eyck and Vincent's Well," for tanner and future fire warden Dirck Ten Eyck and the family Vincent, which owned several houses there. Farther up Broad was "Tunis De Kay's Well," named for the former baker and future overseer of public works and buildings. Just west of the head of Smith (now William) Street on the street newly laid out along the inside of the wall was "Frederick (Francis) Wessel's Well," its proprietor the son of a prominent Dutch distiller. In Broadway was the "Well of Suert Olpkerts [Olpherts]," who in 1688 was involved with substantial repairs to the fort. Also in Broadway was the 1677 well that became known as "Mr. Rombouts's Well," for former schepen, alderman, and mayor Francis Rombouts, a Frenchman whose substantial property extended west from Broadway to the Hudson River. Three other new wells—two in Broad Street and one in Wall—were not known by any particular name.[7]

All this civic digging refocused attention on water at the fort. Presumably because its quality had faltered, the city's first public well had been filled sometime during the tenure of Governor Thomas Dongan, between 1682 and 1688. His successor, Edmund Andros, ordered extensive repairs to crumbling Fort James and intended to dig a new well. He never got the chance. Word of the overthrow in England of James II, the city's namesake Duke of York, in favor of William and Mary reached American shores in the spring of 1689, leading to Andros's imprisonment at Boston in April and the surrender of Fort James in May to rebellious and short-lived Jacob Leisler. Leisler promptly set to work "with sixteen carpenters & twenty men," repairing the fort and reopening the old well. At the same time, he began work on a great new well just outside the fort's northern entrance, a site first considered by the Dutch back in 1658.

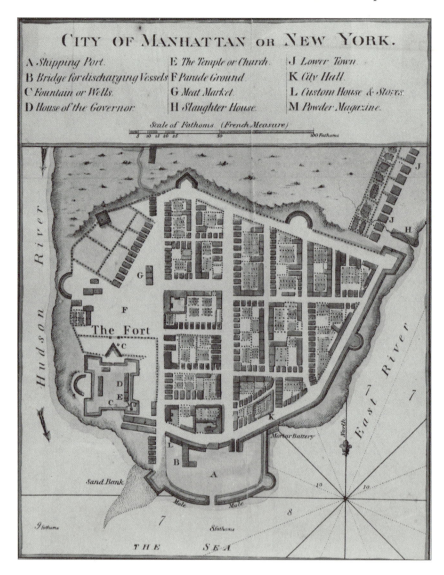

FIGURE 4. New York, 1693–1694

This lithograph, drawn for the 1861 *Manual of the Common Council* from the original "Franquelin Plan" circa 1694 (first published in 1764), shows the locations of the 1666 well inside the fort, as well as the newly installed pump in front of the fort. (Photo by Barry Rosenthal.)

Leisler reported the new well completed in August; lined with wood expropriated from ex-mayor Van Cortlandt, it was thirty-six feet deep, with "very good water," according to Leisler. In the meantime, Leisler wrote to his king and queen that the old well in the fort had been "made new againe and gives good water enough."[8]

Leisler had little time to drink to his waterworks. In January 1690 his imagined benefactor William appointed a new governor, though Henry Sloughter didn't arrive in New York for another fourteen months. After a deadly exchange of gunfire between troops and rebels, Leisler gave up his fort and, two months later, his neck. His contributions to the city's water supply survived him in fine style. In 1694, the well outside the fort became the first and, for a number of years, the only well in New York to be equipped with a pump.[9]

A detailed plan of New York in 1695, drawn by former military chaplain John Miller, reveals a town that had spread several blocks beyond its wall (which was shortly to be torn down), up to Maiden Lane, the paved-over Dutch laundry. Reverend Miller numbered some thirty important landmarks, including government and religious buildings, docks, burial grounds, and a dozen public wells.

The efforts of the English to water their city did not go unnoticed. Passing through town in June 1697, Boston physician Benjamin Bullivant observed "many publique wells enclosed & Covered in ye Streetes." He also, however, found those streets "Nasty & unregarded."[10]

By the time of the doctor's visit, the population had reached nearly five thousand people, a relatively modest increase during English rule that, at century's end, left New York behind Boston as the largest colonial town.[11] How the streets came to be "Nasty & unregarded" is seen in the evolution of the town's sanitary laws, and helps explain how the well water came to suffer as well.

Street-level privies had been a problem for forty years. At the dawn of the 1700s, "Tubbs of Odour" were the standard of the day. It was common practice for households to dump their ordure tubs indiscriminately in the streets, "to the Great Nusance" of all. The council ordered forty-shilling fines, to be shared by the city and the informant, for anyone who failed to dispose of "odours" in the proper place: "the River & no where Else."[12]

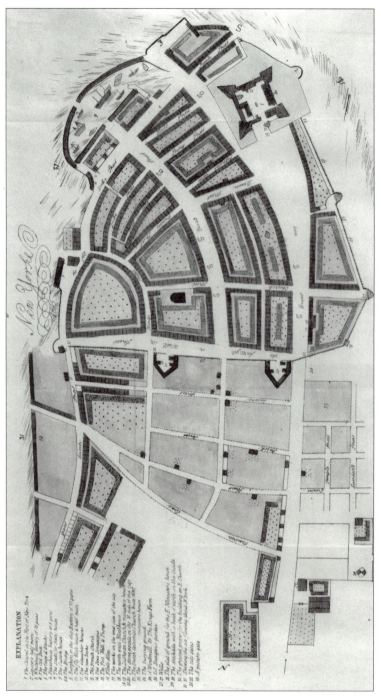

FIGURE 5. New York, 1695

This lithograph, drawn for the 1851 *Manual of the Common Council* from the original "Miller Plan" circa 1696, shows nine public wells in Broad Street, Broadway, and Wall Street; the original indicates three more public wells along the East River waterfront. (Photo by Barry Rosenthal.)

New York's tidal rivers remained the sewers of choice for decades. A 1731 law reinforced river dumping of "any Tubs of Dung, Close Stools or Pots of Ordure or Nastiness," while restricting dumping to late night hours and imposing a new fine of six shillings for spilling anything on the delicate journey through the darkened streets.[13]

General sanitation laws attempted to keep pace with the town's growth. Dutch street-sweeping regulations were constantly renewed and expanded by the English, with the burden for garbage removal split among residents, professional cartmen, and public scavengers. The sanitary law of 1731 combined various sweeping and dumping regulations under one head; as a general rule, the town was supposed to gather up its assorted animal and human wastes on Fridays and Saturdays, disposing of them in the rivers or in dumps north of the city limits. At the same time, while fines increased for the apparently frequent breach of the regulations, more wells were sunk in the less than sanitary streets.[14]

Epidemic disease, never recorded during the Dutch period, became a regular feature of the English decades, beginning with an "unusual sicknesse" in September 1668, when untold numbers were "dayly swept away." Governor Lovelace blamed his subjects' "wickednesse . . . inordinate & intemperate . . . drinking & all manner of Impietyes," though a more sober modern assessment points to typhoid or malaria.[15]

Smallpox outbreaks disrupted city life in 1679–80, 1689–90, and in the spring of 1702, but a different epidemic broke out that summer in historic proportion. For lack of better understanding then it was called a "malignant distemper." It was in fact yellow fever, a term not coined until 1739 and, like cholera, a disease not fully understood until the twentieth century. An acute infectious viral disease that attacks liver cells causing jaundice, yellow fever is spread among humans by mosquitoes. The unsewered town of 1702 with swamps and filth all around was a superb breeding ground.

"Here is a mischevious insect call'd a musqueta," prominent merchant and future mayor Charles Lodwick had noted in extraordinary detail ten years earlier in a report eventually presented to the Royal Society in London. "The musqueta, a small sort of fly, is also venomous, has a small body not much bigger than ye head of a pin, 6 long leggs, and a trunk almost 1/4 of an inch long, by wch it sucks blood from Man and Beast, and wherever it bites, that part swells immediately itching extreamly, which by scratching often proves a venomous sore, but if lett alone it vanishes quickly."[16] A half-century later, a visiting botanist observed that New Yorkers were still "greatly troubled with mosquitoes" breeding "near the town, in the low meadows saturated with salt water" in such numbers that "the skin is sometimes so covered over with little swellings from their stings that people are ashamed to appear in public."[17]

The understanding of the connection between mosquitoes and yellow fever was still two centuries off in 1702. Blaming "our Manifold sins Immorality & profaneness," the Common Council at the end of September reported "great Numbers" dead and as many "in A Languishing Condition." Setting a precedent for future epidemic disease response, many more "Retired into the Country." Not until the chill of November did governor (and scandalous cross-dresser) Lord Cornbury report "the sickness, God be Praised, quite over." By then the death toll had reached 570, nearly 12 percent of the population, a withering unmatched even by the cholera epidemic 130 years later.[18]

In 1729, measles came to town, in a relatively mild form that seems to have killed mostly children. After regular outbreaks starting in 1679, smallpox killed at least 549 New Yorkers in 1731, then roughly 6 percent of the population. Yellow fever returned in 1732 and in 1743, when 217 burials were reported by Mayor John Cruger in the space of two summer months.[19]

The 1743 epidemic followed two summers of fevers of undetermined pathology that had aroused serious concern about the unsanitary condition of the city. Cadwallader Colden (1688–1776), Scottish-born scientist, scholar, provincial surveyor-general, and later hated Loyalist administrator, established himself as New York's first influential medical figure with an essay that year on the fevers. "It is well known," he wrote, "that the part of the town chiefly afflicted with the epidemical distemper these two last summers, is built upon a swamp, or moist slimy ground . . . ; that some other parts of the town are likewise built upon low swampy grounds, and that the moisture of these grounds is to be observed almost in every cellar of the houses built on them." He complained the cellars were rarely drained and "seldom or never cleaned after the settling of corrupted slime."

The situation was no better along the waterfront, Colden wrote, where nobody could escape "the filthy smell" emanating from the slips into which "by an intolerable carelessness, the nastiness of the town is thrown . . . at such a distance from the stream of the river that it is not carried off, but remains there . . . to ferment to such a degree, that it appears, as it were, boiling to the eye of the spectators."

Colden recommended that the city drain its wet grounds, fill in polluted slips, and make sure that waste was deposited fully into the river stream. He recognized that individual action was unlikely: "Some people are so wretchedly stupid, that rather than take some trouble for a few days, will risk their own health, and even the destruction of the whole community." Government would have to step in, with a tax and "the direction of men of known industry, and zeal for the welfare of the town." He suggested the city apply to the provincial legislature for the necessary authority.[20]

Colden's authoritative paper got the reaction it intended. In November, the Provincial Assembly, meeting in its City Hall chambers, began pondering a petition from certain inhabitants for a law to remove and prevent "Nuisances."[21] In the meantime, a grand jury indicted the local government for failing to keep the city clean.

Compelled to act, in February 1744, the Common Council ordered a citywide posting of the much-ignored 1731 street cleaning law. On the recommendation of committees, the council allocated a substantial £200 for cleaning or filling several filthy East River slips, including two that took the noxious outflow of Beekman's Swamp, home of the tanning trade.[22]

In early May, the assembly took the next step, passing an historic law "to Remove and Prevent Nuisances within the City of New York." Endorsed immediately by the Common Council, it was a remarkable piece of legislation, commanding immediate and significant changes in the sanitary condition of the city. New York would become a much cleaner and healthier place for the remaining three decades of colonial rule.[23]

Seeking to eliminate the "Noisom Smells" that had pervaded the city during the previous several summers, the sanitary lawmakers targeted not only the garbage-clogged dockside regions, already being cleaned by the city, but also any perceived source of bad smells and ill health. The leather trades, with their vats and pits of standing water and mounds of uncured skins, were banished from the city limits to the area of the Fresh Water

Pond; all existing pits were to be filled with clean dirt, though skin trades already located at Beekman's Swamp were grandfathered. Hogs, the bane of street life for a hundred years, were likewise banished from south of the Fresh Water. The polluted waters of dyers, hatters, starchmakers, and others were henceforth only to be drained into the streets during cold-weather months, and in no case were to remain on premises located south of the Fresh Water. The 1731 cleaning law was updated to prohibit any dead animal materials from remaining longer than a day on private property below the Fresh Water, with limited cold month exceptions. Finally, waste dumping on any public property was forbidden.

It is likely no coincidence that there were no significant outbreaks of yellow fever in New York for the rest of the colonial period. Not that the locals would have made the connection, but the 1744 law at the very least must have diminished the breeding grounds for the mosquitoes that carried the disease.

It is also likely that the simple geography of urban expansion was at play. As the 1700s got under way, the city leaped over its wall and expanded north, directly exposing its population to the mosquito-infested regions of Smith's Fly and Beekman's Swamp. As those marshy areas were gradually filled and developed, the mosquitos moved their breeding grounds north to the Fresh Water, the next center of foul industry. Sure enough, yellow fever returned with a vengeance at the end of the 1700s when the city's population reached that degraded region.

Whatever the cause for the elimination of yellow fever in the 1740s, the damage was already done to the town's fragile groundwater supply. In an introductory note to his essay on New York's fevers, Colden observed that all in all you'd have been healthier in Philadelphia. He saw two reasons: "first, the poor people at this time eat abundance of watermelons and other such kinds of fruit more than they do in Philadelphia; the other is, that the water in the town is not near so good as there, being brackish and so hard (as it is commonly termed) that it will not dissolve soap."[24]

Approaching midcentury, New York had fallen to the third most populous colonial town; with some thirteen thousand people, it trailed both fading Boston and surging Philadelphia.[25] But like its competitor cities, New York had become a favored stop for American and foreign travelers.

From those who left a record comes confirmation of the city's growing water problem.

Just two months after New York's sanitary law was passed in May 1744, Dr. Alexander Hamilton (1712–56), prominent Annapolis physician and intellectual, passed through town on a tour of the northeast. "They have very bad water in the city," he wrote in a private journal, "most of it being hard and brackish."[26] Like Colden, whose fever study he perhaps had read, Dr. Hamilton had found Philadelphia different: "They are stocked with plenty of excellent water in this city, there being a pump at almost every fifty paces." So well stocked that "the people . . . at sunset throw bucketsful of water upon the pavement, which gives a sensible cool."[27]

The contrast between the drinking water of Philadelphia—built between the fresh Delaware and Schuylkill Rivers—and New York—squatting at the confluence of salt waters—was most completely drawn a few years later by Swedish botanist and Linnaeus disciple Peter Kalm (1716–79). Kalm's North American travels to research plants for the Swedish Academy of Sciences first brought him to New York in November 1748. "There is no good water in the town itself," he discovered, "the water from the wells [being] very bad," so bad that the "want of good water is hard on strangers' horses that come to the place, for they do not like to drink the well water." Like Hamilton, Kalm had found better in Philadelphia. After noting its favorable climate, Kalm added that "the good clear water in Philadelphia is likewise one of its advantages. For even though there are no fountains in the town, there is a well in every house and several in the streets, all of which furnish excellent water for boiling, drinking, washing and other uses."[28]

Kalm's host in Philadelphia, Benjamin Franklin, thought the scholar's study "full of idle Stories, which he pick'd up among ignorant People."[29] But clearly Kalm had taken an accurate measure of New York's water. In 1750, visiting sea captain James Birket found the well and pump water brackish at best.[30] By 1760, the verdict was inescapable. "[New York] is subject to one great inconvenience," observed visiting English scholar Andrew Burnaby, "which is the want of fresh water."[31]

Tea Water and the Works That Weren't

It is hoped that New York will very soon be abundantly supplied with a quantity of water.
                    —St. Jean de Crèvecoeur, *Letters of an American Farmer*

Tea Water Time

As New York's free well water deteriorated, the search for something better began. Like moderns favoring bottled water over the common tap, fastidious late colonials eschewed the neighborhood well for "tea water" brought by pail and barrel from springs on the fringes of town. The first source of this new supply was also the most notorious, not for the product but for the atmosphere surrounding it.

Gerardus Comfort was a cooper, with several irons in the fire. He ran a dock on the Hudson just above Wall Street and at his adjoining house he had a well, dispensing "Comfort's Tea Water." The water was considered superior to that of all the public wells. Morning and evening, the slaves of the town's principal citizens carried it away in kegs. Just when Comfort went into the water business is unclear; it most definitely ended early in 1741 with the "Great Negro Plot."[1]

It was a nervous time in New York. The winter of 1741 had been the coldest and most severe in years, money and work were still scarce from a 1737 recession, and colonial resources had been drained by England's ongoing war with Spain. Adding to the tension of the town's whites were rumors the previous year of a plan by blacks to poison the public wells.[2]

After a generation of unrestricted slave importation and the recent addition of a captured and questionably enslaved shipload of justifiably angry black Spaniards, in 1741 one in five New Yorkers was black. Used less for labor than as house and personal servants, New York's slaves easily become familiar with their masters' anxieties and had plenty of occasion in the pause of their duties to discuss these anxieties amongst themselves.[3]

One of their daily duties was fetching water. The list of leading citizens whose servants went to Comfort's well is a veritable Who's Who of mid-century New York, provided in the contemporary account by city recorder Daniel Horsmanden: a "tall slender negro" belonging to Widow Schuyler; Jacob Kip's Harry; Adolph Philipse's Cuffee; alderman John Pintard's Caesar; Cornelius Ten Eyck's Bill; Peter DeLancey's Antonio (one of the "Spanish negroes"); John Roosevelt's Quack; tipsy tavernkeep Richard Todd's Dundee; Brash, belonging to patriot John Jay's father Peter; and Jack and Adam, belonging to jurist Joseph Murray, whose private library would later help establish the library for King's College, now Columbia University.[4]

The trouble with Comfort's was twofold. First, Comfort was often away, leaving his allegedly crafty slave Jack in charge. Jack had every opportunity to enlist supporters for any of his plots. Second, Comfort's place happened to be next door to John Hughson's "very disorderly house," where the scheming Hughson, his wife, daughter, and assorted sons scandalously offered entertainment and liquor to a mixed crowd.[5]

What plots actually were hatched at Hughson's and Comfort's is unclear to the ages but, after a series of thefts and seemingly related fires beginning in late February 1741, nervous white New Yorkers were certain there was a design to massacre them and burn the city. The gathering hysteria was fanned by sixteen-year-old Mary Burton. She was John Hughson's white servant girl, and she had vivid descriptive powers and a keen interest in the whopping £100 reward offered for information on the crime wave. Turning on her employer of several months, Burton offered spectacular testimony at trials through the summer of a "Negroe plot" run by Hughson, aimed at crowning him "King of New York," his wife queen, Pintard's Caesar governor, and his white prostitute mistress, Peggy Kerry, governess.

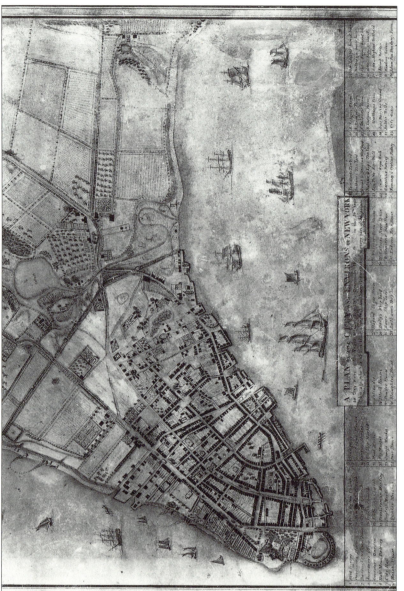

FIGURE 6. New York, 1742–1744

This detail of a lithograph, drawn from memory by merchant David Grim in 1813, depicts numerous city features, including the Fresh Water or Collect Pond, tanyards, several public wells, and the execution place for those convicted in the 1741 "Negro Plot." Notably absent from Grim's recollection is the newly established Tea Water Pump. (© Collection of The New-York Historical Society.)

In the end, after hundreds of arrests and months of trials, four whites—the elder Hughsons, Peggy, and an unfortunate Catholic schoolteacher—and eighteen blacks lost their necks. Thirteen more blacks were burned at the stake, and seventy blacks and seven whites were banished. Comfort's Jack, who likely was running a theft ring with Hughson but nothing more, testified skillfully and falsely to the greater plotting of others, and escaped with banishment. Mary Burton, who soon enough unnerved the righteous investigators with wild new accusations against prominent citizens, collected her reward and promptly disappeared.[6]

Though other "tea water" wells were likely operating at the time, the events at Comfort's had a chilling effect on water procurement by blacks. As court proceedings were winding down in early 1742, a law was passed requiring blacks to get water from no farther away than the nearest neighborhood well.[7]

By the time Dr. Alexander Hamilton came to town in 1744, the method of obtaining tea water had changed. He found that suburban spring water was being carted to the city in great casks.[8] Four years later, Swedish botanist Peter Kalm discovered only one notable source of clean spring water, "which the inhabitants use for their tea and for other kitchen purposes."[9] This was the famous Tea Water Pump. Located at the hilly intersection of country roads a few steps above the eastern outlet of the Fresh Water Pond, the Tea Water Pump became New York's single source of good water for the remainder of the colonial period.

The pump seems to have begun service in the late 1730s or early 1740s. Who dug the well that tapped the underground spring, who equipped the well with a pump, and who turned its water into a treasured commodity is unclear. The best evidence suggests the flourishing Hardenbrook family, whose various members owned plots of land containing the spring and nearby tanyards as early as the late 1600s and well into the 1800s.[10] One imagines that with the downfall of Comfort's Tea Water after 1741, the industrious Hardenbrooks stepped into the breach with some tea water of their own.

It's not clear whether the Hardenbrooks ran the water concession or leased their pump to others, but by midcentury, an industry was born: several people were earning their living carting the water and selling it by the cask or pail. The law prohibiting blacks from fetching water was allowed to lapse because water delivery had passed to a professional class of "Teawater Men." By 1757, their business was significant enough for the Common Council to consider regulations, though no law was enacted. In the meantime, the Tea Water Pump spawned a catch phrase for good water. In 1768, an ad for a Pearl Street tavern to rent noted "a very good Pump of excellent Tea Water, in the Yard" among its amenities.[11]

Despite the growing dependence on the Tea Water Pump, not every colonial New Yorker could afford the forty-five shilling annual cost.[12] The city recognized the need to maintain the free, if lamented, public wells. By the early 1740s, several had been fitted with wooden pumps. In the wake of the 1741 "revolt" and attendant arson, the Provincial Assembly hastily passed a law for the upkeep of the city's wells and pumps, aimed specifically at ensuring a sufficient supply of water to fight fires.[13]

Under the law, each ward's alderman and assistant had overall charge of its wells. They appointed an overseer to repair and maintain the wells and, when ordered, fit them with pumps. Residents were assessed well taxes, with forced property sales to cover unmet obligations. For his troubles, the overseer was paid one shilling for every twenty collected. Such vandalism as cutting well ropes, breaking pump handles, and "other Mischiefs" merited a forty-shilling fine. Originally written to expire after three years, the law was regularly extended and revised for the duration of the colonial period.[14]

The law was a boon to the public water system. The records of the Common Council indicate numerous payments for the sinking of new wells, the installation of pumps, and their continuing maintenance. As the system evolved, the city generally contributed a modest £8 toward the significantly higher cost of a new well, and the standard well width grew from six feet to eight. The significant technology advance during the period was the installation of brass pump chambers; from 1753 to 1764, the city paid nearly £100 for thirty brass pumps. As the English period drew to a close, dozens of public wells and pumps were scattered through the streets of the city.[15]

To Their Health

As the laws promoting the public wells and pumps make clear, the greatest interest was in having plenty of water to douse fires. When colonial

New Yorkers drank, it was not straight well water but more than likely water boiled and mixed with other ingredients, especially alcohol, the lubricant of commerce and society.

In 1704, Boston shopkeeper Sarah Kemble Knight observed that New York market auctions featured the liberal consumption of liquor. In 1744, Dr. Hamilton found that prominent visitors were well regarded only if they were "bumper men" and "good toapers." The game doctor "tossed about the bumpers so furiously" at the best supper club with Governor George Clinton and others that he often retired drunk; he tired of nothing in New York but the "excessive drinking." In the end, he "was glad to remove from a place where the temptation of drinking ... threw itself so often in my way."[16]

Alcohol consumption was hardly the exclusive pursuit of the elite, but it was New York's special offering. In the year of Hamilton's visit, the city of some eleven thousand souls had 166 licensed taverns, more than either Boston or Philadelphia, both of which had larger populations. By 1773, New York's population had merely doubled but the official number of taverns hit 396; there were untold numbers of unlicensed liquor sellers.[17]

Rich and poor had plenty of potions to choose from. From the beery Dutch days, English New York proceeded to Madeira and rum. New York imported greater amounts of Madeira than any other American city; the vintage of 1767 obtained an unequaled reputation. The heavy wines of Spain, Portugal, and the Azores were favored over lighter wines. In 1768, New York boasted seventeen distilleries, producing over half a million gallons of rum. It was no coincidence that the leading sugar houses were run, to great profit, by the city's leading families: Bayard, Livingston, Roosevelt, Van Cortlandt, Cuyler, and Rhinelander.[18]

Rum, "the staple drink of the century," was freely mixed with fruit concoctions at social, business, and official events. The prime ingredients of "Rack punch," likely as not served in a communal bowl, were rum, brandy, porter, sugar, lemons, and a dash of arrack. Flip was "a universal and 'most insinuating' drink," concocted of beer, sugar or dried pumpkin, and rum, heated to a foaming boil with a red-hot poker called a loggerhead, and topped with a batter "flip" of cream, egg, and sugar. Mimbo, or mim, was rum drunk with loaf sugar; calibogus, or bogus, was rum and beer or molasses; black-strap was rum and molasses with assorted herbs.[19]

Many of the rum drinks, especially the punches, required at least a dash of water and, given the quality of the local supply, boiled tea was the common substitute for plain water. Good drinking water was so dear and distilled spirits so plentiful that in 1770, the Common Council started paying "for divers Quantitys of liquor Delivered out" at fires, a perk that became increasingly common. In 1773, the council repaid tavern keeper John Simmons for the liquor supplied to a coroner's jury, a common practice apparently designed to ease the deliberative process.[20]

Still, not all of New York was routinely drunk. Hot chocolate, introduced by the Dutch, was the most popular nonalcoholic drink of the early colonial period, only slowly giving way in the mid-1700s to tea and coffee. As seen in the rise of "tea water," tea drinking increased in popularity as well water declined in quality. Dr. Hamilton drank tea at four most afternoons at his lodgings, often in the company of young women. By the end of the English period, New Yorkers routinely paused for the tea-washed late-day meal now known as "high tea."[21]

Tea was not drunk at breakfast; the morning brew for late colonial New Yorkers remained warm beer. Coffee was slow to percolate into colonial home life. It was first drunk in New York at public coffeehouses by sober merchants, and soon enough by caffeinated revolutionaries. Pub-crawler Hamilton recorded no visits to either the Merchants' Coffee House (opened in 1737) or the Exchange Coffee House (1709), though the latter was just next door to his favorite tavern. Two more coffeehouses opened in the 1750s, and three in the 1760s, which still made for a rather limited cafe society.

Water, as a general rule, was not a beverage by itself. In one of his drinking groups, Hamilton did come upon a fellow doctor who "would drink nothing but water," though this form of intoxication left his discourse "copious and insipid."[22]

The public wells and pumps served for fire fighting and some domestic purposes, but the Tea Water Pump gradually became the city's only source for drinkable water. A plan depicting the city, drawn by the British military engineer John Montrésor in 1766, clearly identifies the "Fresh Water Engine, from whence the Town is supplied." By 1774, one interested observer estimated there were "3000 Houses that receive Water from the Tea Water Men," meaning that every house in the city was taking at least

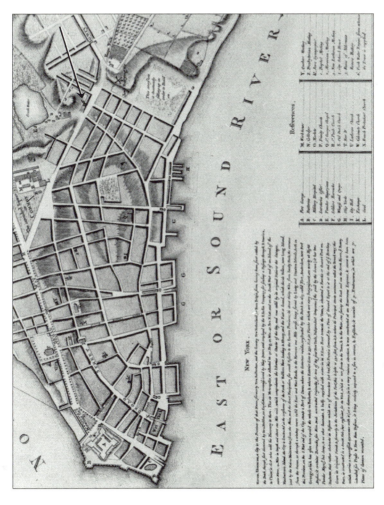

FIGURE 7. New York, 1766

This detail of a hand-colored copperplate engraving by French military engineer John Montrésor in 1766, reissued in varying editions over the following decade, shows (arrow) the location of the Tea Water Pump, "from whence the Town is supplied." (Historic Illustrated Plans; photo by Barry Rosenthal.)

FIGURE 8. *The Tea Water Pump, late 18th century*
This often-reproduced drawing of uncertain vintage depicts the famous pump in
its heyday.

some of its water from the pump. There was no demonstrable concern
as yet that the pump sat just downstream from the Collect Pond's growing assortment of tanyards, slaughterhouses, and other noxious industry.[23]

The Colles Try

"Had I been brought up a hatter," Christopher Colles often lamented,
"people would have come into the world without heads." The star-crossed
engineer and inventor arrived in New York in 1774 with a plan to change
both the city's water misfortunes and his own bad luck.[24]

Colles (1739–1816) had emigrated to Philadelphia two years earlier from
Ireland, leaving behind a trail of youthful indistinction. Born into a withering Dublin branch of an otherwise distinguished Anglo-Irish family, Colles
was raised and educated by his genius uncle William, whose marble mill
in Kilkenny was famed throughout Ireland. Among William Colles's
many successful endeavors were several water projects that failed: marble water pipes for Dublin and Cork, and a long-standing effort to turn
Kilkenny's rapids-strewn river Nore into a navigable canal linked by

FIGURE 9. *Christopher Colles, circa 1809*
Here Colles is shown as an older man by painter John Wesley Jarvis. Colles failed to put his New-York Water Works into operation just before the Revolution but remained active in the city's water searches for twenty-five years. (© Collection of The New-York Historical Society.)

others to Dublin. It was these projects that apparently seized the imagination of his inquisitive but restless nephew, whose brief first employment was as pay clerk on the doomed canal project.

Over the next ten years, doting William bailed out headstrong Christopher from business ventures that failed, set him up in architectural and engineering positions that he abandoned, frowned at his apparently happy marriage to a social inferior, and generally feared for his nephew's self-destruction. After William died of gout in 1770, Christopher hoisted anchor. With his wife, several of an eventual six children (five others died young), and a small advance on his living mother's estate, Colles sailed off to America, "convinced it would be a proper place to make money in for one of my way."

Colles landed in Philadelphia with letters of introduction from an old Quaker schoolteacher. In two years time, he did not find his fortune but he did establish a reputation, of sorts. He sought work as an engineer and architect, gave scientific lectures at the preeminent American Philosophical Society, and labored to produce a machine practically unknown in America: a steam engine. After failing to secure financial backing from the Pennsylvania Assembly, Colles was hired by a local distillery to build an engine to pump water into cooling tanks around the distilling coils. It is considered to be the first steam engine made in America.[25]

In part because England actively discouraged industrial independence in the colonies, only one other steam engine had been at work in America. Imported in parts from England in 1753 to pump water out of the famous Schuyler copper mines in New Jersey, the engine was assembled and operated by its English builder, Josiah Hornblower (1729–1809), whose father had been an early associate of engine inventor Thomas Newcomen. A refinement of the Newcomen engines long in service at English mines, the Hornblower engine had a boiler some eight to ten feet around, a cast iron cylinder three feet across and eight feet high, and a piston performing up to twelve strokes a minute. With a ten-inch-diameter pump and a pump rod one hundred feet long, the engine was able to extract two hundred thousand gallons of water a day. But the £1,000 engine was wrecked by a fire in early 1773; with revolution approaching and business uncertain, Hornblower made no effort to rebuild it.[26]

Thus, when Christopher Colles was building his engine in Philadelphia that summer, he had no model to draw on. Whether Colles ever saw the Hornblower engine in operation is unknown. By his own admission, Colles's engine was no match.

Colles humbly sought support from the Philosophical Society. Limited finances had forced him to build an undersized boiler; a favorable review from the society would help him raise money from a public subscription for a better effort. A committee featuring scientist and inventor David Rittenhouse promptly had a look. They saw the machine "perform several strokes, tho' some of the materials not being sufficiently large and strong, owing to his attempting the execution at a very low expence, it did not continue in motion long." The society experts concluded that Colles was well acquainted with the necessary mechanical principles, very capable of building a better engine, and "worthy of Public encouragement," though the society itself provided none.[27]

Encouragement came in New York eight months later. Why Colles moved from Philadelphia is unknown, but at the Common Council session of April 22, 1774, he presented a detailed proposal "to Erect a Reservoir, and to Convey Water thro' the Several Streets of this City."[28] The "New-York Water Works" would, if built, be the city's first piped water supply, a solution to the city's largest problem.

It was an inauspicious day to launch such a radical idea. Most of the town's attention that Friday was focused on events in the harbor. The ship *London,* approaching from England, was boarded at noon by members of the newly formed Committee of Observation, and escorted to the town wharf in the late afternoon. After repeated patriotic inquiries, the harried royalist captain confessed that his ship carried £2,000 worth of tea purchased and heavily taxed in England. In the evening, a mob inspired by earlier actions in Boston entered the ship's holds and dumped her cargo into the East River. The next morning, the New York Tea Party was celebrated with the largest public gathering yet held in the city.[29] Though for a time both the waterworks and the revolution proceeded apace, it was impossible that both could succeed.

The plan that Colles proposed to the council and promoted in public broadsides was revolutionary in itself, a grand vision of urban living unknown in provincial America.

Boston had built the first colonial water supply system back in 1652. "The Conduit," as the private project was known, consisted merely of a twelve-foot-square reservoir at the intersection of Union and Ann Streets, gravity-fed by wooden pipes from nearby wells and springs. The reservoir primarily supplied water to fight fires and for the laundry needs of neighboring families. It apparently had fallen into general disuse by the turn of the century, when several individuals reported laying their own pipes from the reservoir.[30]

The first pumped water supply in America was completed in 1755 for the tiny Moravian community established at Bethlehem, Pennsylvania, fourteen years earlier. Built by Danish millwright Hans Christopher Christiansen, the ingenious system featured an undershot wooden waterwheel, iron crankshaft, and three water-powered forcing pumps. The system sucked spring water through a lead and wood pipe to a water tower 320 feet away and ninety feet high, then distributed it by gravity to four cisterns. "Every house in the town is supplied with an abundance of excellent water," remarked a visitor forty years later. "Some of the houses are supplied with water in every room." The works survived into the 1830s, when the growth of the community overwhelmed its limited capacity.[31]

Providence, Rhode Island, was the only other colonial town with a piped water supply. In 1772, two private companies brought water by gravity through wooden pipes from springs a mile distant, but these efforts in a town of barely four thousand people were short-lived.[32]

Colles's plan, as it evolved during the spring of 1774, envisioned a waterworks on high ground just north of town, and a large network of distributing pipes to furnish the city "with a constant supply of FRESH WATER." To raise water from a large well, Colles proposed a steam engine with a forty-inch cylinder and a twelve-inch pump, housed in a tile-covered brick or stone building, and capable of raising two hundred thousand daily gallons of water as it consumed some eighteen tons of coal a week. Colles indicated an awareness of James Watt's ongoing experiments with a separate condenser that would burn half as much fuel as a Newcomen engine, but a working prototype was still several years and an ocean away.[33]

To save fuel, Colles suggested a reservoir large enough to allow the steam engine to work only half the week: 126 feet square, with twelve-foot

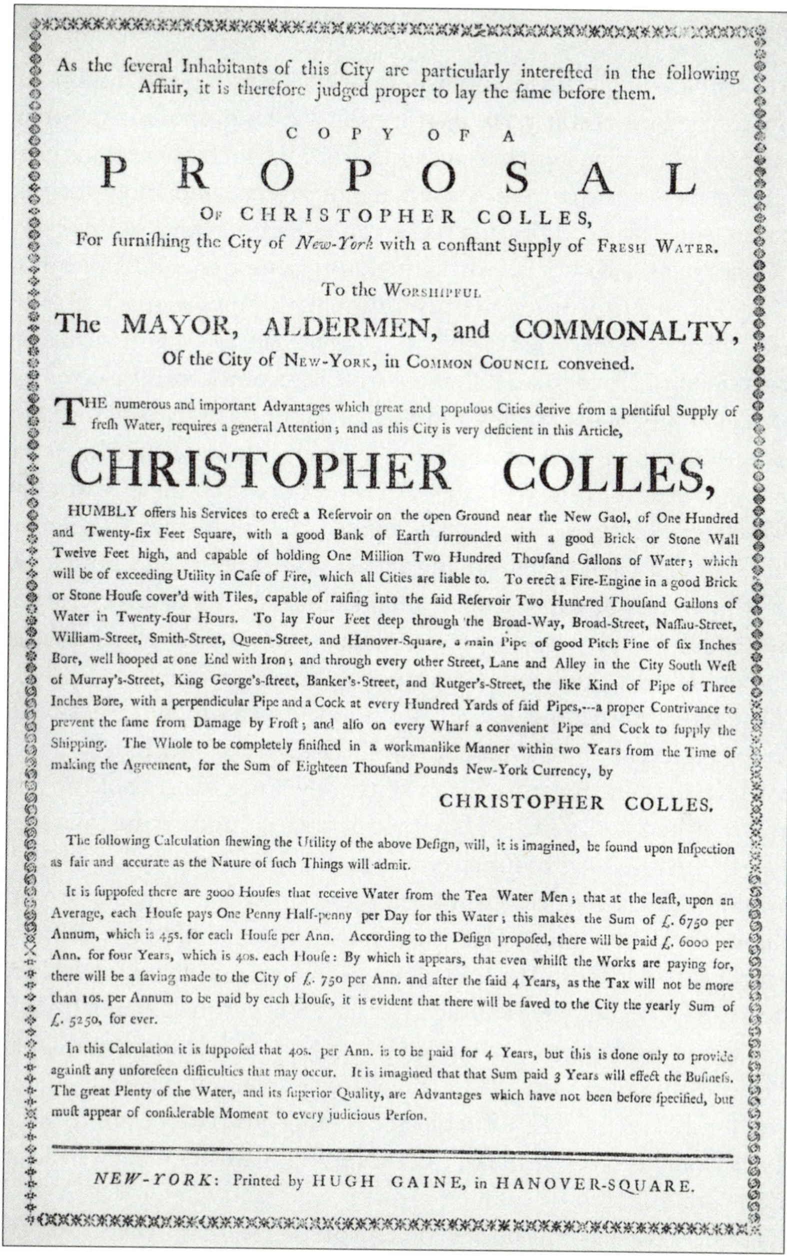

As the several Inhabitants of this City are particularly interested in the following Affair, it is therefore judged proper to lay the same before them.

COPY OF A

PROPOSAL

OF CHRISTOPHER COLLES,

For furnishing the City of *New-York* with a constant Supply of FRESH WATER.

To the WORSHIPFUL

The MAYOR, ALDERMEN, and COMMONALTY,

Of the City of NEW-YORK, in COMMON COUNCIL convened.

THE numerous and important Advantages which great and populous Cities derive from a plentiful Supply of fresh Water, requires a general Attention; and as this City is very deficient in this Article,

CHRISTOPHER COLLES,

HUMBLY offers his Services to erect a Reservoir on the open Ground near the New Gaol, of One Hundred and Twenty-six Feet Square, with a good Bank of Earth surrounded with a good Brick or Stone Wall Twelve Feet high, and capable of holding One Million Two Hundred Thousand Gallons of Water; which will be of exceeding Utility in Case of Fire, which all Cities are liable to. To erect a Fire-Engine in a good Brick or Stone House cover'd with Tiles, capable of raising into the said Reservoir Two Hundred Thousand Gallons of Water in Twenty-four Hours. To lay Four Feet deep through the Broad-Way, Broad-Street, Nassau-Street, William-Street, Smith-Street, Queen-Street, and Hanover-Square, a main Pipe of good Pitch Pine of six Inches Bore, well hooped at one End with Iron; and through every other Street, Lane and Alley in the City South West of Murray's-Street, King George's-street, Banker's-Street, and Rutger's-Street, the like Kind of Pipe of Three Inches Bore, with a perpendicular Pipe and a Cock at every Hundred Yards of said Pipes,---a proper Contrivance to prevent the same from Damage by Frost; and also on every Wharf a convenient Pipe and Cock to supply the Shipping. The Whole to be completely finished in a workmanlike Manner within two Years from the Time of making the Agreement, for the Sum of Eighteen Thousand Pounds New-York Currency, by

CHRISTOPHER COLLES.

The following Calculation shewing the Utility of the above Design, will, it is imagined, be found upon Inspection as fair and accurate as the Nature of such Things will admit.

It is supposed there are 3000 Houses that receive Water from the Tea Water Men; that at the least, upon an Average, each House pays One Penny Half-penny per Day for this Water; this makes the Sum of £. 6750 per Annum, which is 45s. for each House per Ann. According to the Design proposed, there will be paid £. 6000 per Ann. for four Years, which is 40s. each House: By which it appears, that even whilst the Works are paying for, there will be a saving made to the City of £. 750 per Ann. and after the said 4 Years, as the Tax will not be more than 10s. per Annum to be paid by each House, it is evident that there will be saved to the City the yearly Sum of £. 5250, for ever.

In this Calculation it is supposed that 40s. per Ann. is to be paid for 4 Years, but this is done only to provide against any unforeseen difficulties that may occur. It is imagined that that Sum paid 3 Years will effect the Business. The great Plenty of the Water, and its superior Quality, are Advantages which have not been before specified, but must appear of considerable Moment to every judicious Person.

NEW-YORK: Printed by HUGH GAINE, in HANOVER-SQUARE.

FIGURE 10. New-York Water Works proposal, 1774

Published in mid-1774, this broadside by Christopher Colles outlines his proposal to build a water works consisting of a well, steam engine, reservoir, and log pipes. (Chapin Library of Rare Books, Williams College, Williamstown, Mass.)

earth embankments lined with wood, brick, or stone, and holding over a million gallons of water. For distribution, Colles proposed a network of hollowed pitch pine logs, hooped with iron: six-inch bore mains buried four feet beneath the town's seven major streets, and three-inch pipe beneath the rest. Access would be by cocks placed every hundred yards.

Colles put the cost of his works, including a modest salary for himself, at £18,000, at a time when the city's annual revenues were about £3,000 and its debt £13,000.[34] He carefully showed the fantastic figure represented a cost savings. He estimated that tea water currently cost the city's three thousand households a penny and a half a day or forty-five shillings a year, for a total annual cost of £6,750. If households were taxed just forty shillings a year for four years to build his waterworks, the city would net £24,000, providing a large surplus against any "unforeseen difficulties." After four years, a mere ten-shilling annual tax per household would maintain the system at £1,500, an annual savings on water of £5,250. The wisdom of the plan, Colles concluded, "must appear of considerable Moment to every judicious Person."

The judicious people of the Common Council ordered city surveyor Gerard Bancker to take a measure of the city. With Colles in tow, Bancker took levels in June from the Fresh Water down to a liberty pole on upper Broadway near today's City Hall Park; he then computed the total length of all the city's streets at fourteen miles.[35]

On July 21, the council, after some debate, voted eight to two to go ahead, followed by a unanimous vote to issue an initial £2,500 worth of promissory notes to pay for it. The council was informed that Augustus and Frederick Van Cortlandt were willing to sell, at £600 per acre, as much of their land as was needed between Great George Street (the northern extension of upper Broadway) and the northwestern portion of the Fresh Water as a site for the waterworks. On a hillside sloping down to the pond, this was largely virgin territory, with none of the noxious industries that were located on the other side of the pond.[36]

The newspapers immediately took up the banner of the New-York Water Works. A "useful and Laudable Design," reported the *New York Journal;* "Water will be conveyed through every Street and Lane in this City," the *New York Gazette and Weekly Mercury* affirmed. "It is hoped," wrote French essayist Jean de Crèvecouer, then cultivating his nearby farm,

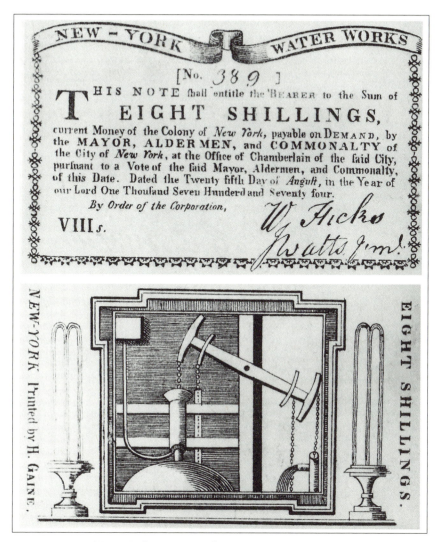

FIGURE 11. New-York Water Works money, 1774

This eight-shilling note was part of the first issue of money to finance the Colles waterworks; the back of the note features an engraving of a Newcomen-type steam engine flanked by fountains. (General Research Division. The New York Public Library. Astor, Lenox and Tilden Foundations.)

"that New York will very soon be abundantly supplied with a quantity of water sufficient for the use of houses and washing of the streets."[37]

In early August, the council agreed to buy a portion of the Van Cortlandt land, provided that upon the sinking of a well, good water was found. Colles promptly set to digging. Two and a half weeks later, members of the council tested the waters and pronounced them "of a very good Quality." They ordered Colles to enlarge the well and "prosecute the undertaking." After a Bancker survey, the city purchased 1.75 acres of the Van Cortlandt plot for £1,050 in bonds, redeemable in a year at 5 percent interest.[38]

It cost £230 to complete the well. It was thirty feet across and twenty-eight feet deep, with eight feet of water and a "very fine running sand" at the bottom. Dr. Samuel Bard, the colonial city's leading man of science, used a silver solution to compare the water with that of the Tea Water Pump: "the Tea Water had a visible tinge of white, about as much as if two drops of Sweet Milk had been put into it; whilst that of the great Well was no more discolored, than if two drops of clean Water was put into it."[39]

At the end of August, the council ordered the printing of £2,500 worth of notes, in denominations from six pence to eight shillings. Local engraver Elisha Gallaudet, who later cast the die for the Continental Dollar of 1776, designed the notes with the denomination on the front and an illustration of a Newcomen engine flanked by fountains on the back. Printed in red and black ink, the "water works money" was the first paper currency issued by an American city, and rapidly became "current as other Money."[40]

After advertising for a pipe supplier in early September, the city signed a contract two months later with the Isaac Manns senior and junior, of Stillwater, New York, above Albany on the Hudson. Colles, a superstitious man, perhaps saw destiny in their selection: the Protestant Lord Bishop of Cork—the city William Colles had proposed to water and from which Christopher took his departure to America—was also named Isaac Mann.[41]

The Manns agreed to provide sixty thousand feet of logs for £1,250, of which they received an advance of £250. They were to deliver the logs, fourteen to twenty feet long, "straight and free from Shakes and large Knots," in three shipments from July to October 1775. The total cost of the distribution system, including pipe, street digging and repaving, clay to lay around the pipes, and the cocks to fit into them, was later estimated at nearly £12,600.[42]

While Bancker continued taking levels around the city, Colles completed a reservoir much larger than originally planned, some 165 feet square with a capacity of two million gallons, at a cost of roughly £1,850. The structure's sloping earthen embankments were forty feet wide at the base, tapering up their twelve-foot height to six feet thick at the top. The vertical interior wall was brick or stone, with a coping wall 3½ feet wide along the top, sealing the joint between the interior wall and the embankment.[43]

At the same time, Colles was hard at work designing his engine. Unlike when he built his Philadelphia machine, money was in good supply. The builders were Peter Curtenius and Richard Sharpe, whose New York Air Furnace, on a lot now featuring the Woolworth Building, had opened for business in 1767 with the boast that its pots, kettles, skillets, forge hammers, anvils, stoves, weights, and chafing dishes would be better and cheaper than any European imports.[44]

The waterworks engine was the company's greatest project. The cylinder was cast on February 10, 1775, reportedly "the first performance of the kind ever attempted in America, and allowed by Judges to be extremely well executed."[45] It was, though, only seven feet long and a mere twenty inches in diameter, a good bit smaller than the Hornblower engine cylinder and the cylinder proposed by Colles.[46] The boiler, presumably also fabricated by Sharpe and Curtenius, had a reported capacity of just twelve hundred gallons, a fraction of Hornblower's boiler. Still, that machine was fabricated in industrialized England by the leading manufacturer of steam engines. The Colles engine, the second made in America, was created by colonial craftsmen working with limited supplies and plans drawn at best from images of what a steam engine should be. It was a valiant effort. By the time the engine was put into operation a year later, the cost for all its parts and labor had risen to £1,500.[47]

As Colles and various waterworks contractors labored away, spending £2,400 by February 1775, the rush of patriotic events closed in. After word reached the city of the Battle of Lexington, riot became the chief activity in early April 1775, followed by forming various kinds of revolutionary government. "Many families are retiring into the country," wrote a New

Yorker in early May, "all business declining fast, and in a few weeks we expect will totally cease." The *New York Mercury* reported in midmonth that "The Martial Spirit diffused through this Province is almost beyond Conception." The following week, the Provincial Congress met in New York for its first session.[48]

Incredibly, Colles remained on the job and the still-functioning Common Council continued to lavish support. In August 1775, the council ordered a second issue of waterworks notes totaling £2,600, followed by £2,000 more in January, and a final £2,000 in March 1776. The works had become an industry in itself; Common Council records indicate payments to numerous craftsmen for tile, rope, pumps, and iron work.[49]

The winter of 1776 was unusually cold and miserable. "This City is in Terror and confusion," wrote Governor William Tryon in early February, after repairing some months earlier to the comparative safety of a ship in the harbor. Mayor Whitehead Hicks quit town with other Loyalists in mid-February, after American forces arrived to prepare New York's defense. "To see the vast number of houses shut up," wrote steadfast New Yorker Frederick Rhinelander in late February, "one would think the city almost evacuated. Women and children are scarcely to be seen in the streets. Troops are daily coming in; they break open and quarter themselves in any houses they find shut up."[50]

But on March 4, Christopher Colles had some cheerful news. "The Fire Engine of the Water Works being now completely finished," reported the *New York Mercury,* "Mr. Colles proposes to keep it going for several Days successively, to give every Gentleman an Opportunity of seeing it." To announce the times of the engine's operation, workers raised a flag that was visible down the length of Broadway. The engine was worked many days that week, "greatly to the Satisfaction of vast Numbers of People who went to see it."[51]

The city's money seems to have been well spent. Josiah Hornblower had needed a year and a half to assemble a prefabricated engine; Colles had accomplished the design, building, and operation of his own engine under vastly deteriorated conditions and in less time. The *Mercury* enthusiastically described the engine, burning wood instead of scarce coal, raising twenty-nine gallons per six-foot stroke; at ten strokes a minute, the engine reportedly was capable of raising 417,600 gallons a day, though

Colles's own later account indicated the engine raised just under three hundred thousand gallons when it was worked only once for a whole day.[52] Still, in a city with a prewar population of just under twenty-five thousand, even the lower figure would have provided nearly twelve gallons of water a day per person, an astounding supply for a preindustrial community then making do with a daily gallon or two of pumped and carted water.

Steam engines were mysterious machines in colonial America. The Hornblower engine in New Jersey was known to a privileged few; it was wrecked in 1773. Colles's Philadelphia engine attracted the passing attention of a handful of scientists. But his New York engine—belching wood smoke, hissing steam, driving metal machine parts, and lifting water from deep beneath the ground—was a sight to be seen.

Watching the engine in action was high on the agenda of Isaac Bangs, a Harvard-educated surgeon in a Massachusetts militia who arrived in New York in April 1776. The young Bostonian, who would die of war wounds in 1780, kept a detailed journal during his several months in and around the city. On April 20, he visited the works that were to replace the city's "very bad & unwholesome" well water. Bangs's description remains the most complete on record and illustrates the wonder of it all.[53]

The most difficult part, as Bangs saw it, had been accomplished: a pump in the well would raise water through a wooden pipe uphill for a distance of eighty feet to the reservoir. "All of this I could easily understand," Bangs confided to his journal, "but the grand Question was how was the Machiene in the Well first actuated & continued in Motion? This I was surprised to find was wholly done by the Power of Boiling Water." Trained to be intellectually curious, Bangs made a closer inspection, attempting "a perticular discription of this curious Engine," which unfortunately he never saw running:

> I found that by Means of a large Copper (which is kept boiling when it is requisite for the Works to be set in Motion) the Steem or Vapour of the Water is conveued from thence into a strong Copper Tube . . . which stands perpendicularly. The lower part or end of this Tube is tight; but the uper [*sic*] End hath in it a moveable Stopper which may move upwards or Downwards with as much ease as possible, and at the same time to keep any of the Air from without from entering into

the Tube & to keep it as tight as possible another part of the Works
constantly supply the Top of the Tube above the Stopper with a small
stream of Water. The Steem of the Hot Water (as I take it) entering
into the Tube rarifyeth the Body of the Air contained therein to a great
degree, when the Stopper is let loose and flyeth upwards with great
Rapidity to the upper End of the Tube, when the pressure of the Air
from without throweth [it] back to the Bottom of the Tube with as
great Force as it came upwards. When it gets to the bottom it is again
drove upwards by the same cause, & repelled when it arrives at the Top:
thus the Stopper is kept in constant Motion by the Means of Steam
or Vapour, & to this Stopper is fastened a stout Wooden lever by a bar
of Iron. The Lever is Fastened in the Middle upon an Axis; and as the
Stopper of the Tube moves upwards and downwards, it moves the Lever,
which worketh the [pump] in the Well, which forceth (as I before
described) the Water into the Pond at the Top of the Hill.[54]

The person best equipped to report on the Colles engine would have
been Josiah Hornblower. In fact, he had been hired by the Common
Council in May to do just that. Unfortunately, his report, for which he collected a £12 fee after the war, has been lost.[55]

By the time of Hornblower's inspection, the city had become a lawless
camp. Amid rumors of British invasions and Tory conspiracies, patriotic
mobs took over, until the city was abandoned to the British without a fight
in September. By then, the population had dropped to perhaps five thousand, most of them Loyalists.[56] In the early morning of the 21st, a fire of
unknown origin swept through the emptied city, destroying a quarter of
its buildings and any remaining semblance of normal city life.

It is unclear precisely when patriotic Christopher Colles took his leave.
One account has him chased through the occupied city by British soldiers,
escaping their probing bayonets in the tall grass of the Trinity Church grave-
yard. A Loyalist cousin arriving in 1778 was told that Christopher, his wife,
and children were last seen crossing the Hudson into New Jersey. "His wat-
ter works," John Colles wrote home, "were almost finished when he
flead."[57]

How much of the Colles project was actually completed? The best measure comes from Colles's own hand. In 1784, in the first of several memo-

rials to city officials after the war, he made a claim for £600 owed him and various contractors, the difference between £3,000 in bills paid and £3,600 for "the part executed." Colles claimed completion of only the reservoir, well, and steam engine, a small fraction of the £18,000 project; he made no mention of any work on the £12,600 distribution system.[58] Indeed, when the younger Isaac Mann made an unsuccessful claim in 1798 for the balance of his unpaid log contract, the Common Council could not find any evidence that the logs had even been delivered.[59]

The 1776 fire did not reach as far as the waterworks, but the British did. Testimony to British failure to discourage American industry, New York's budding waterworks, along with David Rittenhouse's famous orrery at Princeton, were reported by February 1777 to have been "wantonly destroyed."[60] A wanderer in the occupied city, venturing up the road not yet called Broadway, would have come upon only remains of what had promised to be colonial New York's greatest civic project.[61] But for the great well, which would be tapped again, nothing else of Colles's New-York Water Works survived the Revolution.

New City, Old Trouble

The water is very bad to drink, except at . . . the tea-water pump.
—Henry Wansey, *Henry Wansey and his*
American Journal 1794

It will be very difficult for the city to command a river.
—Joseph Browne, *Memoir on Supplying the City*
with Pure and Wholesome Water

New York did not fare well during the Revolution. A fire two years into the British occupation destroyed much of what the 1776 fire missed, leaving the city "almost half Burned to Ashes." Shelter, food, and fuel were in short supply. In the winter of 1780, river traffic was blocked by ice and people froze to death from lack of firewood; during a 1781 reconnoiter, George Washington reported the island "totally stripped of trees."[1]

Drought and deforestation played havoc with the groundwater. There was no rain for two months in the spring of 1780; in the summer of 1782, the town wells were dry and Hessian soldiers dug holes forty feet deep without striking water, arousing fears of death from thirst.[2]

Sanitation, moderately efficient since the 1740s, had broken down by the first summer of occupation. A newly arrived Englishman believed a "treatise upon stinks" could be written about New York; a 1780 proclamation ordered all garbage dumped into Beekman's Swamp, an unhappy prospect.[3]

Maintenance of the public wells and pumps fell to an ad hoc vestry. As civic order was breaking down just before the Revolution, control of well and pump overseer appointments had passed from the Common

Council to the city's secular, elected vestrymen, whose primary responsibility since the 1740s had been ministering to the poor, collecting and
distributing the poor tax, and overseeing the almshouse.[4] This ward-
based vestry disappeared under occupation, replaced by a group of loyalist citizens appointed by the British commandant of New York. The
occupation vestry eventually took over the duties of the elected vestry, as
well as most of the functions of the disbanded Common Council. Without tax collection, the appointed vestry did what it could about the poor,
the pumps, sanitation, and other government duties by collecting dona-
tions, exorbitant rent on abandoned houses, criminal fines, and tavern
license fees.[5] This was no easy task; by the end of the war in 1783, the occupied town was bloated with some thirty thousand people, most of them
impoverished loyalist refugees.[6]

What became of New York's favorite tea water during the war isn't clear.
A July 1780 advertisement promoted a new tavern near the Tea Water Pump,
its water available on demand. As to the pump itself, the vestry advertised
the following March for a renter for the ensuing year; there is no indication when the previous renter departed or if a new one was found. Apparently the patriotic Hardenbrooks had taken leave of their property during
the English occupation.[7]

New York became an American city on November 26, 1783. A couple
of months later, the Hardenbrook family announced its intention to sell
by April the "noted and valuable" lot containing the pump, itself "supplied
by never-failing Springs," the good water and privilege of vending it "too
well known to want any encomiums."[8] In the meantime, the restored Common Council again cast its eye on the pump, after a suggestion that the
Tea Water Men be required to assist at fires. As before the Revolution, the
effort failed; a fire prevention law passed in March 1784 made no mention of the water carters.[9] Despite the regulatory escape, the Hardenbrooks
failed to sell off their property by April, which perhaps prompted the July
suicide of Abraham Revere, "who lately occupied the 'Tea-Water Pump.'"[10]

Revere's demise coincided with the start of a declining local image for
the pump. A correspondent to the *New York Packet* that summer called
attention to the fact that many people were washing their dirty linen in
a section of the Collect Pond near the pump, "a practice which has a manifest tendency to affect the health of the inhabitants of this city."[11]

Laundry was the least of the trouble. In the dawning days of Recon-
struction, noxious industry beat a path to the Fresh Water's southern and
eastern shores. Furnaces, potteries, breweries, tanneries, rope-walks, and
other manufactories sought the pond's plentiful waters.[12] The negative relationship between industry and drinking water wasn't immediately clear
to all. An October 1784 advertisement for a group of lots between the pump
and the pond praised the location as excellent for a distillery because the
pump was fed through those lots.[13]

Some otherwise satisfied customers were likely given pause by a long
open letter to city officials published in the *New York Journal* at the end
of August 1785:

> It is remarked by the citizens, that the Tea Water, with which this city
> is supplied, grows worse every day, so that the common pump water,
> used only to scrub houses, etc. with, is now preferred in cooking to
> our Tea Water. The reason is very obvious,—let any one view the pond,
> which is the spring and source of that pump, and you will find it to
> be a very sink and common sewer. It's like a fair every day with
> whites, and blacks, washing their cloths blankets and things too nau-
> seous to mention; all their sudds and filth are emptied into this pond,
> besides dead dogs, cats, etc. thrown in daily, and no doubt, many buck-
> ets [bodily waste] from that quarter of the town.

The anonymous writer suggested a small tax to pay for two watchmen,
"and in 6 or 9 months our water would be as good as it was before the war."[14]

There is no indication that guards were posted around the Collect, but
the prewar effort to water the city from the far side of the pond was increasingly on local minds. In August 1784, newly returned Christopher Colles
came calling on the Common Council for his £450 share of unpaid
accounts; after another two and a half years of detailed memorials and partial payments, he received a total of £300. The process was confounded
by the absence of records, many of which were either lost during the war
or removed to England. Often with Colles's certification, various contractors
pursued their claims as well, collecting some £250 by the end of the
decade. In January 1786, Josiah Hornblower staked his claim to the £12
owed him for inspecting the Colles works in 1776; he collected in 1788.[15]

The partial success of the Colles project and the continuing pursuit of related claims inspired a flow of proposals modeled on the Colles plan. In March 1785, wealthy iron founder and land promoter Samuel Ogden and associates sought approval from the Common Council for a nearly identical plan; it was referred to a committee, the first of several that would receive water supply proposals.[16] In May, architect Joseph Newton and Jonathan Emery proposed a Colles-like £30,000 plan, to be funded by a lottery; this plan never reached the council.[17] In January 1786, the Common Council heard proposals from Chancellor Robert R. Livingston, scion of New York's most prominent family, longtime chief judge of the state Court of Chancery, and keenly interested in steam engines (he backed Robert Fulton's *Clermont* in 1807); a committee was appointed to review Livingston's plans.[18]

The council discussed the various plans during February 1786, but decided to return them and advertise for sealed proposals for a privately owned supply. Hampered by a shortage of public funds, the council reckoned it best to grant "the privilege of supplying the city with water . . . to such persons or companies as will engage in the undertaking on the most reasonable terms."[19] This earnest intention marked the beginning of decades of official abdication of responsibility on the subject of water and of private interest choking off real solutions to New York's growing water needs.

A correspondent to the *Daily Advertiser,* approving of the council's good intentions to water the city, nevertheless warned about private interest:

> As an important and permanent revenue may result from it, and tend to diminish our heavy taxes, it becomes a subject of the most serious nature, and I make no doubt, the corporation, as upright guardians to every citizen, will prevent a few interested persons making what is called a *job* of it—and as they have too much delicacy to interest themselves in the contract, either directly or indirectly, I flatter myself their wisdom and integrity will conduct and guard us through every stage of this momentous undertaking.[20]

Over the two-month bidding period, council members informally discovered that public opinion was decidedly against a private water company. Three sealed proposals received in April were returned unread and council members assigned themselves the task of soliciting written opinions from their constituents on whether a private or a public supply, funded by taxes, was most desired.[21] Establishing the pattern of official inaction that would intensify over the next half-century, no such opinions appear to have been gathered.

It was nearly two years before a petition began circulating through the city, favoring a public waterworks funded by an average household tax of twenty-six shillings a year. In February 1788, the council took up the petition, which had been signed by "a great number of Inhabitants." Despite its mandate to come up with a Colles-type plan, a council committee promptly let the matter lay.[22] If the petition signers were upset, there's no record.

The next proposal came from out of town. After many experiments, James Rumsey had successfully tested a steamboat on the Potomac River in 1787. In January 1789, his Philadelphia backers informed the Common Council of his engine, "far superior to any other for supplying Towns with Water." They promised that a plan would be forthcoming. The council replied that the city would consider the matter, and nothing further was heard from Rumsey, who died several years later in London after failing to put his engine into production there.[23] The Rumsey flirtation was the last noteworthy water supply proposal in New York for nearly a decade.

Instead, New Yorkers drank ever deeper from their cherished but tainted Tea Water Pump, which remained the property of the Hardenbrook family through the 1790s. After attempts to sell or lease the land failed in 1793 and 1794, the plot that included the pump was conveyed in December 1796 to Hardenbrook in-law William Thompson, a leather dresser.[24] He promptly ran an ad promoting the family franchise, which had suffered some bad publicity:

> A report having been in circulation that the water of the Tea-water Pump begins to fail, and also, that the proprietor will not allow any more water to be drawn from it than is absolutely necessary for the use of the citizens for *tea* and *drinking;* the subscriber begs leave to contradict the said report, and inform the citizens that notwithstanding the extremely dry season, the source of the Tea Water has not

in the least diminished; and so far from his refusing any demand for Water, he hereby offers the citizens a plentiful supply for *washing* or other family uses. Any order for one or more hogsheads of water, directing the place where to be delivered, sent to the *pump,* will be immediately attended to. The price of the water is 4s. per hogshead, containing 140 gallons.[25]

Indeed, the pump was still capable of producing a prodigious supply. A few days before Thompson's ad ran, a fire had spread north from the foot of Wall Street along the waterfront to the Fly Market at Maiden Lane. The pump, which reportedly supplied sixteen thousand gallons of water on a usual day, "was kept constantly employed for eight hours," providing fifty thousand gallons of water to fight the fire.[26] Still, about seventy buildings were destroyed and a million dollars in damage done before the fire was broken, not by water carted from the distant pump, but by tearing down the wooden roof and other fixtures of the city fish market.[27]

Though doubts about the pump's purity had begun to sink into the local consciousness, European travelers flocking to America in the 1790s were quick to praise the Tea Water and join in the general condemnation of the public wells. "The water is very bad to drink, except at . . . the tea-water pump," observed English textile manufacturer Henry Wansey in June 1794. A water drinker, Wansey tried many public pumps "before I found this out, and suffered sometimes sickness, with very severe pains in the bowels, from its bad quality."[28] Moreau de St. Méry, then a Philadelphia bookseller in exile from the French Revolution, noted on his October arrival in New York that "people were drinking excellent spring water" from the great pump. According to his information, the pump then was leased for a thousand dollars a year and operated by two horses driven by a child; the water was sold for sixteen cents a barrel to twenty-four tea water men who distributed it by horse-drawn cart to every house in the city at ninety-six cents a bucket.[29] Three years later, fellow exile La Rochefoucauld-Liancourt, a social, scientific, and agricultural reformer from one of France's noblest families, found much the same: the public wells were bad, but the Tea Water Pump was thriving, with the annual lease up to twelve hundred dollars and daily sales of as much as twenty thousand gallons.[30] A contemporary study of post-Revolutionary War America by William Win-

terbotham likewise noted the "want of good water" from New York's
public wells and the manifest abundance from the Tea Water, its well reckoned at twenty feet deep and four feet across, meeting a demand for nearly
thirty thousand gallons on the hottest summer days.[31]

One gets the sense that the Europeans' New York hosts tended to boast
of their Tea Water Pump to deflect attention from the wells. And, as
tourists tend to do, the city's 1790s visitors likely gushed about an attraction that the locals quietly knew had once delivered better. Absent a suitable alternative, mythologizing the Tea Water's quantity was perhaps a cover
for its increasingly questionable quality.

The city gained an average of two thousand residents a year from the
end of the Revolution to the end of the century, creating a population of
sixty thousand, with New York poised to overtake Philadelphia as the
nation's largest city. Visitors compared Philadelphia to London and New
York to Liverpool but recognized that sooner or later New York would come
out on top.[32]

The 1790s was a decade of fantastic physical and institutional expansion for New York. The city's first commercial bank, Alexander Hamilton's
Bank of New York, won a long-sought state charter in 1791. Together with
a branch of the Bank of the United States that opened the following
year, Hamilton's Federalist-dominated bank financed the city's commercial growth. When both banks laid cornerstones on Wall Street in 1797,
the locus of global finance was born. The growing business class sought
fraternity in organizations like the Society of Saint Tammany, founded in
1786 by merchant-intellectual John Pintard and others. The society's
innocuous patriotic trappings were soon shed and by the end of the
next decade Tammany emerged as the Democratic machine that remains
a byword for political corruption.

To better count upisland progress, the city's seven wards were renamed
by number in 1791; in sixty years, twenty-two wards divided the entire
island. A 1797 plan by city surveyor Benjamin Taylor and engraver John
Roberts depicted the effects of a dozen years of postwar development. The
once-distant Fresh Water Pond had become a blot on the peopling of the
Sixth Ward. Increasingly referred to simply as the Collect, the pond was
surrounded by new streets but for as yet unleveled hills and marshy outlets to the northwest. The pond's eastern outlets had all been filled and

built over. Streets, albeit with few buildings, were laid well beyond the pond to North (now Houston) Street, encompassing today's Soho and Lower East Side. Downtown, many of the older streets were being Americanized under a 1794 order removing names with royal associations: Great George Street became the northerly continuation of Broadway, Queen became Pearl, King Pine, Duke Stone, Crown Liberty, and so forth.[33]

The proud American city was making much less progress on the old problem of sanitation. In 1784, the Common Council had re-enacted the colonial cleaning regulations and appointed three commissioners to police the weekly sweeping of dirt by residents and its removal by carters. Suitable for a small English town, this system quickly proved unworkable in a commercial city. Jailed vagrants were pressed into sanitation service, scavengers were hired at £150 a year, and constables were empowered to enforce the various sanitary laws. Grand jury indictments against the city in 1788, 1792, and 1795 for filthy streets suggest little headway had been made. A visiting English officer in mid-1793 found some of the streets "so abominably filthy" that he could "scarcely refrain from sickness in passing them."[34]

Progress on water was similarly negligible. With no plan to build a piped water supply, the city set about making the best of its much maligned wells. Beginning in 1785, the Common Council awarded an annual contract for repairing and cleaning the public wells. The first contractor was paid £140; the low bid the following year was £120. Typically, however, the contractor did as little work as possible and the alderman and assistant of each ward were often ordered to follow up.[35] In 1787, the Common Council obtained passage of a state law reprising the colonial arrangement of annually appointed well and pump overseers in each ward.[36] As the city grew, this decentralized arrangement became less workable. In 1799, the council appointed longtime Third Ward assistant Nicholas Carmer to oversee the overseers.[37] In 1792, the council finally updated the colonial system of paying a fixed £8 ($20) toward the cost of sinking any public well; now the city agreed to contribute $1 per foot depth of any new well, provided "that it is at least six feet diameter in the clear at Bottom, that it is compleatly stoned or bricked up, that it hath a sufficiency of Water, that it hath a good new pump, brass chambered, therein and that the well is properly covered."[38] Funding came from a state-authorized tax, which also covered

FIGURE 12. Broad Street, 1797

This watercolor by John Joseph Holland, looking north toward the second City Hall on Wall Street, shows several of the city's oldest street pumps. (I. N. Phelps Stokes Collection. Miriam and Ira D. Wallach Division of Art, Prints and Photographs. The New York Public Library. Astor, Lenox and Tilden Foundations.)

the cost of repairs and cleaning. Under these provisions, annual city spending on wells and pumps during the 1790s rose from under £200 ($500) to just over $2,300.[39]

Despite increased spending on the wells, their product remained unsavory. The rapidly increasing population stressed the wells' supplies, street paving and new buildings prevented rain from entering the groundwater, and inadequate sanitation ensured that whatever moisture did seep down was harmful to the supply. Efforts to seek good water at greater depths with new technology were unavailing as well. For the better part of the 1790s, prominent merchants Ebenezer Stevens and Abijah Hammond experimented with a "boring apparatus" that Hammond had procured in Boston. The Common Council offered to cover some of their expenses if they met with any success, but there is no record that they did.[40]

The mid-1790s brought a new parade of would-be water suppliers into the Common Council chambers. In 1794 and 1795, city surveyor Taylor and three others made separate proposals of unknown detail; all were referred to committees that took no action. A public solicitation by the council in February 1796 brought only two recorded responses, with similar results. In the summer of 1796, the city took steps to bury a nagging link to its water supply past. After rejecting a state offer to purchase the old Colles waterworks lot for a new prison, the council ordered the ground "appropriated as a Place to deposit the Dirt & Filth taken out of the Streets." In December, two more water proposals came before the council and were again forgotten in committees. One of the proposers was a Westchester doctor named Joseph Browne, who would be heard from again.[41]

Early in 1797, the council again advertised for sealed bids from "any persons who are disposed to contract or undertake the business" of a water supply.[42] By May, there were seven bidders, including several of some note. Previous proposers Newton and Taylor joined forces and exhibited a model of their planned waterworks at City Hall, charging fifty cents a head to see it.[43] Nicholas Roosevelt, forebear of two American presidents, had established the country's first steam engine plant at the old Schuyler copper mines in New Jersey several years earlier.[44] Luckless Christopher Colles, then a fifty-eight-year-old veteran of failed canal and mapping ventures, was still seeking an elusive fortune.[45] No details were recorded and

FIGURE 13. The Fresh Water or Collect Pond, late 18th century
In this lithograph for the 1860 *Manual of the Common Council,* the view looks north, with the "Little Collect" in the foreground. (Photo by Barry Rosenthal.)

no action was taken on any of this latest batch of proposals. All were adaptations of Colles's old Collect-sourced supply, novel when attempted a quarter-century earlier but dubious now that the city had grown around the once rural pond.[46]

The Common Council dealt best with less conceptual matters. Responding to complaints, it ordered the spout of the Tea Water Pump raised and lengthened so water carts could line up to receive the water without blocking recently paved and increasingly busy Chatham Street (now Park Row).[47] At the same June session, the council ordered the tanyards of John R. Livingston (the chancellor's cousin) and others near the Collect fenced in, after complaints that open vats posed great danger to neighborhood children. Responding to a petition of local residents, the council also ordered the filling of the pond's southern extension. Once a natural inlet of the main pond, the "Little Collect" had been putrefied in recent years by "a number of Dead animals being thrown into it," as well as the "pernicious matter" running from a glue factory. The order to fill certain of the pond's sunken lots began a process that eventually led to the pond's disappearance.[48]

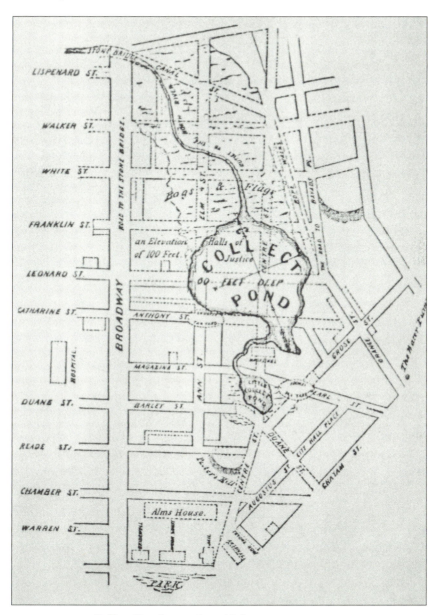

FIGURE 14. *Collect Pond map, late 18th century*
One of several versions issued in 1846, the map depicts the pond's position in relation to streets laid both before and after its filling, as well as the Tea Water Pump
and the area's natural topography.

The council made no progress on new sources of water, but after yet another unsolicited supply proposal was received and sent to committee in February 1798, the council was forced to deal with some very old business. Perhaps inspired by all the water talk, Isaac Mann, Jr., initiated a claim on his log contract from the Colles waterworks. Stumped by the passage of time and absence of records, the council eventually suggested Mann sue; two years later, he settled for £843.15, a good bit less after inflation than the £1,000 outstanding balance on his contract.[49]

The lack of official action on water suggested to some New Yorkers early in 1798 that the city had "given up." One despairing newspaper correspondent indicated that his annual cost of Tea Water had risen to £6 ($15), "a great tax for one small family." He saw no reason why a $40,000 public works couldn't be built with an average annual tax on the city's four thousand households of £4 ($10), a small fee to bring the "City Guardians much honor—and preserve the city from the great danger of fire, etc." The city guardians, however, did nothing.[50]

There was good reason for the New Yorker of 1798 to be concerned about his or her health and well-being. After a lapse of nearly half a century, yellow fever had returned with a vengeance.

A few New Yorkers had died in the late summer of 1791 from a "malignant fever" said to have spread from the filthy environs of the East River docks.[51] Two summers later, the city watched in horror as Philadelphia endured an unprecedented yellow fever epidemic that killed four thousand people and sent half that city's fifty-five thousand people fleeing.[52] In New York, the Common Council spent £1,400 ($3,500) cleaning the worst pollution, but the city most likely escaped an epidemic because a summer drought cut the mosquito population.[53] Although 1794 was fever free, 750 deaths were reported in 1795; half the population fled. The city spent well over $10,000 on prevention measures, but it was a sultry, wet summer; physicians Valentine Seaman and young Elihu Smith marveled at clouds of mosquitoes, in greater numbers and remaining longer than anyone could remember.[54]

After yellow fever killed several dozen people in 1796 and 1797,[55] the city took its first steps toward organized public health. By the spring of 1798, all existing health laws had been repealed, replaced by a new state law sought by the city granting broad powers to the Health Office, which previously had been limited to quarantine authority. Under the "Act to provide against infectious and pestilential Diseases," three state-appointed health commissioners were empowered to make and enforce sanitary regulations and enter private property to remove nuisances, with which the ill-watered and minimally sewered city was rich.[56]

The Health Office was led by innovative doctor Richard Bayley, who had been a founder of the state Medical Society four years earlier. In close cooperation with the Common Council, Bayley ordered swamps drained, slips cleaned, and health law violators prosecuted.[57]

The well-intentioned efforts failed. In the summer of 1798, New York got the fever like Philadelphia had in 1793. In late July, Revolutionary War hero Melancton Smith was the first New Yorker to die; by early August, a hundred deaths were reported. "The Town full of Trouble," wrote printer Hugh Gaine in his journal. "People moving out very fast." Business picked up for opportunistic carpenters; one sent a handwagon about town loaded with coffins, which his two young boys hawked at exorbitant prices: "stopping at intersections of the streets, they would sing out 'Coffins! Coffins of all sizes!'" Grant Thorburn, a young Scotsman with a new hardware store, did a booming business making coffin nails. At the same time, vehicles "from the humble dungcart to the gilded carriage" were requisitioned to remove families, furniture, and property. Many of the fleeing went no farther than the village of Greenwich, hastening its eventual incorporation into the city proper.[58]

Among those remaining was doctor Elihu Smith, who wrote with hope on September 2 that the desertion of the most affected neighborhoods was minimizing the number of new cases.[59] Medical pioneer Samuel Latham Mitchill soon concluded otherwise: "New York this time has got a plague indeed," he wrote to editor and health reformer Noah Webster.[60] A week earlier, the Common Council appointed a temporary Health Committee to minister to the needy; in three months' time, the committee spent a considerable $5,000.[61]

The city's official efforts were not nearly enough. A thousand New Yorkers died in September, including the wife, father, mother, brother, sister-in-law, and other relatives of Alexander Anderson, a young doctor whose suffering turned him permanently from medicine to engraving, for which he later became famous. On September 13 alone, sixty-three people died, including the father of future mayor and diarist Philip Hone; five days later, the seventeen-year-old's mother succumbed. The following day, steadfast Elihu Smith lost a two-day battle with the fever. Editor Webster warned at the end of month that

> The present sickness will subside and soon be forgotten . . . and men will proceed in the same round of folly and vice . . . piling together buildings, accumulating filth, and destroying fresh air, and preparing new and more abundant materials for pestilence, which will continue to assume greater virulence and to prove more destructive to human life, in proportion to the magnitude of our cities.[62]

Despite Webster's predictions, the present sickness wasn't quite ready to subside. In October, the death toll was over four hundred. By November, the total number of dead New Yorkers reached more than two thousand. Tens of thousands of state, local, and charitable dollars were thrown at the disease, which was finally mastered only by November's mosquito-killing chill.[63]

While the fever raged, healthy New Yorkers got hot about their water supply. Letters began appearing at the end of August in those newspapers that were still publishing. "GET WATER INTO THE CITY," demanded an anonymous physician in Webster's *Commercial Advertiser;* "WATER WILL WASH AWAY PESTILENCE—AND ONE VISITATION OF THE PLAGUE WILL COST YOU MORE THAN WILL WATER YOUR CITY FROM A DOZEN SOURCES."[64]

A remarkable screed appeared in Webster's paper the following week, under the heading "Machinery for getting clean cool uncontaminated Water into New York": "The New-Yorkers are like the rich man told of in the Parable, they have no clean cool water to slack their thirst, when the flames of the plague are devouring their vitals. Yet they pretend their city-water is very pure and nice. It is no such thing." The item described the Collect as "a shocking hole," a collection "of all the leakings, scrapings, scourings, p--s--gs, &-----gs, for a great distance around." The pond was the source of the "nasty wash and slops" that the Tea Water had become, "grown worse manifestly within a few years" and "less and less wholesome every day." The paper doubted claims the water still refreshed: "Can you bear to drink it on Sunday's in the Summer-time? It is so bad before Monday morning as to be very sickly and nauseating; and the larger the city grows, the worse this evil will be."

"Already it has been whispered by some vigilant travellers thro our city," confided the paper, "that the New-Yorkers are like the Dog in the Manger, they will not provide aqueducts themselves, nor let anybody else do it." A great civic effort was urged:

Take the matter into consideration, and resolve every man for himself, to leave no stone unturned to have this grand object of watering carried thro. Stick to it, until you do it.—Work every mother's Son, until the noble job is done.—For plague will make a yearly slaughter until you furnish better water.—Then New-York will be as famous as old Rome was, and the other cities may learn from us how to do clean things.[65]

Webster was perhaps aware of a radical new plan to water New York that had been penned two months earlier.

"It may be laid down as a general rule," wrote Joseph Browne in a twenty-one-page memorial dated July 2, 1798, "that the health of a city depends more on its water, than on all the rest of the eatables and drinkables together." What Browne had proposed two years earlier is unknown; his 1798 document was profoundly original, and would influence the city's water fortunes for the next thirty-five years.[66]

In an earlier treatise, Browne theorized that yellow fever arose atmospherically from the decay of "animal vital air" and "vegetable vital air."[67] Without discounting that theory, he now recognized that plentiful water was somehow "essentially necessary" to limit the effects of disease.

Tapping local egos, Browne prefaced his 1798 plan with a brief lesson on urban water supply. Ancient Rome had provided hundreds of millions of gallons of water daily from its regional springs and rivers. London drank mainly from the Thames, raised by water wheels and steam engines, but also from "New River," the twenty-one-mile-long open canal built by Hugh Middleton in the early 1600s that brought suburban spring water to a local reservoir for distribution by hollowed elm logs. Central Paris took water from the Seine; better neighborhoods brought spring water by pipes to reservoirs and street fountains. Louis XIV had spent £500,000 on "the most celebrated water works now in the world" at Versailles, where hundreds of pumps raised a million and a half gallons of suburban Seine water hundreds of feet for the palace's famous fountains and gardens. Browne envisioned a more democratic water system for New York that would fight disease and fire and be used "for the constant daily consumption of families, for drinking, washing, cooking, &c."

From whence would such a supply come? Most decidedly, wrote Browne, not from the "large stagnating filthy pond, commonly called the Collect, which now is or soon will be at the center of the city." Others suggested continued reliance on the pond, but Browne was "under no apprehension that the Corporation will ever seriously think of forcing the inhabitants to drink [its] disgusting water." As development would eventually overwhelm all of Manhattan's ponds and springs, Browne argued that only an off-island supply would do. This was a new idea.

Browne considered the two rivers originating in his native Westchester. On the west was the Saw Mill River, emptying into the Hudson at Yonkers, nineteen miles from City Hall.[68] Although he conceded the Saw Mill's water was of excellent quality and ample supply, Browne found the distance too far, the country too rough, and the likely cost too high. Water for New York, Browne decided, must come from "THE RIVER BRONX."

As accurately described by Browne, the Bronx originated in a small lake just above White Plains, meandering south twenty miles through central Westchester until emptying into the East River at Hunt's Point, twelve miles northeast of City Hall. Bronx water was "remarkably pure and pellucid," Browne claimed, and local inhabitants were "in the constant habit of using it in preference to other water." It passed the popular tests of the day, boiling "leguminous vegetables tender" and readily dissolving soap. Best of all, the river contained "more than 40 times" the three hundred thousand daily gallons that Browne believed the city needed.

Bringing the Bronx to New York would take some work. The Westchester part was easiest. Browne proposed a dam five feet high across the Bronx near Williams's Bridge, several miles above the river's outlet.[69] The diverted river would flow six miles southwest, first in a short canal through a low meadow, then in a creek that divided the lands of Lewis and Gouvernor Morris before emptying into the Harlem River, just eight miles from

City Hall. There were times, Browne claimed, that the Bronx naturally flooded into the Harlem by this route.

At the Harlem, the situation took on greater gravity. Browne initially had hoped the Bronx could have flowed over the Harlem and down to the city in pipes without the aid of any machinery, but he could find no way to do it. Where the Bronx would be dammed it was only fifty feet above mean high tide; the location for an intended city reservoir fourteen miles away was forty feet above tide, "a fall perfectly inadequate to any design of conveying the water in a pipe of conduit only." Browne conceded that the diverted waters of the Bronx would have to be mechanically elevated at the banks of the Harlem.

Browne laid out a detailed plan of hydrostatics and hydraulics for a water-powered works. A dam six feet high would span the Harlem; a tide-powered water wheel sixty feet around would work six pumps and assorted machinery to raise the Bronx water into six-inch wooden pipe across the Harlem and down Manhattan to a receiving reservoir five miles north of the city and eighty feet above tide, an elevation sufficient for the water to make its final pipe run down to the principal city reservoir.

Not especially clear on just how the pump works would be built or how the pipes would lay across the Harlem, Browne seemed eager to plan his waterworks and make use of an "excellent bridge" recently built across the river by John B. Coles.

The history of this bridge bears some recounting. Back in 1774, Lewis Morris and John Sickles won permission from the city and the colonial Assembly to link their respective Westchester and Manhattan properties with the first bridge across the lower Harlem. As with other projects of the period, nothing was done until after the Revolution. In 1790, the legislature passed a new act authorizing Morris to build a toll drawbridge, but a construction tontine failed in 1792. The following year, a state commission was named to make sure that a good road would be laid to the as-yet unbuilt bridge; one of the four commissioners was United States Senator Aaron Burr, a name to remember.[70]

Tiring of his bridge dream, Lewis Morris transferred his rights to wealthy Federalist flour merchant John Coles, who for some time had been seeking permission to throw a mill dam across the Harlem. In early 1795, his petition was finally granted by the legislature: a stone dam would provide power to his mills and serve as the foundation for the long-sought toll bridge, which after sixty years would revert to the state. By the time of Joseph Browne's water proposal in 1798, Coles had completed the bridge but not the mill works.[71]

Sensitive to the controversial issue of blocking the Harlem with bridges, Browne suggested that the Bronx water pipes might cross the river on Coles's bridge, and that the millworks might in some way be constructed for the dual purpose of elevating the Bronx. He expected this idea to carry "some weight" with the cost-conscious Common Council.

Despite the obvious question marks, Browne priced the cost of the whole affair at $200,000: $20,000 in damages to four mills below the diverted Bronx; $20,000 for the dams, canal, waterworks, and Harlem crossing; $22,000 for the six-inch mains; $10,000 for the two reservoirs; $28,000 for superintending the works and incidental costs; and $100,000 for twenty miles of distributing pipe in the city.

Browne recommended haste in moving forward. Relatively few mills had located on the Bronx; as more were established, values would rise, and "it will be very difficult for the city to command a river." If not able to proceed immediately with his plan, Browne urged the city at least to purchase the rights to do so in the future.

Browne's ideas showed great insight; however, his suggestion that a private company undertake the works was controversial. Clearly aware of both public sentiment for a city-owned supply and the city's inadequate resources to build one, Browne carefully laid out details for a public-spirited private enterprise. He proposed a company authorized to issue two thousand shares of stock at $100 each, with no person initially entitled to more than one share. The company would be required to supply three hundred thousand gallons of Bronx water a day, distributed through all the principal streets in such a way that the entire supply could be diverted into any one street to fight a fire. A watchman at the principal reservoir would constantly monitor water use; any of the daily supply not used by the company would be at the disposal of the city for street washing. The company would provide free of charge "an ornamental fountain and *Jet d'Eau*" at the Battery or Bowling Green.

Households would be charged an average of $10 a year for thirty gallons of water a day, fed from the street conduit by service pipe installed at householder expense. Though seemingly high, the annual water charge was "probably less" than the cost per household of building and maintaining the public wells. Households that chose not to hook up would pay an average of $2 a year, "a trifling consideration" for protection from fire and disease. Browne estimated that half the city's then six thousand houses would take the company's water, making for annual receipts of $36,000, which, after management and maintenance expenses of $10,000, left annual revenues of $26,000 and a very reasonable 13 percent return on investment after ten years.

Who was Dr. Joseph Browne that he knew so much about providing water to cities and profit to investors? His proposal identifies him as a Westchester doctor, but little is known about him. His ideas about watering New York would elevate him to great prominence in the next several years, but he eventually would follow fortune elsewhere and die in mysterious circumstances on the western frontier around 1811. The date of his Bronx proposal does offer a hint at the source of his designs: July 2, 1798, was the sixteenth anniversary of Dr. Joseph Browne's wedding.

It had been a double wedding that day at the Dutch Reformed Church in Paramus, New Jersey. Joining then-wealthy Browne and Catherine De Visme at the altar in the dwindling days of the Revolution were her older half-sister, the recently widowed Theodosia Bartow Prevost, and Theodosia's ardent suitor, an ambitious but threadbare young attorney and war hero named Aaron Burr.[72] Where Burr went, intrigue always followed; his brother-in-law knew this well.

Aaron's Water

*Aaron Burr with his rod struck the rock Manhattan and
the waters flowed. Drink, O Israel, of Aaron's water!*

—Gore Vidal, *Burr: A Novel*

*Alas! I have turned my cock repeatedly, but nothing
comes from it.*

—Manhattan Company customer, 1803

If England had won the Revolution, Aaron Burr might, with time, have become a prince. As it happened, the proponents of democracy prevailed, and patriotic Colonel Burr, who had served the American cause with distinction, was happy for the opportunities presented in a liberated nation.

The facts of his life are well known. Descended in his paternal line from a Puritan English carpenter who reached Massachusetts in 1630, Burr (1756–1836) was the maternal grandson of Calvinist theologian and American philosopher Jonathan Edwards, who died in 1758, just months after succeeding Burr's prematurely deceased father as president of the College of New Jersey (now Princeton University). After Burr's mother died a month later, and his grandmother Edwards six months after that, the orphaned two-year-old (and his four-year-old sister Sally) came into the care of young uncle Timothy Edwards, a Princeton graduate and prosperous merchant with a new home on New Jersey's Elizabeth River.

A restless and rebellious youth, Burr entered Princeton at age thirteen, where he formed a lifelong friendship with future U.S. Supreme Court justice (Henry) Brockholst Livingston. Burr graduated with distinction in

FIGURE 15. Aaron Burr, circa 1792

This portrait by Gilbert Stuart depicts Burr when he was a thirty-six-year-old New York lawyer, some seven years before launching the Manhattan Company. (From the Collections of the New Jersey Historical Society, Newark, N.J.)

1772 and began law studies in 1774 after first considering theology. His war service, begun the following year, featured staff positions with George Washington and Israel Putnam, but was ended by ill health in 1779, when he resigned from the army and finished his legal education. In 1782, he married the widowed Theodosia Prevost in a double ring ceremony with her half-sister and Joseph Browne. Frail Theodosia died in 1794, leaving their daughter Theodosia, whom Burr adored.

After establishing a successful law practice in New York during the 1780s, the future vice president entered politics on the Anti-Federalist side, first as state attorney general, and from 1791 to 1797 as U.S. senator. Burr enraged Federalist treasury secretary Alexander Hamilton by opposing his financial policies, but the two were also leaders of the New York City bar, co-counsels as well as rivals. Burr also regularly alienated factions of his Democratic-Republican party by hewing most closely to personal agendas but, after losing re-election to the U.S. Senate, he was elected to the first of two terms in the state Assembly in April 1797. The election of Burr and several other party cronies unsettled Federalist-dominated New York politics and helped pave the way for the national ascendancy of Jefferson and Burr in 1800.

Burr was a slender, handsome man, with piercing eyes and a suave manner. He was inscrutable and unscrupulous, generous and self-indulgent, a libertine in financial and intimate relations, a genius tainted by unarticulated ambitions. After Vice President Burr shot and killed statesman Hamilton in a duel in 1804 over alleged character insults, Burr's political star exploded. Ahead was a long, strange trip: a notorious "conspiracy" with Joseph Browne and others to colonize America's western and southern frontiers; exile in Europe; relentless liaisons, a modest legal practice, and social exile back in New York, following the heartbreaking loss at sea of his daughter and only grandchild; a brief but scandalous marriage to a prostitute turned heiress; invalidism and death at poverty's door. An orphan and widower turned loose on a virgin nation, he became and remains its most infamous famous man.

The evolving elements of Burr's complex nature were amply displayed in 1798, when he embarked on what proved a brief adventure for him and an enduring agony for New Yorkers. The seeds of Aaron Burr's Manhattan Company were planted that July, when brother-in-law Joseph Browne proposed to water New York with the Bronx River.

The topic of water was not revisited in the city until that summer's devastating yellow fever took its leave in November. The Common Council had Browne's Bronx plan in its hands but continued to receive other ideas. In early December, Nicholas Roosevelt revived his proposals and Judge William Cooper, the upstate land speculator and father of James Fenimore Cooper, wrote a letter proposing to lay water pipes in the city. As with so many communications on water, though, the details of these are unknown; the same council committee that had received Browne's Bronx proposal took these. Nothing more was heard of them.[1]

In the fever-traumatized city, the committee charged with evaluating the various plans must have felt compelled to focus their attentions on Browne, who had fully described the city's health salvation in the rural waters of the Bronx. The committee of four aldermen—Gabriel Furman, John Bogert, Jacob de la Montagnie, and Harlem bridge builder John B. Coles—issued their report on December 17. It was not exactly what Browne had had in mind. The committee were of the opinion that the Bronx was ample and pure and Browne's plan the only one worth pursuing, but with "some few variations."

Wary of "incalculable mischief" from mistakes, the committee recommended a second opinion by English canal engineer William Weston (c.1752–1833), who had been building and consulting on American canals for most of the decade.[2] More significantly, the committee dashed Browne's suggestion of a private company, which would undertake the work only "under the prospect of considerable gain" at the expense of the city. After some debate, the committee recommended that the council seek a state law granting the necessary authority for "the great end they have in view," with financing either from loans or a tax on auction sales.

The council as a whole embraced the committee report, which was published as a pamphlet along with Browne's memoir. Longtime Federalist Mayor Richard Varick wrote to Weston, then in Philadelphia, and Federalist recorder Richard Harison drafted the law.[3]

Harison completed his work in ten days, presenting the council with a draft bill "for supplying this City with pure & wholesome Water," along with ostensibly unrelated anti-fever legislation granting the city broad sewerage and drainage authority. The council ordered the bills delivered to the thirteen Assemblymen representing the city and county in the state legislature, beginning its session in Albany the following week. The leader of New York's Assembly delegation was Aaron Burr.[4]

Though the Democratic-Republicans were still the minority party in the Assembly (and the state Senate) for the 1799 legislative session, they had become the overwhelming majority in the city and county delegation.[5] Burr's position on the bill would soon become apparent; the full explanation for his position would not become known for several months.

In the meantime, William Weston accepted the city's offer and arrived in New York on February 4, though by then the situation was evolving faster than Weston's good intentions. The publication of the Browne plan had aroused a public debate in the newspapers over the quantity and quality of the Bronx and the cost, complexity, and necessity of bringing its waters to New York.[6] The smoke of divided public opinion provided excellent cover for the purposeful Aaron Burr; New Yorkers were not certain how to proceed, but Assemblyman Burr was. The devil was in the details.

Up in Albany during January and early February, the Assembly delegation was having trouble preparing the water bill for full Assembly consideration. Burr, it seems, was pressing his fellow committeemen to reverse course on a city-owned water supply and recommend a private company along the lines envisioned by brother-in-law Browne. It was later alleged that Burr went so far as to intercept the correspondence of certain members of the committee and exclude them from meetings. At the very least, the committee was uncertain about what to do. Members of the delegation were leery of confounding the expressed intentions of the city they represented. Two of the assemblymen, Democratic-Republican Philip Arcularius and Federalist Richard Furman, were also Common Council members who had voted for a city-owned supply; Democratic-Republican assemblyman and assistant alderman Thomas Storm had been absent for the Common Council vote but presumably supported the bill sent to Albany. Arcularius, Furman, Storm, and Democratic-Republican assemblyman Elias Nexsen were later reported opposed to Burr's intentions.[7] There was also doubt about Burr's claim that the public favored a private company. By February 11, it was clear to Burr that he would have to return to the city to shore up his position. On Saturday the 16th, the delegation agreed that he should get a better sense of the Common

Council and the public, and the full Assembly approved a ten-day leave. On horseback, Burr rushed south.

He had a full agenda. The first results of his private consultations became known on the 22nd, when Mayor Varick and Recorder Harison were paid an interesting visit by Burr and a group of five other notables organized by him. John Broome was a leading merchant grown rich in the China tea trade, president of the New York Insurance Company and the state Chamber of Commerce, and a future lieutenant governor; today's Broome Street bears his name. Peter H. Wendover was a prosperous sail-maker, president of the Mechanics Society, a future alderman, assembly-man, and congressman, and an ardent Jeffersonian. Broome, Wendover, and Burr were the Democratic-Republican half of the politically bal-anced group. John Murray was a wealthy Quaker merchant, president of the city Chamber of Commerce, and an active humanitarian; the Mur-ray Hill section of Manhattan is named for him. Gulian Verplanck was a descendant of the earliest Dutch settlers, past speaker of the Assembly, and president of the Bank of New York. Rounding out the Federalist contin-gent was Alexander Hamilton, the architect of federalism. His best days, though, like those of his party, had passed. Out of public office for some years and troubled by shaky finances, he had been forced to pursue a pri-vate legal practice.

It is easy to understand how the four merchants in the group cast aside political differences to unite behind Burr's plan for a private water com-pany. It was clear to everyone, especially business and civic leaders, that something needed to be done about the water supply; private enterprise was not an unfamiliar concept to these businessmen. Burr's deepest motivations, though, were still not in evidence. Why Hamilton was will-ing to be led by his longtime rival may never be completely answered.

As Varick recounted to the Common Council the following Monday, his distinguished visitors had told him that "great difficulties" had arisen in Albany concerning the powers requested by the city in the water supply and sanitation bills. Varick was told that passage of the bills in their exist-ing form was "problematical" and that unspecified changes might be made by the legislature. Varick and Harison asked that their visitors' proposals to remedy the bills' defects be put in writing for full Common Council consideration. At some point over the weekend, Hamilton delivered "a paper without Signature" to Harison; Varick presented it on Monday to the council.

The council rejected the unsigned document. It wanted a signed statement specifying "the Nature and Circumstances of the Difficulties" that the draft laws had met in Albany. This demand was to be communicated to Burr and Hamilton "without delay," and once Varick received "the Proper communications" the council would consider them at a special meeting.[8] The council did not have the benefit of independently confirming the alleged difficulties in the legislature because the council's three members also serving in the Assembly—Arcularius, Storm, and Richard Furman—remained in Albany.

Varick received the "proper communications" the next day in the form of a signed letter from Hamilton, which was brought before the council two days later. This incredible document could not have served Burr's purposes better.

First, Hamilton sought to clear up the council's apparent misconception concerning the status of the members of the Burr group that had first visited Varick. They did not have an official capacity, Hamilton explained, but were merely private individuals offering useful information to the city. Hamilton also labored to make clear that the original unsigned document was not a proposal per se from the group but merely an informal response to Varick's request. Now, though, Hamilton acknowledged that the propositions represented the results of the group's discussions, authenticated with his signature; the suggested changes in the city's water supply plans now had Hamilton's "full concurrence." The Federalist-dominated Common Council had no choice but to consider them.

Hamilton's primary concern was financing the proposed water project. He doubted the legislature would fund a public venture from auction duties, as this would divert revenues from the cash-short state to the city, and he questioned whether a new city water tax would cover the expected cost, which Hamilton now curiously estimated at $1 million. How Hamilton arrived at a figure five times Browne's estimate is unknown; perhaps it was calculated to impress upon the council the city's financial inadequacy for the task.

Instead, Hamilton laid out how a private company, working with the city, might accomplish "the main object." Incorporated by the state, the company would be capitalized at a million dollars in $50 shares. The city would be entitled to a third of the shares, the purchase of which would be funded by state auction duties, local taxes, or loans. The company would be managed by seven directors, six chosen annually by shareholders, and the other being the sitting city recorder. As a further check on the company's activities, the project would be overseen by appointed commissioners, instead of the easily distracted Common Council.

Hamilton suggested that if the council agreed with his ideas, it should let the legislature know. The overmatched council promptly folded. Having no "wish for any peculiar Agency in this business," the city fathers voted that they would be "perfectly satisfied if the objects in View are pursued in any Way that the Legislature may think proper." A copy of the resolution and related documents were sent to Arcularius, Furman, and Storm in Albany.[9]

Burr, meanwhile, remained in the city. While he used Hamilton to extract the city's blessing for a private company, Burr was lining up a set of directors for the prospective company, a much different company than that portrayed by Hamilton to the city.

Instead of using six elected board members, Burr selected twelve. Unlike the politically balanced group that had conferred with Mayor Varick, Burr's board had a distinctly Republican flavor. But for Burr and John Broome, it was a new cast of characters. The seven new Republicans were prominent merchants William Edgar, William Laight, Daniel Ludlow, and Paschal N. Smith; former soldier, legislator, and first U.S. postmaster-general Samuel Osgood; Burr's college friend Brockholst Livingston; and Chancellor Livingston's brother-in-law John Stevens, a wealthy Hoboken landowner and steam engine pioneer.

Heading the slender Federalist contingent was venerable merchant and lawyer John Watts, a former city recorder (during the Colles project), speaker of the state Assembly, and U.S. representative, and currently a director of the Bank of the United States. Watts's same-named Loyalist father had once observed famously that the law was a "System of confounding other People and picking their Pockets, which most of the Profession understand pretty well." Whether Watts *fils* understood what fellow lawyer Aaron Burr was cooking up is unclear.[10]

Next among the Federalists was alderman John B. Coles, the flour merchant with a bridge across the Harlem where Joseph Browne envisioned a pipe of Bronx water. Coles, of course, had been on the Common Council committee that dashed Browne's plans for a private company. What Burr had done to change Coles to a company man is unknown.

The third Federalist was even more intriguing, and perhaps the key to all of Burr's plans. John Barker Church (1748–1808) was a renegade in Burr's image. Church arrived in America from England at the outset of the Revolution and, as a principal investor in the Bank of North America under the alias John Carter, made a small fortune off the bank's loans to supply the Continental army.[11] After the war, Church married Angelica Schuyler, the beautiful and wealthy daughter of war hero and Federalist statesman Philip (John) Schuyler, who already had one prominent son-in-law: in 1780, Angelica's sister Elizabeth had married Alexander Hamilton.

With peace restored, Church and his bride removed to London, where he as a member of Parliament and she as a stunning hostess were prominent players in the high-flying "Carlton House set" led by the Duke of Windsor, the future King George IV. The Churches returned to New York in 1797, setting up an elaborate household for entertaining at 52 Broadway, a few doors up the street from the Hamiltons. Hamilton, who had retired as the nation's first secretary of the treasury in 1795 due to short personal finances and had become moderately successful with his private law practice, counted Church as a friend, client, and occasional partner in speculative business ventures. Hamilton, like Burr and Church a man of many women, is said to have taken on his sister-in-law Mrs. Church as a partner as well.[12]

As to Church's federalism, it was apparently like Burr's republicanism, more of economic convenience than political conviction. Federalists still controlled the bulk of America's wealth, which Hamilton's English in-law was eager to share. How, when, and why Church entered Burr's plans is unclear. The likeliest explanation is that Church's company board position was the quid pro quo for Hamilton's efforts on Burr's behalf.

While he was assembling his company's board, Burr also set about signing up its future stock. Among prominent Federalists, merchant, land speculator, and Hamilton friend Nicholas Low pledged for one hundred shares. But Republicans snapped up the lion's share, led by Chancellor Livingston and Burr ally John Swartwout (two thousand shares each) and De Witt Clinton (one thousand shares).

At the tail end of his whirlwind city visit, Burr secured a number of petitions, one drafted by Hamilton, attesting to public support for a private company. Burr returned to Albany in early March with all the support he needed for a private water company. Why a man with no known interest in water wanted a water company was still unknown.

For the better part of March Burr did not play his cards. Back in the city, the month's chief water headline was William Weston's report, delivered to the Common Council on the 16th. Despite having spent only six winter weeks at his researches, Weston produced a plan significantly different and much more specific than Browne's.[13]

First, Weston determined that at least three million gallons of water would be needed a day, ten times Browne's estimate. Weston sized up the city at 750 acres, of which four hundred acres were built over or paved and needful of "cleansing and cooling." Two and a quarter million gallons would be necessary to provide the equivalent of a quarter of an inch of rain a day. The remainder would be "adequate" for domestic use.

As to the source, Weston recognized a "general bias of opinion" in favor of the proximate Collect, but he dismissed it. Large steam engines could be used, but the pond's capacity was uncertain and its quality deteriorating. To the Bronx the city should go. Europe's principal cities were supplied by rivers; Weston saw every reason for New York to do likewise.

Weston was aware of claims that the Bronx would provide an inadequate supply. His examinations concluded otherwise, provided that the river's principal source was dammed. Rye Pond, "a beautiful sheet of water" covering five hundred acres four miles north of White Plains, was bounded by high shores "admirably calculated for the formation of an immense reservoir." Dammed into a billion-gallon basin, Rye Pond would discharge eight million gallons a day, plenty for both the city and Bronx mills that would otherwise be harmed by diverting the river.

Like Browne, Weston called for a dam on the Bronx to divert a portion of the river west through an open canal and Morrisania Creek to the Harlem. Like Browne, Weston estimated a fall of six inches per mile along this stretch but, although Browne thought this insufficient to propel the water by gravity across the Harlem, Weston believed otherwise. A small, elevated reservoir fed at six cubic feet of water per second would be more than sufficient to send the water across the river in a two-foot

cast iron pipe, a nascent technology just coming into general use in
Europe and nowhere present in America. Weston pegged the fall across
the Harlem at eight feet, producing a velocity of nearly twenty-three
inches per second and maintaining a water flow of roughly six feet per second. By Weston's calculations, he had done away with the complex tide-
powered machinery thought necessary by Browne.

On the Manhattan side as well, Weston parted company from
Browne. Browne, with few specifics, had envisioned bringing the water
down the east side of the island; Weston proposed an open canal leading west across the upper portion of Manhattan and then south along
the Hudson shore for six miles, negotiating "numerous ravines" with
small raised aqueducts. Two miles from the city where the ground
dipped significantly, the canal would give way to iron cylinders, leading all the way to a "Grand Reservoir," in the Park (later City Hall
Park) or a couple of blocks north on Broadway. Either location was sufficiently elevated to distribute water throughout the city. Weston estimated
a descent of twenty-three feet in the fourteen miles from the Bronx dam
to the city reservoir.

The reservoir was the most original part of Weston's plan. To counter
any questions about the purity of Bronx water, Weston's reservoir would
consist of five linked basins. The largest would be the "reservoir of reception," the water's first stop out of the delivery cylinder. Next, the water would
flow, on a daily alternating basis, into one of two subdivisions where "adven-
titious matter" would be deposited. After twenty-four hours, the water
would be drawn off at the bottom into a filtering basin where remaining
sediment would be deposited. Finally, the water would percolate through
a bank of washed sand and gravel into a distributing basin which, as a final
precaution, would be covered.

The originality of Weston's reservoir plan, featuring what is now called
"slow-sand filtration," was astounding. The first sand filtration system in
the world would not be built until 1829 to purify London's Thames River
water; not until the 1870s, in Poughkeepsie, New York, would such a
water purification system go into operation in the United States—which
is to say that Weston's plan would go unbuilt.[14]

Though Weston offered no cost estimate, the Common Council was
happy to pay his $800 bill. The council was so taken with his report that

it was ordered published, like Browne's, and sent immediately in manu-script form to Furman, Arcularius, and Storm in Albany.[15]

Perhaps the report's arrival in Albany was a signal to Burr, who was spending the better part of March fitting one more piece of his puzzle into place. It had to do with the sanitary legislation sent to Albany back in January with the water bill. The Common Council, acting on the recom-mendations of city health officials investigating yellow fever, was seeking authority to make by-laws regulating privies, deep cellars, sunken yards, slips, burial grounds, and other potential nuisances, as well as authority to hire carts and laborers to carry away garbage. This was the same leg-islation that Mayor Varick had been warned was "problematical." In fact, the Federalist-dominated Senate had promptly passed the bill and sent it on March 9 to the Assembly, which referred it to Burr's city commit-tee. On the 15th, the Assembly passed the bill, featuring a Burr commit-tee amendment that the city be granted auction duties as a credit for borrowing $100,000 to pay for its sanitary projects. Burr knew that the Senate would reject that authority, which it did on the 25th. Facing upstate opposition to city financial privileges, the following day, the Assembly did likewise. When finally passed, the bill contained no financ-ing authority for the city except for assessments on owners of offending property. The significance of all this to Burr was that the legislature, as he had expected, was now on record as opposed to auction duties for the city, the likeliest source of funding for a public water supply.[16]

Now Burr felt confident to spring his water company on the Assembly, which had just decided to extend its busy session a week to April 3. At the morning session on the 27th, Burr crony James Fairlie introduced before the whole chamber the various petitions for a privately owned supply and a draft bill entitled "An act for supplying the city of New-York with pure and wholesome water."[17]

The bill, ostensibly prepared and approved by the Burr committee, was read aloud and, by unanimous consent, read a second time. Normal pro-cedure would have called for debate on the bill by the entire Assembly; Burr, though, quickly arranged for it to be referred to a special commit-tee of three: two upstaters and himself. They made quick work of what Burr is said to have dismissed as "a trifling act." Burr reported that after-noon that his special committee had approved the bill and no discussion or other reading was necessary. At the morning session on the 28th, the full Assembly approved the act, having considered it for less than twenty-four hours.[18]

The company that the Assembly authorized was a remarkable entity, nothing like what the city had empowered its representatives to pursue and, by the late inclusion of one simple clause, nothing like any company that existed in America.

The "Manhattan Company" would be capitalized at $2 million, double what Hamilton had proposed. The city was entitled to purchase only two thousand of the $50 shares, a fraction of the one-third stake proposed by Hamilton. And, as Burr had arranged, the number of directors was doubled from Hamilton's proposed six to twelve, plus the city recorder, effectively minimizing whatever influence the city official might have.

The twelve directors were listed in a middle paragraph of the eleven-paragraph act. Daniel Ludlow and John B. Church were named as well in the first line of the act, "together with sundry other citizens," as having "associated for the purpose" of supplying New York with water. In the second paragraph, Ludlow and Church, along with John Watts and one other person, were named with "their present and future associates" as the "President and Directors" of the company. That other person, who was not named as a company director, was Joseph Browne.

The structure of the company as it evolved up in Albany was significantly different from what had been conceived in New York, and its powers were wholly original. Hamilton had laid out no specifics about how the company was supposed to go about its business, a void that Burr readily filled.

The company's substantial rights of eminent domain over lands, rivers, and streams were similar to the rights of the state's two private canal companies but, unlike other American water companies, the Manhattan Company did not have to repair streets torn up for pipelaying, could set water rates as it saw fit, and did not have to provide free water to the city to put out fires.[19] Additionally, the company's charter was perpetual, provided that within ten years it "furnish and continue a supply of pure and wholesome water sufficient for the use of all such citizens . . . as shall agree to take it on the terms to be demanded."

With these provisions alone, Burr was proposing a precedent-setting company, with broad rights and few obligations. But deep in the charter, in the ninth and second-shortest of its paragraphs, was the most novel provision:

And be it further enacted, That it shall and may be lawful for the said company to employ all such surplus capital as may belong or accrue to the said company in the purchase of public or other stock, or in any monied transactions or operations not inconsistent with the constitution and laws of this state or of the United States, for the sole benefit of the said company.

Here was Aaron's rod turned serpent. The power to do anything legal with a company's capital was unheard of in American or English corporate law, which tended to restrict corporate entities to their specified purposes, such as canals, bridges, or roads. Only a handful of New York City business concerns were incorporated by the state between the Revolution and the end of the century: three insurance companies, one manufacturing company, and two banks, all of which had specific and limited mandates.[20] By its "surplus capital" clause, the Manhattan Company would be able to engage in practically any business it chose. For Burr, the company offered him the power to turn water into wine, a water company to be swallowed by a bank serving Republican interests, a rival of what was then the city's only other state-chartered bank, Alexander Hamilton's Bank of New York.

Though there was much to digest in the bill presented to the Assembly, the swiftness of its passage was especially stunning to Assemblyman Thomas Storm, who reportedly heard the "surplus capital" clause for the first time when the bill was read on the Assembly floor, even though he was a member of the Assembly committee that supposedly drafted and recommended the bill. Just what this clause meant was not discussed, on the record at least, until the bill was considered in the Senate, more Federalist and conservative, and seemingly less influenced by Assemblyman Burr.

Accordingly, instead of risking consideration of the bill by the Senate as a whole, on the afternoon of March 30, Burr went into the Senate chamber and asked his friend, Western District senator Thomas Morris—a Federalist with Democratic-Republican leanings—to get it moved to a select committee. According to Burr friend and biographer Matthew Davis, Morris told Burr that although he had no objection to trying "the experiment," the Senate routinely refused committing bills to select committees. Burr then suggested that Morris take to the Senate floor and "intimate" that Senator Samuel Jones was contemplated as chairman of such a committee.

Jones, "the father of the New York bar," had been the city's recorder from 1789 to 1796, when he published a compendium of local and state laws affecting the city. He had been the state's first comptroller since 1797, and was a major landowner on Long Island, where today's Jones Beach bears his name. A Tory during the Revolution, Jones was an influential Anti-Federalist during the Constitution-writing period after the war, until that party's chauvinism for Robespierre brought Jones and others permanently into the Federalist camp. Jones was also a brother-in-law of Alexander Hamilton. Burr surmised that Jones's presence might induce the Senate to name a special committee.[21]

As usual in political matters, Burr was right. Federalist Lieutenant-Governor Stephen Van Renssalaer, the richest man in the state, the largest landowner in the country, and also a Hamilton brother-in-law, promptly named a committee of Jones, Morris, and Ambrose Spencer, who had been a Federalist until the previous year when he launched a two-decade run as the dictator of Republican state politics, mostly as a judge and chief justice.[22] As Jones's committee went, so would the Senate.

The position of Morris and Spencer on Burr's bill was clear, especially considering that Spencer was in for a hundred shares of the proposed company's stock. Jones's position was less clear, perhaps favorably influenced by his brother-in-law Hamilton's record of support. But there was no time for Jones to have conferred with Federalist leaders days away in New York City about the various changes Burr had introduced in Albany; Burr was moving things along in the capitol by the hours and minutes.

The Senate records show that Jones was concerned about "surplus capital." It had already been suggested to him by unnamed persons that the clause be stricken. He inquired of Burr who, according to biographer Davis, frankly acknowledged that it was intended to let the company directors use surplus capital in any way they thought profitable. They might start a bank, an East India Company, or any thing else they desired, because merely "supplying . . . water would not, of itself, remunerate the stockholders." Irate Federalists would later accuse Burr of hiding his intentions, but Burr plainly told Jones he was free to discuss Burr's explanation with others. It is unknown if he did so, but two days later Jones reported the bill favorably with no amendments, and the full Senate accordingly passed it.[23]

The final stop for the bill before it became law was the Council of Revision. Consisting of the governor, the chancellor, and the judges of the state Supreme Court, the Council of Revision was charged with reviewing the constitutionality and public good of all bills passed by the legislature.[24] Here, on April Fool's Day, Burr's scheme came up against second-term Federalist Governor John Jay, Republican Chancellor Livingston, Federalist Judge Egbert Benson, and Republican Chief Justice John Lansing. Jay was two years from retirement from a long and distinguished career in public service and had no taste for partisan politics; he was also a brother-in-law of Manhattan Company director Brockholst Livingston.[25] Chancellor Livingston was the largest investor in the company. Erudite Judge Benson was a famed patriot, first chief judge of the U.S. Second Circuit Court, prospective governor, and considered by many the rival of Hamilton in legal knowledge.[26] Justice Lansing was an eminent and independent-minded Albany jurist who would succeed Livingston as chancellor in 1801. In 1800, Lansing's instructions to a New York City jury in a celebrated murder trial would bring an unpopular acquittal of a young man defended by Brockholst Livingston, Hamilton, and Burr. Thirty years later, Lansing would step out of a New York City hotel for a business meeting and never be seen again.[27]

The Manhattan Company bill was committed to Lansing, who the next day reported his objections to Burr's "novel experiment." Worried about a $2 million company that could use those immense funds in any legal manner, Lansing suggested that at the least the company's charter should be of a limited duration, as all charters then were.[28]

Lansing, though, stood alone. His objections were taken into consideration and overruled: for reasons unknown, Benson sided with Livingston and Jay "had no vote." On April 2, 1799, "An act for supplying the city of New-York with pure and wholesome water" became law.[29] The unsuspecting believed a water company had been born; Burr knew he had sired a bank.

The Manhattan Company set to work immediately. A copy of the company's charter was delivered to the Common Council by company president Daniel Ludlow on April 10.[30] The next day, at the first meeting recorded in its corporate minutes, a committee of three directors—Samuel Osgood, John Stevens, and John B. Coles—was appointed "to report with all convenient speed" on the best plan for supplying the city with water.[31]

The popular assumption was that the Bronx River was the only real choice. Its promotion by Joseph Browne, validated by William Weston, had excited great discussion; the broad aqueduct-building privileges granted to the Manhattan Company seemed designed to facilitate such a project. The company water committee met that night and decided otherwise.

As described in a long letter the next day from Stevens to brother-in-law Livingston, Coles was a "strenuous advocate" for the Bronx; Osgood and Stevens "fell into his ideas" only so far as to admit that the Bronx might be "ultimately necessary." Harlem bridge-builder Coles feared that the Bronx would be "neglected perhaps forever," but after much discussion, he was brought around to the "temporary expedient" of the Collect Pond. "Thus," Stevens assured the company's largest investor, "you may perceive that this Business is in proper train."[32]

The Manhattan Company had no intention of spending its money on a historic but expensive water supply for New York. A supply from the Collect, thought Stevens, might be accomplished for just $200,000 and completed in several months: "This will put the Citizens in good humour with us, but should we do nothing we shall raise a violent clamor against us." Though the city had been compelled by the deadly yellow fever outbreak of 1798 to support any action on water, the company's interest in cleanliness and health would be decidedly antagonistic: "As to watering the streets it can never be expected from us, unless [the city] will agree to pay us amply."[33]

In its report to the company board the following week, the committee discredited the Bronx plans of Weston and Browne: sections of open canal would freeze in the winter; neither gravity alone nor Harlem-powered pumps could be relied on without time-consuming investigations; costs might well run beyond the company's capitalization. The Collect, though, would do just fine. A large steam engine (Stevens's special interest) could be built for $15,000, and a pipe network completed by year's end to supply over three hundred thousand daily gallons for all domestic purposes to the city's six thousand households. The board embraced the committee report and, at the suggestion of Burr, the committee was granted $1,000 for a survey of the pond to determine a proper spot for a well and make an estimate of the expected expenses. The water committee placed newspaper ads soliciting information on where to dig a well, and what quality and quantity of water might be obtained.[34]

Advertisements of the company's Collect intentions were the first public indication that something was terribly wrong with the Manhattan Company. A correspondent to the *Commercial Advertiser* warned that the company would have the deaths of thousands on its hands from the Collect's "fetid" waters.[35]

Nonetheless, the company promptly received two proposals for watering the city from the Collect. One came from Elias Ring, a Quaker dry goods merchant of no known expertise or interest in water supply matters. Alleging that the Collect was as pure as the Tea Water (a dubious position) and preferable to the Bronx, Ring suggested an underground, stone culvert from the pond to a steam engine, well, and reservoir down at the park; he imagined his plan could be completed for $100,000 by the following summer.[36]

The other proposal came from Christopher Colles, a quarter century to the day of his first proposal to water New York. The years had done little for Colles, then a couple of weeks short of sixty. His visionary projects of the 1780s—a canal linking the Hudson River and Great Lakes, and a map book of American roads—had been decades ahead of their time but come to naught, as had a geographical atlas in 1794. In 1792, he had conducted the initial surveys on the Connecticut River for what became the first lock canal in America, but he had not been selected for the work itself.[37]

The Manhattan committee actually had sought out Colles, then living in Westchester. Despite a lengthening record of flawed genius, which would continue until his impoverished death in 1816, Colles remained New York's expert on water supply matters. He also was personally known to Aaron Burr, who in 1786 was Colles's lawyer when Colles and his wife were assaulted on a city street.[38]

After exploring the site of his pre-Revolution waterworks with company officials and furnishing his notes on that failed effort, Colles offered his thoughts about the current situation. He dismissed the idea of a waterworks in the park, where he believed the water would be brackish and the well digging difficult. He warned of "many difficulties" with the Bronx: an open canal would freeze in winter and a pipe conduit would be expensive and difficult to lay and maintain; in summer, Bronx water was "not fit to drink," as he had learned during a year's residence along the river. Instead, Colles offered an updated version of his old plan: a new well, reservoirs, and steam engines at the original site near the Collect, plus log pipe distribution for just $68,500.[39] If the venerable Colles was living in the past, the Manhattan committee were happy he was there with his convenient opinions.

The committee also solicited the opinions of Bronx advocate William Weston. A month after detailing a grand plan to harness the Bronx and "unsurmountable" objections to the Collect, the English engineer now embraced the pond. Incredibly, Weston recommended using the old Colles waterworks site, cleaning out the old well, building a new reservoir, and employing a single steam engine to raise just three hundred thousand daily gallons of water, a tenth of what he had told the Common Council was needed a month earlier. With a distribution system using English cast iron pipe instead of logs, Weston suggested an overall cost of under $50,000.[40] Nearing the end of his seven lucrative American years, Weston perhaps was content to provide whatever opinions clients wished to purchase.

Also at the end of April, the Manhattan committee received a short letter from steam engine maker Nicholas Roosevelt, the natural choice to build an engine for the Manhattan Company. Roosevelt had been proposing to water New York himself for a number of years. He was running a diversified foundry business at the old Schuyler copper mines in New Jersey, with a focus on steam engines; among his assistants was Charles Stoudinger, formerly of the thriving English firm of Boulton & Watt, which turned out the most advanced steam engines of James Watt's invention.[41]

Roosevelt was well known to Manhattan Company men: Hamilton in-law Philip A. Schuyler was a foundry backer; Hamilton and John B.

Church were upstate land partners of Roosevelt's. More significantly, Roosevelt, John Stevens, and Stevens in-law Chancellor Livingston were involved in steamboat collaborations: in 1798, a Livingston-designed boat with a Roosevelt engine had failed grandly; just as the Manhattan Company was gearing up, Roosevelt built a Stevens-designed, Livingston-funded boat that fell apart from lightweight construction and engine vibration.

Despite those expensive and contentious setbacks, Roosevelt was negotiating with Philadelphia officials for a $30,000 contract to build two steam engines capable of raising three million daily gallons each for a planned waterworks. Roosevelt informed the Manhattan Company committee that in a year's time, he could build a $15,000 steam engine capable of raising two million gallons of water a day, or in four months a $9,500 engine that could raise three hundred thousand gallons.[42]

Before making its decisions, the committee was to hear from one more person. Ten months earlier, Joseph Browne had disdained "the disgusting water of the Collect." Now, the company incorporator felt the Collect less impure than he first imagined. Burr's pliant relation offered a "temporary" plan of his own.

Assuring the committee that the "situation of New-York is a very happy one for being watered at a small expence," Browne advocated a well and a steam engine with a mere sixteen-inch diameter cylinder, capable of raising three hundred thousand daily gallons, curiously in line with Roosevelt, Weston, Colles, and Ring. For the location of the principal reservoir, Browne rejected the old Colles site as too costly and not central enough; he favored Ring's suggestion of the park. Browne called for a reservoir 110 feet square and ten feet deep, holding a million gallons, "the least quantity that it ought to contain." Two seven-inch pumps would force the water through an eight-inch diameter cast iron pipe from the well to the reservoir. For distribution, Browne proposed two wooden mains down Broadway feeding lateral pipes on several principal streets sloping east and west to the rivers. He thought only four miles of distributing pipe would be needed for the time being, none larger than four-inch bore, at a cost of fifty cents per foot for the pipe plus the costs of ripping up and repaving the streets.

For street cleaning, Browne envisioned plugs in the mains at every intersection, so water could be thrown into any street which could "easily be overflowed, by making a small temporary Dam of old blankets, &c. below the part to be washed." Browne gave no indication of who was to supply the blankets.

The happy planner estimated the whole project at $60,000 and completeable by August, just in time for the feared onset of yellow fever. But he made clear that the water would not be drinkable by then: "It is not impossible that the water taken from the vicinity of the Collect, after it has been renewed by a constant pumping, for a few months, might be thought sufficiently pure for culinary purposes." Browne offered no estimate of the costs associated with service pipes into private houses.[43]

Before the Manhattan committee reached any formal conclusions from the array of options, there was some heavy political fallout. A withering anti-Burr, anti-Manhattan Company campaign in the Federalist press at the end of April brought a Federalist sweep in the city's legislative elections.[44] Into the state Senate went John Coles, whose company directorship was seen as a brake on the company's Republican-dominated board. Out of the Assembly went Burr cronies Storm, Arcularius, and Elias Nexsen, as well as Burr himself.

Days after the startling election results, the company water committee presented its recommendations at a special board meeting: the old Colles waterworks site should be purchased from the city, the old well should be re-opened and deepened if necessary, a reservoir should be built of unspecified size, and a contract for Roosevelt's smaller steam engine should be made "without delay." Twenty thousand feet of log pipe could be laid by summer, 120,000 more throughout the city by the end of 1800. Two thousand households could be signed up by winter at an annual $8 fee, substantially offsetting an anticipated construction cost of only $50,000. Impressed with what was in effect little more than an updated Colles plan, the company board empowered its water committee to proceed.[45]

The company tried to put on a good show about its water obligations. After resolving in April that water matters be discussed first at board meetings (an intention that would be honored most often in the breach), in early May, the board resolved that the company's capital should never be spent in such a way as to defeat the "primary object" of supplying water, exemplified in its corporate seal: the sea god Oceanus pouring water

from an urn into a lake. All of these decisions and future water-related proceedings were published in two local (albeit Republican) papers.[46]

Still, banking was the base reason for the company's existence and, with
nothing politically to lose and everything financially to gain, the board
resolved in mid-May to open "an office of discount and deposit." The decision prompted director William Laight to resign the next day, not because
he was conflicted about water but because he was already a director of the
New York branch of the Bank of the United States.[47]

Outrage over the company's apparent priorities was left to the Federalist press. "This Company must and will be destroyed," wrote a correspondent to the *Commercial Advertiser.* It was not. The Bank of the
Manhattan Company opened for business at what is now 40 Wall Street
on September 3. The rest, as what is now Chase Manhattan proudly
boasts, is banking history.[48]

While actively pursuing profit, the company did move forward on
water. By mid-June, the company had advertised for and made the first
of several pine log contracts, as well as contracts for boring and laying the
logs, and for supplies for a million-gallon reservoir. As laborers began clearing out the old Colles well, health-conscious editor Noah Webster signaled
cautious approval: "We believe it will be a source of infinite gratification
to the citizens, provided they find the current of water is made to keep
pace with the current of discounts."[49]

A few days later, the company chose a superintendent from among four
applicants; with a supporting letter from brother-in-law Burr, Joseph
Browne was the winner of the job and its generous salary of $1,500.
That expected decision followed a stunning one: the board rescinded its
decision to make a steam engine contract with Nicholas Roosevelt, opt-
ing instead to raise 250,000 gallons of water a day with "pumps to be worked
by horses." Seemingly unthinkable, Manhattan Company water would be
raised not by the machine of the future but the beasts of the past, the same
four-legged force raising the lately lamented Tea Water.[50]

Why were Roosevelt and steam power abandoned? The obvious and
likeliest explanation is that the company was seeking to conserve capital
for its banking operations. Yet, whereas many of the company's early
decisions on water were less than pioneering, this one showed some
foresight. Though Roosevelt would become a true steam pioneer, running

the first steamboat on the Mississippi in 1811, his New Jersey operation would fail in 1801, after delivering engines to Philadelphia that were poorly made, undersized, inefficient, and eventually the subject of seven years of lawsuits. Company investor Livingston may have shared concerns about Roosevelt with the directors, perhaps in Livingston's own self-interest; in September, he wrote to the water committee, questioning the use of horses and suggesting a steam engine of his own design, better, he alleged, than even a Watt engine.[51]

The Manhattan Company had reasonable inducements to hesitate not only on Roosevelt but steam engines generally. Though Roosevelt was building double-acting, separate condenser engines of the type successfully pioneered in England by Boulton & Watt, America was not quite ready to build steam engines, even a generation after Christopher Colles had produced the first ones. At the turn of the century, there were few if any steam engines in industrial use in the country. It was not until 1806 that genius inventor Oliver Evans established the country's first successful steam engine factory, near Philadelphia. Standing at the brink of the American steam age, the Manhattan Company directors, some with memories of Colles's short-lived New York engine, had some justification to take a step back.[52]

By the end of June, the company had a contract for horse pumps with Robert McQueen, soon enough a steam pioneer in his own right. A protégé of Robert Fulton, McQueen would shortly open the Columbian Foundry, the first New York City ironworks specializing in steam engines and soon one of the city's leading manufacturers, with over eighty employees by 1820. In 1802, the Manhattan Company would begin replacing McQueen's low-capacity horse pumps with a succession of his increasingly powerful steam engines.[53]

Superintendent Browne had no trouble for the time being with horses. Beyond the $9,500 for his engine and pumps, Roosevelt apparently had demanded additional money for an engine house plus a $4,500 annual fee to maintain the works. McQueen had agreed to pump nearly the same amount of water and furnish the horses, a pump house, stables, and related machinery for $4,500, plus a two-year maintenance fee of only $200. "If McQueen complies with his Contract," Browne informed brother-in-law Burr, "it appears to me the company will never be found fault with for making it."[54]

FIGURE 16. Manhattan Company water pump, 1800–1803

One in a series of mural paintings by Ezra Winter installed in the company head-quarters at 40 Wall Street in 1930, this scene depicts Robert McQueen's original horse-powered pump and (from right to left) original directors Samuel Osgood and John Stevens, and first superintendent and Burr brother-in-law Joseph Browne. (Courtesy Chase Manhattan Archives.)

In his lengthy letter to Burr, Browne indicated a fair understanding of modern hydraulic theory, then in its infancy. He apparently was familiar with the theories of French hydraulic pioneer Edme Mariotte (1620–86) and English natural philosopher John Theophilus Desaguliers (1683–1744), the only modern hydraulic writings available in English. Mariotte's basic contribution to hydraulics was showing that pipe length affected the height to which piped water would rise; Desaguliers had added approximations of the effects of pipe length on velocity. The theories of both men, though, stressed the difference in height between the water's starting and finishing points; practical application resulted in much lower flows than predicted. Accurate predictions of water flow would have to wait until subsequent hydraulic theories focused on the slope the water traveled.[55]

Using the knowledge he had, Browne suggested that the well and pump works be as close to the reservoir as possible: the shorter the connecting pipe, the less friction the pumps would have to overcome and the higher the water could be elevated for distribution. Princeton-educated Burr, in a marginal note that the pipe could be large enough to eliminate friction, demonstrated somewhat less knowledge.

Ultimately, the rudimentary hydraulic understanding available to the Manhattan Company would come to a confounding head in its pipe distribution system. For the time being, though, the company believed it was accomplishing good works. Backtracking from his earlier projection, Browne doubted that any water could be supplied by summer but hoped that "enough will be done to satisfy the Public and particularly the Legislature that the Institution is not a speculating Job, but an undertaking from whence will result immediate and incalculable advantages to the City of N. York."[56]

Luckily for the company, yellow fever returned that summer with less devastation than the previous year. Dockside areas were evacuated, the poor were moved to tents on high ground, the wealthy removed themselves from the city, and some 350 deaths were recorded from July through October.[57] It was reason enough for laborers throughout the summer to build the Manhattan Company works.

As the effort proceeded, Browne was responsible for relocating the intended reservoir and waterworks from the old Colles site to lots farther south, between the northeastern corner of the park and the filled south-

FIGURE 17. Laying Manhattan Company pipe, early 19th century
Another in the mural series, this scene features company "facilitator" Alexander
Hamilton at the extreme right. (Courtesy Chase Manhattan Archives.)

ern extremities of the Little Collect. In August, on newly laid Reade Street a block north of the park, McQueen began assembling his horse-works and a massive, iron-plated water storage tank over a new well. Elevated twenty-three feet above the ground on a massive stone foundation, the round tank was forty-one feet across and fifteen feet deep, holding a maximum of 123,354 gallons of water.[58]

"The Water-Works of the Manhattan Company progress with astonishing rapidity," observed Philadelphia's *Gazette of the United States* at the end of August. A half mile of pipe had been laid from McQueen's works southeast along Chapel (now Beekman) Street over the long-filled Beekman's Swamp nearly to Pearl Street, then running several landfilled blocks inland from the East River.[59]

By late September, another half mile of pipe had been laid down Pearl Street, but a bit of trouble had developed with the pumping system. "The machine for raising Water performs perfectly what was promised," Burr advised Chancellor Livingston, "but we are embarrassed with quick sand which is drawn up in such quantities as to choak the pumps every hour—we shall avoid this inconvenience by deepening the Well."[60] This was the cost of building a waterworks beside the filled swamps of the Collect Pond's southern reaches.

By mid-November, workers had laid pipe in several other streets. The company announced that it was ready to supply water: "Notwithstanding the intervention of a malignant fever, which occasioned so great and so large a desertion of the city, the works have never been suspended. . . . From actual experiment there is no doubt that one of the wells already opened will yield to five thousand families a daily supply of at least 50 gallons each, a quantity excellent for drinking and good for every culinary purpose."[61] How the company intended to supply 250,000 gallons of water a day from a tank half that size was not explained.

The announcement also contained a set of regulations. Prospective customers would have to apply in person or in writing; the water company would not come to them. Applicants were responsible for the purchase and installation of their own service pipe; the company recommended lead, astounding now but the popular malleable choice of plumbers from ancient Rome to modern America. Only a company worker could make the tap into the main. Water rates were $5 a year for private houses with fewer than five fireplaces, $1.25 for every additional fireplace, up to a maximum of $20. Payments were to be made quarterly, in advance. Rates for manufacturing buildings, taverns, and stables were to be set by agreement. Shipping would be supplied at twenty cents per hogshead from fountains to be built along the waterfront.

Apparently there were few initial takers. The first revenue in the company's books, a grand total of $162, doesn't appear until June 1800. In early July, another $325 was recorded, two-thirds being for one hundred thousand gallons of water provided to shipping over the preceding three months. If every private customer was paying at the lowest rate, in mid-1800, the Manhattan Company was serving no more than 220 households.[62]

By then, six miles of pipe had been laid, half of it purchased from Caleb Leach, who had lost out to Browne for superintendent. At the end of the year, Leach was hired as the company's "agent," reporting to Browne and earning a $1,000 salary. Leach had charge of all pipe purchases and maintenance, and was authorized to hire service pipe installers and set the price of installation; Browne was authorized to cut off the pipes of customers deemed to be wasting water.[63]

The company revisited plans for its unbuilt reservoir in the opening months of 1800. Shortly after becoming superintendent, Joseph Browne had modified his original idea of a simple square into a landmark octagon of stone walls twelve feet high, layered with clay and brick, holding the same million gallons. The frugal board discarded that idea in favor of a lead-lined reservoir of only 250,000 gallons, from a plan submitted by John McComb, the young architect who several years later co-designed and built the current City Hall. But a vote was repeatedly deferred until April, when the board finally approved a reservoir of merely one hundred thousand gallons.[64] In its broad retreat from a million-gallon reservoir, the Manhattan Company ensured it would never serve the water needs of its rapidly expanding city.

The immediate answer to getting water was: more horses! After approving the meager reservoir, the board ordered another well dug at the Reade Street site, as well as additional machinery to pump up the full 250,000 daily gallons that McQueen had not yet had the capacity to store. By October, he was keeping a herd of twenty horses in fireproof pumpworks and stables.[65]

FIGURE 18. Manhattan Company Reservoir, circa 1825

This lithograph, drawn for the 1855 *Manual of the Common Council* from an 1825 original, shows the Chambers Street reservoir, surmounted by the company symbol, the god Oceanus. (General Research Division. The New York Public Library. Astor, Lenox and Tilden Foundations.)

As McQueen built up his horse power, the reservoir slowly took shape. After much negotiation, in mid-June, the company paid $3,000 for three privately owned lots facing the park on the north side of Chambers Street, extending back toward the waterworks on Reade Street. With a new plan, perhaps drawn by McComb or by City Hall co-designer Joseph Mangin, construction finally began. The reservoir was completed (at a cost of $17,428) and filled during 1801.[66]

Although not nearly as grand as superintendent Browne had first envisioned, the Manhattan Company reservoir was a sound and attractive structure that became something of a New York landmark. Built of stone and cement, and lined with clay and tar, the reservoir's outer walls rose nearly twenty feet in an area roughly fifty by one hundred feet. The side walls were vertical (soon adjoined by a house for the superintendent and a public bath concession he ran); the front wall sloped back from Chambers Street. The middle of the front wall was adorned with a portico of four Doric columns, surmounted by a statue of water-pouring Oceanus.

If there wasn't much water behind the walls, at least the reservoir was pleasing to the eye.[67]

With the additional storage capacity, the company moved forward boldly on pipe. By the end of 1802, twenty-one miles had been laid throughout the city, at a cost of some $45,000. A battalion of laborers earning a generous dollar a day cut logs, carted sand and stone, and dug trenches.[68]

Rarely, though, did the company repair the streets it ripped up; indeed, nothing in its charter required it to do so. In July 1801, the Common Council first approached the company about the city's wrecked pavement, marking the beginning of three years of legal wrangling and the end of the tentative honeymoon between the city and its would-be water bearer. After two years of fruitless negotiations, in July 1803, the city secured the appointment of a state commission to evaluate the damages done by the company. The company in turn hired a lawyer who had kept his counsel about the company he had helped found. Privately, Alexander Hamilton considered the Manhattan Company "A perfect monster in its principles, but a very convenient instrument of profit and influence." Legally, he had no hesitation defending it. In November, though, the commissioners determined that the company owed the city $6,881.14; advised that the judgment was double what was due, the company rejected it.[69]

The advice came from Joseph Browne, who played both sides of the street battle. Late in 1802, he was appointed the city's first street commissioner, at a salary of $1,250, while happily retaining his Manhattan Company superintendent's job. After writing a July 1803 report with his street commissioner's pen recommending that the city and company share street repair costs, the company had fired him (and hired Caleb Leach), but it was Browne's private advice in a letter to company president Ludlow that induced the company to reject the high damage judgment.[70]

Another round of negotiations and legal action ensued before the company finally agreed in September 1804 to pay just under $5,000.[71] By then some institutional guilt was perhaps at play: five weeks earlier, their attorney in the matter had been shot dead in his duel with company creator Aaron Burr.

Burr had long since joined the procession of departing board members. John Stevens was the first prominent departure at the end of 1801, after losing a head-to-head competition with Robert McQueen to push the company into the steam age; after rejecting a Stevens's trial engine, over the next two years, the company purchased two large McQueen engines and retired his pump horses.[72] Burr, then the country's vice president, was removed at the end of 1802 after living up to his reputation as a fiscal libertine. A $48,000 loan from the bank in 1800 to pay off old debts had blossomed by mid-1802 to $120,000, only slightly less than the company's entire investment in its waterworks. Negotiations to retire the debt in exchange for Burr's cherished Richmond Hill estate and other real property are practically the only business in the company's recorded minutes from August 1802 until Burr's ouster in December.[73]

The bank was not hurting for money. Since the second half of 1801, its semiannual banking profits had been about $100,000, from which investors were receiving dividends of $2.50 per share.[74]

The water ledger told a different story. By the end of 1802, the company had invested only $132,000 on its waterworks. With annual water revenues of just $12,500 and operating expenses of $11,500, the water business was turning a meager profit, counting only 1,683 household customers. As the city's population grew from sixty thousand in 1800 to nearly seventy-six thousand five years later, an increasingly small percentage of New Yorkers were drinking Manhattan Company water.[75]

The summer of 1803 was a turning point for the company. Having already alienated official New York over street repairs, the company suffered the first of many failures to supply even its few customers. Yellow fever returned with a virulence not seen since the company was incorporated, ostensibly to limit the devastating effect of such fevers. After the first of over six hundred deaths, superintendent Browne (nearing the end of his company service) informed customers that well repairs would limit water distribution "for a few days." By the end of July, a customer in Pearl Street had not had water for two weeks: "Not long since I discharged my tea-water man, and had a Manhattan Cock introduced into my cellar, and for the first ten days I was highly pleased with it, as it afforded me good water—But, alas! for the last fourteen days, I have turned my cock repeatedly, but nothing comes from it." The luckless patron was forced to take water from a local street pump. A succession of other customers took to the papers with complaints of as many as nine weeks without water.[76]

By the end of 1804, the Manhattan Company had shed many of the characters of its founding days. Hamilton was dead, John Stevens was off inventing steamboats, and Burr and Browne were shortly to pursue the western adventures that would permanently wreck Burr's reputation and eventually leave Browne's wife and children destitute on the frontier.[77] Brockholst Livingston had resigned and John Watts and Samuel Osgood had been dropped in 1803. John Coles and John Church, whose pistols were used at the Burr-Hamilton duel, were dropped in 1804.

Not only was the company struggling to provide water to few people, it had assisted in the demise of the venerable Tea Water Pump. After William Thompson had finally succeeded in selling off the Hardenbrook family land containing the pump early in 1804, company superintendent Leach informed his employers "that the supplying of the tea water carts at that place will soon be discontinued, and . . . it may be said that the introduction of the Manhattan Water Works has discouraged the tea water interest." The company ignored Leach's suggestion that it take over the Tea Water concession.[78]

By 1804, the Bank of the Manhattan Company was firmly established as one of the nation's most powerful and influential financial institutions, tethered to the single obligation of providing "pure and wholesome water." For the next thirty years, the company would claim fulfillment of that duty while alternately brandishing its bank-affirming water rights against other would-be suppliers or attempting carefully to pawn off its waterworks on the city. As for New Yorkers, drinking no more Tea Water and scant Manhattan, it was once again back to street wells and carted spring water. New York had entered the first American century with less good water than the Dutch had bequeathed the English.

Fools of Gotham

Oh! Gotham, Gotham! most enlightened of cities!
—Washington Irving, *Salmagundi*

Legend says that in the early days of the thirteenth century, England's King John was hunting about for a new castle. All the king's men had eyes for a Nottinghamshire village named Gotham, meaning "goat town" and accordingly pronounced GOAT-em. The men of Gotham were none to pleased with the royal news.

Fearing a tax hike to pay for the king's new digs (John was a tax-happy monarch), as well as the attendant troubles of having a treacherous and lecherous neighbor (John killed a captive nephew, starved to death the wife and son of a recalcitrant baron, fathered a fistful of bastards, and took great pleasure in his twelve-year-old second wife), the Gothamites conspired to put on quite a show for the Crown's location scouts. The plan was to behave like complete idiots. By day, they tried drowning eels in a pond; by night, they took rakes to the pond to remove the moon's reflection. They joined hands round a thornbush to shut in a cuckoo and hoisted carts to the roof of a barn to shade it from the sun. All this foolishness sent the king's heralds packing, which for the time being seemed wise.[1]

In the long run, people forgot about Gotham's method and repeated only its madness. The "foles of Gotham" appeared in the Wakefield mystery plays, around 1460. A century later, Andrew Boorde issued *The Merrie Tales of the Mad-Men of Gotham*. In 1659, James Howell's *English Proverbs* noted the disparaging expression "wise as the men of Gotham"; three years later, a popular history by Thomas Fuller observed that "a hundred fopperies are feigned and fathered on the town-folk of Gotham." London tavernkeep and Hudibrastic sketcher Edward (Ned) Ward brought the lore forward to 1703: "I happen'd to be a hopeful branch of that ancient and renoun'd family of the wise-men of Gotham."[2]

Inevitably, the wise men of Gotham went to sea, making stops in varied American writings between 1741 and 1806, from Georgia to Boston to Lancaster, Pennsylvania.[3] In 1807, the men of Gotham found their permanent American home.

In the second of an eventual twenty numbers of *Salmagundi; or the Whim-Whams and Opinions of Launcelot Langstaff, Esq. and Others,* Washington Irving, in pseudonymous collaboration with his brother William and William's brother-in-law James Kirke Paulding, skewered a musical performance in the tea-room of the celebrated City Hotel, the leading showplace for the musical arts in New York: "The person who played the french horn was very excellent in his way, but Snivers could not relish his performance, having sometime since heard a gentleman amateur in Gotham play a solo on his *proboscis,* or nozzle, in a style infinitely superior." By the next issue, Irving was delighting in the popularity of *Salmagundi's* anonymous mockeries of New York: "One of the most tickling, dear, mischievous pleasures of this life is to laugh in one's sleeve—to sit snug in a corner unnoticed and unknown, and hear the wise men of Gotham, who are profound judges (of horse-flesh), pronounce from the style of our work, who are the authors."

As *Salmagundi's* single year progressed, Irving's razor quill whittled the image of "Gotham, Gotham! most enlightened of cities!" By November, Irving told New York's tale (with a nod to Ned Ward) in "The Renowned and Ancient City of Gotham," a chronicle of its conquering by the nimble-toed Hoppingtots.[4]

Responsible for the eventual launching of a thousand proud Gothams—from bistros to Batman locales—young Irving had practical reasons to question the wisdom of his city. The last-born of eleven children to a wealthy merchant, in 1807, Irving was an aristocratic young Federalist, uncom-

FIGURE 19. The Tea Water Pump, circa 1807
This watercolor drawing on cardboard by tinsmith and amateur artist William P. Chappel is the last known depiction of the pump that once supplied water to all of New York. (The Metropolitan Museum of Art, the Edward W. C. Arnold Collection of New York Prints, Maps and Pictures, Bequest of W. C. Arnold, 1954 [54.90.504].)

fortable with the increasing democratization of Jeffersonian America, masking his politics in whimsical satire.

The ethnic hordes that "capered towards the devoted city of Gotham" horrified Irving, but they came with a vengeance. In the first decade of the 1800s, New York's population swelled from sixty thousand to just under one hundred thousand, at last overtaking Philadelphia as the country's most populous city.[5] Unlike that amply watered place, though, New York was still drinking in the colonial ages. In no way had Gotham been more foolish than in failing to procure good water.

Water, Water Everywhere . . . Else

On the whole, you would have rather been in Philadelphia. Unlike salt-ringed Manhattan, Philadelphia had the fresh Schuylkill and Delaware Rivers running by its doors. When Philadelphia's long-praised wells and pumps succumbed to dense habitation and yellow fever in the 1790s, the city promoted pioneering efforts at a public water supply.

In the same year that Aaron Burr conspired to poison New York's water future, in Philadelphia, English-born architect and engineer Benjamin Latrobe created the Centre Square Waterworks, the country's first public urban water supply. It demonstrated that an American city could direct its best resources toward a civic purpose, and move forward from the imperfect results.[6]

In December 1798, Latrobe conceived a plan to water Philadelphia from the Schuylkill by the following July for $125,000, but it was three years and twice the money before the works were fully operational. The biggest delays arose from convoluted contracts worth $30,000 for two large steam engines, poorly built by future Latrobe son-in-law Nicholas Roosevelt, from whom the Manhattan Company concurrently shied away.

A large marble basin collected ebb tide Schuylkill water, which then flowed through sluices to a smaller basin and, via a short tunnel in solid rock, into a large well at the Lower Engine House. There, a forty-inch cylinder Roosevelt steam engine raised the water into a brick tunnel for a run by gravity under Chestnut and Broad Streets east to the Upper Engine House at the Centre Square intersection of Broad and Market Streets, which was still open land west of the settled portions of the city. Inside the pump house, the second engine, with a thirty-two-inch cylinder, raised the water to two wooden tanks holding a total of just under twenty-one thousand gallons. From the tanks, the water dropped to a cast iron distribution chest on the outside of the building, from which wooden mains carried the water east for distribution in small hollowed logs to dozens of public hydrants throughout the city.

The Centre Square building was no mere pump house. Set in landscaped grounds with statuary and fountains, the neoclassical marble building with columned porticoes was sixty feet square and surmounted by a windowed drum and stately dome with a chimney-concealing oculus nearly one hundred feet high. The triumph of the building's design was its external harmony with the parkland setting, which gave no indication of its internal, throbbing, industrial function: boiler, steam engine, pump, and water tanks were jammed inside its walls, along with the offices of the engineer and city water officials.

A site to behold, Latrobe's waterworks were nonetheless an endless headache. The system's storage capacity was far too small and Roosevelt's steam engines, made with many wooden parts, frequently broke down. The system required both engines to work in series. When one engine was being repaired, the system stopped; when both were working, they consumed fantastic amounts of wood and coal fuel. After years of retooling, the engines reliably pumped a million gallons a day (a third of their contractual capacity), filling the small reservoirs in the same half hour that the distribution system emptied them, which required the over-matched engines to run nonstop. Roosevelt and the city spent many years reaching a financial settlement. Latrobe's accounts were only settled in 1805, long after his departure and a vote of no thanks from the city government.

Still, Philadelphians embraced their flawed works and others took notice. After yellow fever glanced Philadelphia and plagued New York in 1805, New York's resident physician Edward Miller pointed to Philadelphia's "noble and costly . . . provident and wise plan." The following summer, Scottish cartographer John Melish observed Philadelphia's "great luxury" of abundant, clean, and free water, and New York's deficiency of the same.[7]

Worse than Centre Square's technological faults were its economics. By 1811, it had only 2,127 paying customers and annual revenues of half the $20,000 operating costs. By its last year of operation in 1815, total gross receipts of $105,000 were a sixth of total expenses. "Yet it cannot be said this sum has been lost to the City," a water department report rationalized many years later; "character and impetus was given to the City, [and] much was done to improve the sanitary condition, an important feature which was added to its many attractions as a place of residence."[8]

By the time Latrobe's system was retired, a new system designed and run by his former assistant, Frederick Graff, had come on line. After early design problems, the Fairmount Waterworks would gain international fame.

As announced late in 1811 and approved the following August, Graff's $150,000 plan called for a steam-pumped works a mile upriver on the Schuylkill. At the base of a rocky suburban elevation called Fairmount, a new engine and the transplanted Centre Square engine would pump river water up to hilltop reservoirs holding a million gallons; the water would flow south by gravity for distribution in the city by the existing Centre Square network.

Keeping in mind the aesthetic pleasures of Centre Square, Graff created an engine house in landscaped grounds that mirrored the Federal-style country estates then sprouting along the Schuylkill River. With a stuccoed exterior (the city economized on Graff's intended bluestone), pedimented and arched windows and doorways, columned porticoes, and eventually adorned with allegorical sculptures of a river god and water-works goddess by William Rush, the Fairmount Waterworks building disguised the furious machinery inside.

A low-pressure Boulton & Watt-type engine by local foundryman Samuel Richards was put into operation in 1815; alongside it went not Roosevelt's cranky beast, but a radical new machine: Oliver Evans's non-condensing high-pressure engine, truly capable of pumping over three million gallons of water a day. Produced at his renowned Mars Iron Works, Evans's massive engine operated at pressures exceeding two hundred pounds per square inch, infinitely more efficient than low-pressure engines. Delivered for trials early in 1815, the Evans engine went into full operation in 1817. By then, an expanded distribution system, featuring thirty-two miles of spruce and yellow pine pipes, supplied thirty-five hundred customers and three hundred public pumps.

"New York would do well to take a lesson from the rival city," observed Scottish traveler John M. Duncan in 1818.[9] The lesson, though, was still being learned by Philadelphia; Graff's steam-driven system proved shorter lived than Latrobe's.

The two steam engines burned tremendous amounts of fuel, pushing annual costs over $30,000; revenue lagged at $20,000. Boiler explosions in the high-pressure engine in 1818 and 1821 killed three men. Twice burned by steam, the city, in coordination with a canal company seeking to make the Schuylkill navigable, turned to water power. In the spring of 1819, work began on a low dam across the Schuylkill to create power for a series of waterwheels to pump water up to the reservoirs, concurrently expanding to a capacity of seven million gallons.

Completed by early 1822 and built largely of stone-filled hickory log cribs fastened to each other and the river bedrock, the dam was laid diagonally across the river to deflect spring floods and winter ice. Accom-

FIGURE 20. Fairmount Waterworks, 1835–1836
Replacing Benjamin Latrobe's flawed Centre Square Waterworks, Fairmount was famed in the 1830s as the finest modern urban water supply. This Nicolino Calyo gouache shows the navigational canal, the low dam, the waterworks buildings, and the hilltop reservoirs; replaced by larger works upriver and closed in 1909, the Fairmount buildings remain a tourist attraction. (Collection of Mellon Bank.)

modating navigational locks and a canal on the far shore and a mill race blasted out of solid rock on the waterworks side, the entire structure stretched sixteen hundred feet and created a lake six miles long for water storage.

In July 1822, the first wooden waterwheel—fifteen feet around and across—went into operation; two more were working by the end of the year. Concealed in a monumental neoclassical mill house built to accommodate an eventual eight wheels, each wheel worked a pump forcing over a million gallons a day through an iron main up to the reservoirs. The new works cost nearly half a million dollars to build but required only one person to watch over them and only slight incidental costs. The grand but costly steam engines were shut off in 1822 and ten years later sold for scrap.

Finally, Philadelphia had hit on the right formula. "The celebrated works on the Schuylkill are beyond all praise," observed a visitor from Detroit in 1825. "From the power of the works, a city of perhaps twice the extent of Philadelphia, could be supplied." Major improvements were made in the pipe system during the 1820s. Inefficient, small-diameter wooden mains linking the reservoirs to the old distribution chest at Centre Square were replaced by twenty- and twenty-two-inch cast iron pipe, the first metal pipe used in an American public water supply; by 1829, the distribution chest had been bypassed and Latrobe's Centre Square landmark was torn down. Gradually, the aging, leaky wood distribution system was also replaced with iron pipe, featuring novel but soon standard "spigot and faucet" joints and curved sections at water-slowing corners.[10]

By 1830, the works at Fairmount were a model of American industry and pastoralism. The rhythmic creaking of waterwheels and gushing of pumps harmonized with the sound of river water spilling through the race, mesmerizing to visitors in the gallery above. Graff's original engine house was converted to a graceful reception hall serving refreshments. With extensive landscaped gardens, the whitewashed buildings with colonnades, porticoes, and gazebos appeared as an ancient acropolis set into the rocky hillside, fortifying the downstream city. Frances Trollope, notorious British observer of America's domestic manners, was uncharacteristically overwhelmed: "It is, in truth, one of the very prettiest spots an eye can look upon."[11] In 1830, the Fairmount system was supplying two million gallons a day to over ten thousand customers, including several suburban districts, leading Philadelphia to its first waterworks profit in thirty years.

Fairmount entered a half-century golden age in the 1830s. In 1837, six waterwheels were in operation, the newest three made of cast iron; twenty thousand households and businesses, generating over $100,000 in annual revenue, received over three million gallons of water a day, from linked reservoirs then holding twenty-two million gallons. Nearly fifteen hundred Philadelphia houses boasted bathrooms with running water. "No city can be better supplied with water than this," enthused Irish actor Tyrone Power, great-grandfather of the American movie star. English novelist Frederick Marryat felt sorry for the Schuylkill: "As I presume that river has a god as well as others, I can imagine his indignation, not only at his waters being diverted from his channel, but at being himself obliged to do all the work for the benefit of his tyrannical masters." "It is impossible to examine these works without paying homage to the science and skill displayed in their design and execution," observed English-born inventor and future U.S. Commissioner of Patents Thomas Ewbank. "In these respects no hydraulic works in the Union can compete, nor do we believe they are excelled by any in the world." All eight waterwheels were pumping as much as ten million gallons of water a day when Charles Dickens visited in 1842: "Philadelphia is most bountifully provided with fresh water, which is showered and jerked about, and turned on, and poured off, everywhere."[12]

Dickens and his fellow English travelers were certainly aware of the water situation in London. Supplied hodgepodge by a handful of unregulated and noncompeting private water companies, most of London drank from the Thames, dangerously polluted by the early 1800s. It was "disgusting to the senses," concluded a royal commission in 1828.[13]

Philadelphia was unique among America's largest cities in committing at the outset to a public water supply. In 1796, Boston had cast its lot with a private company, incorporated to pipe water by gravity from nearby Jamaica Pond; forty years later, it sporadically supplied fifteen hundred homes in a city of eighty thousand people. At the same time, a quarter of the city's 2,767 public wells were deemed undrinkable; only seven provided water suitably soft for laundering purposes. It was not until 1848, after decades of dispute and debate, that the city completed a proper public supply, the Cochituate Aqueduct, which brought the water of Long Pond twenty-five miles to the west.[14]

Baltimore, which had overtaken Boston as the third-largest American city at the opening of the 1800s, was served with some success by a civic-minded private company from 1804 through midcentury, when the city purchased the works; by then, though, only a third of the city's 170,000 people were using the system that involved a complex pump works at nearby Jones Falls. The city was naturally supplied by many clear springs, but they and the waterworks failed dramatically in 1832, when Baltimore recorded nearly as many cholera deaths as twice-larger Philadelphia.[15]

New Orleans, the fifth-largest American city in the first half of the nineteenth century, in 1811 granted Benjamin Latrobe and associates the exclusive right to supply water by steam engine from the less than pristine Mississippi. Latrobe's son Henry oversaw the project, which proceeded very little before he died of yellow fever in 1817. His father took over two years later, but the fever-plagued city claimed his life as well in 1820. Already outdated when the city completed them two years later, the works were replaced by a private company's similar system in 1837.[16]

Cincinnati, "the imperial city of the west," was still a frontier town when it was incorporated in 1819, but two years earlier it had granted exclusive water supply rights to private investors. As constructed during the 1820s, a tunnel led from the deepest part of the Ohio River to a well on shore where steam-worked pumps forced the water to reservoirs; cast iron mains carried the water by gravity into town, where oak logs distributed the water along the few principal streets. The system worked reliably well for the forty thousand people who voted for a city takeover of the works in 1839.[17]

Smaller American cities and towns of the early 1800s developed adequate water supply systems from local sources. Troy, New York, with a population of about fifteen thousand in 1840, spent slightly over $100,000 to bring water from Piskawin Creek, a third of a mile east. An iron main, tapering from sixteen to twelve inches, lead a million gallons of water a day by gravity from a two-million-gallon reservoir. On the opposite bank of the Hudson in neighboring Albany, the state capital of thirty thousand people, a private company supplied twelve hundred houses, at $8 to $16 a year, with water brought to a distributing reservoir by a six-inch iron pipe from a creek three miles north of the city.[18] A hundred and fifty miles down the Hudson, a much larger city was having much less success.

Meanwhile, Back at the Manhattan Company . . .

"Some wells have been dug in the filthiest corners of the town; a small quantity of water has been conveyed in wretched wooden pipes, now almost worn out, for family use; and in a manner scarcely, if at all, preferable to the former method of supplying water by the carts."[19] This was how the decidedly Federalist *Evening Post* viewed the decidedly Republican Manhattan Company in January 1808. At the time, De Witt Clinton (1769–1828), then the leader of Republican state politics, was trying to engineer both an extension of the company's 1799 charter, which was limited to ten years if the company failed to supply sufficient good water, and a waterworks transfer to the city that would preserve the company's banking privileges and relieve its water burden. Two months later, while concurrently mayor, state senator, and company director and major investor, Clinton accomplished a charter extension that allowed the company another ten years to provide sufficient water and thirty more years of corporate life after a possible city purchase of the waterworks.[20]

Politics aside, the *Evening Post*'s take on the Manhattan Company was no exaggeration, especially regarding public service. In the summer of 1802, the company had agreed to provide water for street cleaning, at up to $750 a week; that costly "experiment" was soon abandoned. Two Augusts later, the city was forced to hire people to flush the streets three times a week with public well water; private well owners were compelled to flush and sweep the gutters and sidewalks in front of their houses twice a day. When the city made use of company water, acrimony followed; a company water bill in 1806 was referred to arbitration before the city finally agreed to pay $1,244.[21]

The company was initially more accommodating at fires, allowing free (and often wasteful) water use by the city's volunteer fire companies. Arriving at a fire, the firemen would drill into the nearest log main, leaving a wooden "fire plug" when they were done. But beginning in 1807, the company introduced wooden street hydrants, allowing the company to regulate water use at fires and charge for it. The following summer a rare deadly fire killed five people and destroyed several schools and businesses, including Grant Thorburn's seed store. This time, the Manhattan pipes yielded little water to pay for. As late as 1814, the Common Council was still debating how the company ought to provide water at fires.[22]

If streets went unwashed and buildings went aflame for lack of Manhattan water, the company's private customers had it worse. Though the company's third superintendent, John Fellows, insisted shortly after his hiring in 1806 that ample water was available, the company's pipes were rapidly becoming useless. Always prone to leaks, the small-diameter pine logs were under subterranean attack at their joints from the roots of the Lombardy poplar, introduced from France in 1790 and infesting the island in the first decade of the 1800s. Though a staminate tree, the poplar propagates relentlessly from root sprouts; the moisture-seeking fibrous roots worked their way into the dank Manhattan pipe with an insatiable thirst. Alarmed by the obstructions, Fellows eventually suggested that the poplars be cut down, though a new tree protection ordinance made that solution unviable.[23]

By 1809, the company had become one of the city's "greatest vexations." Few customers in the lower wards ever had any Manhattan water; one customer, paying $10 a year, had not had a drop in four months: "if a remedy is not soon found, I shall have my pipe cut off . . . and be obliged once more to rely upon our pumps, and I am confident my neighbors will all follow my example." "The complaint is indeed universal," noted the *Commercial Advertiser:* "We know of no family which is regularly supplied with Manhattan water."[24]

Privately, the company recognized that its water system was "very deficient" and would even worsen until it was "improved or abandoned."[25] This candor, posing a threat to the company's continuing banking privileges, remained within the confines of the boardroom.

After struggling with repeated distribution pipe blockages, steam engine and other mechanical breakdowns, and the extended absences of service pipe repairmen, the company tried a new approach in 1811, replacing harried superintendent Fellows with an independent contractor working on commission. The ten-year run of F. Huguet was distinguished by the company's failure ever to record his first name. Huguet was responsible for the addition of a large McQueen steam engine, a new engine house, a blacksmith shop for on-site machinery repairs, and two wooden settling tanks on the intake side of the reservoir; he also engineered higher rates (especially for leather tanners, who came to use 20 percent of all Manhattan water) and continued claims against the city for fire water, while bloating his staff and failing to solve rampant root blockage. Huguet's death in 1821 (after a year's incapacity) revealed other troubles: he hadn't balanced the water revenue ledger for seven years; on company time and machinery, he'd been running a side business in service pipe; and he'd been selling for his own profit the valuable ash from the voracious wood-burning steam engines. Alarmed, the bank-distracted board reinstituted the superintendent job, with specific controls and oversight.[26]

New superintendent John Lozier, who would serve for two decades, conducted an internal report on the system in his second year on the job. Two eighteen-horsepower steam engines were pumping 691,200 daily gallons into the reservoir and twenty-five miles of pipe were distributing the water to just over two thousand houses and a number of free fire hydrants. Lozier certified that the system was capable of serving an additional 11,520 houses with "perfectly clear" water: "I drink it," he alleged, "and have experienced no unwholesome effects from it, nor have I ever heard of any. The water appears as pure and clean as any I ever saw." No wonder company man Lozier, who apparently never saw Philadelphia water, kept his job for so many years.[27]

Most revealing in Lozier's report is that the company had barely increased its customer base or its pipe mileage since superintendent Joseph Browne's accounting two decades earlier. While the city's population and settled area had tripled, the Manhattan Company had added a few hundred customers and four miles of pipe. In a public announcement a year later, Lozier slashed his estimate of potential new customers to one thousand, and boldly guaranteed subscribers "a regular supply at all seasons of the year." At an annual rate that had risen as high as $12, few took the bait.[28]

Under Lozier's earnest management, the company did pick up the pace of improvements, spending over $170,000 from 1825 to 1838. The efforts began with a contract for the services of artesian well zealot Levi Disbrow, who was singularly convinced for years that a bounty of pure water laid trapped in bedrock deep beneath the city. Having bored with reported success at regional distilleries, and armed with the first of several water boring patents, Disbrow started drilling the rocky earth in a Manhattan Company lot up at Broadway and Bleecker Street in 1825. Seven discordant years and 442 vertical feet later, the effort reached its natural conclusion: $12,000 spent and no water suitable for distribution.[29]

On sounder technological footing, the company started replacing its wood pipes with cast iron late in 1827. By the following June, longtime company nemesis the *Commercial Advertiser* noted the ongoing "great improvement"; ex-mayor Philip Hone was pleased to record in the opening pages of his later famous diary the "laying down [of] large Iron Pipes in Broadway, opposite to my House." By 1832, some $80,000 worth of iron pipe had been laid in place of wood, much of it supplied by Philadelphia's Samuel Richards. During the 1830s, the company spent $50,000 on additional real estate around its Chambers and Reade Streets waterworks operations, and paid over $30,000 for an iron tank and buildings at Bleecker and Broadway, where Disbrow's boring efforts had been suspended.[30]

No matter how it was stored and delivered, Manhattan Company water still traced its source to the subterranean regions of the Collect Pond, improvidently filled and buried beneath a sprawling slum in the opening decades of the 1800s. Recorder Richard Riker, longtime company apologist and ex officio director, testified in 1831 that he drank a pint of Manhattan water every morning and enjoyed good health, but Gothamites ridiculed Riker's claim for years afterward.[31] An anonymous "Water Drinker" told a different story:

> I have no doubt that one cause of the numerous stomach affections so common in this city is the impure, I may say poisonous nature of the pernicious Manhattan water which thousands of us daily and constantly use. It is true the unpalatableness of this abominable fluid prevents almost every person from using it as a beverage at the table, but you will know that all the cooking of a very large portion of this community is done through the agency of this common nuisance. Our tea and coffee are made of it, our bread is mixed with it, and our meat and vegetables are boiled with it. Our linen happily escapes the contamination of its touch, "for no two things hold more antipathy" than soap and this vile water.[32]

Suffering Gotham

As New York fiddled for three decades with the Manhattan Company, the city burned with disease. City inspector John Pintard put the 1805 population of New York at 75,770, of which three hundred died in that year's yellow fever outbreak, while some twenty-seven thousand fled, including 80 percent of the moneyed first and second wards downtown. This was no way to run the nation's commercial capital. "The embarrassments of our commerce on this account in foreign ports have become oppressively great," resident physician Edward Miller warned the Republican governor Morgan Lewis; "they are likely hereafter to become greater still."

Miller, who discounted the imported contagion theory of yellow fever and gave no thought to mosquitoes, believed *"a pernicious exhalation or vapour floating in the atmosphere,* is the primary and essential cause of this disease." The popular "miasma" theory at least enabled him to focus on New York's abundant, summer-heated filth: "yellow fever, arising from a deleterious principle floating in the atmosphere, and produced by the operation of solar heat upon vegetable and animal filth, ceases to prevail soon after this heat is reduced so low that it can no longer exhale a sufficient quantity of the miasmata of putrefaction." Atop Miller's list of remedies (including sewers, better drainage, improved privies, street paving, and a ban on burials within the city) was "*Water,* obtained from a distant source, of pure quality, and in quantity sufficient to allow a constant, plentiful, and increasing expenditure."[33]

No distant water was brought any time soon, though the procuring of water from the city's once great local resource was soon ended. With the city crowding around by 1806, the Collect had become less of a pond than a convenient bog to dump murder victims. Even longtime iceman Joseph Corre informed his customers that the "putrid state" of the Collect had rendered its seasonally frozen waters "unfit to be made use of in liquors," and henceforth his ice would come from a fresh spring three miles upisland. Ad hoc filling of degraded lots at the Collect had been going on since the turn of the century. In 1803, the city started razing the hill where the Colles waterworks had been erected and using the dug earth to fill swampy portions of the pond; the city also began paying five cents per cartload of "any dirt for filling in the Collect." By 1807, nearly $40,000 worth of dirt had been dumped into the degraded natural landmark of old New York.[34]

Unfortunately, this unscientific process had some undesirable results. As recalled by John Randel, Jr., the city's great surveyor, the earth fill was often as not mixed by the industrious carter with rubbish. The earth "being of greater specific gravity than the debris, or mud at the bottom of [the pond] caused it to rise, and mix with the rubbish and stand out; forming a very offensive and irregular mound of several acres; which appeared to me . . . to be from 12 to 15 feet in height above the level of the . . . water remaining in the Pond."[35]

In 1809, the city began selling off lots in and around the Collect. The old Colles plot of 1.75 acres was divided into some thirty lots, of which twenty-one went at auction in November for just over $25,000, a rate of return on the city's original purchase of about 900 percent.[36]

The Collect itself proved more difficult to transform into valuable real estate. A survey on its frozen surface by the street commissioner early in 1810 determined that only 26,400 more loads of earth would be needed to fill the pond completely; by July, twice that amount had not accomplished the matter. A year later, the Common Council ordered up another fifteen thousand loads but was still considering whether it might not be proper "to leave some of the Springs or [natural] fountains of it open." Another $2,000 was spent that year trying to make the Collect disappear. A grand jury toured the site in June 1812, finding "much to complain of; besides great quantities of stagnant water it seems to be made the common place of deposit for dead animals & filth of all kinds, where they are left to corrupt the air and endanger the health of the City."[37]

A state commission made up of Baltimore surveyor Thomas Poppleton, New England inventor Eli Whitney, and venerable local engineer Robert Fulton warned late in 1812 that impromptu filling of the Collect and irregular building over it would create "a curse upon the City and posterity ... a prolific source of Contagion and disease." The team recommended that the Collect first be drained with a large, tapering, vented tunnel from the pond to the Hudson; the design would allow the Collect's foul waters to drain constantly, while clean tidal water would regularly flush the tunnel. The tunnel would run beneath Canal Street, which took its name from earlier notions of Collect drainage through the old Lispenard's Meadow. The Poppleton-Whitney-Fulton plan demonstrated that only a tunnel would work and, in the process, eliminate development-hindering bridges.[38]

Typically, Gotham torpedoed this wisdom, debating the matter until 1819, when an open sewer was laid. The stopgap pond filling continued.[39] Briefly fashionable, the new neighborhood over the former Collect began to go down after 1820, literally. As predicted, buildings on the poorly drained landfill sagged, putrid gases rose, and the notorious low-rent district of Five Points, the nation's first great slum, was born. It was an ugly death for the once glorious Fresh Water.

The crude filling of the Collect was just a small part in the paving over of Manhattan, induced by the unfortunate success of a different set of com-

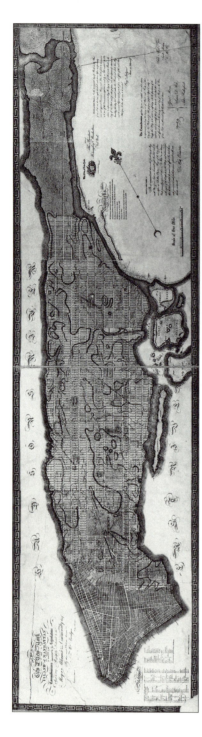

FIGURE 21. The Commissioners' Plan, 1811

Ordered in 1807, the plan laid the familiar grid of avenues and streets over most of Manhattan's natural topography, leveling hills, filling valleys, and burying watercourses in the decades-long process. (Print Collection. Miriam and Ira D. Wallach Division of Art, Prints and Photographs. The New York Public Library. Astor, Lenox and Tilden Foundations.)

missioners. Four years after their appointment, retired statesman Gouverneur Morris, leading lawyer John Rutherford, and longtime state surveyor-general Simeon DeWitt produced the "Commissioners' Plan," the most important document in the history of the city's development: a blueprint for the modern city and a death warrant for old New York.

As drawn by surveyor John Randel, Jr., on a map eight feet long, the plan presented a relentless rectilinear grid of two thousand rectangular blocks north of the already settled areas: streets from Houston Street to Washington Heights and avenues from river to river. "[A] city is to be composed principally of the habitations of men," wrote the commissioners, "and . . . strait sided, and right angled houses are the most cheap to build, and the most convenient to live in."[40]

The grid encountered few of Manhattan's hills and watercourses that couldn't be turned into neatly sectioned potential real estate. State Chancellor James Kent pronounced the plan "an everlasting monument," but scholar Clement Clarke Moore deplored planners "who would have cut down the seven hills of Rome" (though the "Night Before Christmas" poet later made a fortune developing his estate into lots that became the Chelsea neighborhood). To Manhattan's great historian I. N. Phelps Stokes, writing a hundred years later, the grid "destroyed most of the natural beauty and interest of the island which . . . might have possessed the charm and variety of London."[41]

Because the island was embraced by "large arms of the sea," the commissioners planned few parks or public spaces. Among the small areas they did suggest was a five-block rectangle at 5th Avenue and 89th Street, "a space sufficient for a large Reservoir, when it shall be found needful to furnish the City, by means of aqueducts, or by the aid of hydraulic machinery, with a copious supply of pure and wholesome *water*."[42] As it turned out, neither this square nor any other envisioned in the Commissioners' Plan was set aside; only with the carving out of Central Park in the 1850s was any substantial open area preserved on Manhattan.

Back to the Wells, Again

The future did not come so fast where water was concerned. Their ponds and upisland springs facing permanent interment, the people of Gotham

FIGURE 22. Corner of Greenwich Street, 1810

This contemporary watercolor by Baroness Hyde de Neuville depicts a typical street scene, with one of the ubiquitous public pumps in active use a decade after the Manhattan Company had failed to make them unnecessary. (I. N. Phelps Stokes Collection. Miriam and Ira D. Wallach Division of Art, Prints and Photographs. The New York Public Library. Astor, Lenox and Tilden Foundations.)

settled in for decades more of public wells and pumps and the assorted schemes of public and private water seekers.

Beginning in 1806, public pumps that had stood in the streets since English colonial days were banished to the sidewalks. "Pumps, of a large size, with long, clumsy, wooden handles, are found in the middle of many of the streets," observed a summer visitor from abundantly watered Philadelphia; "Their removal is said to be gradually taking place, and it is expected they will soon be succeeded by something less clumsy and unsightly." Old pumps in lower Broadway were moved "in the usual Mode" in May 1807; as early as 1809, the great well sunk back in 1752 opposite St. Paul's Church on upper Broadway was shifted with its popular pump to the curb.[43]

The public pumps were pushed aside but not abandoned. In the summer of 1808, the city counted 238; six months later, after the Common Council ordered that new wells be at least six feet wide and contain at least three feet of water, another eleven had been built.[44]

If the quantity was rising, the quality certainly was not. Former Manhattan Company director Brockholst Livingston "found nothing so disagreeable as the water" during an 1810 visit to the city: "Inhabitants Literally in their water [are] drinking a proportion of their own evacuations, as well as that of their Horses, Cows, Dogs, Cats and other putrid liquids so plentifully dispensed." Ten years later, resident physician David Hosack estimated that one-twelfth of the city's inhabited area was occupied with cesspools, sinks, and privies. Most privies of the period had stone walls and unsealed bottoms as deep as twelve feet but as shallow as two and a half, equipped with removable tubs. The city had established its privy cleaning policy at the beginning of the century and didn't change it much for thirty years: a superintendent oversaw city scavengers who were supposed to empty privies at night and, as in Dutch colonial days, dump the waste in the rivers. Under cover of darkness, New York's nightsoil often missed the tide.[45]

To improve their water, some New Yorkers took to adding French brandy or gin to make it safe to drink. The rage, though, was for gas. In 1818, a Swedish visitor found "artificial soda water . . . for sale on every corner."[46]

Natural sparkling mineral water, discovered in upstate New York in the 1780s, was first brought to the city around the turn of the century by health pioneers Samuel Latham Mitchill and Valentine Seaman. This gave rise to a treatment for the local waters. By one account, artificially carbonated water was first offered in New York's City Hotel in 1809 by Noyes Darling, who became a leading manufacturer of "soda water." In 1811, Sophia Usher, claiming her late husband George was "the first person who introduced the use of Soda water in this City or in the United States," won permission from the Common Council to sell "her most excellent waters" in the vestibule of City Hall. After fending off a competing claim of priority from a relative, Sophia's business flourished until 1820, when she sought permission to put up "a small building for the purpose of vending Soda Water" in a city-owned lot next to City Hall. Her petition was rejected as "an improper incumbrance."[47]

The carbonated house of Usher fell but the industry thrived. "Iced soda water from the fountain is the liquid in universal use by all descriptions of persons, and is admirably prepared," Scottish traveler James Stuart observed in 1828, "the pleasantest beverage, as it appeared to me, that I had ever tasted in warm weather. It is frequently mixed with a small por-

tion of lemon syrup; the price threepence sterling for a tumbler. It is prepared and sold in almost every street. The demand at the fountains is so
great, that very large sums of money have been made by the manufacturers."
Four years later, Englishman John Matthews set up a soda water factory
out at 26th Street, becoming the first exclusive manufacturer of soda
water machines and for decades the country's leading bottler, with an international reputation.[48]

Even as New York went mad for temperate bubbly, misty sentiment rose
in the local conscience. In 1826, Knickerbocker editor and poet Samuel
Woodworth published "The Old Oaken Bucket," a pastoral reverie on his
childhood memories. Set to music by Frederick Smith, the gushy verses
became one of America's most popular songs:

> That moss-covered bucket I hailed as a treasure
> For often at noon, when returned from the field,
> I found it the source of an exquisite pleasure,
> The purest and sweetest that nature can yield.
> How ardent I seized it, with hands that were glowing
> And quick to the white-pebbled bottom it fell.
> Then soon, with the emblem of truth overflowing,
> And dripping with coolness, it rose from the well.

Wags thought the rhapsody was inspired during Woodworth's reflec-
tive moments in a bar. Another account has him sampling a street pump
on a sultry walk home and wishing for better.[49]

Nearly as famous as Woodworth's maudlin poesy was an anonymous
parody, "The Old Oaken Bucket (As censored by the Board of Health)":

> Oh, had I but realized in time to avoid them
> The dangers that lurked in that pestilent draft,
> I'd have tested for organic germs and destroyed them
> With potassic permanganate ere had I quaffed.
> Or perchance I'd have boiled it, and afterwards strained it
> Through filters of charcoal and gravel combined;
> Or, after distilling, condensed and regained it
> In potable form with its filth left behind.[50]

FIGURE 23. *City Hall and Park Row, circa 1830*
This watercolor by John William Hill shows a spring water cart and a hand-pumped fire engine. (I. N. Phelps Stokes Collection. Miriam and Ira D. Wallach Division of Art, Prints and Photographs. The New York Public Library. Astor, Lenox and Tilden Foundations.)

New Yorkers of the 1820s could take just so much sentiment about well water, but there was abiding fondness for the old Tea Water Pump. Much as Woodworth drank memories from an old well, seedsman Grant Thorburn long remembered his final encounter with the Tea Water, in 1827: "I found the water brought by a pipe into a liquor store, in the house No. 126 Chatham Street. I drank of it to revive recollections."[51]

Contemporary accounts of other drinkable water procured within the city during this period are hard to come by. Most often recalled was Knapp's Spring, located at the northern fringes of Greenwich Village near the Hudson shore. As the only information on Knapp's comes from recollections, it seems likely that the waters were a pale semblance of the late, great Tea Water.[52]

For those who could afford it, spring water carted by the hogshead from upisland was the best but limited and imperfect alternative at the opening of the 1830s. "This water, although far from good, is much better than that obtained from wells in the city," observed the *New York Evening Journal.* At six cents a day for three pails, a typical family paid $20 a year for carted water, nearly twice the cost of precious Manhattan water. "This amount is paid for warm water—water that has been carried several miles in a hot sun, and if we could have cold water, or water approximately fresh, we must have ice; this is another tax."[53]

The limited availability of water also stymied fire-fighting efforts. Increasingly disastrous fires beset the city during the first third of the nineteenth century. In 1804, the worst fire since the Revolution destroyed up to $2 million worth of property in the Wall Street area; it was one of sixteen fires that year. There was an average of over twenty fires a year through 1814, including a fire in 1811 that destroyed more than a hundred houses. Twenty volunteer firemen were severely injured in an 1816 blaze. In 1820, the famous Park Theatre burned to the ground. The dramatic Bowery Theatre fire of 1828 killed two people, destroyed $600,000 worth of property, and was notable for the lack of any water in private or public cisterns to fight it.[54]

Lacking a public water supply, the city had begun building rain-fed cisterns in 1811, when the wings of City Hall were adorned with twin two-hundred-hogshead stone cisterns, "to be supplied from the roof thereof, ... the water [to] be used only at fires." After the city's churches balked at a Common Council request to build public cisterns, in 1817, the state legislature authorized the city to build them in the same manner as it had been digging public wells—wherever the council thought best and at the expense of those living nearby. At first cisterns only went up in neighborhoods that requested them and could afford the $600 cost, but by 1830 forty-three public cisterns had sprung up around town. Each had a capacity of about one hundred hogsheads but, as the Bowery Theatre fire proved, due to frequent drought they often contained less.[55]

Even as the climate limited the effectiveness of cisterns, geography increasingly diminished the effectiveness of fire buckets, hose, and hand-pumped fire engines that relied on river water. The city was not only stretching lengthwise but doubly so in width. Narrow at its southern tip, Manhattan widens dramatically above the regions of the old Collect. The island is roughly two miles wide in its one-mile length from Grand

Street to 12th Street. This was the area, including Greenwich Village on the west, that New Yorkers rushed to pave and populate starting in the 1820s. New York, 123,706 strong in 1820, was home to 270,089 souls by the middle of the next decade.[56] The rivers, source of much fire-fighting water, receded from central neighborhoods, which no number of cisterns could protect.

The Worst-Laid Schemes Go Awry

Reeling from yellow fever and the failings of the Manhattan Company, in 1804, the Common Council appointed a committee "to devise an effectual plan for furnishing this City with a more abundant supply of water for public emergencies." City inspector John Pintard was sent "exploring the source of the River Bronx." He returned with the cautious advice that the council go look for itself, prompting the committee to seek the trusted opinion of original Bronxite Joseph Browne, then the street commissioner. Browne promptly responded with a detailed proposal for a $263,820 Bronx supply, a good bit pricier than his 1798 estimate. Shortly thereafter the Democratic-Republicans won control of the Common Council for the first time; the party of mayor and Manhattan Company director De Witt Clinton would not be putting the company at risk for a public go at the Bronx.[57]

The Manhattan Company's exclusive water rights stifled all official discussion for the next dozen years. In 1816, a Common Council committee was appointed to investigate whether the legislature might grant the city the right to build a public water supply. It appears that the committee never issued a report.[58]

The next flurry of activity began in 1819, with similar results. Robert Macomb offered to supply the city "for all Domestic and Public Purposes" with water from Rye Pond, crossing the Harlem where he had built a bridge, dam, and mill in 1813. Macomb and his associates asked for no money, just the city's permission to lay pipes in the streets and sell the water. A Common Council committee, including then-alderman Robert McQueen, the engine manufacturer who had brought the Manhattan Company into the steam age, reported favorably on this modest proposal early in 1820. On the same day it crushed Sophia Usher's soda water fiefdom, the council issued a conditional approval to Macomb. He could lay distribution pipes only after he had built and filled a reservoir up at the Harlem. On an amendment from assistant alderman Samuel Stevens, the city retained its rights to regulate water rates and reserved its right to purchase the works at cost after forty years. These surprisingly wise provisions apparently scared off Macomb, who perhaps had other intentions: some weeks earlier, he had offered unsuccessfully to buy or operate the Manhattan Company's water business.[59]

Concern for the city's water troubles was expressed up in Albany in January 1820. In his annual message to the legislature, Governor De Witt Clinton (separated from the Manhattan Company since 1812) wrote that the growing city could never furnish water from within its borders. He suggested renewed explorations of Westchester's Bronx and Saw Mill Rivers.[60]

Clinton's call to action was heard by New York's mayor, Stephen Allen.[61] A sailmaker's ragged apprentice in Revolutionary New York, Allen had grown rich in the sail business. "Industrious, scrupulously exact, and rigid in justice," with a "reputation for integrity," Allen was among the city's wealthiest citizens by the 1810s. He was "a self made man, with a clear head and sound heart," conceded powerful Whig opponent Thurlow Weed; "though cold and stearn [*sic*] in look and manner, [he] relaxed and warmed in conversation." A Tammany grand sachem and oft-elected Democrat, Allen was "an energetic and decided man," wrote Moses Beach, condescending biographical sketcher of New York's wealthiest, "always adopting a policy of his own, and carrying it out with great self-reliance. He is just, but not generous; and in mind and manners rude and unpolished."[62]

His fortune made, plain-speaking Allen soon enough took on civic challenges. His interest in changing his city's water misfortunes would not meet with success for many years, however. Then he would base the primacy of his claim as New York's water savior on his frustrated efforts as mayor.

The first move under Allen's stewardship was the formation of yet another Common Council water supply committee in January 1822, with himself as its chairman. The committee was assisted by three knowledgeable men: architect, engineer, and former city surveyor and street commissioner John McComb; Harlem dam builder Robert Macomb; and upstate civil engineer Canvass White. White was then the principal assis-

FIGURE 24. Stephen Allen, date unknown

Shown here in a portrait reproduced in the 1863 *Manual of the Common Council,* Allen ended years of frustrating involvement in the city's water searches as mayor and state legislator by leading the Water Commissioners who oversaw the planning and building of the Croton Aqueduct. (General Research Division. The New York Public Library. Astor, Lenox and Tilden Foundations.)

tant on the Erie Canal construction, during which he discovered hydraulic cement that hardened underwater and for which the state paid White $10,000 to obtain his patent rights.[63]

Their researches were focused on the Bronx. White determined that the 270-acre Rye Pond (actually a large pond and a small pond) discharged a million gallons of "very good" spring-fed water a day; Macomb provided details from his earlier investigations. The committee issued its report on April 1, often a bad day for serious announcements.

The plan was incredibly familiar. The Bronx would be diverted near Mill Brook to Morrisania Creek and thence to the Harlem at Macomb's Bridge. There a dam and pumps would raise the water across the Harlem to a reservoir on the Manhattan side and down to the city through pipes.[64]

Somewhere under the western frontier, the late Joseph Browne was rolling in his grave. But for some details, Stephen Allen's earnest committee was proposing just what Browne had twenty-four years earlier! Rejected then by the Manhattan Company, the reincarnated plan was heartily endorsed by the Common Council, which immediately appropriated $500 for a detailed survey and estimate of the project's probable cost.[65]

New York's last yellow fever epidemic delayed matters. Largely in remission for nearly two decades because the city's mosquito breeding grounds had been gradually filled in, the fever killed four hundred people by October.[66]

In the fall, Canvass White was asked to make a formal examination of the Bronx and its source ponds. "*The bringing* in of good and wholesome water," Allen wrote in his private journal, "ought never to be lost sight of *until its accomplishment was consummated.*" Alas, engineer White, who was otherwise heavily engaged on the Erie Canal, didn't get the message. His report didn't arrive for another year and a half, just after Allen was replaced as Gotham's mayor by William Paulding, brother of Washington Irving collaborator James Kirke Paulding.[67]

In the meantime, Allen was involved in another water ploy. Earlier in 1822, the promoters of a planned canal from the Housatonic River at Sharon, Connecticut, through Westchester to the Hudson thought to enhance their charter pitch to the New York legislature by offering to extend their canal south to thirsty New York City. Encouraged by state officials, the canallers won the enthusiastic backing of Mayor Allen's water committee. On Allen's recommendation, the Common Council supported the incorporation of the New York and Sharon Canal Company and requested the right to purchase company stock from the proceeds of a half-percent duty on city auction sales.[68]

If eager for any improvement in his city's water fortunes, Allen was certainly no dupe. Less than convinced of the canal company's engineering or financial viability, he wanted the city to be able to choose whether or not to invest and, more importantly, be able to spend the auction duties on any other water plan.[69]

The city's hedged bet did not play well in Albany. The legislature did incorporate the canal company later in 1823, but denied auction duties to the city. Without that substantial backing, the company had difficulty raising money. Allen, turned out as mayor in January 1824, declined a directorship in the troubled company the following month. It went further downhill from there. The company president was accused of misconduct, other directors went bankrupt, and the company went to court. No canal materialized but, once invited to the city's table, the company would refuse to excuse itself, asserting its water rights and complicating future city plans into the next decade.[70]

While all this was going on, Canvass White finally settled down to his water surveys for the city. The engineer had voluntarily left his number-two post on the grueling Erie Canal project early in 1823 to pursue more lucrative short-term consulting work, such as advising New York on its water options. He was hard at work by the fall of 1823, when at his request the city brought in to assist him his friend and former boss on the Erie Canal, Benjamin Wright, the "father of American civil engineering." White and Wright presented separate conclusions to the city's water committee in January 1824, two days after its chairman Mayor Allen left office.[71]

White thought the Bronx, if its natural flow of three million gallons a day were augmented by the damming of the two Rye Ponds, could supply New York with over six and a half million gallons, a per capita supply of over forty gallons a day, well beyond the twenty-seven daily gallons then available to every Philadelphian. If more were needed later, the adjacent Saw Mill River could be linked by an open cut to the Bronx, and the nearby Byram River by canal or tunnel to the Rye Ponds. These combined sources might serve until the city's population tripled. For good measure, White dismissed the Croton River forty miles north in rugged upper Westchester; there was no way to connect it with the Saw Mill, and an aqueduct along the Hudson River valley directly to the city would be of inconceivable time, expense, and engineering in the making. This dismissal of the Croton would influence city decision making for another decade.

Not that Bronx water would come cheap. Of four different suggested methods, White favored a plan that dammed the river at a sufficient elevation, sixty-two feet above City Hall Park, to deliver its water by gravity in either a brick conduit or open canal across the Harlem at Macomb's Dam and into a receiving reservoir on the Manhattan side, from which a line of thirty-inch cast iron pipe would send the water down to a distributing reservoir near the city. Backed by Benjamin Wright's separate report, White priced this plan at $1,949,542.65.[72]

For the cash-poor government of Gotham, this was a king's ransom. Three months passed before the full Common Council formally considered White's plan. He was thanked with a $1,100 fee and the council quietly shelved the luxurious proposals.

In the meantime, others had entered the fray. In March, a select committee of the state Assembly reported favorably on a bill to incorporate the "New York Water-Works," an association of prominent New Yorkers led by pioneering chemist, social reformer, and educator John Griscom. Though the Manhattan Company was nowhere mentioned, Griscom's effort was clearly intended as an antidote. The proposed company would be limited to the single business of procuring water in metal pipes (from unspecified sources), would (somehow) not interfere with other water company rights, and would not be granted land condemnation rights enjoyed by canal companies. Griscom marshaled support from botanist friend David Hosack and other leading physicians in the city, who issued statements that Manhattan Company water was "highly injurious" to New Yorkers' health. Still, the legislature took no action on the bill during the 1824 session. "Year after year is allowed to pass without a single step being taken to obtain the necessary supply," moaned the *Evening Post* that summer.[73]

The legislature's attention to water was refocused in January 1825 by Governor Clinton's annual message, calling for "a liberal hand" in approving "all laudable attempts," whether public or private, to water the city.[74] These were loaded words to corporate pretenders old and new.

The Sharon Canal Company petitioned the legislature to engage in banking to generate capital; a Senate vote came up three votes short of the two-thirds majority needed to amend charters. Manhattan Company president Henry Remsen, successor to Daniel Ludlow, advised ex-company man Clinton that new company wells at the city limits had recently improved Manhattan water. Remsen questioned the quality of any water brought by open canal from Connecticut and criticized ex-mayor Allen for seeking such new supplies instead of negotiating the city's purchase of the Manhattan works. The company also sharpened its opposition to the as-yet uncharted New York Water-Works, whose leaders in turn questioned the company's monopoly power.[75]

The Common Council's position in these hostilities was typically mixed. In January, the council made tentative moves to establish a public water supply; in February, it first opposed a Water-Works Company charter, then voted overwhelmingly to support one. The *Evening Post* was pleased with the prospects:

> The present filthy state of our wells ... and the impurity of the water now brought to this city ... would likely have continued so for many years to come, had not a few spirited individuals undertaken to remedy the evil; not by applying for banking privileges, but by asking for a charter which will enable them to apply their money in safety, and realize a fair and honorable compensation for its use.[76]

The paper would come to regret its enthusiasm.

Getting into the immediate spirit of things, the legislature chartered the Water-Works Company at the end of March. Capitalized at $2 million and granted no land condemnation rights, the company was to supply the city from unspecified sources through iron or other metal pipes within six years or lose its charter.[77]

The company got started with a bang. After eager subscribers signed up for $9 million in stock certificates at the Franklin Bank on April 18, the company was forced to reassign the shares within its $2 million limit. By June, the familiar pair of Canvass White and Benjamin Wright had been hired to complete surveys and manage the works. The *Evening Post* had "not the smallest doubt" that all would be well.[78]

The engineers spent a busy summer, during which Wright was elevated to president of the company. In late November, he announced that the company had "contracted for a number of valuable Water rights," and secured on favorable terms "the shores of Byram and Rye ponds with their outlets." White's nearly completed surveys suggested the city could expect six million gallons a day of "the best quality" water, obtained for less than the company's capitalization. Giving assurance that "no unforeseen or unexpected difficulty exists," Wright also mentioned in passing that the company would be applying at the next legislative session for a charter amendment to gain "powers similar to other aqueduct companies of this state."[79]

In fact, Gotham had been fooled again. In their enthusiasm for the new company, many had failed to look closely at the act of incorporation. Days after Wright's seemingly cheerful news, a series of anonymous letters in the *Evening Post* showed that the Water-Works Company had nowhere to take water from: the Manhattan Company and the Sharon Canal Company claimed exclusive rights to water sources from Manhattan to Westchester. At the same time, resentment was simmering among investors who had been denied assignment of the over-subscribed stock. Indeed, it was suggested that the whole operation was nothing more than "a bare-faced bubble," a windfall of deposits to the suspicious Franklin Bank, which soon failed from an unrelated scandal.[80]

A large group of anxious stockholders passed a resolution in mid-December to dissolve the company and distribute its funds. They appointed a committee to negotiate with the company's directors, who pleaded for a delay until White's engineering report came in. In the meantime, public charges and countercharges appeared in the press almost daily.[81]

White's early January report was not especially compelling. He proposed diverting the Bronx some thirteen miles from the Harlem, much farther north than he had considered two years earlier for the city. The water would flow in a closed canal or tunnel to the Harlem, crossing onto Manhattan in iron pipes laid on a stone bridge, and then south along the line of Third Avenue to the city. Sensitive to the company's $2 million capitalization, White conservatively estimated his works at $1.45 million, "exclusive of the sums which may be necessary for purchasing water rights on the Bronx, and to pay damages to those whose lands the tunnel shall pass thro."[82] Years earlier, the city had ignored Joseph Browne's advice to purchase cheaply those then-undeveloped lands; the Water-Works Company faced a premium to acquire them.

A week prior to White's report, the Sharon Canal promoters had published their own engineer's estimate that only $1.2 million would be needed to build their works. They also claimed to have taken legal possession of Rye Pond and the Byram and Saw Mill Rivers. The promoters renewed their case in the legislature for banking privileges.[83]

The corporate battle for Westchester's rivers and ponds was promptly joined in the press, with assertions about the poor quality and low quantity of the contested waters. At the same time, the industries of the Bronx River valley were petitioning the legislature to preserve their precious power source.[84]

Albany had its hands full of New York water troubles in the opening weeks of the 1826 legislative session. In the lower house, new assemblyman and former mayor Stephen Allen tried to sort things out to his city's perceived advantage. As chairman of a select committee, Allen backed the hometown Water-Works Company over the Connecticut canallers with whom he had declined to associate a year earlier. A proponent of a public water supply when he had been mayor, Allen now portrayed the annually elected and debt-fearing Common Council as unequal to the task; his committee recommended that the embattled Water-Works Company be granted a charter amendment that would allow it to claim water rights and land by condemnation.[85]

Alas, Allen again had backed a loser. Steering clear of this turbid bend in New York's water adventures, the legislature denied a charter amendment. Chemist Griscom, as president in Wright's absence, acceded to the stockholders' demands and cashed them out at nearly full value. The company was dissolved the following year and its incurable charter surrendered.[86]

As a consolation prize of sorts to Gotham water seekers, at its 1826 session, the legislature did incorporate yet another water company, one having no apparent conflicts with existing corporations. The New-York Harlaem Spring Water Company, organized by wealthy metals merchant

Anson G. Phelps and engineering authority James Renwick, was capitalized at only $500,000 and given only ten months to procure water for the
city from springs on upper Manhattan. After early prospecting near
Yorkville, the effort failed.[87]

At its 1827 session, the legislature empowered the New York Well
Company to dig for water on Manhattan's most northern high ground.
The company found no water but did earn a place in the city's water history: it was the last private company chartered to supply Manhattan
with water.[88]

Back in the city proper, there were more schemes. Levi Disbrow, trading on his still-promising Manhattan Company contract, began a series
of drilling operations in April 1827 intended to impress the citizens with
the benefits of artesian wells.[89] He met with little success but remained on
the New York water scene for years.

One deep well, which may have been dug by Disbrow, caused some excitement in the summer of 1827. When prosperous Jacob Lorillard and other
tanners announced that fine water might be had from beneath their estab-
lishments over the long-filled Beekman's Swamp, the ever-credulous Common Council agreed to let them bore a well. Predictably, diggers struck a
bubbly spring 128 feet down, but the water tasted terrible. Undaunted, the
tanners engaged respected chemist George Chilton, who concluded that the
water, while not useful for household purposes, had excellent medicinal properties. Lorillard's leather shop was promptly furnished "with the instruments
of a *spa*" and a corporation was organized. The curative waters of "Jacob's
Well" sold briskly at six pence a glass for some weeks, until it was suggested
that "as the locality was surrounded by tan-pits, which had retained tan-
bark, lime, and animal skins for half-a-century or more," the "sparkling" of
the waters might be significantly less than natural. By fall, business ceased;
in February, the council with rare wisdom "found it inexpedient" to purchase the operation.[90] "Jacob's Well" was the fitting end to private profiteering
in the quest for water in New York.

Dirty Water Quenches Fire

In the late 1820s, the divining rod for watering New York passed from
earnest but misguided Stephen Allen to his local political adversary

Samuel Stevens. By 1829, Stevens had served in seven of the previous four-teen annual Common Councils, none during Allen's terms as mayor. "Alderman Sam" possessed the "inborn energy and power of mind" of his "meritorious and gallant" father General Ebenezer Stevens, the late Rev-olutionary artillery officer who had toyed with bored wells for New York back in the 1790s. In December 1828, the council fire department com-mittee, chaired by Samuel Stevens, recommended that the city contract with the Manhattan Company to keep the public cisterns filled, an idea that was quickly shot down.[91] A few months later, he came up with a bet-ter idea.

Incoming mayor Walter Bowne made water a major part of his inau-gural message in January 1829. He and Peter Cooper, prominent mem-bers of the council's water committee, were soon distracted, though, and the "great object" fell to Stevens's fire committee.[92] The tall order for water would be half-filled by Stevens; for Gotham, that wasn't half bad.

Though it focused only on fire prevention, the committee's March report contained the first glimmer of a permanent solution. Stevens dismissed cisterns, the surrounding rivers, and the Manhattan Company as inade-quate or unsuited to the task. The committee suggested wells and an iron tank reservoir near 13th Street and the Bowery (then at the northern fringes of the city), a horse-driven pump to raise the water, and cast iron mains down Broadway and the Bowery to distribute the water to hydrants. The concept was both humble and keen: "laying down permanent iron pipes through the two main entrances into the City, does contemplate the time as not far distant, when the City will be ready to meet the expense of intro-ducing good and wholesome water, sufficient for all purposes into the City." The 13th Street system could become part of a grander, future solution, and no money would be lost. This was vision never before encountered in New York.

The committee put the construction cost at a mere $26,000, readily paid out of general revenue. In council debate, Stevens successfully countered questions about whether water was to be had beneath 13th Street: "Give us the tank and pipes, and we engage to fill them, if we have to carry the water in quart bottles."[93]

Under Stevens's guidance, the work proceeded with unusual speed. In April, the council approved a pipe contract with a Philadelphia manu-

FIGURE 25. *The 13th Street Reservoir, 1830s*
This contemporary engraving shows the octagonal reservoir building, the main feature of the system devised by alderman Samuel Stevens to deliver fire-fighting water
by pipe throughout the city; the pump in the foreground is a reminder of how New
Yorkers of the period still got their drinking water. (Photo by Barry Rosenthal.)

facturer. By June, $12,250 had been spent on empty 13th Street lots
between Third Avenue and the upper Bowery (now Fourth Avenue). By July,
Philadelphia's Thomas Howe had begun work on the iron tank. By
November, an excavation fifty feet deep had found water of a sufficient
quantity for fire fighting, and the council approved a wooden building
(Stevens had proposed brick) to enclose the works.[94]

At the same session, the council showed that it had not lost sight of the
broader picture. In December, the water and fire committees were coupled
in a joint mission to investigate all rivers in Westchester that might serve
the city's greater purposes. In January, Mayor Bowne's second inaugural
address stressed that even the distant Croton River in northern Westchester
should be "within our reach."[95]

Water far off won't quench fire, the saying goes, and Stevens's fire
committee remained true to its primary mission. By April 1830, a stone
tower twenty-seven feet high had been completed, onto which an octag-

onal iron tank—forty-three feet across and twenty feet high—was being raised. By the committee's calculation, the tank held just over three hundred thousand gallons of water (though basic geometry and other accounts suggest about 230,000 gallons). The well was dug to a capacity of just over a hundred thousand gallons. Running south under Broadway and the Bowery, three and a half miles of twelve-inch iron pipe was laid, equipped with thirty fire plugs and six stop cocks. The system would be capable of delivering water to a height of sixty feet above the elevation of the highest streets. Pleased with Stevens's work, the council granted his request to replace a horse-worked pump with a $5,000 steam engine capable of raising nearly half a million daily gallons.[96]

While pipe laying and well deepening continued, the works were officially opened in April 1831. Within weeks, "the most sanguine anticipations" were met. A fire in early May was put down with 13th Street water, preventing thousands of dollars in property damage and providing the "most practical evidence of the certain success of this enterprize." The council immediately appropriated another $27,000 for pipe to continue spreading south toward the city's oldest neighborhoods. That same month, under a charter revision that divided the Common Council into two houses of aldermen and assistants, Samuel Stevens was chosen by his peers as the first president of the Board of Aldermen.[97]

In June, Stevens reported that over $100,000 had been either spent on or appropriated for the works. Six miles of iron pipe had been laid, with only a single burst and no leakage, and several more miles were under way. The well was now sixteen feet across and ninety feet deep, with excavation continuing.[98]

Stevens left the Common Council in 1832, but work on his creation continued unabated. By November 1833, the city had spent $185,000 on the 13th Street system, two-thirds for pipe in six-, ten-, and twelve-inch diameters. The distribution system ran beneath Broadway, the Bowery, Pearl, William, Hudson, and a dozen other major streets, servicing over 150 street hydrants in every ward. The massive well was approaching its ultimate depth of 112 feet, much of its lower reaches blasted through solid rock; at a depth of 100 feet, two lateral chambers were cut, creating an immense quarry of over 175,000 gallons of water. The excavations had come with certain costs: $89.46 had been spent on funerals for three men killed in the well, the first lives lost in New York City's pursuit of water.[99]

Standing on high ground at the fringes of 1830s New York, the works eventually were housed in a handsome octagonal stone building and became a notable landmark. *The Family Magazine* of 1839 reprinted a scenic engraving of the "New York City Reservoir" and reported a favorable impression: "The whole building rises seventy-five feet above the ground to the top of the tank and is surmounted by a cupola, making in all one hundred feet. It forms a very picturesque object to boats passing through both the East and North Rivers."[100] It was nothing so prideful as Philadelphia's famous Fairmount, but for Gotham it was a palace of civic virtue.

Built of iron and the will of Alderman Stevens, the 13th Street system was the beginning of New York's public water supply. But the real work of providing drinkable water was still ahead. A visiting English geologist echoed the comments of Swedish botanist Peter Kalm some eighty years earlier: "The chief disadvantage of New York is the want of good water."[101]

Samuel Stevens had limited his mandate to ending destructive fires, and in this he was successful. Earlier, Stephen Allen's vision of a clean and disease-free city had extended, without result, only as far as the Bronx River, which would never do for Manhattan. It would take greater calamities and inspiration to bring abundant pure water to Gotham.

Catching the Croton Bug

The supply for the City [should] be taken from the Croton River.
—Col. De Witt Clinton, Report to
Fire and Water Committee

Despite the creation of the 13th Street Reservoir system, New York remained an ill-watered city in the 1830s. The Manhattan Company frustrated repeated efforts to bring Bronx River water to the city, until the cholera of 1832 shocked farsighted civic leaders into focusing on the distant Croton River. Yet, four years after the cholera's devastation, and nearly two years after New Yorkers voted for a public supply, not a single brick had been laid for the Croton Aqueduct.

Setting the Stage

In August 1832, the man who dubbed New York Gotham, safely removed to the spas at Saratoga Springs, wrote to a friend abiding in the beleaguered city: "As the cholera is proving so powerful an ally of the temperance society and ruining the liquor trade I wish you would endeavor to interest it in the cause of good water . . . which is nearly as important to health as the air we breathe." Chased by cholera from Europe, the celebrated Washington Irving had just returned to New York after seventeen years abroad. "It is a pity," he lamented to New York *American* editor Charles

139

King, "that so rich and luxurious a city which lavishes countless thousands upon curious wines, cannot afford itself wholesome water."[1]

Not that the city hadn't been trying. For the previous two years, alderman Samuel Stevens, creator of the 13th Street system, had repeatedly sought to break the Manhattan Company's water monopoly and obtain a proper public supply. It had proved a frustrating and misguided endeavor.

In the spring of 1830, Stevens chaired a special Common Council committee that concluded the Manhattan Company was not complying with its charter. It had never supplied "pure and wholesome" water; the citizenry relied on dangerous wells and expensive carted water; in the absence of adequate Manhattan water, hundreds of thousands of dollars had been spent on the 13th Street system, well and cistern construction and maintenance, and property losses from fire. Yet there was nothing the city could do until the company's water rights were limited. At best, Stevens advised the council to support efforts in Albany to bring the company to heel through its banking operations.[2]

An 1829 law, the Safety Fund Act, attempted to protect creditors by forcing all state chartered banks, then numbering forty, to pay into a fund to cover the debts of any that became insolvent; new or extended charters would only be granted to participating banks. After the Manhattan Company, emboldened by its unique perpetual charter, refused to participate, Attorney General Greene C. Bronson (an upstate Democrat) finally sued in October 1830 to dissolve the company's charter. Bronson argued in state supreme court that the company was fraudulently engaging in banking because its charter nowhere conferred the privilege; that "surplus capital" could not be applied to purposes other than water because the company had not yet supplied sufficient water; and that in failing to supply water to all who wanted it, the company had failed to meet its primary charter obligation. Company lawyers attacked all of the state's arguments, noting particularly that the state had failed to name one person who had requested water and been dissatisfied with the service.[3]

While the case slowly moved toward a verdict that would not come for two years, Alderman Stevens tried a new approach in the Common Council. In February 1831, he opened what seemed a historic council debate. At issue was whether to ask the legislature to transfer the Manhattan Company's water powers to the city, allow the company to retain its banking rights, and authorize the city to raise $2 million in loans to build a public water supply from the Bronx.

The debate in regular and special sessions over the next several weeks was intense, much of it reported in unprecedented detail by the *Evening Post*.[4] In a broad attack on the Manhattan Company, Stevens included a calculated appeal to the budding teetotaler movement, tagging Manhattan water as the chief cause of intemperance.[5] Stevens's mostly Democratic opposition, led by Fyler Dibblee, George Strong, and recorder Richard Riker, defended the company and its legal rights, derided the Bronx, and questioned the city's ability to plan, fund, and administer a public supply, as well as its right to leave a large debt to future generations. Riker added his soon-lampooned claim of fine health derived from morning pints of Manhattan water. Stevens's support was led by fellow Whig Peter S. Townsend, a world-traveled physician and health expert. On the final day of debate, he presented a report on New York's water by the fiercely apolitical Lyceum of Natural History, the city's leading scientific institution (flourishing today as the New York Academy of Sciences).[6]

The Lyceum scientists described Manhattan's gneiss and sand geology as a poor host for bored or dug wells, and the city's human and animal occupants as the source of an "almost incredible" hundred tons of excrement a day. Chemical analysis on gallon samples of well water yielded 126 grains of organic and inorganic waste; Bronx River samples yielded just two grains. Wells in the vicinity of graveyards offered "very offensive" water with "a ropy appearance." Untold gallons of urine helped soften the otherwise hard wells, though the Lyceum recognized that "the fastidious may revolt from the use of water thus sweetened to our palate." Dyspepsia and the often fatal bowel ailments of children were among the obvious health effects of drinking from city wells. The Lyceum concluded that "no adequate supply of good or wholesome water can be obtained on this island for the wants of a large and rapidly increasing city like New York."[7]

Among other materials pondered by the council was a petition from several of the city's brewers, complaining that the poor quality of New York water was rapidly causing a market preference for Philadelphia beers. This was no idle concern in a city whose brewers had been rich and leading citizens for two hundred years; indeed, annual city beer sales of $460,000 were

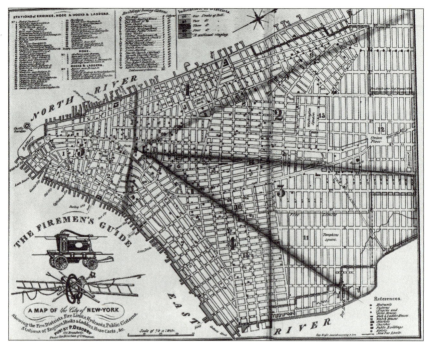

FIGURE 26. The Firemen's Guide, 1834
This lithograph, conceived by famed fire engineer Uzziah Wenman, shows the location of 13th Street system hydrants, public cisterns, and fire stations, where reproductions of the guide were posted. (© Collection of The New-York Historical Society.)

nearly double what New Yorkers were then paying for carted spring water.[8]

After much discussion, the council finally took votes on three resolutions. The first, for a general memorial to the legislature outlining the city's water needs, passed twenty to four, with Dibblee, Strong, and Riker leading the nays. The second, stating that the Manhattan Company had failed to comply with its charter obligations and asking the legislature to transfer to the city the company's exclusive but unused rights to natural water courses, passed seventeen to five.

The third and briefest resolution was the linchpin. Though Stevens originally had argued for a $2 million fund for a public water supply, the resolution on the table asked only for $1 million. Even so, the matter lost. Stevens gathered only seven other votes (including Townsend, fire and water committee co-chairman James Palmer, and civic improver Peter Cooper); the Dibblee-Strong bloc garnered fifteen. When the resulting city petition for water-seeking authority was sent to Albany without a funding mechanism, the toothless measure died in the Assembly.[9] The council had tested the waters of a public supply but failed once again to take the plunge. Though much of Mayor Bowne's annual address in May to the new bicameral council urged a renewed effort on water, the council paused for the rest of 1831 and Stevens returned his attentions to completing the 13th Street system.[10]

The limited utility of that system was demonstrated by a fire on the Fourth of July, an inauspicious Independence Day. In the afternoon, at his son-in-law's home on Prince Street near Broadway, James Madison became the young nation's third ex-president to die on a Fourth. That same evening, on Charlton Street (the western extension of Prince), firecrackers touched off shavings in a carpenter's shop. In a short time, nearly forty buildings were destroyed in a block square area, burning out nearly one hundred families.[11]

Stevens made his final assault on the citadel of bad water at the last council session of 1831, presenting with co-chairman James Palmer a new fire and water committee report. It was time, they implored, for the "municipal authorities no longer to satisfy themselves with speeches, reports and surveys, but actually to raise the *means* and strike the spade into the ground."[12] It would prove to be Stevens's greatest failure, though it raised the image of a future solution.

After tracing New York's lamentable water history, disparaging the Manhattan Company, and praising the works of Philadelphia and several European cities, Stevens's report toyed with the notion of the Croton River, Westchester's largest and northernmost river, rising in the highlands of neighboring Putnam County and emptying into the Hudson forty miles north of the city. The report presented two documents, not publicly discussed since received by the Common Council the previous year: a letter from Sharon Canal Company president Cyrus Swan suggesting that only the Croton could satisfy the city's future water needs, and a thinly detailed plan by metallurgist Francis B. Phelps for bringing the Croton in a twenty-inch-diameter cast iron pipe. Though impressed with the Croton's potential, Stevens considered the cost prohibitive and the abundant water "not for centuries, if ever" required.

Instead, Stevens returned to his old standby, the Bronx. Synthesizing three decades of Bronx plans, he suggested a tunnel or pipe from the Bronx to the Harlem, Harlem-powered waterwheels, a new bridge over the river, two upper Manhattan reservoirs, and iron mains leading to the 13th Street pipes and two new distribution networks. With the supporting opinions of the new street commissioner and his assistant, familiar Bronxites Benjamin Wright and Canvass White, the report estimated that four million daily gallons could be had for $2 million in loans. A council-appointed board of commissioners would administer the project.

With reports of cholera in Europe already reaching New York, the council supported Stevens's designs this time. In January, both boards approved a draft law by large majorities, which was sent to Albany in February. There, the trouble began. As the legislative session dwindled down by mid-March, the city's Senate and Assembly delegation, as always sitting in committee on city issues, had done nothing with the bill. Alarmed at the prospect of yet another wasted effort, the council dispatched water committee co-chairman James Palmer and Board of Assistants president James Murray to lobby the hesitant delegation, whose chairman was former mayor and assemblyman and new senator Stephen Allen.[13]

Murray later alleged that Allen's "decided hostility" killed the bill, which eventually was reported by a select committee but never came to a full Assembly vote. Allen, when forced to explain his role, contended that he merely was among a group of legislators who questioned the ability of the annually elected, politically divided Common Council to appoint independent commissioners and oversee the project.[14]

Allen later won backhanded credit for rejecting the bill. His wise hesitation on the Common Council's role incidentally prevented the city from wasting $2 million on the Bronx, which "would in all probability, at no distant period, have failed to answer the large calculations of the engineers . . . and the increasing demands of the city." This was the opinion of Myndert Van Schaick, the man who would make the Croton a reality.[15]

1832: Myndert Makes the Rules, De Witt Shows the Way

Myndert Van Schaick is not a household name but he, first as alderman and then as state senator, more than any other New Yorker was responsible for changing household life in the city. The Van Schaick line in America stretches back to a 1652 Dutch land grant at Beverwyck (now Albany), where the family flourished through the generations. Myndert's father was a patriot hero in the Revolution; his mother was from an equally distinguished Dutch family in New York City, where Myndert was born in 1782. In 1815, he married Elizabeth Hone, wealthy niece of Philip Hone. The couple lived in the city's finest residences, collected art, and were noted philanthropists. A committed Democrat, in 1830, Van Schaick was a founder of the University of the City of New York (now New York University), organized as a liberal antidote to aristocratic Columbia College. After what proved a ten-year labor to water New York with the Croton River, Van Schaick asserted "there was no person but myself who was familiar with all the springs and movements from first to last." Provoked by the publication of rival claims, it was an unusual public boast from a discreet man, but it was true.[16]

The year that began with the latest disappointment over the Bronx ended with greater hopes for the Croton. The April 1832 elections started things rolling. The turnover was typically substantial, with twenty of the thirty council seats newly filled, but good for water. Van Schaick was elected alderman of the 5th Ward. "Alderman Sam" Stevens departed the council he had first served in 1817; he was replaced by Democrat Henry Meigs as board president. Assistant James Murray moved up to alderman of the new 15th Ward. Anti-water Democrats Dibblee and Strong were voted out. Council water policy fell to a new but pliant committee: chairman James Palmer and five new members, including alderman Charles Henry Hall and assistant Peter Titus. Around these players, Van Schaick wrote a winning script: "The favor of heaven conferred on Palmer, Hall, Meigs, Murray and Titus, a most conspicuous part in the opening scenes of the Croton theatre."[17]

Van Schaick's power play was prefaced by tragedy. Within weeks of the seating of the new council, cholera paralyzed New York. Over one hundred thousand people fled and thirty-five hundred died, leaving only the destitute, the disbelieving, and the duty-bound like Van Schaick. As the

FIGURE 27. Myndert Van Schaick, date unknown

As a forward-thinking alderman and state senator, Van Schaick prepared and secured passage of the laws that led to the Croton Aqueduct; after its completion, he served for many years on the Croton Aqueduct Board. (New York University Archives.)

council-appointed treasurer of the Board of Health that summer, he observed at close hand the strange disease that left its dehydrated victims pleading for scarce clean water. As early as August, he began informal investigations into solving the city's perpetual shortage. He had already been impressed, he later claimed, by Cyrus Swan's opinions on the Croton, which "established a strong bias" in Van Schaick's mind against the Bronx.[18]

In order to work his will once the cholera had passed, the alderman had some lobbying to do. He was chairman of the finance committee and a member of the street committee, but not a member of James Palmer's fire and water committee, which on October 1 was ordered to investigate a proper water supply for New York "with the least possible delay."[19]

Invited by his friend Palmer to attend some of the committee's deliberations, Van Schaick was pleased when the committee recommended in mid-October that rather than risk another application to the legislature, the council ought merely to hire engineers to examine all possible sources of water. Van Schaick could not have been pleased, though, when street commissioner and Bronxite Benjamin Wright was put in charge of the inquiry. At the end of October, Wright sent a surveying team led by Timothy Dewey and William Serrell into the field, with primary instructions to take levels of the country from the Harlem River north to the Bronx River and its source, the Rye Ponds, and the Byram River and its Wampus and Byram Pond sources. The surveyors' instructions on to the Croton were only to examine whether one of its eastern tributaries could be led by a tunnel into the Bronx River.[20]

Van Schaick knew that in the 1820s Canvass White had concluded that the Croton could not be connected to the Bronx because the intervening ground was too high and rocky. Van Schaick thought Wright "a very able and experienced engineer," and surveyor Dewey "a gentleman of some practical ability," but clearly the Croton was not on their agenda.[21]

The need for new thinking was bolstered that month by a broad win for the Manhattan Company's banking rights in the case brought by the attorney general two years earlier. The question of whether the company was providing "a plentiful supply of pure and wholesome water" did not even reach consideration on its merits. As the company lawyers had argued, the court ruled that the state had failed to provide the names of anyone who had been denied water: "How could the defendants supply water to those of whose wish to take it they were ignorant." The court read the famous "surplus capital" clause as authorizing the use of any "unemployed" funds before the "complete fulfillment" of any duty to supply water. As to the company's corporate status, the court ruled that the company's 1808 charter extension, an 1804 exemption from a law restraining future "manhattan companies," and decades of government banking with the company all demonstrated the state's implied approval of the company's existence.

The court decision was silent on the company's presumed exclusive water privileges. Later this would come to be interpreted as rejecting them. As the focus began to shift from the Bronx, the original supposed source for the Manhattan Company, to the Croton, which the company had never contemplated, a way was opened for the city to skirt the company's claimed water monopoly. In any case, the thriving bank was increasingly less insistent about its water rights.[22]

The company had the late De Witt Clinton to thank for crafting its strong corporate status. His work in the first decade of the 1800s had fortified the company's legal and business standing, to the detriment of the city's water interests. Within weeks of the 1832 court ruling, Clinton's heir made amends. While Wright waited for his surveyors to report on the Bronx, Colonel De Witt Clinton, the late governor's son, was hired to show the way to the Croton.

De Witt Clinton, Jr., was an up and coming civil engineer. Born in 1805, by his mid-twenties he was "a Gentleman hugely respected . . . both for his promising talents & his amiable private character," in the opinion of President Andrew Jackson.[23] He had begun professional life in New York City in 1829, doing surveys for prospective railroads. In 1831, Clinton won a spot with the War Department's newly established Topographical Bureau; early that year, as a member of the budding Army Corps of Topographical Engineers, he ran a survey of the Connecticut River. Early in 1832, Clinton began government surveys for a railroad from the portage summit of the Ohio Canal to the Hudson; that work brought him back to cholera-plagued New York, from which he promptly fled.[24]

When Clinton returned to the city in the fall to continue his government work, he was first enlisted to investigate the Croton by Van Schaick, to whom Clinton owed a favor: at the request of a mutual friend, Van

Schaick had used his influence to secure Clinton's government post. A fellow descendant of "the old revolutionary stock," the young man had impressed Van Schaick with his professional enthusiasm and creative suggestions for difficult railroad projects. Clearly, Clinton was the man to support his patron's designs on the remote Croton.[25]

Confronted in postcholera New York with a water committee and engineers still tilting at the Bronx, Van Schaick recommended to the committee that Clinton be appointed to make his own examinations, "particularly in reference to the Croton." Chairman Palmer complied.[26]

The appointment of Clinton *fils* was not the first orchestrated event of early November. While he was lobbying Palmer's committee, alderman Van Schaick also got himself elected to the state senate, quite intentionally replacing Stephen Allen. As James Murray recalled, "the friends of the Croton project" united behind Van Schaick, while the gruff Allen, according to Van Schaick, "had rendered himself the most unpopular man in the democratic party," largely because of his hesitations on water.[27]

While Van Schaick awaited the January opening of the Albany legislative session, official support gathered for the Bronx. In late November, Palmer's committee received favorable reports on Bronx water samples from several prominent chemists, including John Griscom of New York Water-Works Company infamy. At the same time, Dewey and Serrell gauged the total output of the Bronx and Byram Rivers and their source ponds at an ample nineteen million daily gallons; Dewey alone pressed north to the Croton Valley, where he determined that only with great difficulty could a single southeastern tributary of the Croton, the Cisco (or Kisco) River, be connected to the Bronx, via canals to and from the intervening Saw Mill River.[28]

Van Schaick countered with a Bronx tour of his own. He led Clinton, Palmer, and Murray to the shores of the main Rye Pond, where the party beheld "a very small body of water to be relied on as a main resource." Tales told during a stormy evening reinforced the impression. The party was obliged to put up at the farmhouse of a Van Schaick business acquaintance who had retired to his ancestral home near the pond; Oliver Matthews assured his storm-bound guests that "no dependence could be placed" on the declining pond, whose outlet had been progressively widened to service a growing number of mills downstream. For Van Schaick's party, this information was "much more striking and indelible than any of the acts or opinions of a report." When the new day dawned bright, the party headed back to New York: "A cloud was removed from our sight. The question was settled against the pond."[29]

At the end of November, Dewey and Serrell turned in a relatively brief report to Benjamin Wright, who passed it on to Palmer's committee. The surveyors reported that the waters of the Bronx, augmented by the Byram, would be sufficient and obtainable at modest cost; the Croton itself was untappable but "cannot ever be needed." Nevertheless, citing Philadelphia's several "hasty conclusions" on water, the surveyors advised extensive investigations before any final decision.[30]

Clinton's Croton Plan

Colonel Clinton's report, with one hundred fifty-six lengthy paragraphs, numbered and indexed, was a much different document from Dewey and Serrell's. He presented it to Palmer's committee three days before Christmas.[31]

Predicting that New York would be inhabited by a million people within sixty years (it would take only forty), Clinton expressed surprise at the city's profound lack of good water and at hesitations to grant the power to obtain it. The engineer quickly dismissed all sources of water on Manhattan. The 1831 Lyceum study and his own investigations proved pump water dangerous and getting worse. Even costly spring waters, some 37,500 daily gallons purchased at two cents a gallon, were "losing their goodness" and would inevitably fail as dense habitation overwhelmed nature. The wells Disbrow bored promised expensive disappointment; the Manhattan Company system was too meager to dwell on.

In Westchester, neither the Byram River source ponds nor the Saw Mill River would do: tapping the ponds would require the unlikely sanction of Connecticut, through which the lower Byram flowed; the slender Saw Mill, running from the county's central highlands to the Hudson at Yonkers, had been diminished and heavily encumbered by mills that had barely enough water themselves.

In order to squash the latest hopes pinned on the Bronx, Clinton produced a swirl of conflicting numbers from the plans of Browne, Weston,

Macomb, White, Wright, and Dewey and Serrell. Clinton was careful to use information where it suited him. He trumpeted the judgments of White and Dewey that the Croton could not be led into the Bronx, making much of White's conclusion that the Croton itself could be diverted at a suitable elevation and conducted along the banks of the Hudson to the city. White had recognized the river's potential but considered it unneeded; Clinton concluded that the time had come for "the supply for the City [to] be taken from the Croton River."

Unlike the low-lying, oft-examined Bronx, the Croton ran through a "primitive landscape" with elevated banks forbidding to future dense settlement. Conveniently for Clinton, who conducted no surveys, the river had been already gauged: Westchester surveyor George W. Cartwright had measured several branches of the river, apparently for White's 1820s surveys. Not publicly reported before, Cartwright's data were supplied to Clinton and prominently displayed in his report. At Pines Bridge, three miles below the confluence of the river's east and west branches and nine miles above the river's mouth at old Van Cortlandt family land near Sing Sing, Cartwright had gauged some twenty million gallons a day. Observing the many ponds feeding northerly branches of the river (and sagely anticipating today's twelve-reservoir Croton system), Clinton believed the Croton watershed promised an inexhaustible supply.

His plan for harnessing the river was naive, though its simplicity was compelling. Using Cartwright's determination that the riverbed at Pines Bridge was elevated 183 feet above tide, Clinton proposed diverting the entire river into an open channel for a forty-mile run by gravity to the city. There would be no risky dam or expensive tunnel or pipeline. At a descent of eighteen inches per mile, the current would be rapid enough to prevent winter freezing. As to the purity of an open supply, Clinton noted that London's New River, a winding, timbered canal thirty-nine miles long, and Philadelphia's Schuylkill, with mines, factories, and cultivated lands upstream of Fairmount, both delivered good water.

Clinton laid out a general route south through Westchester with few engineering details. From Pines Bridge, the canal would follow the high, broken banks of the Croton down to the Hudson shore, where it would curve south along the rugged slope of the Hudson valley. In order to negotiate a deep kill at Sing Sing, the Mill River at Sleepy Hollow (made legendary in 1820 by Washington Irving), and numerous other watercourses and hills, the canal would require unspecified embankments, pipes, and elevated sections. At some point, the Saw Mill River had to be crossed but Clinton offered no certain plan. The canal might cross the Saw Mill somewhere near its mouth and continue on to the Harlem at Manhattan's northern tip (Clinton's preference), or cross the Saw Mill farther inland and meet the Harlem at Macomb's Dam. By either route, the Harlem would be crossed by a new, high bridge, specified only by length (a thousand feet) and elevation (138 feet).

Having gained Manhattan by gravity alone, the water would continue by canal south to a reservoir "near Madam Jumel's," a notorious landmark of northern Manhattan and a fitting place for the water's pause. Elizabeth Jumel was a madam in more ways than one. Prior to maneuvering wealthy French-born wine merchant Stephen Jumel to the altar with a deathbed feint in 1804, Eliza Bowen had been the leading courtesan in post-Revolutionary America. Born to a Providence prostitute in 1775, Eliza had brought her trade to New York, where she flourished famously. Made an "honest" woman by marriage but not immediately by society, Madam Jumel was soon installed by her adoring husband in the elegant Roger Morris estate overlooking the Harlem River (today's Morris-Jumel Mansion at 160th Street). From her aerie, Madam Jumel descended into society as the richest woman in America after 1826, when she returned from the couple's long sojourn in France ahead of her husband but with his lucrative power of attorney. After Stephen Jumel bled to death in the attic of the mansion (not accidentally said some), in May 1832, the industrious widow took possession of whatever else of his fortune she had not already made her own. In a year's time she would take a new husband of repute equal to her own, a man who had started in the water business thirty years earlier.[32]

Clinton provided no details for the Jumel reservoir or others at unspecified Manhattan locations, or for distributing the water in the city. After consulting with legendary fire engineer and 13th Street system superintendent Uzziah Wenman, Clinton did suggest that the 13th Street pipes, but not the well, pumps, or tank, could become a small part of a Croton distribution system.[33]

Clinton priced the whole works at $2.5 million, a higher cost than ever officially suggested for supplying New York with water and at the same time a deliriously low number. He provided no indication of how he arrived at this sum, other than that the canal, supporting structures, and land purchases would cost $850,000, and the reservoirs and distribution system the rest.

Instead, Clinton offered a unique analysis of annual economic benefits. Croton water would eliminate some or all of the public and private costs of maintaining the fire department, property losses from fire, fire insurance premiums, street cleaning, public pump maintenance, carted spring water, and Manhattan Company water fees. All told, $576,634 would be conserved annually after the introduction of Croton water. Thus, Clinton reasoned, the Croton project could cost as much as $11.5 million and the city would pay no more in annual 5 percent interest than what was already being paid for not having Croton water. Looked at another way, the $2.5 million project was "capable of paying twenty-three per cent. interest on the cost" of not having Croton water. "This must therefore completely settle the question of the productiveness of the undertaking," Clinton artfully deduced.[34]

Concluding his report, Clinton recommended detailed surveys before a Croton route was determined. Once done, he believed the work would take no longer than three years to complete. In fact, it would take ten years and even more than Clinton's own $11.5 million exaggeration before New Yorkers drank from the Croton.

Despite its glaring inadequacies, Clinton's report won high marks. For water committee chairman Palmer, it "decided the question in favor of the Croton." As Myndert Van Schaick put it, "The Bronx, the pond, and the unreliable tributaries, were soon forgotten."[35]

For his part, young Clinton had not so much planned a Croton Aqueduct as legitimized the idea of building one, lending his famous name for the purpose. His role in New York's water story proved brief. Clinton returned to his government work; less than a year later, after seeking out the milder climate of Cuba to cure a mysterious illness, the promising young engineer died.[36]

His report on the Croton reached the Common Council just in time. Days before, the Dewey and Serrell report had met a favorable reception in the Board of Assistants, which passed a resolution to seek anew the legislature's approval for a $2 million loan for a Bronx supply. The resolution had been referred to Palmer's committee, which in turn reported it, the Dewey and Serrell report, and the just-received Clinton report to the Board of Aldermen for debate on the evening of December 22, a Saturday.[37]

Palmer's committee took no position on the competing reports but urged prompt approval of any one, ensuring a typically divisive debate. Advocates of the Bronx and Croton argued late into the night, until board president Meigs delivered a long speech favoring the Croton. When a Bronxite questioned a Harlem crossing by gravity alone, a highly animated Meigs countered, *"Why, sir, we'll build a bridge of gold to let the silver stream pass over."*[38]

Alderman and incoming senator Van Schaick was too wise to wade into the ballyhoo. With valid fears of the council's unsuitability to the task ahead, he and others espoused a slower approach. The aldermen's raucous session, gilded with images of silver and gold, ended with an order for further consideration by Palmer's committee.[39] Van Schaick would use the next forty-eight hours to divert the city's water fortunes from anguish to expectation.

Paving the Legal Road to the Croton

Employing a risky gambit, Van Schaick invited the water committee to his house on Sunday evening, December 23, for discussions. For reasons unknown, only Peter Titus showed up, joined by council attorney Robert Emmet, whom Van Schaick had also invited. "If I had questioned my position at that moment, I should have dissolved the meeting without action," Van Schaick later wrote, but, shedding his alderman's hat for senatorial mantle, he pressed on, presenting a draft law of his own that merely called for surveys, water quality analysis, and cost estimates. Nowhere was the Croton, the Bronx, or any particular source named, nor was any loan or cost amount mentioned. The draft law called only for a report to be made in a year's time.

The provision potentially most controversial was who would be in charge. Van Schaick's draft law proposed that five commissioners serve not at the pleasure of the Common Council but be appointed in Albany by the governor, with the senate's concurrence. Reasoning that a legislative body like the council "was not to be intrusted with executive business" such as public works, Van Schaick implied that his city government not only *could* not handle great projects but *ought* not. Fortunately, Titus agreed, and Emmet departed with the draft to work it into a report for Palmer's committee to present to the aldermen's session the next evening.[40]

When Stephen Allen read Van Schaick's public account of the episode years later, he was incredulous at Van Schaick's enterprise of questionable legality, but the full committee and board proved to have no argument with what he had done. Indeed, Van Schaick claimed, the bill was written as generally as possible to avoid the opposition of certain aldermen and such "citizens out of doors" as Allen.[41] Still, Van Schaick had plans for the man he was replacing in the Senate.

The draft law unanimously passed the Board of Aldermen on January 7, 1833; taking no chances, newly seated Senator Van Schaick traveled from Albany to cast his alderman's vote. The Assistants gave their unanimous approval a week later, and Mayor Bowne signed on three days after that.[42]

Van Schaick immediately convened a special meeting of the city's Albany delegation, which promptly gave its necessary approval. The full Senate and Assembly in turn gave affirmative votes, and on February 26, 1833, the bill became law, under the innocuous title "An Act for the Appointment of Commissioners in Relation to Supplying the City of New York with Pure and Wholesome Water." It was, in Van Schaick's words, "the pioneer law to the Croton."[43]

Newly elected Governor William Marcy, a Democrat, did not have to think hard about whom to appoint as water commissioners: Van Schaick supplied the names. Resisting a temptation to reward supportive Common Council members, Van Schaick made a list of men who had not been involved in promoting the Croton. All were good Democrats, four with no direct prior involvement in water affairs: grocer Charles Dusenberry; hardware merchant Benjamin M. Brown, Mayor Bowne (who declined and was replaced by Whig William W. Fox, a Quaker of impeccable business reputation), and retired merchant Saul Alley, who despite lowly birth was regarded by society as "an agreeable man."[44]

"Agreeable" was not a word often ascribed to Alley's close friend, a similar rags-to-riches success who topped Van Schaick's list. The last person one might have expected him to tap for water commissioner was ousted senator, ex-assemblyman, ex-mayor, and old Bronxite Stephen Allen.

Van Schaick never explained his choice, alleging years later that he was privately blamed for the "unpopular appointment." Allen, who later claimed he'd been a Crotonite all along, believed his long and earnest involvement in the city's water searches had inspired his selection.[45] In any case, it proved a wise choice.

Despite his political unpopularity and unrefined manner, Allen's reputation for honesty and integrity induced his fellow commissioners to name him their chairman, a role he pursued with vigor. Given the long history of civic frustration over water, Allen noted that all of the commissioners accepted their unsought positions with some reluctance: though all were wealthy, they initially were not paid for the increasingly time consuming work.[46]

Getting Down to Business

As if to demonstrate to the commissioners how challenging their job would be, they were no sooner settled in their offices than artesian well zealot Levi Disbrow came calling, disparaging the "far-fetched, and dear bought water of the Croton." Backed by Harvard-educated former canal engineer John Langdon Sullivan, Disbrow sought the commissioners' support for a $2 million company to supply the city from deep wells. Public support for Disbrow's plan waxed with fear of another cholera summer but waned as the disease failed to reappear.[47]

Keeping Disbrow at bay, the commissioners got down to serious business, engaging two prominent engineers to conduct separate examinations of the Croton, Saw Mill, and Bronx Rivers. The employment of familiar Canvass White was brief. After two visits to the Croton Valley, White returned to ongoing canal work in New Jersey; he took ill that fall and died a year later in Florida.[48] For better or worse, the commissioners were left with Major David Bates Douglass.

Douglass (1790–1849) was a rigid man.[49] Born and privately tutored in New Jersey, he graduated from Yale College in 1813 with high honors in civil engineering, and took a commission as second lieutenant in the Army's Corps of Engineers. After training at West Point, he distinguished himself under fire during the British siege of Fort Erie in 1814. Promoted to captain and remaining with the army after the war, in 1815,

FIGURE 28. *David Bates Douglass, date unknown*

From 1833 to 1836, Douglass conducted surveys and determined the course and basic shape for the Croton Aqueduct. He also planned many of its prominent structures, before disputes with Water Commission chairman Stephen Allen led to his firing as chief engineer. (Archives, Warren Hunting Smith Library, Hobart and William Smith Colleges.)

Douglass became assistant professor of natural and experimental philosophy at West Point, the only American college then offering formal engineering education. In that first of many years at West Point, Douglass married the daughter of longtime mathematics professor and surveyor Andrew Ellicott. When Ellicott died in 1820, Douglass was named to his chair in mathematics; three years later, he was promoted to major and made professor of civil engineering.

During his West Point years, Douglass participated in numerous government surveying projects; an 1825 appointment to supervise final construction of an Erie Canal section led to lucrative positions on numerous private canals. He finally resigned from the War Department in 1831 to become chief engineer of the nearly completed Morris & Essex Canal across New Jersey to New York Harbor.

Setting up house in Brooklyn, Douglass became a civilian for the first time in his adult life, but he did not surrender the ivory tower. In 1832, he took the first of several professorships at the newly formed University of the City of New York; by agreement, he was allowed to take outside engineering jobs, such as surveys for what is now the Long Island Rail Road. Douglass remained closely attached to the university, designing its great marble and brick building on Washington Square, for which the cornerstone was laid in July 1833; when completed three years later, the massive Gothic structure was hailed as New York's finest public building, and its spire was the highest point in the city.[50]

One assumes that during his university days Douglass made the frequent acquaintance of founder Myndert Van Schaick. If Van Schaick had something to do with Douglass's hiring by the water commissioners, he never took credit for it, perhaps because Douglass's water work would end badly.

Later a cemetery designer (notably Brooklyn's influential Green-Wood Cemetery) and Kenyon College president, Douglass proved to be a civil engineer more attuned to theory than practice. His three years in the service of the water commissioners ended with no construction begun, and his termination was followed by years of recriminations.

There was no suggestion of trouble at the outset. In the first week of June, the Common Council appropriated an initial $5,000 for the survey work, and Douglass went into the field with an eleven-man team. Leading an instrumental survey from the mouth of the Croton was top sub-ordinate George Cartwright, the Westchester engineer whose 1820s Croton information had helped Col. Clinton recommend the Croton River.[51]

Under Douglass in the summer of 1833, Cartwright was the traverser who took the actual survey measurements; among Douglass's assistants was Henry T. Anthony, destined for long engineering service to the city. By the end of August, the party had leveled two hundred miles and traversed thousands of courses in Westchester, Putnam, and upper Manhattan, much "in woods or upon ground otherwise difficult and rough."[52]

Douglass handed in his report to the water commissioners on November 1 as required, with findings quite satisfactory to the Croton crowd.[53] The questions of linking the Croton to either the Bronx or Byram Rivers was quickly settled in the field; the Bronx and Byram themselves were inadequate, offering less than six million daily gallons. Douglass made no effort to defend this number against Dewey and Serrell's thrice-higher estimate; the Major's mission was not to debate the Bronx but make the case for the Croton.

Douglass recommended only the Croton for New York, delivered by gravity in a closed masonry aqueduct along one of two routes: a "river route" along the Hudson River Valley or an "inland route" via the upper Saw Mill River Valley. Although the river route largely followed the course suggested the previous year by Colonel Clinton, all of Major Douglass's plans were significantly more detailed, practical, and expensive.

The inland route began with a "confluent reservoir" in a natural rock basin nearly twelve miles from the mouth of the river and 268 feet above tide level; iron pipe would feed seven Croton tributaries into the reservoir. Douglass estimated the inland route supply (including the Cisco River entering the system farther south) at a minimum of twenty-six million daily gallons, after deducting 20 percent from his gauges for the worst possible drought. The water's journey to New York would begin with a three-mile excavation through the massive ridge into the upper Saw Mill River Valley, and then continue twenty-four miles south to a deep cut or tunnel through a rocky ridge into the valley of Tibbet's Brook at Yonkers; two storage reservoirs were possible along the way. Another eight miles of aqueduct, featuring deep cuttings and embankments, would bring the line to the Harlem opposite the upper Manhattan highlands, at today's East

174th Street. Arriving at the Harlem at an elevation of 126 feet, the water would have rushed thirty-five miles at the hydraulically steep descent of four feet per mile.

The river route arrived at the same place more gently and with more water. A thirteen-foot high dam across the Croton at Muscoot Hill, a mile or so downriver of the inland route's confluent reservoir and three miles above Pines Bridge, would create an eighty-acre reservoir fed naturally by all the Croton tributaries. The river's worst-drought supply at Muscoot would be forty-four million gallons; this gauging, which proved quite accurate, was nearly triple the flow gauged by George Cartwright in the 1820s.

The surface of the Muscoot reservoir would be 175 feet above tide, nearly a hundred feet lower than the confluent reservoir. Instead of immediately cutting south into the Saw Mill River valley, the top of the river route approximated Clinton's route, arcing southwest along rugged Croton hillsides until reaching the Hudson and then turning south to the village of Hastings, twenty-seven miles from the dam. Whereas Clinton had noted only generally what was needed, Douglass specified many excavations, embankments, culverts, deep cuts, tunnels, and arches to negotiate Sing Sing kill, Mill River, a large ridge at Tarrytown, and numerous hills and streams. Clinton's route continued south to an unspecified crossing near the mouth of the Saw Mill River, but Douglass's river route turned east at Hastings, cutting through a rock ridge into the lower Saw Mill River valley, crossing the river on a triple-arched bridge, and finally meeting his inland route that had entered the valley many miles north. As it continued on to the Harlem, the river route's descent averaged out to a gentle fifteen inches a mile over the thirty-nine-mile course.

By either route to the Harlem, Douglass imagined Croton water entering Manhattan in dramatic fashion. Many years after his departure from the project, the crossing took shape much as he envisioned: a towering bridge spanning the Harlem between natural rock abutments, supported in the Roman style by a series of semicircular arches on piers sunk deep into the river bed and the rising plain on the Westchester shore. The grade-level bridge would be "a work of considerable labour and expense, but by no means of paramount difficulty," Douglass avowed, citing a half-dozen larger modern arched bridges in Europe. "With such examples of enterprise and skill before us, many of them undertaken for objects far less important than that of supplying the city of New-York with water, we may certainly look upon the design of the Harlem aqueduct without fear." Still, although he specified the works needed, Douglass provided few engineering details.

Boldly gaining Manhattan, the aqueduct would angle southwest toward the village of Manhattanville, on a Hudson cove at today's West 130th Street. As with Clinton's plan, this would take the line past the Jumel place, which had opened its doors in the summer of Douglass's surveys to a prominent if temporary habitant.

Readily dropping her mourning clothes in the season's heat, fiftysomething Madam Jumel took a second husband on the first of July, the everamorous septuagenarian Aaron Burr. "It is benevolent in her to keep the old man in his latter days," noted diarist Philip Hone; "One good turn deserves another." It was rumored that bride and groom had been familiar for decades before their legal bonding. Within months, however, the wise old wife tired of her new husband's offenses, including his speculations on her hard-earned assets. Separated by fall on friendly terms, Madam Jumel (as she never ceased to be known) sued Burr for divorce the following year, citing his adulteries with a twenty-one-year-old and "divers other females."[54]

At the deep valley of Manhattanville, Douglass planned either a sixteen-acre receiving reservoir between two rock ledges or a crossing by bridge or inverted siphon to a receiving reservoir farther south. Wherever the receiving reservoir was placed, the masonry aqueduct would end, and iron mains would lead downisland to one or two "equalizing reservoirs" and farther south to an eight-acre distributing reservoir on Murray's (or Murray) Hill, a wooded high ground surrounded by old farms and homesteads some seven miles south of the Harlem crossing and a mile north of the city limits, at today's Fifth Avenue and 38th Street. Holding fifty-two million gallons inside twenty-foot walls, the reservoir's surface would be at an elevation of 117 feet, nine feet above the highest point in the city, the spire of Douglass's university building at Washington Square.

Douglass priced the inland route at $5.8 million, the river route at $4.7 million; either way, this was uncharted financial territory. Confident that the Croton could be delivered "without any insuperable difficulty" by either route, Douglass suggested that future examinations determine the better one. Thus, even in the mind of its author, the Douglass report of 1833 was a step toward the Croton but not the final word.

Eleven days after Douglass handed in his report to the water commissioners, they presented it along with their own report to the Common Council. Professing great pleasure with their engineer's findings, the commissioners agreed that the Bronx would be "barely sufficient" even for present needs and all attention should be focused on the Croton. Tracing the city's unfortunate water history from Christopher Colles to Levi Disbrow, the commissioners determined that each New Yorker deserved at least the amount of fresh water available to Londoners (twenty-seven gallons a day) and Philadelphians (twenty-four). Playing to the legislature, the commissioners made the point that a healthy and clean city was essential to the prosperity of the state, which had built the infinitely more difficult Erie Canal. Having personally observed their engineer's researches in the field, the commissioners also expressed no preference as to the route from the Croton and expected further examinations to decide the question.[55]

The reports were sent for consideration and recommendation to the council fire and water committee, which typically had been completely reconstituted but for chairman Palmer after the spring elections. Reporting back to the council at the end of December, his committee found "no reasonable doubt" of the project's feasibility and no concern about the cost: if $5 million was needed, a mere $5 annual water charge on each of the city's forty thousand buildings would equal the likely 4 percent interest on the principal.[56]

The committee got far off the track, though, with its proposed law to replace the expiring law written by Van Schaick, who had left the council after one term. The draft in every one of its provisions attempted to shift power back from state-appointed commissioners to city government: the mayor and Common Council would appoint five water commissioners who would superintend the work under the direction of the council. The draft was read and laid on the table. The regressive legislation would be dealt with later by the full council, and after that by Senator Van Schaick in Albany.[57]

Another of the committee's reports submitted at the same council session, on a proposed purchase by the city of the Manhattan Company's water operations, displayed more wisdom. The committee advised that only after the legislature passed a new law for a public supply should the city consider buying the Manhattan works, after an appraisal; the committee apparently recognized that the value would be considerably less once a public works had been approved.[58]

Van Schaick Seals the Deal; Westchester Aroused

All the tramping around Westchester by surveying crews aroused the county's interest, which was chiefly expressed in its single newspaper, Sing Sing's *Westchester Herald*. The Democratic weekly was run by Caleb Roscoe, whose keen editorials were said to have been composed and set in type "without having been written even in outline." When Roscoe weighed in with "Pure Water" in his February 4, 1834, issue, it was likely true as he claimed that almost all of Westchester's citizens appeared to favor the Croton project.[59]

Roscoe was writing for a county of thirty-six thousand people, spread thinly across 480 square miles of mainland above Manhattan. Westchester presented a rolling landscape in its narrower southern reaches, rising above the county seat at White Plains to steep, wooded, granite ridges and numerous lakes and streams. Large manor tracts (many held by the descendants of their Dutch grantees) and farms (many acquired after the Revolution from forfeited English estates) dotted the county. The farmers, especially in the north, scratched out their existence in rugged terrain; wealthy city dwellers played seasonal country squire on Hudson valley estates. Of the county's twenty-one villages in 1834, Sing Sing was the largest, counting 4,832 residents.[60] Despite Roscoe's rosy editorial, a number of Westchester's landed few would soon give Manhattan's thirsty a run for their water.

A month after the Common Council fire and water committee recommended a $5 million Croton project administered by the city, the full council halved the amount but otherwise instructed the city counsel to prepare the law as drafted. The lower figure may have been intended to demonstrate to the legislature that the council was taking a conservative approach, but Senator Van Schaick still would have none of it.[61]

The chaotic city elections in early April renewed his fears about local government. The three-day balloting, featuring the first direct election for mayor in a major American city, was a moveable riot. "Respectable persons were beaten and trampled in the mud," howled Philip Hone, who blamed Tammany Democrats for inciting Irish immigrants against law-abiding Whigs like himself. After outgoing mayor Gideon Lee (a Democrat) himself was attacked, the militia put an end to things. When the dust settled, Democrat Cornelius Van Wyck Lawrence had won the mayor's office over Gulian Verplanck by 181 votes out of the thirty-five thousand cast. Of greater significance, Whigs gained a majority in the Common Council and potential control over water policy. The chairmanship of the fire and water committee for the 1834–35 session passed from outgoing Democrat Palmer to Whig John Labagh, the committee's only returning member.[62]

Van Schaick seized the day. Though the Douglass report had ended any personal hesitation on the Croton project, Van Schaick recognized that the next law had to "paralyze any opposition which might remain." Later claiming that the draft law from the Common Council was delayed in reaching him and in any case "laden with the numerous mischiefs of an irrelevant power," he simply "laid it aside." The senator had been drafting a bill of his own, which "was not submitted to the Common Council for want of time."[63]

Yet Van Schaick drafted his bill uneasily, not because he feared outcry from newly Whiggish Gotham, but because the American political and monetary systems were imploding. President Jackson vetoed a recharter of the Pennsylvania-dominated Second Bank of the United States in 1832; the removal of government deposits from that bank to certain "pet" institutions was the wrenching national issue of 1833, a motivating force in the rise of the national Whig party early in 1834, of which the Whig Common Council victory was a piece. In the winter of 1833–44, the "Bank War" provoked a panic in New York City, as elsewhere, shocking Whigs and driving deep wedges among Jacksonian Democrats as railroad and canal stocks crumbled, banks failed, and trade slowed to a crawl.

Van Schaick wondered if it was right "to impose a new and perhaps a very heavy debt on the city at this alarming juncture." He decided to press ahead: money could always be borrowed, the local economy would be stimulated by the purchase of materials and labor, the great project would become a topic of discussion as work progressed, "and all sensible men would at last discover that they had been fighting against the inestimable blessing" of abundant fresh water.[64]

Van Schaick's bill restored complete authority over the work to state-appointed commissioners. They were to hire engineers, adopt a plan, determine its cost, make contracts, enter private land for surveys, and offer compensation to landowners for property to be taken, with a panel of state-appointed appraisers settling disputes. The commissioners were to report their plan to the Common Council by the end of 1835; the council's role would be merely to approve or reject it. If approved, the plan then would have to cross a most democratic hurdle. At the next city elections, New Yorkers would vote on whether the project should go forward. This was a wholly original notion in New York's water saga, inspired by the troubled times. "It seemed necessary to rouse the citizens," Van Schaick later explained, "and to call out a strong sentiment in favor of the measure. . . . Was it not prudent that the people should be pledged for the payment of the debt by their own act and deed, and by their favorite rule of a majority?"[65]

One component of the council's draft law retained by Van Schaick was the limited $2.5 million loan authority. Knowing that the project could not be done for that price, he calculated that the amount could be increased once work had begun and the economic panic was over.

The bill breezed through the Senate and Assembly during April. On May 2, 1834, the second great law on the road to the Croton, simply titled "An Act to Provide for Supplying the City of New York with Pure and Wholesome Water," was signed by Governor Marcy. As with its forebear, the law nowhere mentioned any particular water source. Though Stephen Allen found Van Schaick's claim of exclusive authorship of the law "passing strange," he and the other commissioners were pleased to be reappointed at Van Schaick's behest.[66]

After rehiring Major Douglass for a new round of surveys to determine the aqueduct route and lower its anticipated cost, the commissioners contended with official anxiety about a return of cholera, brought on by a dry early summer. The Whig-dominated council ordered the commissioners to investigate any possible upisland water sources, but an unwanted junket to the villages of Manhattanville and Harlem revealed only dried up springs and nearly empty wells. Fortunately, the cholera proved epidemic in rumor alone, with no more than several dozen deaths.[67]

The summer brought a more significant flourishing of opposition to the Democratic commissioners from the Whig press, notably in August issues of the influential *New-York Mirror,* George Pope Morris's conservative literary weekly. The over-abundant and expensive Croton could hardly be needed with the cheap and ample Bronx close at hand, argued the *Mirror,* fearful of heavy new taxes on its wealthy readers.[68] The commissioners' only response was consulting with Albert Stein, a German-born engineer who had just completed a water supply for Nashville; with the commissioners in tow, Stein conducted gauges of the Croton in September and prepared a brief supportive report.[69] Any festering political opposition to the commissioners in the Whig-controlled Common Council fizzled after the early November state elections, when Democrats humbled Whigs in the city, state, and county.

The real trouble for the commissioners was in deciding just how to design their aqueduct. After their consultation with Stein and while Douglass's surveys continued into the fall, the commissioners sent two new engineering parties into the field.

For some months earlier in the year, the council and the commissioners had been solicited with sketchy Croton plans by Daniel Rhodes, who suggested ponding the Croton with a much higher dam and much farther downriver than initially planned by Douglass, either at Quaker's Bridge two miles from the river's mouth or up a few more miles at Garretson's Mill.[70] Though they had little confidence in the overall proposals of the otherwise unknown Rhodes (who sought millions of dollars to do the work himself), the commissioners were impressed with his thoughts on dam location. In late October, they hired Erie Canal veteran John Martineau to offer a plan for conveying the Croton from "a lofty dam" at Garretson's to a reservoir at Murray Hill.

How Martineau, whose life and engineering career are relatively obscure, came to his important assignment is unclear, but after obtaining the necessary instruments and collecting a team, Martineau commenced his surveys early in November from the mouth of the Croton. There is no indication that Douglass opposed Martineau's work.[71]

For a more limited assignment, the commissioners hired a third engineer, one possessing much local knowledge. George Cartwright, Croton gauger in the 1820s and Douglass party traverser in 1833, was now employed to run levels upriver from Garretson's Mill to determine how much land would be overflowed by a thirty-eight-foot-high dam. Again, there is no indication of how Douglass felt about yet another engineer's entry into the field that had been his exclusively; Cartwright had worked with Douglass and there is no suggestion of any tension between them. Cartwright ran his levels early in January. It seems that the commissioners were adding engineers not from any misgivings about Douglass but because they wanted many answers quickly.[72]

The Commissioners' Report

By early February, the water commissioners had received reports from Douglass, Martineau, and Cartwright. On February 16, 1835, nearly a year ahead of the deadline set by the 1834 law, they handed in their own recommendations to the Common Council, urging its prompt decision so that the public vote could take place during the city elections in eight weeks. By leaving such a small window for council consideration, the commissioners effectively limited interference from the city government.

The council had plenty to digest. With the appended reports of the Croton engineers and city officials, route profiles and maps, and assorted communications from interested schemers, the commissioners' report ran over two hundred pages, the most comprehensive accounting to date of New York's water situation. The council ordered twenty-five hundred copies distributed throughout the city, and pondered the commissioners' blueprint for seizing the Croton.[73]

After conscientiously explaining their rejection of numerous unsolicited ideas (including damming the Hudson at Greenwich Village), the commissioners proceeded to the varying findings of their engineers. Sensible to the shifting focus downstream from Muscoot Hill, Douglass now favored a thirty-three-foot-high dam at Garretson's; at the head of steep rapids and surrounded by bold shores forming natural abutments, the dam would create a two-hundred-acre reservoir, 155½ feet above tide. From Garretson's, Douglass recommended his 1833 river route, at a grade reduced by the shorter distance and lower elevation to a foot a mile but requiring more tunnels than deep cuts through Westchester ridges. The high Harlem crossing would remain the same, with a simplified route down

Manhattan: arches across Manhattanville Valley and a reservoir only at
Murray Hill. Douglass described the natural terrain along each of the route's
thirty-nine miles, and detailed the construction costs for the masonry conduit and its supporting structures. At just under $5 million, the plan was
still more costly than his original river route.

Martineau had reached different and less expensive conclusions. Following his instructions, he priced a route from a dam forty-four feet high
at Garretson's to a distributing reservoir at Murray Hill at $4.2 million,
but he favored a plan with two significant differences: a much higher dam
down at Halman's Hill near the mouth of the river, where the Croton was
only twenty feet above tide; and a Harlem crossing of multiple, eight-foot
pipes laid on a low embankment across the river. The dam would create
a seven-hundred-acre lake (backing up the Croton beyond Garretson's)
and allow a foot-per-mile grade along a shorter aqueduct course; the Harlem
pipe siphon would likewise save money and also avoid the significant engineering questions of a Harlem high bridge. With several required Westchester and Manhattan reservoirs, Martineau's favored plan was only
$4 million.

After the commissioners sorted out significant differences of opinion
on the Croton's daily flow (they rejected Cartwright's mistaken new
gauging of one hundred million gallons, believed Douglass's and Stein's
fifty million, and trusted Stein's worst-drought reduction to thirty million), they decided on a plan that mingled the recommendations of Martineau and Douglass: a high dam at Halman's (eliminating five miles of
aqueduct), pipe siphons at the Harlem (half the cost of a high bridge), arches
across Manhattanville Valley, and masonry conduit to a single reservoir
at Murray Hill (less than half the cost of a Manhattanville reservoir and
iron pipe to Murray Hill). Recalculating their engineers' various estimates, the commissioners put the cost of delivering the Croton to Murray Hill at $4,250,709.71. As the work later took shape, changes would be
made by and for the commissioners, but for the moment they believed
they had come up with the best aqueduct at the lowest cost.

For distributing Croton water, the commissioners relied on a report from
city water engineer Uzziah Wenman, who detailed how 167½ miles of pipe
(ranging from twenty-inch mains to mostly six-inch branches) would run

under all the city's streets. Happily, the entire fifteen miles of the 13th Street system could be incorporated into this grid but, with the addition of some two thousand stop-cocks and street hydrants (and the purchase of 1.4 million pounds of lead), the cost of the distribution system would be nearly $1.3 million, raising the cost of delivering the Croton from river to residents at just over $5.5 million.

To determine the number of potential water users and how much they might be willing to pay, the commissioners drew a broad statistical portrait of 1835 New York. From information supplied by city surveyor Edwin Smith and others, the commissioners found that below its limits at 21st Street, New York contained 30,000 houses, over 2,000 back tenements, 240 boarding houses, and 40 large hotels; 2,646 taverns and 100 victualing and refectory houses; 267 bakehouses, 63 distilleries, 12 breweries, 10 porter cellars, and 7 sugar houses; 178 printing offices, about 60 silversmiths and jewelers, 58 soap and candle factories, 43 marble and stone-cutting works, and 10 type foundries; 73 hatteries and 19 curriers and morocco manufacturers; 5,000 horses, 237 butchers, 100 slaughterhouses, 86 livery stables, and 1 tanyard; 26 classical schools, 23 primary schools, 22 female boarding schools, 12 public schools, and 7 "African free schools"; 60 steam engines (exclusive of those at distilleries, sugar houses, and stone works), 2 gas works, and 1 chemical factory.

Presuming that two-thirds of the houses and all other potential users would immediately sign up for Croton water, and after studying water use information solicited from other cities, the commissioners offered a table of estimated water revenue, from a gas works that might pay $1,000 a year to a horse whose owner might pay $1.50. Households would pay an average of $8, double earlier anticipations but lower than the $9.20 average for water in six American cities: Boston ($12), Albany ($11.07), Providence ($10), Troy ($6.50), and Philadelphia ($6), as well as New York's own Manhattan Company ($9.63). The commissioners expected that some two thousand homes would pay an additional $4 a year for the luxury of private baths, long enjoyed by hundreds of Philadelphians; a booming business was also expected in public baths.

Projected total annual revenues of $310,000 would neatly cover 6 percent annual interest on a $5 million budget, which the commissioners saw as the extent of their financial duty; the principal would be paid off by subsequent generations. Still, the commissioners acknowledged that it might take a few years for income to meet interest, as it had in Philadelphia. Philadelphia's expensive patience had banished cholera, though, while New York remained destitute of abundant, good water.

The commissioners recognized the psychological barriers presented by the project to water New York. Steamboats, gas lighting, canals, and railroads were all doubted, the commissioners noted, until time and usage convinced the public of the advantages. Well aware of the pending referendum on their Croton plan, the commissioners appealed to civic pride. New York spent millions of dollars on great public buildings when cheaper structures would do. At immense expense, public squares, parks, and wide streets were built to improve the health, beauty, and comfort of the city, yet the great evil of bad water remained.

The Common Council referred the commissioners' report to the fire and water committee, which issued its approval on March 4; with little opportunity for debate, the full council gave its unanimous assent two weeks later, and Mayor Lawrence issued an official proclamation on March 24, informing voters that at the April city elections they would hand in ballots marked with a written or printed "Yes" or "No."[74]

The People Vote

After decades of indecision, New Yorkers had exactly three weeks to decide their water future. Anti-Croton pamphleteers blanketed the city: Disbrow well promoter John Sullivan hit the streets with his *Exposition of Errors in the Calculation of the Board of Water Commissioners;* Moses Hale entered the fray with *Spring Water Versus River Water,* a fifty-page argument for up-island springs; the Manhattan Company, reconciled to the loss of its monopoly but facing a diminished value for its unsold waterworks, was rumored to be inciting anti-Croton sentiment. "We regret to see Expensive Pamphlets out in circulation to defeat the great Water project," observed the Whiggish *New-York Daily Advertiser,* "and in favor of Boaring, and keeping up the odious monopoly of the Manhattan Company."[75]

Unified by civic interest, the press crossed party lines for Croton. Worried about the tax-fearing opposition of "the poorer classes," the Democratic *Evening Post* ran long abstracts of the Commissioners' Report and banner illustrations of the proposed work. Water was no subject "for party boast or party action," asserted the *Commercial Advertiser;* the Whig mouthpiece ran report abstracts and editorialized favorably for what promised to be "the crowning glory of the Commercial Queen of the Western World."[76]

The press battled the pamphleteers and also a Westchester prince. Theodorus Van Wyck, squire of the vast Dutch-era Cortlandt patent downriver from the proposed Croton dam, came to town on horseback to distribute anti-Croton handbills at city polling places.[77]

Van Wyck, who would later lead legal opposition to Croton plans, had a chilling task. Fair weather the preceding week gave way to extraordinary cold for the duration of the three-day election that began on Tuesday, April 14. The city was swept by a northwest gale that night, followed by a severe frost that coated the streets with ice. At daybreak on Thursday, a driving snowstorm set in and continued until noon, when the wind backed off and the bitter day brightened.[78]

It was hardly voting weather, and apathy was running strong. Popular Democrat Mayor Lawrence ran unopposed; the Whigs, still smarting from the November elections, seemed resigned to losing their council majority. The Democrats took no chances, prevailing on Myndert Van Schaick to resign his Senate seat to run for 5th Ward assistant. He immediately had a role to play. In the days leading up to the election, he had become aware that few water ballots had been printed by the Common Council. Guiding the final act of the process he had put in motion, Van Schaick saw to it that equal numbers of yes and no ballots were distributed throughout the city.[79]

Without partisan issues, the newspapers seized on water as the election's headline event, for three days and nights printing alarming reports that the Croton initiative might be defeated. The poor and the rich, "agrarians," immigrants, and tax-fearing landlords were all rumored to be voting no, or not voting at all. On the election's final evening, the Whiggish *American* frantically urged men of business to cast their ballots before returning home: "Is his dinner for a *single day* of more consequence to him than good water during a life time?"[80]

The first formal returns made the evening papers of the 17th. True to the Whigs' worst fears, they had lost control of both boards of the Com-

mon Council by substantial margins; Van Schaick was among the Democrats sweeping back into the council.[81]

As to the water vote, either the papers had done their editorial jobs with
remarkable success or had excited unnecessary alarm. After three days of
dire predictions, the first returns allowed the *Commercial Advertiser* to
"anticipate that within a very few years, the Croton River will flow into
the city of New-York, sparkling and pure as it gushes from its mountain
springs." The turnout proved light but the answer was decided: the Yeses
were 17,330, the Nos 5,963.[82]

The margin was decisive and the demographics were illuminating.
In the first three wards, the oldest and wealthiest, the margin was 4,121
to 97; large margins prevailed in other wealthy wards. Only three
wards had majorities against. Narrowly opposed were the two poor-
est, the cramped, sunken, immigrant neighborhoods of the future
Lower East Side with the worst wells, no Manhattan pipes, and no
money for spring water. The 9th Ward had different reasons for its decisive opposition (1,015 to 631). Comprising the former country village
of Greenwich, it had the best wells and nearest access to suburban
springs.[83]

Chairman and Chief Engineer

On the Monday following the vote, the Common Council began struc-
turing a water loan. It cast a wide financial net: Europe-bound commissioner Saul Alley was instructed to seek the most favorable terms from
bankers he met there. In early May, the city issued the first of $2.5 mil-
lion worth of "The Water Stock of the City of New York," payable at 5 percent over twenty-five years. After some debate, the council also agreed to
modest salaries for the long unpaid commissioners: $1,500 for Chairman
Allen, $1,000 for the others.[84]

In early June, the commissioners named Major Douglass their chief engineer, at an annual salary of $5,000.[85] Douglass was gratified with his
selection (from among unnamed rivals), despite his knowledge "of certain peculiarities in the character of Mr. Allen, which were likely to render my situation a difficult one." The gentleman engineer previously had
noted the unpleasant roughness of Allen's manner, but believed Allen's devo-

tion to the work "would secure me against any undue asperity in his intercourse with *me*." He was wrong about this.

The fireworks began immediately. It seems unlikely that Allen was already intent on undermining Douglass, as Douglass later claimed, but the military engineer and self-made merchant possessed different visions of how to proceed. Previous surveys by Douglass and others had been conducted merely to win approval for the project; now that plans would actually have to work, Douglass sought to hire "some of the highest order of assistant engineers." Allen, though, wanted a hand in Douglass's selection process; overruled to some extent by his fellow commissioners, Allen succeeded in imposing what Douglass saw as significant restrictions: "His idea was, that two or three young gentlemen with the Chief Engineer, were quite sufficient to lay out the whole work in a few weeks—he had no doubt, that *he himself*, with such assistance *could do it in that time*. There was no reasoning with him on the subject—every attempt to do so was treated with sneers and rudeness."[86]

Douglass entered the field in early July at the head of a seven-man corps, a fraction of the team he had sought. Nevertheless, he forged ahead. His first assignment was to stake out a line above the anticipated level of a five-hundred-acre lake to be created by a dam not at Halman's but at Garretson's Mill. What had shifted the commissioners' thinking since February back upriver is unclear. Next, Douglass was to stake out the aqueduct line down to the Harlem River, specifying the exact amount of land necessary for the conduit, excavations, culverts, and embankments. Then he was to make surveys and determine the locations of any necessary reservoirs on Manhattan. In the meantime, George Cartwright was engaged again, this time to survey the land to be overflowed by the dam. Douglass and Cartwright were to deliver maps of all the land affected by the dam, aqueduct, and reservoirs to the commissioners as soon as possible. Construction could not begin until lands were acquired from their owners and maps were necessary first to negotiate land purchases and then to bid out and award construction contracts.[87]

Allowed to increase his corps only marginally into the fall, Douglass worked without rest, "obliged to take upon myself, for some time, the duty of sub-assistant," a humiliation that no doubt delighted his low-born boss. After four months of work "which an efficient corps would almost have accomplished in as many weeks," Douglass was permitted to augment his staff, but November was a bad time of year to hire the best engineers. The corps expanded to seventeen (four assistant engineers, plus rodmen, chainmen, and laborers) only as winter closed around them. Still, after enduring backbreaking work, hard frost, and deepening snow, Douglass was proud to have staked the entire route from the dam to the Harlem River before removing to winter offices in the city.[88]

Cartwright turned in his report in late November. "Beginning at a peeled ash sapling in the west boundary of [William] Ricket's farm," Cartwright had marked the outline of New York City's primary storage reservoir using the landmarks available in a primitive country: near a large walnut in a buckwheat field, past a shell bark hickory, through Isaac Tompkins's potato field, in the orchard of David Webber's widow, along a road near the farms of the Flewellen family, in Joseph Hyatt's garden, at a blazed apple tree near the Cornelius Ferris farm, and so on to a fence bordering Purdy family property.[89]

Cartwright had staked out a lake in the lands of Westchester's oldest families; Tompkins, Webbers, Flewellens, and Purdys had staked their own claims in the Croton Valley for generations, the Purdys as early as 1700. The water commissioners immediately began negotiations with some three dozen landowners, but not all would be easily bought.[90]

As 1835 drew to a close, Chairman Allen seemed pleased. The lone December entry in his private journal betrayed no disappointments: "The work is now progressing with all the speed that a project of so much importance and magnitude will warrant . . . and we entertain no doubt whatever, if our lives are spared, that we shall be enabled to complete what we have undertaken to the perfect satisfaction of our fellow citizens."[91]

New York Burns

Allen's journal entry carries no date, but the reference to the sparing of lives suggests it was written after December 17, when New York learned the hard way that it had waited too long for water. "How shall I record the events of last night," mourned Philip Hone in his own diary on the 17th, "or how attempt to describe the most awful calamity which has ever visited these United States? . . . I am fatigued in body, disturbed in mind, and my fancy filled with images of horror which my pen is inadequate to describe."[92]

The Great Fire of 1835 was a conspiracy of the worst circumstances. Two large fires on the night of the 15th had depleted both the energy of the city's volunteer firemen and the supply of water in the 13th Street reservoir. After rainy, snowy weather started the week, the temperature had dropped below freezing; on the 16th, a northwest gale drove the mercury down toward zero and beyond. When the first fire alarms sounded just before nine that evening, the streets were clogged with ice and snow; the rivers were frozen solid at the shore and choked with ice in their streams.

Engine Company No. 1 arrived just minutes after a watchman's report of fire in a warehouse on crooked, narrow Merchant Street (today's eastern extension of Beaver Street). After briefly holding the blaze in check with their hand-pumped engines, the firemen soon retreated as the fire spread along both sides of the street.

The wind-driven flames fanned south and east, consuming forty buildings by midnight, as 13th Street water slowed to a trickle and street hydrants froze shut. Neighborhood cisterns and public pumps were useless from the beginning; what water they held was frozen solid. If any Manhattan water was available, none of the many accounts mention it. Firemen had diminishing luck cutting through river ice to draw frigid salt water through stiffening hoses to the engines. In the first hour of the 17th, helplessness set in; to Philip Hone, unsuccessfully attempting to remove goods from his son's store, "the firemen appeared to look on with the apathy of despair"

The fire reached epic proportions when the Merchants' Exchange came into the flames' relentless path. Completed only eight years earlier, the Greek Revival temple of business fronted on three streets, with a grand entrance portico on Wall Street and a towering domed cupola over the central trading room. In March, an acclaimed larger-than-life marble statue of Alexander Hamilton, standing watch over the city's financial transactions, was added to the rotunda. Like the man, the life of his likeness would be foreshortened.[93]

Thought impervious to the flames, the Exchange had been hurriedly filled with valuable dry goods from the more vulnerable buildings around it. But, just as the flames began to lick at the Exchange, all fire fighting with

FIGURE 29. Ruins of the Merchants' Exchange, 1835
This Nathaniel Currier lithograph of a J. H. Bufford drawing depicts the scene on
Wall Street during the Great Fire of 1835. (© Collection of The New-York Historical
Society.)

water stopped. The goods inside heated into fuel. "A single stream would
have saved the Exchange," officials later testified, but "not an engine could
play" on it. The massive stone edifice resisted the flames for two hours before
becoming engulfed. At about three in the morning, a party of would-be
rescuers rushed up the marble steps and into the rotunda to see if Hamilton could be saved; they succeeded only in partly bringing him down from
his pedestal before "the warning cry was uttered that the roof was about
to fall, and they had to seek safety in flight." At four, the dome came crashing down, and the marble Hamilton fell, the broken victim of the city's
water want, for which the living Hamilton had earned a share of blame.

Fire overwhelmed the bitter night, "an ocean of flame" illuminating
mountains of smoke. The heat was so intense that metal roofs and shut-
ters ran off in streams. Wind-driven embers scorched buildings across the

East River in Brooklyn. New York's torment lit the night sky as far away as New Haven and Philadelphia, where firemen turned out supposing the fire was in their own suburbs.

At about the time the Exchange was collapsing, the first significant action to stop the fire was accomplished, when two nearby buildings on Exchange Place were intentionally blown up. Four hours earlier, Mayor Lawrence reluctantly had made the decision to round up gunpowder, after pleadings from prominent citizens—including United States district attorney Colonel James A. Hamilton, Alexander's son, who believed the entire south end of the city in imminent danger. "The whole fire department [was] so deranged and demoralized, that there was no direction, and no head to give orders." Hamilton, Lawrence, and Charles King (whose *American* was burning to the ground) were among those who heroically rushed north by foot and to Brooklyn and Governor's Island by open boat to gather powder, which was required to be stored away from the city's center. Incredibly, enough was collected so that just as his father's statue came down, James Hamilton himself applied the match at 48 Exchange Place, after the fire department's chief engineer refused the honor.

In the remaining hours before daylight, other buildings were blown up in the southerly path of the fire, halting its progress. It was the first time the city had destroyed private property in order to save others from fire. In the last of many lawsuits, brought seventeen years later by the printing company whose buildings were the first to be blown up, the jury found for the city, having followed the judge's instructions that gunpowder had been the only means available to contain the fire. Water, fire's best master, had retired early.

When daylight came, a twenty-block area covering fifty-two acres was "a mass of burning, smoking ruins, rendering the streets indistinguishable." The commercial heart of the city, from Wall Street south to Coenties Slip, and from Broad Street to the East River, was a "burnt district" of wrecked buildings and streets piled with ruined merchandise. Fires amidst the smoldering ruins broke out for days afterward.

Because few homes were involved, only two people died, but some seven hundred buildings were destroyed in the city's oldest streets, most of them laid out when New York was New Amsterdam. The greatest single loss was the Merchants' Exchange, which also contained the main post office and the Chamber of Commerce. Nearly all the other wrecked buildings housed shipping, dry goods, and grocery concerns; many were of recent construction and readily rebuilt. But the fire also destroyed perhaps the oldest remnant of Dutch New York, the 1642 cornerstone of the church in Fort Amsterdam, excavated in 1790 and stored in the belfry of the South Dutch Reformed Church on Exchange Street. The fire reduced the Reformed Church to rubble, the stone relic of oldest Manhattan mingled and lost among it.[94]

A conservative estimate of lost property was about $20 million, 10 percent of the assessed value of all property in the city. "There is not perhaps in the world," lamented Hone, "the same space of ground covered by so great an amount of real and personal property as the scene of this dreadful conflagration."[95]

Businesses were wrecked, fortunes were ruined, thousands were put out of work, and recriminations were many. The volunteer fire department shouldered most of the blame but it was unclear precisely what the firemen could have done better, except perhaps to have laid off the imported spirits after their own and the water had run out.[96]

The destruction of what had been the commercial center of the United States was a shock in the already nervous economic times. Yet the city set to work rebuilding, even as the fire smoldered. "It is gratifying to witness the spirit and firmness with which the merchants meet this calamity," Hone observed on the 19th, the day he was among 125 prominent citizens named to a special committee to administer the rebuilding. Among the fourteen men directing the effort was Stephen Allen, who as a boy had survived the fire of 1776 and as a man was most aware of the city's tragic lack of water.

The Allen-Douglass Debates

Up in the Croton Valley, Major Douglass weathered the same bitter wind that spread destruction in the city. When he left the field on January 8, Douglass returned not only to a charred city but to an employer burning with intolerance for any delays.

Now in daily contact with Allen, Douglass endured what he saw as a series of petty persecutions that sent tempers flying: a dispute over a few hundred dollars worth of summer disbursements; Allen's demand that Douglass present a pass book for all winter season purchases; a three-week delay in furnishing the engineers' eight-man winter office while Allen selected a joiner.[97]

When Douglass's charges were made public four years later, Allen denied ever using "uncivil or insulting language," having spoken to his chief engineer only "with energy and decision, as I am in the habit of doing, when improper acts are the subject of debate." But clearly, a class struggle was under way: "because I am unable to clothe my observations in the feminine utterance of a learned sophist like Mr. D. am I to be charged with rudeness?"[98] Convinced that Allen "was determined to persecute" him into quitting, Douglass remained on the job only after persuasion by friends.[99] It was a chilly winter.

The central issue, as Allen saw it, was the maps essential to the purchase of land. The trouble with producing them was that Douglass had met with incomplete success in discussions during the summer with some two hundred affected landowners. Little resistance had been offered from certain Westchester gentry who were also city folk and knew the value of a land sale, but many other locals had been less accommodating: some were away from home when called on, others were off in their fields, most wanted time to decide what compensation they were owed for their land, and more than a few promised legal action.[100]

In at least one instance, Allen and Douglass found common ground that winter, though it further delayed Douglass's other work. Smarting from December's fire, Mayor Lawrence asked for an investigation into whether river water could be pumped into the proposed reservoir at Murray Hill until it was filled with Croton water. In some detail, Allen and Douglass advised the mayor in February that a steam-pumped river works could hardly be cost-effective or good for a distribution system designed for fresh water.[101]

With the first twitchings of spring, Douglass, Allen, and certain Westchesterites came out of their corners slugging. In mid-March, Allen rejected the engineer's request for "a *strong* corps" of up to seventy men, ostensibly because landholder movements threatened to stop the work. Allen also rejected Douglass's request for a land agent to make amicable arrangements with resistant owners. Having attended several of their meetings, Douglass urged the commissioners to make a conciliatory visit to Westchester, but this suggestion was ignored.

For weeks, Douglass pared his corps request, until "the golden period" of hiring the best engineers had passed and some of the past season's corps had found other work. Nearly a month after his first request, Douglass returned to the field with a "pitiful" corps of thirteen, though it did include at least two trusted assistants: Henry Anthony, who had worked under Douglass since the first surveys in 1833, and Edmund French, a former Douglass student at West Point.[102]

Despite deep snow, Douglass began his fourth and final Westchester survey in mid-April. The necessity of this survey was a point of contention. Douglass claimed it was required because some landowners had demanded shifts in the line's location and because the commissioners had demanded a larger conduit and gentler grade than previously planned. The commissioners claimed it was Douglass who insisted on certain improvements that would shorten the distance and smooth some curves in the aqueduct's course.[103]

Douglass and the commissioners finally agreed that the aqueduct would run thirty-three miles from dam to Harlem bridge, on a grade of thirteen and a quarter inches per mile. The masonry conduit, lined inside with brick and stone, would be arched at top and bottom, with side walls angling slightly outward toward the top. The walls would be just over four feet two inches high, and the conduit interior as much as seven feet five inches wide and eight feet five and a half inches high.[104]

With the prospect nearing of actual aqueduct construction, the anxious voices of Westchester opposition were heard in Albany and New York. In a petition to the legislature that spring, a large group of landowners contested the commissioners' land-taking privileges under the 1834 law. The landowners demanded that the city pay for taken land but that legal possession remain with the owner; that land paid for but ultimately unused revert to the owner without repayment; that owners be protected by trespass provisions and be allowed to purchase some of the water running through their land; and that land appraisals be conducted by Westchester County judges instead of state-appointed appraisers. The water commissioners opposed all of these demands as threats to their authority. The legislature rejected them outright.

At the same time, the commissioners were approached directly by a different set of landowners, with more tempered complaints about the security of their rights under the 1834 law. This group asked that land only be acquired by the city for the purpose of supplying water and if ultimately unused revert back to the owner for the purchase price; that fences be maintained around the aqueduct; and that "convenient passes" be made under or over the aqueduct's elevated crossings of private land. The commissioners endorsed these demands in an act passed at the end of May.[105]

The commissioners believed this law would show Westchester that they were acting in good faith. The *Westchester Herald* was convinced, printing the law's full text and expressing "satisfaction with its provisions."[106] A calm settled briefly on the Westchester front.

Believing he had defused landowner tensions, Chairman Allen returned to his squabbles with Douglass. It wasn't until the end of June that both parties agreed that all the necessary Westchester maps had been delivered. Douglass considered his final placing of the line a job extremely well done, meticulously accomplished despite "incessant rain" and other impediments:

> The location was probably the most difficult ever undertaken in this country. The ground was excessively uneven; the advantage of lockage (in giving choice of convenient levels) *unavailable,* and the character of the work itself, such as to involve the most serious consequences from errors *apparently* the most trifling. The work required in short extraordinary attention, and I am happy that notwithstanding the smallness of the corps and impediments thrown in my way, it *received* it.[107]

No gratitude was forthcoming from chairman Allen. Instead, claimed Douglass, the commissioners fiddled about in New York as July rolled around and Westchester again began to burn; a large group of landowners was "daily becoming more and more exasperated" and holding public meetings; the commissioners hadn't visited the line in eight months. The engineer could not understand why they stayed away, with full knowledge that militant landowners were on horseback through the county gathering support. Douglass himself was cordially received at public meetings in Westchester, but he could see what lay ahead.[108]

A meeting of disgruntled Westchesterites in Tarrytown in early July resulted in a threat to test the constitutionality of the 1834 law in the U.S.

Supreme Court. A committee was formed to seek a blanket indemnification by the city for all damages to landowner property, including theft or other crimes committed by aqueduct workers during and after construction.

One defect of the 1834 law was that it had no provision for regular reporting by the commissioners; indeed, for eighteen months, they had issued no public statements on the progress of their great work. Ignoring the *Westchester Herald*'s suggestion that they attend the landowners' next meeting in early August, the commissioners instead addressed Westchester concerns in nearly half of an eight-page report voluntarily submitted to the Common Council that week.[109]

The commissioners argued that land compensation questions were covered by the state-appointed appraiser mechanism in the 1834 law. Blanket indemnification would encourage the worst behavior: people would steal without fear of prosecution and the victimized would simply present bills to the city. To soften their legal hard line, the commissioners appealed directly to Westchester egos and purses. Yes, New York had the most direct gain from Croton water, but it was paying a heavy price. Westchester, by contrast, would obtain many benefits without cost: the city's increased prosperity "insured a good and unfailing market" for Westchester produce; Westchester land "chiefly of second rate quality" would be purchased for the aqueduct at greater values than could be derived from farming; and the great sums to be spent in the county building the aqueduct would "naturally tend to increase the trade of the place, and thereby not only benefit the farmer, but the merchant and mechanic also."

The commissioners noted that they had recently applied for the appointment of land appraisers to settle initial disputes with Joshua Purdy and other families in the dam area. The state named three popular Westchester men to handle all appraisals. The commissioners' ingratiating arguments calmed Westchester's "unfortunate prejudices" for the remainder of the year, though plenty of action lay ahead.[110]

Back in the city, the commissioners forged ahead with pipelaying. By midsummer, new pipe was being trenched (at Uzziah Wenman's direction) in several streets downtown, and uptown in some of the numbered streets and alphabetical avenues that make up today's East Village.[111]

While extending pipe lines, the commissioners were reaching the end of the line with Douglass. After marginally increasing his corps to nineteen for the summer, they laid a fresh resolution on the engineer in mid-July. The commissioners demanded forthwith the specifications for every aqueduct structure, including the dam and Harlem crossing, so that at least some of the work could be put under contract before year's end. As the commissioners reported it, Douglass promptly promised to furnish all of the information; for his part, Douglass thought the request unreasonable but was repeatedly rebuffed when he sought additional staff to meet it.[112]

Relations got rockier at the end of August. Having failed both to turn in the required specifications and to hire additional assistants, Douglass wrote from Westchester for permission to employ day laborers in quarrying at the site of the dam, the better to determine its specifications. The commissioners had denied similar requests before, believing that the 1834 act required all work to be done under contract approved by them. Now Allen requested specifications for the quarrying so that it might properly be put under contract as excavation. Writing two weeks later from his home in Brooklyn, Douglass repeated his request to hire quarrymen, nominated a head of the quarry party, and sought the appointment of a chief assistant engineer at a salary of $3,500. Incredulous, the commissioners resolved again to make no further appointments until Douglass complied with their July order.[113]

In the midst of Douglass's final scenes, the oldest living relic in the city's water epic passed from the stage. In June, friends ferried a spirited but bedridden Aaron Burr down New York harbor to a boardinghouse on Staten Island. The eighty-year-old creator of the Manhattan Company had suffered a debilitating stroke after parting ways with Eliza Jumel several years earlier and had progressively weakened. On September 14, 1836, the dark prince expired.

Six days after Burr's death, Douglass sealed his own professional fate with another request for additional staffing. The commissioners read it as a desperate call for engineering help. "The conclusion was irresistible," Allen later wrote, "and it was unanimous with the commissioners, that Mr. Douglass doubted his own ability to perform the duty required of him in preparing the necessary specifications." A change was required.[114]

On October 1, Allen summoned Douglass to his office and suggested he resign. As Douglass recalled that unpleasant interview, Allen "did not pretend to make any *charge* against me either *professionally* or *personally*" but based the commissioners' request on "the *disagreements* between Mr. Allen and myself." Douglass thanked Allen for his suggestion but indicated that the commissioners would have to take the responsibility of firing him. Three days later, they did.

In official documents, the commissioners avoided naming any reasons for Douglass's dismissal. In his private memoirs, however, Allen wrote that the commissioners were "woefully disappointed" with Douglass's operations. When Douglass raised the issue publicly four years later, Allen responded in kind: "Mr. Douglass was a ripe scholar, a good mathematician, *and in theory,* well acquainted with the science of engineering. But my opinion, nevertheless, was . . . that he does not possess that practical knowledge which I deemed necessary to carry on a work of so much importance to the city as that of the Croton water works."[115] Before he disengaged Douglass, Chairman Allen selected a more politic and "practicable" replacement.

The Work Begins

*This work when completed will compare with anything of the kind
in this country or in Europe, . . . an illustration of what the ingenuity
of man led on by the pure light of science can accomplish.*

—Fayette B. Tower, letter

The Plans of John Jervis, a "Practicable Engineer"

The delays in putting spade to earth on the Croton Aqueduct did not go unnoticed in the press. "Two years have now elapsed, and yet we hear nothing of the murmering [*sic*] Croton," complained the scandal-seeking New York *Herald* on October 14, 1836. "The Commissioners are in the regular receipt of their salaries, and that appears to be all they are doing or intending to do."[1] In fact, the water commissioners had been actively engaged in dumping David Douglass and securing the services of a American engineering pioneer. To Stephen Allen's thinking, John Bloomfield Jervis was an "energetic and practicable Engineer" who would not waste time.[2] In a few months, he would move the Croton project from stalled plans to the start of construction.

Jervis (1795–1885),[3] the first-born of seven children, was raised on a struggling farm and lumber mill outside Fort Stanwix (later renamed Rome) in central New York State; his father had sold the old family homestead on Long Island when Jervis was three. Rome was notable for one of the first lock canals in the country, connecting the Mohawk River with Wood

FIGURE 30. *John Bloomfield Jervis, circa 1835*
The successor to Douglass, Jervis built the Croton Aqueduct from 1836 to 1842, remaining as chief engineer until completion of the High Bridge in 1848. The Croton project was one of many highlights in his long and successful engineering career. (Jervis Public Library.)

Creek; it was designed in 1795 by William Weston, the English engineer who four years later advised New York City to tap the Bronx River for its drinking water. Jervis's formal education ended at age fifteen, and he worked alongside his father for the next seven years, farming and lumbering. The family were members of the local Congregational Church, where Jervis adopted Calvinistic beliefs that guided him for the rest of his long life. Distant and reserved by nature, Jervis was honest and industrious, and expected the same in others.

Jervis might have remained on the heavily mortgaged farm had it not been for a combination of fortunate events and the influence of two men. Uncle John Bloomfield directed his inquisitive young nephew to his copy of the *Edinburgh Encyclopedia,* one of the few English-language reference works with authoritative articles on engineering. Local family friend and future New York City water consultant Benjamin Wright was chief engineer of the middle section of the Erie Canal, for which the ground breaking ceremony was held on July 4, 1817, in Rome. Jervis's father was hoping to contract for canal work and Wright was looking for axemen from Jervis's lumbering operations. To gain information for his father, the slender but "very handy" John Jervis became an axeman on the Erie Canal. The rest is engineering history.

Under the tutelage of Wright, who became a lifelong friend and mentor, Jervis rose quickly in the "Erie School of Engineering." Promoted to rodman in 1818, Jervis befriended Canvass White, then himself rising fast as Wright's principal assistant. By 1819, Jervis was a resident engineer; over the next four seasons, he became known for careful engineering and contracting records, delighting his superiors and saving tens of thousands of dollars in attempted contractor fraud. Jervis came to the attention of, and forged lasting relationships with, numerous state canal officials, especially Canal Commissioner William C. Bouck, a leading Democratic politician who was elected governor in 1842. In the spring of 1823, Jervis was made superintending engineer of a fifty-mile stretch of the canal, a position he shared for a few months with future Croton consultant John Martineau and then held alone until leaving the canal in the spring of 1825, the year the "Big Ditch" was dedicated. By then, White and Wright had moved on, and Jervis, too, was eager for new opportunities.

They came quickly. Within days of leaving the Erie, Jervis was hired on to the Delaware and Hudson Canal, as principal assistant to chief engineer Wright; John Sullivan, later the promoter of Levi Disbrow's bored wells, had done the preliminary surveys for the canal company. Two years later, Jervis succeeded Wright, who had shifted to other canals. Among Jervis's assistants on the Delaware and Hudson was Horatio Allen (1802–99), a Union College math professor's son and Columbia College graduate who would become a famous Jervis protégé.

The Delaware and Hudson work called for a railroad over a Pennsylvania mountain from the canal's western terminus at Honesdale (named for company director Philip Hone) to the coal mines at Carbondale. This brought Jervis into the pioneering development of locomotives. The *Stourbridge Lion,* procured in England by Allen at Jervis's instructions, became the first steam locomotive operated in America when Allen drove it on company track in 1829. The overweight engine was a failure; Allen was faulted privately by Jervis for failing to convey his exact specifications to the builder. Still, Jervis recognized that the technology was new and, when both men soon left for other railroad projects, they remained friendly competitors.

Allen spent the early 1830s in South Carolina perfecting locomotives while superintending the construction of the Charleston & Hamburg Railroad, the world's longest when it was completed in 1833. During the unhealthy southern summers, Allen visited Jervis, then working on the Mohawk and Hudson Railroad in upstate New York. The company's directors included John Jacob Astor, fast becoming the richest man in America, and James Renwick, the Columbia College engineering authority who had consulted on Jervis's first locomotive designs. For this railroad in 1832, Jervis designed the successful *Experiment,* built (as were several previous engines) by the West Point Foundry Association, established by Renwick and others in 1818.[4] It was the first locomotive with a swiveling, four-wheel "bogie" truck supporting its front end, allowing the engine to make high speed turns, a design that soon became standard in American railroading.

After completing the Mohawk and Hudson Railroad, in 1833, Jervis was named chief engineer for the hundred-mile Chenango Canal, a state project linking the Erie Canal at Utica to Binghamton. Jervis's great innovation for this work was the construction of rain-fed reservoirs to supply the canal's summit. Using a rain gauge and runoff sluice of his own design, Jervis determined that 40 percent of the rainfall was retained in artificial reservoirs; this landmark of American hydrology upset the European theory that only a third of rainfall remains after evaporation and soil absorption.

Jervis's personal life was simpler. A budding romantic relationship during his Erie Canal work in 1821 ended when Jervis learned that the young woman had married; surprised and disappointed, Jervis swore off passion and submitted to "God's will" for his emotional deliverance. This took another twelve years, when the thirty-eight-year-old engineer married Cynthia Brayton, a hometown woman twelve years his junior and of fragile health. The couple's lifestyle was soon established: he lived wherever work took him and she mostly remained with her family near Rome. Still, it was not an unhappy arrangement; through frequent correspondence, she relieved her husband's need for companionship and eased his loneliness on remote projects.

By the spring of 1836, the Chenango Canal was nearly complete. Though the canal would prove a financial failure, Jervis had brought the work in at just under $2 million, less than 6 percent over his original estimate. While overseeing the Chenango construction, Jervis had many informal and official consultations with William Bouck about a significant enlargement of the Erie Canal. When the state committed to the work early in 1836, Jervis was appointed chief engineer. By the fall, though, New York City had tapped him to tap the Croton.

Jervis did not just happen onto the scene. In fact, as it was revealed four years later, he had been quietly in contact with Stephen Allen for at least a year before his appointment. Late in 1835, Jervis had provided copies of Chenango Canal contracts and specifications to guide Commissioner Allen's Croton work. In return, Allen had appointed one of Jervis's younger brothers to Douglass's engineering corps. For several months in early 1836, Timothy Jervis had kept his older brother informed on the Croton, especially about the escalating tensions between Douglass and Allen. Douglass, who protested against Allen's consultations with the elder Jervis, succeeded in making Timothy's employment brief.[5]

Allen was not Jervis's only pre-appointment advocate. Never far from the Croton action, Myndert Van Schaick claimed (nearly ten years later) that during the opening of the 1836 legislative session he discussed with Jervis in Albany the possibility of his replacing Douglass. By Van Schaick's account, he recommended the switch to Allen during a winter walk in City Hall Park.

Well aware of the implications, Jervis later claimed to have remained fully engaged on the Erie Canal enlargement until Commissioners Allen and Alley visited him in Albany at the end of September with what he considered "the first official proposition" to hire him.

The issue of his accession to the Croton project followed Jervis for the rest of his professional life. "I have been charged with intrigueing [*sic*] for the engineership of this work," Jervis wrote in an 1868 memoir, "but that is an entire mistake, as I had not mentioned the subject to any one, and consequently was quite surprised at receiving the proposition." Indeed, when Allen and Alley offered him the job, Jervis claimed to have initially declined, "not feeling willing to interfere with" Douglass's employment. Only when the commissioners made it clear that Douglass was out and *somebody* would replace him did Jervis see "no impropriety" in accepting the unsought position.

Assured that Jervis would take the job, the commissioners returned to the city and fired Douglass on October 4. Jervis's appointment the following week "solved the mystery" for Douglass of his strained relations with the commissioners. Jervis assumed the chief engineer's salary of $5,000 and from October 12, 1836, the Croton was his to build.[6]

Far from the *Herald*'s accusations of inactivity, newly appointed Jervis found the commissioners "very urgent" to prepare the work for contract. Eight days after his hiring, Jervis was at Garretson's Mill, which he agreed was "probably a good" site for the dam. With Commissioners Allen and Fox and Douglass engineers French and Anthony in tow, Jervis spent the next fortnight walking the staked, thirty-three-mile line south to the Harlem. The contribution of Douglass to the work that Jervis would build would be debated to the ends of their lives. Still, Jervis conceded that Douglass had done a good job determining the aqueduct's route in Westchester: "It was in the main, well located." To reign in the commissioners' "natural urgency" to go forward immediately with contracts,

Jervis convinced them that little work could be accomplished before winter, giving him several months to determine the many construction details not specified by Douglass.[7]

Jervis found his predecessor had not done much: "From the long time he had been engaged on the work I did expect to find more progress in preparation." Douglass's line from the Croton needed only minor improvements, and his determination of the shape and inner dimensions of the conduit was "mainly satisfactory," but that was all Douglass had established. The line on Manhattan had not been determined; there were no engineering plans for the dam, ventilators, waste weirs, culverts, supporting walls, masonry in tunnels, valley crossings on Manhattan, or the receiving and distributing reservoirs and related piping; Douglass had not drawn specification and contract forms. In other places, Jervis considered changing plans, such as the Sing Sing kill crossing, where Douglass had called for a series of small arches. As to the Harlem crossing, which had troubled planners back to Joseph Browne and would make much trouble ahead, Jervis found few details for the high arched bridge that Douglass grandly had envisioned. "It was easy to propose a bridge," Jervis later wrote, but to make specifications from the tops of the arches to the depths of the river "was quite a different thing."[8]

If there would be no construction in the remaining months of 1836, there was plenty of surveying to do before the snows came. Perhaps as a measure of expedience, but also to avoid "wounding the feelings or disappointing the expectations" of Douglass's twenty-one-man corps, for the time being Jervis retained all of them. But he made clear after his tour of the line that the engineering parties led by French and Anthony would be conforming to rigorous Jervis standards. "The days are short, and to make much progress in the field work it is indispensable to have an improvement of their early hours," Jervis wrote to Anthony in early November. "This remark is made, not that I have the least doubt of your industry and application— but because I have observed the parties commence at a later hour in the morning than has been usual in the operations I have heretofore conducted." Jervis wrote to French the same day about his Sing Sing office:

> Have Pitcher, bowls, glasses, candlesticks, etc. properly cleaned and set up and the instruments and table so arranged as to admit of

being kept in order. Remove from the office articles that do not belong to it and which only promote confusion. Allow no one to derange the order of the office, or to remove papers of any kind without direction. Allow no smoking and no play of any kind in the office. In all respects let it be strictly a place of business.[9]

Jervis quickly sorted out relations with his employers. Based on his proposals, in mid-November, the commissioners passed a resolution detailing rights and responsibilities. Jervis would recommend engineers and other salaried employees, but the commissioners would approve them; he could employ day or temporary workers under his authority, but they had to be reported promptly to the commissioners, who could then discharge them. Jervis would prepare all the drawings, maps, and profiles according to the overall plan adopted by the commissioners. Jervis would make all working plans, with material and workmanship specifications, subject to revision by the commissioners. Jervis was to draw up all contracts for approval or revision by the commissioners, who would have the chief engineer's assistance in their letting. He was to certify that contracts were faithfully performed before payment was authorized by the commissioners, who retained the right to reject the engineer's certification if the work appeared to them improperly executed. Jervis was required to enforce discipline among his engineers, who were expected to provide their own instruments. Finally, the chief engineer was to make monthly reports to the commissioners on his progress.[10]

Jervis had no objection to any of these rules, but he notably reserved the right to resign from the project if he deemed any commissioner-mandated revisions of his plans "unsafe" from an engineering point of view, or otherwise "hazardous to his reputation as an engineer."[11]

The perception that the Croton project now had the engineer to build it induced another flurry of deal making between the city and the Manhattan Company. After the failed discussions of a sale in 1833, city and company negotiators had reached a tentative agreement early in 1836 for a twenty-one-year lease of the works at $16,000 a year, but the company board abruptly rejected the deal and ended discussions. Now, the parties returned to a possible transfer. As with the earlier negotiations, the company was willing to sell at a price determined by arbitrators, but this time the city insisted that the price be agreed between the parties themselves. By January, this latest effort was dead.[12]

Not especially concerned about the Manhattan Company's fate, Jervis spent the fall and early winter preparing plans, specifications, and contracts, and analyzing labor and material costs. He was ready to abandon his own ideas when others, carefully considered, appeared better: "Originality was regarded as subservient to success."[13]

As far as printed guidance, there were no books on American civil engineering, and precious little on European hydraulics in English, Jervis's only language. His major reference was the *Treatise on Water Works for Conveying and Distributing Supplies of Water,* a summary of European hydraulic works, theories, and formulae just published in 1835 by Charles S. Storrow, a young and soon to be distinguished engineer who had studied at Harvard and in Paris. Jervis also referred frequently to his copy of late Scottish professor John Robison's four-volume *System of Mechanical Philosophy,* first published in 1804; Robison offered and refined the water flow mathematics of his continental contemporaries, including France's Pierre DuBuat and Baron Riche de Prony, and Germany's Johann Albert Eytelwein.[14]

Jervis's inherited engineering corps worked the line until late December, French's party from the Croton down to Tarrytown, Anthony's party from Tarrytown to the Harlem. At Jervis's instruction, French prepared a map, a profile, and sectional drawings of his portion of the line, enabling Jervis to determine the location and dimensions of tunnels, excavations, embankments, bridges, and protection walls; French also sunk test shafts every two hundred yards to determine the geological support for the aqueduct in the rugged terrain of the northern section. In separate operations in northern Westchester, Thomas J. Carmichael, a draftsman under Douglass, had been assigned to locate sources of stone and sand. Carmichael discovered that most of the stone in the area of the aqueduct was gneiss, highly stratified with feldspar, hornblende, mica, and quartz; this unstable rock would not be suitable for hydraulic use. Some local gneiss, though, was composed mostly of feldstone; this more durable "bastard granite" would be acceptable for certain aqueduct structures. The best local stone, pure granite, was available at only a few local quarries; one, conveniently, was within two miles of the dam site. Carmichael sent Jervis many rock specimens, and also advised that good sand for mortar was in plentiful and proximate supply in coves along the Hudson River. In his flatter, more populous southern portion, Anthony made minor adjustments to the line and was kept busy resetting stakes yanked by increasingly sensitive landowners.[15]

When he brought the corps in from the field, Jervis pared down the Douglass team into the standard, smaller winter corps. It was an unacknowledged credit to Douglass's hiring decisions that dutiful engineers French and Anthony and draftsman turned rock hunter Carmichael headed the list of those retained.[16]

Jervis had numerous public and private issues to contend with during the winter. On the first anniversary of the Great Fire, the *Evening Post* resuscitated the idea of temporary city reservoirs, filled with river water to battle fires during what the paper estimated would be another five to ten years before Croton water arrived. Impatience with the Croton project and fear of fire were not unreasonable. Over eighteen hundred buildings were put up in 1836, almost six hundred more than the previous year, and nearly all of the "burnt district" had been rebuilt. Still, there was no visible progress toward avoiding another devastating fire.[17]

Salt water coursing from temporary reservoirs through pipes meant for fresh water was not a reasonable idea, though, so the Common Council did not act on the suggestion. Instead, a council committee, acting on a request of the water commissioners from fifteen months earlier, prepared a law authorizing the city's purchase of land for permanent reservoirs. They sought land at three locations, identified by future street locations on the city's grid plan: for a receiving reservoir at York Hill (Yorkville) between 79th and 86th Streets and Sixth and Seventh Avenues, an intermediate reservoir between 67th and 69th Streets and Third and Fourth Avenues, and a distributing reservoir on Murray Hill between 40th and 42nd Streets west of Fifth Avenue. These were all locations that had been suggested during Douglass's tenure.[18]

In late December, Jervis began a series of reports to the commissioners laying out the design and organization of the work. The first and most important report clarified how he would build the main conduit. Combining his observations of the line with published hydraulic theories available to him, Jervis retained the basic horseshoe shape of the conduit as described by Douglass, but slightly enlarged its dimensions, reduced the amount of masonry in the conduit's arched roof, and increased the masonry on the arched, load-bearing floor. The result was a conduit that would cost just under $94,000 per mile to build, and in which water would flow at 1.725 feet per second, delivering up to sixty million gallons a day.

Of greater significance, Jervis balked at Douglass's plan, already accepted by the commissioners, for hydraulic cement in only the facing of the masonry, with cheaper quick lime in the backing. Hydraulic cement had been discovered by Canvass White when Jervis worked under him on the Erie Canal; though hydraulic cement throughout would increase the cost by some $250,000, Jervis had long considered it essential in all water-related construction. One commissioner (unnamed in Jervis's later account) objected, and the issue was "earnestly discussed" at several meetings. Jervis exhausted his arguments in favor of the impervious but expensive cement, then announced that if the commissioners insisted on lime, "*they* must assume the responsibility for the measure." Faced with responsibility for the failure of the aqueduct, the commissioners "finally yielded" to the judgment of their new chief engineer. Inspectors of masonry would be appointed for every two miles of aqueduct, paying particular attention to the mortar.[19]

Jervis met no resistance in reorganizing the construction process. Abandoning Douglass's proposal for forty, one-mile sections, Jervis divided the entire project into four divisions of roughly ten miles apiece, comprising a total of ninety-seven sections varying in length to conform to the particular topography. Following the line established by Douglass, the first division traced the southern arc of the Croton Valley from the dam down to the Hudson, then turned south through Sing Sing to the farm of Reverend William Creighton. The second division continued south along the Hudson, crossing the Pocantico (or Mill) River at Sleepy Hollow, and on through Tarrytown and Dobbs Ferry to architect George Harvey's property at Livingston's Landing near Hastings. The third division ran through Hastings down to Yonkers, cutting inland two miles across the Saw Mill River and Tibbit's Brook to Fordham Church, just east of the northern tip of Manhattan. The fourth division ran from Fordham, across the Harlem, and down Manhattan to the planned distributing reservoir near 42nd Street.

A resident engineer would supervise each division. As the title implied, the engineer would be quartered along the line, along with several first and second assistants, plus rodmen and axemen. The resident engineer's major responsibility was to implement the plans and specifications in his division and make sure that the contractors were doing the work correctly. Once a month during the summer construction season (April through October) and several times during the winter, each resident would report to Jervis on how much work the contractors had satisfactorily completed; Jervis would pass the information on to the water commissioners, who would pay the contractors accordingly. Thus, only with the resident's approval could a contractor expect to get paid.[20]

While digesting Jervis's reports to them, the commissioners issued their first report of the Jervis era to the Common Council. They described in the briefest terms their switch to Jervis from Douglass (who had exhibited "much lack of energy"), but noted the continuing problems of land acquisition, which had so confounded the commissioners' relationship with Douglass.

The total amount of land needed from the Croton down to the Harlem was put at just over 813 acres, of which more than half—454 acres—was still not purchased. The three state appraisers named the previous September were popular Westchester men but in their travels along the line during the fall they met with many "unreasonable demands" by landowners sniffing windfalls. Many owners were dividing their woods and fields into village lots in advance of the appraisers, making acquisition more difficult and expensive. For example, Van Brugh Livingston sold a marble quarry and fifteen acres of land near Hastings to George Harvey for $1,200 in 1834; four years later, Harvey sold 1.354 of those acres to the city for $2,500 and required the building of an aqueduct bridge over his inclined railroad from the quarry to the Hudson landing.[21]

The water commissioners announced that they had hired Daniel Tallmadge to act as their attorney in these and other legal issues. The commissioners also reported to the council that significant questions existed about the rebuilding of roads that would be flooded by the Croton dam, and expressed concern about a growing public perception, in Westchester especially, that they were accountable to no one.[22]

Jervis thought the land appraisers "rather liberal," but legal appeals of the disaffected delayed final resolution of many claims for months and years.[23] Still, land troubles did not delay Jervis's engineering plans; by the end of February he had submitted general plans for the entire line, and specifics for the two major structures in the first division: the dam and the crossing of Sing Sing kill.

The dam would be a significant structure, "a mass of substantial stone masonry, combined together with hydraulic cement," fronted by a massive earth-filled embankment lined with stone. Jervis planned a dam fifty feet high, set on the river's rock bed, elevating the water forty feet above its natural level, 166 feet above mean tide. The masonry portion would be sixty-nine feet thick at its base, tapering up its downriver side to seven feet along the lip of a spillway or waste weir a hundred feet long. The embankment, buffering the upriver side of the dam, would span the river's breadth of nearly three hundred feet, and spread 250 feet wide at its base, tapering to fifty feet wide at the top; the embankment would be sixty-five feet high, rising as abutments fifteen feet above either side of the spillway, with a stone retaining wall in its backing down to the masonry lip of the dam. The lake created by the dam would cover four hundred acres, backing up the river five miles and containing some 500 million gallons of water, of which 30 million daily gallons could enter the aqueduct through a channel in the dam's southern abutment.[24]

To cross the 536-foot-wide valley at Sing Sing, Jervis abandoned Douglass's elaborate multiple-arch bridge concept for long, narrow, solid stone walls on either side of a single, elliptical arch, in a "plain and substantial style of architecture." With a span of eighty feet, the arch would have a vertical height of twenty-five feet, seventy feet above the stream.

Jervis recognized that even this single arch was susceptible to a problem that had plagued elevated masonry aqueducts from ancient Rome to America, including the High Falls Aqueduct carrying the Delaware and Hudson Canal, and the Little Falls Aqueduct carrying the Erie, with which he was intimately familiar. The problem was leakage from the waterway and destructive freezing and expansion in the supporting structure; though it had been laid with the best hydraulic cement, Little Falls showed frost damage just a dozen years after its completion. Jervis found the answer in a pioneering work of the great Scottish engineer Thomas Telford. At the beginning of the century, Telford had used fixed cast iron plates in the bottom of the Chirk Aqueduct on the Ellesmere Canal in Wales;

the canal had never leaked. Engineers had fabricated similar troughs on a later Scottish canal with similar results. "After much reflection," Jervis concluded that "the aqueduct over heavy arches, after being made of the best hydraulic masonry, should be lined with cast iron, impervious to water."[25]

Though the plans for both the arch and the dam were soon altered, at the end of February, Jervis and the commissioners placed the first advertisements for sealed bids on the construction of all twenty-three sections of the first division. In addition to the dam and the Sing Sing arch, the division included seven tunnels, several culverts, and roughly eight and a half miles of regular conduit. Bids were due in two months, work to be completed by October 1839. Jervis and the commissioners placed newspapers ads in the city, Westchester, and upstate, as well as in Hartford and Philadelphia.[26] After four and a half months on the job, John Jervis was ready to build an aqueduct.

The Building Begins, Slowly

On the first Saturday after the ad's appearance, angry Westchesterites met to map a strategy against the aqueduct. The meeting, organized by Theodorus Van Wyck, who had demonstrated in the city against the public referendum two years earlier, produced a memorial to the legislature, arguing that the 1835 water law unconstitutionally extended the boundaries of New York City by "invading the historic manor of Cortlandt and the County of Westchester." If the "river waters of Westchester County are to be taken from it, how is it to rise in arts, manufacturing and farming?" the landowners asked. They suggested that New York City, in reaching the limits of its natural water supply, had developed all that it should, and other regions of the state, like amply watered Westchester, should be the focus of development. The memorialists asked that the 1835 law be repealed and that they be left free "peaceably to enjoy, retain or dispose of their respective real estates and property." Whether the memorial was a disingenuous effort to raise the economic stakes or the expression of rural landowners fearing the end of a way of life, the water commissioners dispatched their lawyers to Albany to shut it down.[27]

The grumblings from Westchester were shortly drowned out by ruptures on Wall Street. Days after the inauguration of Martin Van Buren as president, the banking policies of Andrew Jackson came to their natural conclusion. A panic swept the stock market on March 17 when a major lender stopped millions of dollars worth of payments. In the coming days and weeks, dozens of empty credit houses collapsed. When all New York banks announced the suspension of specie payments early in May, the Panic of 1837 was official. "The immense fortunes which we heard so much about in the days of speculation," lamented Philip Hone who only barely escaped himself, "have melted away like the snows before an April sun." The country spiraled into a full depression over the next six years, matching the construction period of the Croton Aqueduct. Water stock, which in its first issue in 1835 had sold at 12½ percent above par, began a free fall past par and beyond.[28]

A further complication for the water commissioners and their chief engineer was a power shift in city government. The April elections swept Whig Aaron Clark into the mayor's office and a narrow Whig majority into the Common Council; a "wholesale" removal of Democrats from appointed offices followed, creating a hostile political environment for the Democratic water officials. "As the Whigs now rule N. York," Benjamin Jervis wrote later that year to his older brother John, "you do not probably feel very certain of retaining your charge of the Water Works." In fact, engineer and commissioners were safe in their jobs until Whig rule extended to Albany, which would take a few more years.[29]

In these sensitive economic and political times, New York City began signing up contractors to build its aqueduct. Still, when the commissioners began opening the sealed bids at the end of April, they found no shortage of applicants. Over two dozen companies had submitted bids, most for multiple sections. Some sections received as many as nine bids.

For the time being, however, it was a smaller class of contractors than first anticipated. Though all twenty-three sections of the first division had been bid on, only thirteen sections were immediately put under contract. Jervis later wrote that this was "in consequence of the proposals being considered too high" on certain sections; the commissioners reported that the early days of the economic panic prevented too much of a commitment as that point. "A deadly calm pervades this lately flourishing city," Philip

Hone remarked that spring; the commissioners reflected this by holding off on contracts for ten sections.

Jervis thought the bid winners "a very able class of contractors." Those who did win contracts did so at prices far beyond what had been antic-ipated, despite the competition. To the chief engineer, this "was not strange, as the work was new at the time, and the contractors felt an uncer-tainty as to its cost." Notable among the winners was a group led by Stephen Clark of Albany, who bid on every section but won only the first five, including the dam at $117,558. Samuel Roberts bid on five sections but won only two; James Faulkner of Yonkers bid on eight but won only one. Timothy N. Ferrell bid on six but won only section 15, the rugged ridge separating the Croton and Hudson Valleys just north of Sing Sing. Calling for two tunnels totaling nearly nine hundred feet through solid rock, section 15 was the most expensive at nearly $145,000. A Philadel-phia company, Young and Scott, won its only bid, section 20, comprising a tunnel and the Sing Sing kill crossing, which went for nearly $91,000, the third most expensive contract of the April letting.

The thirteen contracts totaled $921,698. With eighty-six sections yet to go, it was clear to anyone paying attention that the Croton Aqueduct was going to be substantially more than a $5 million project.[30]

If work began slower than hoped, Jervis was not prevented from hir-ing and assigning the engineers of his choice, a luxury not enjoyed by his predecessor. He brought in Peter Hastie as a resident engineer, tem-porarily assigned to both the third and fourth divisions. Hastie's primary responsibility for the 1837 season was conducting surveys for the aque-duct line on Manhattan, which Douglass had not completed. Edward H. Tracy, who like Hastie had served under Jervis on the Chenango and Erie Canals, was hired as a second assistant on the third division. Hastie's other assistants were also familiar to Jervis: second assistant James Ren-wick, Jr., was the nineteen-year-old son of Jervis's friend and business asso-ciate; first assistant William Jervis was a younger brother of the chief. Also working under Hastie was the versatile Thomas Carmichael; he spent May on a small boat in the Harlem a mile above Macomb's Dam, taking soundings of the riverbed where Jervis expected the aqueduct to cross. Up in Westchester, Jervis stuck with Douglass engineers French and Anthony, who were made resident engineers of the first and section divisions, respectively. They continued to impress the new boss with their knowledge of the northern sections coming under contract first.[31]

Before starting work, contractors signed a standard agreement that detailed their responsibilities, not only pertaining to construction standards but also to behavior. The last paragraph of the "Articles of Agreement" sought to maintain order along the line by prohibiting contractors to "give or sell any ardent spirits to [their] workmen . . . or allow any to be brought on the work by the labourers."[32]

Keeping liquor off the Croton was a noble policy but not one destined for much success. Drinking on the job was tolerated and even encouraged in hard labor jobs throughout the 1830s in New York. Spurred by temperance movements, alcohol gradually gave way to coffee at midcentury as the preferred workplace stimulant, but along the Croton line, whiskey mills sprang up to fill the demand of the laborers.[33]

Various Croton legal issues were resolved that spring in Albany. Casting aside the Van Wyck memorial that sought to halt the project, the legislature passed a law specifying procedures for land acquisition, compensation for property to be flooded by the dam, and rebuilding of affected roads and bridges. The law also called for the water commissioners to report on the progress of the Croton project semiannually; this would help answer complaints of imperiousness by the commissioners, who previously had no obligation to make public reports.[34]

The first building season got under way smoothly. By the end of May, Young and Scott's crews were "actively prosecuting their work" in Sing Sing; dam activity was to begin shortly. "These operations in our vicinity, already add considerably to the business life and activity of our village," gushed the *Westchester Herald,* "and give indication of the coming prosperity and advantages which this work will confer upon our place."[35]

By the end of June, 390 men were employed on the works, most of them unskilled Irish immigrant laborers. The real numbers of Irish were much higher. The men often brought their wives and children, and set up residence along the line in "shantees" provided by the contractors. The Croton's "shanty Irish" proved unwelcome in many of the old Dutch and English enclaves of Westchester.[36]

The men were hired by the contractors at an agreed daily wage of six shillings, or seventy-five cents. This was not much, but it wasn't terribly bad, either. Irish immigrants were the great labor force in New York during the second quarter of the 1800s; of 166,000 immigrants to the United States in 1836 and 1837, nearly fifty thousand were Irish entering at New York City. The average wage for unskilled laborers of a dollar a day during much of New York's antebellum period was more akin to the pay of skilled workers back home but was increasingly hard to find during the economic crisis that had just begun. Six shillings in the spring of 1837 was a relative windfall for workers emigrating from economic collapse and unemployment in Ireland to panic in America.[37]

The Irish did not become American overnight. Many brought with them deeply held and conflicting Irish identities, which divided them into "Corkonians" from the south and "Fardowns" (Anglicized Gaelic for "men of County Down") from the north. These allegiances, often enforced by oath in secret societies upon arrival in New York, had already been manifested in violence on American canal and railroad projects several years before the Croton work began.[38] For the time being, neither patriotic nor wage unrest were in evidence on Jervis's line.

Just before Independence Day, 1837, the water commissioners issued the first of their newly mandated semiannual reports. In forty-four pages, the commissioners mixed the good news with the bad. Noting that contractors were bound to keep "spiritous liquors" off the works, peace thus far existed where construction was ongoing. "As yet, no complaints have been made, and the Commissioners entertain the hope, that the evils anticipated by some worthy citizens of West Chester, will not be realized."

On the other hand, although the commissioners had dispensed only $135,121.57 thus far, they warned that "the total cost of the project will far exceed" the original estimates, though they offered no new estimate. "The country through which our line of aqueduct has to pass, affords, perhaps, as few facilities for the avoidance of labor and expense as any other portion of the State; we are met at every step with deep ravines, which must be passed, either by embankment or bridge; or elevated hills, which must be pierced by a tunnel of more or less extent." None of this was news to the commissioners, who nonetheless found it convenient to lay the blame for higher than expected contract and land prices on "the Engineers originally employed to make the necessary examinations."[39] Chairman Allen rarely missed an opportunity to denigrate ex-chief Douglass.

Privately, Allen later groused that Douglass's estimate of $65,000 for land purchases fell short by four times the actual cost, but high prices could not have been any real surprise. "Being mainly speculators themselves," wrote the *New York Sun* in mid-June, "the Commissioners must have known that landholders are seldom diffident in taking advantage of public improvements, to enhance the price of property."[40]

Though the commissioners did not offer details in their report, chief engineer Jervis was encountering problems with the two major structures then under contract, the dam and the Sing Sing arch.

Despite hopeful local newspaper reports about impending work at the dam, none in fact had been done. The water commissioners had decided upon the location at Garretson's Mill and, for the sake of contracting the work, Jervis has agreed to it over the winter. Come warm weather, though, he began new surveys of the area, which continued into midsummer when the river fell. At the end of July, Jervis decided to shift the dam site about 400 feet downriver from the location staked by Douglass, resulting in several important design modifications. The southern end of the dam could be carried right up to a rock bluff, dispensing with an abutment and other masonry work; water would enter the aqueduct through a short tunnel through the bluff. On the other hand, Jervis found less bedrock than expected in the river bed, forcing him to shorten the waste weir from one hundred to ninety feet. Jervis would come to regret this narrowing of the river's passage over the dam.

More immediately, the new dam specifications actually reduced the cost of the work and brought protests from contractor Clark and company. Jervis advised Clark and the water commissioners that the contract envisioned possible changes and if Clark refused to abide, the contract should be voided. In September, the commissioners did so. They solicited new bids in October, and in November the team of Henry Crandall and William Van Zandt won the contract for the redesigned dam; their low bid of $85,389 was over 27 percent less than Clark and his partners had bargained for. Although it saved money, the redesign meant that no significant construction would be done on the dam during 1837.[41]

The changes at Sing Sing were less momentous. Shortly after breaking ground in May, the contractors discovered that, as with the dam, there was less bedrock than preconstruction surveys suggested. Thus, Jervis had to shorten the abutments and enlarge the arch's span from eighty to eighty-eight feet and its height from twenty-five to thirty-three feet. To support the building of this grander arch, Jervis now specified a wooden centering plan like that employed by the great Scottish bridge engineer John Rennie for London's multiarched Waterloo Bridge, completed in 1817. Unlike with the dam, these and several other new specifications did not materially interfere with Young and Scott's continuing work on the crossing.[42]

A Writer's Eye on the Croton

In the summer of 1837, Jervis added to his engineering staff. His chief objective was bringing in Horatio Allen as his principal assistant. Allen, after concluding his historic railroad work in South Carolina, had married in 1835 and gone abroad with his wife, studying the modern public works of England and France and ancient works in Rome and Egypt.[43] Allen eventually accepted the position, but didn't arrive on the Croton until the spring of 1838. Learning by his side would be an assistant who had joined the project in 1837.

Fayette Bartholemew Tower (1817–57) was a young man with large hopes, a restless nature, and an artist's sensitivities. Tower was born into a family of moderate means in Waterville, New York, in the same upstate county that had spawned Canvass White. After displaying an interest in engineering while attending local schools, Tower enrolled at nearby Hamilton College with the reluctant approval of his older brother Charlemagne who, after the death of their father, controlled the family purse strings. "I think that an education makes a person feel a consciousness of self strength in ability which the man without education cannot feel," sixteen-year-old Fayette wrote to Charlemagne; "If you have any regard for my happiness I wish you would let me go on and get an education."[44] Dissatisfied with Hamilton, Fayette unsuccessfully beseeched his brother to investigate a vacancy at West Point, where Fayette dreamed of formal training as an engineer: "I want a good education or none at all."[45] An appointment to West Point never materialized, but Tower did find his own way in the winter of 1835–36 to Vermont's Norwich University, a military school that at least offered courses in topographical drawing. A Chenango Canal

FIGURE 31. Fayette Bartholemew Tower, 1843

Tower, shown in a wedding portrait with his second wife, served five years as an assistant engineer on the Croton construction; his private letters and published illustrations reveal a sensitive writer and accomplished artist, as well as a young man seeking professional fulfillment. (Helen Tower Wilson.)

contractor for whom Tower had worked the previous summer recommended Fayette to Norwich.[46]

By the summer of 1836, Tower's sporadic education in central New York was over; he was on upper Manhattan in the village of Harlem, working for his Chenango employer on surveys for the New York and Albany Railroad, an important but difficult project that had not progressed much since its incorporation four years earlier.[47] Tower's surveys that summer took him fifty miles north through central Westchester County's rugged terrain, "the *meanest country* that I ever met with," where "the inhabitants have generally corresponded with the face of the country."[48]

After this unpleasant introduction to Westchester, Tower was back upstate by early 1837, conducting surveys for a railroad linking Oswego on Lake Ontario through swamps and forests to Utica, near his hometown. It may have been during his Westchester work that Tower became aware of plans for the Croton Aqueduct, because by early summer he had applied to Jervis for a job. In July, Tower accepted the employment offer that changed his life and brought a writer's eye to life on the Croton.[49]

Engaged at about $83 a month as a first assistant on the first division, the impressionistic young engineer described his entry into the "wild and romantic" Croton Valley in a letter to his mother:

> Leaving Sing Sing the road pursues a northerly direction, winding through lovely groves opening at intervals with a view upon the glorious Hudson, then closing again leaving the imagination to perfect what the eye did not catch of the picture. . . . Leaving the valley of the Hudson, the road winds along diverging here and there to approach some neat cottage and view the beauty of its gay parterre in front; then climbing the steep ascent to its summit it plunges into the landscape beneath, and thus it continues until you come into the "wild region of the Croton."

Immersed in the rugged landscape, Tower was astonished at the engineering difficulties involved but certain of the result:

> This work when completed will compare with anything of the kind in this country or in Europe, and I think it will be visited by foreigners

not only as a model but as an illustration of what the ingenuity of man led on by the pure light of science can accomplish, and they will admire the gigantic undertaking and the boldness of conception. . . . I shall devote myself to the work and let my whole mind be upon it and I shall be happy to have my name identified with the work tho in a small degree.[50]

Life on the remote Croton was both physically debilitating and intellectually lonely for the young engineer, but there were regular diversions, including the visits of official New York, for which Tower and the other engineers served as tour guides. At the end of August, members of the Common Council spent a day of "delightful rustication" in the Croton Valley, "courteously received and entertained by the contractors and workmen, along the work," so far as the *Westchester Herald* could make out.[51]

Getting Up the Irish

The *Herald* did not see fit to disturb the serenity with an account of the Croton's first recorded labor unrest. On the day of the council's visit, a White Plains paper, the *Westchester Spy*, reported that some three hundred laborers on the line north of Sing Sing had "made a strike for higher wages" just a few days earlier. The strikers presently were engaged in "a general fight" with contented workers, in which several combatants were hurt. When word reached Sing Sing, an armed militia was dispatched but arrived at the scene to find the striking and fighting ended.[52]

Wage strikes on the Croton would become more significant in future seasons, but were generally unproductive and hard to maintain. There was no labor movement per se in 1830s New York; few workers were unionized, and job actions were impromptu affairs that often began at the morning muster. The spring of 1836 had been a boom season for spontaneous walkouts over wages, especially at city shipyards, but nascent union activity and further strikes were aborted by the economic panic of the following spring. By 1838, the downward economy ended any hopes for labor solidarity for another decade.[53] Still, a somewhat different economy held on the Croton, an enormous publicly funded project with some immunity from the general business malaise; as construction activity increased, so did the demand for workers, who would occasionally take collective action.

Formal allegations of worker transgressions during the 1837 season were made at land appraisal hearings. During the fall, Gabriel and Joshua Purdy, Henry Lounsberry, and Robert Tompkins, members of the county's oldest and largest farming families, complained of the theft of wood, corn, and apples, though they couldn't be sure aqueduct workers were to blame. It was also alleged that "noises, riots and drunken revels" had made the vicinity of aqueduct construction "extremely unpleasant" and, indeed, "unsafe and imprudent for a respectable female to walk on, or near, or along." Other farmers, though, indicated that "the laborers are a civil people."[54]

If whiskey was the tonic, religion was the opiate of some of the laboring masses, whose numbers had reached over six hundred by midsummer. Few if any Roman Catholics had settled in Westchester before the Croton Irish arrived, who found no established place for religious observances. This changed when Father James Cummiskey came to Sing Sing. Cummiskey, who had established St. Joseph's Church in New York several years earlier, began conducting services for the laborers in a hastily erected "rude frame building" on a plot purchased for the purpose. By one account, the barnlike structure overflowed with worshipers, and the good people of Sing Sing for a time became accustomed to "brawny laborers kneeling on the grass outside." Over the next several years, the interment of several bodies induced the village fathers to clamp down and the site was abandoned. By the time Father Cummiskey left Westchester around 1840, he had given Catholic services in makeshift accommodations all along the line, most notably near the Saw Mill River crossing where a small building became the county's first permanent Roman Catholic chapel.[55]

Of the many thousands of Irish immigrants who put in time on the aqueduct line, few left a record of their lives. One who did was perhaps typical of the minimally disruptive group attracted to the project in its first year. James Delaney was born into a farming family in Cullahill, County Queens, in 1815. Left fatherless as an infant, he eventually learned the stonemason trade and emigrated to New York in the spring of 1836, with a plan to share in the rebuilding boom after the Great Fire. Instead, he first found work on construction projects in the Hudson River valley before being hired on to the Croton in the fall of 1837. Delaney remained with the Croton as a skilled stonemason for most of the next six years. Later, he became a stonework contractor on dams, canals, and other projects from Brooklyn to Maine, and settled in Holyoke, Massachusetts, where he built bridges, mills, churches, the city hall, and the Marble Building, a local landmark for many decades. "He has always done his work in a thorough and substantial manner," wrote a contemporary local historian when Delaney was an older man; one imagines his Croton employers being similarly impressed.[56]

Hard Work, Hard Questions

Delaney came to the work just as a second portion of the aqueduct was put under contract. Jervis had readied plans for the second division during the summer; in early September contracts were made for all of that division, as well as the remaining sections of the first division, making a total of fifty-three sections under contract. Among current contractors, Samuel Roberts won two first division sections that had been withheld in April; Timothy Ferrell and a partner added two second division sections. Among numerous first-time contractors was Thomas Carmichael, the draftsman turned quarry hunter and Harlem bottom sounder; putting his researches to profitable use, Carmichael and partners won sections 21 and 22, south of Sing Sing.[57]

Another new contractor of note was George Law, who submitted winning bids for sections 32 and 33, including the significant Mill River crossing near Washington Irving's Sleepy Hollow estate outside Tarrytown. The youngest of three sons born to an earnest but struggling Irish immigrant farmer in upstate New York, Law had left home in 1824 at the age of eighteen. After various laboring jobs on canals and other works from New Jersey to North Carolina, he had gained enough knowledge of stone cutting and brickwork to win his first subcontract in 1829, to build a lock on the Lehigh Canal. Over the next eight years, Law became a regular contractor on Pennsylvania canal works, accumulated some wealth, married a Philadelphia woman, and moved to New York in the summer of 1837

FIGURE 32.   *George Law, circa 1855*

Law, shown here in an engraving from a presidential campaign biography, rose from poor upstate farm boy to Fifth Avenue millionaire, boosted by his Croton contracts, especially for the High Bridge. (General Research Division. The New York Public Library. Astor, Lenox and Tilden Foundations.)

to bid on the Croton. "He had a talent for making money out of other people," wrote an unkind biographer of the man who eventually owned steamship, railroad, and ferry lines from New York to California, financed foreign intrigues, and was considered for the presidency in 1856 on the Know-Nothing ticket. A coarse, slovenly, and bloated Fifth Avenue millionaire who disdained the masses, "Live-Oak George" allegedly was "one of the most unpopular men" in democratic New York by the late 1860s: "a self-made man [who] worships his creator." Far from made in 1837, George Law was still an obscure contractor taking a big chance in Westchester.[58]

The Mill River crossing presented the most challenging engineering on the second division. The riverbed was over seventy feet below the grade line of the aqueduct, and the hollow through which the river ran was some three hundred feet across. Jervis had spent much time analyzing the options before rejecting a multiarched bridge (as first proposed by Douglass) in favor of a massive embankment with two sixteen-foot culverts (later reduced to one of twenty-five feet) for the river to pass through; it would be the highest embankment on the entire line.[59]

At nearly $100,000 (some 40 percent less than the rejected arched bridge), the structure that George Law would build was among $2 million worth of contracts in the September letting, for a total of over $3 million dollars on just the first two of four divisions. The Croton was proving to be far more than a $5 million project but, by the end of the first construction season, the commissioners and their chief engineer could be satisfied that half of the aqueduct was under contract.[60]

Later that month, the city finally appropriated ground for a receiving reservoir at York Hill and a distributing reservoir at Murray Hill; plans for the intermediate reservoir were scrapped. Also in September, Jervis traveled to Washington for consultations with John Abert about his Potomac (or Alexandria) Aqueduct, the eastern extension of the Chesapeake & Ohio Canal over the Potomac River.[61]

In the meantime, his engineers remained hard at work. "My knowledge of what is going on in the world is quite . . . circumscribed," Fayette Tower wrote his mother in early November. In four months, he had missed only one day of work, when he went to New York to pick up his theodolite sent from home.[62]

In midmonth, Alexander Wells's *Hudson River Chronicle*, a new Whig competitor in Sing Sing to the Democratic *Westchester Herald*, took a tour of the line north of Sing Sing and found several sections nearly complete, including one large embankment: "a wall some fifteen thick is carried to nearly thirty feet in height, composed first of layers of large flat stone, compactly laid, and then a course of stone pounded to the size of pebbles, that every crack and crevice are filled up; and upon this is a thick laying of stone and water cement, that the whole may become as one solid rock." Elsewhere, tunnel blasting had reached two hundred feet in some sections. "It is supprising [*sic*] to observe how beauty and solidity are blended in the construction of this stupendous work," enthused Wells, who believed "that better or finer cannot be found in the United States, than that now being done on the Croton Works." Over-optimistically, the paper calculated that the aqueduct would be completed on schedule and for less money than estimated.[63]

Progress reports from Westchester slowly made their way into papers in the city. "There are more than twenty miles of this work under contract and in progress," the *Evening Post* informed its readers early in December. The labor force had reached twelve hundred men, and some three thousand were expected to find employment in spring. During the winter season, though, no masonry could be laid and laborers were let go; those who remained saw their daily wages reduced from six to five shillings.[64]

Excavation and tunneling was the only work that could be done during the winter season, and it was becoming a deadly task. In December, one man was killed and two others injured while setting a charge inside a tunnel on Ferrell's increasingly dangerous section 15. "The accident is supposed to have occurred from small stones which were carelessly thrown into the charge while tamping," reported the *Hudson River Chronicle*, which noted that the dead Irishman's body was conveyed to a Hudson River steam boat by three hundred of his countrymen for burial in New York. The paper also related the circumstances of another Irish laborer's death on a different section. "He had prepared a blast and laying down a short train of powder, imprudently applied a match: he was thrown a number of rods, his head nearly blown off, and his body cruelly lacerated; his death must have been instantaneous." Setting a precedent, these first reported deaths on the Croton were blamed on the victims: "It is but justice to say that both the above accidents were the result of carelessness"[65]

Workers had blasted out over six hundred feet of tunnel by the end of December, when the commissioners issued their next semiannual report to the Common Council. It included significant reports from their chief engineer on the Harlem crossing and the reservoirs and other structures on Manhattan.[66]

Jervis had studied the general ideas of Canvass White and John Martineau, who had each suggested an embankment carrying a pipe siphon, and David Douglass, who had envisioned an arched high bridge carrying the Croton in masonry conduit at grade level. Jervis submitted plans for both.

As Douglass had observed back in 1833, the length and height of a grade-level Harlem crossing demanded a structure of unprecedented size in the United States. Stone arch bridges, of course, had been pioneered in grand style by the ancient Romans and refined in modern Europe, but there were no successful models in America of the dimensions required at the Harlem.

Jervis was well aware of troubles with two of the country's most notable bridges. The Erie Canal crossing of the Genesee River at Rochester had been accomplished with eleven Romanesque arches fifty feet wide; when it was completed in 1823, the structure, 802 feet long, was the longest stone arch bridge in the United States. Unfortunately, local sandstone was used for its construction and ten years later fear of collapse had induced Canal Commissioner Bouck to ask Jervis to examine its design; by the late 1830s, a new bridge was built, which, like its predecessor, was less than thirty feet high. At Schenectady, near the eastern end of the Erie Canal, two low, unarched stone bridges crossed the Mohawk River—one of them 1,118 feet long, rested on twenty-six piers, the longest bridge of any type in the country—but both bridges had proved costly to maintain, and in 1835, consultant Jervis had urged without success that they be replaced with a new canal segment along the Mohawk.[67]

Nonetheless, Jervis offered a plan for a Harlem high bridge of larger dimensions than imagined by Douglass. Jervis's bridge would be 1,450 feet long and rise 138 feet above high tide. It would consist of a series of sixteen arches, of eighty-foot spans across the river and fifty-foot spans across the rising plain on the Westchester side. The river arches would be supported on piers with foundations sunk as deep as thirty-two feet below the river's surface. The piers would have to be built inside massive cofferdams, from which water, mud, sand, and other untold elements would have to be evacuated until bedrock was reached.

Although pier work of comparable depths had been accomplished recently for a railroad bridge over the Schuylkill outside Philadelphia and for the Potomac Aqueduct in Washington, construction time and costs far exceeded original estimates. And, as with the Erie Canal bridges, neither the Philadelphia nor Washington bridge approached the size of the Harlem crossing.[68] Bearing all of this mind, Jervis put the cost of his Harlem high bridge at $935,745, and the frugal engineer did not favor building it.

For a mere $426,027, he could build a low bridge. Four thirty-six-inch pipes could be laid across a stone embankment with a single central arch eighty feet wide and fifty feet high to allow passage of what little navigation was then pursued on the river. (Jervis later enlarged the planned arch to 120 feet wide and sixty-five feet high.)

As they had favored Martineau's Harlem crossing over Douglass's, the commissioners were inclined to support Jervis's low bridge plan. It was cheaper, quicker, and easier to build, and would be no impediment to navigation: the central span would "admit the passage of vessels of sufficient burthen and capacity, for every useful and necessary purpose, and the high bridge could do no more." In any case, mills up at Kingsbridge, and Macomb's Dam and Coles Bridge downriver had restricted navigation of the river for many years. Additionally, the commissioners had secured an opinion from their lawyer Daniel Tallmadge that no special legislation would be needed to build the low crossing.

Still, the commissioners conceded in their report "so far as architectural display is involved, that the high bridge has the preference." Unwilling just yet to decide for themselves, the commissioners simply laid the options before the Common Council.

Jervis also submitted to the commissioners, and they to the Common Council, the location and plans for the remaining work on Manhattan, again using street locations that existed as yet only on paper. From the

Harlem crossing at 173rd Street, the masonry aqueduct line would follow the lay of the undulating highland southwest for a mile to the line of
Tenth Avenue; featured along the way would be several high embankments
and a 234-foot tunnel near Madam Jumel's mansion. Running straight
another mile toward the village of Manhattanville, the conduit would
encounter Manhattan Hill, which would be tunneled for some 1,215
feet, the conduit emerging at the entrance to Manhattan Valley, where a
0.8-mile siphon of two three-foot pipes would transit the depression, dip-
ping over a hundred feet below the grade line at its deepest point. Rising
out of the southern side of the valley, Asylum Hill would be tunneled for
640 feet; this would be the last of the aqueduct's sixteen tunnels, totaling
6,841 feet. Continuing again as brick conduit, the line would run south
for half a mile before angling over just west of Ninth Avenue to enter Clendening Valley, fifty feet deep and nineteen hundred feet long. Here the conduit, lined with iron in a similar fashion to that in the Sing Sing arch, would
be carried along an elevated bridge, hollowed again like the Sing Sing structure, and featuring a series of arches to accommodate six future cross streets
and sidewalks; two arches twenty-seven feet across would cross the widest
of these streets, 96th Street, with fourteen-foot arches over sidewalks on
either side. From the Clendening Valley, the final mile of brick conduit
would curve down to the northwest corner of the upper of two, linked basins
of the receiving reservoir at York Hill, a great rectangle covering thirty-
five acres of rocky open land that would later be in Central Park.

The reservoir, 1,826 feet long and 836 feet wide, would have massive
sloping walls of puddled earth (i.e., earth lined with a watertight "puddle"
or paste of wet clay and sand) on the interior, unadorned stone on the outside, eighty feet wide at the base, tapering to eighteen feet at the top, as
much as thirty feet high. After excavation of earth and rock, the north basin
was to hold twenty feet of water, the south basin twenty-five feet, making for a capacity of 150 million gallons. By contrast, the total capacity
of the reservoirs and tanks of the Manhattan Company and the 13th Street
system was no more than half a million gallons.

From the York Hill Reservoir, three lines of three-foot pipe would run
east to the line of Fifth Avenue, then south along a still-rolling terrain for
nearly two miles to the distributing reservoir at Murray Hill. At 420 feet
square and containing 20 million gallons of water in two basins, the

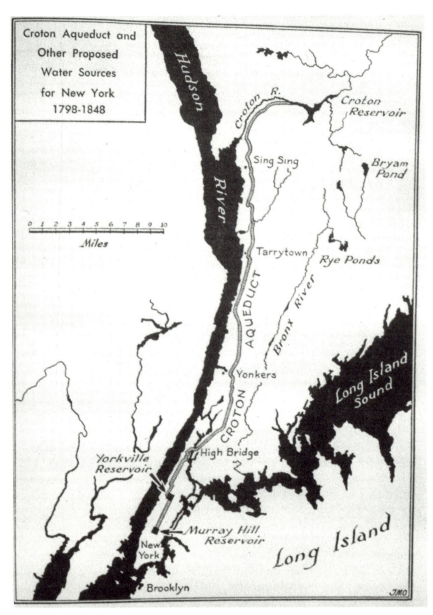

FIGURE 33. Map of Croton Aqueduct and proposed New York City water sources, 1798–1848

This map shows the major rivers and ponds considered for supplying the city. The unnamed river emptying into the Hudson River above Tarrytown is the Mill or Pocantico River; not shown is the Saw Mill River, which runs between and parallel to the Croton Aqueduct and the Bronx River before emptying into the Hudson at Yonkers. (From *Water for the Cities,* by Nelson Blake, courtesy Syracuse University Press.)

Murray Hill reservoir would be a fraction of the size of the receiving reservoir but clearly the display object of the works on Manhattan. In order to maintain a suitable elevation for the water, the reservoir's sloping masonry walls would be on average forty-five-and-a-half feet high, allowing for a water depth of thirty-six feet and a waterline 115 feet above mean tide, some fifty-one feet lower than the water level up at the Croton Dam. The adornment of the reservoir's outer walls, beveled at one to six, would be Egyptian, with raised pilasters at the corners and temple-like entry doors in midwall pilasters. An Egyptian-style cornice would ring the top of the reservoir's walls, some seventeen feet wide, where there would be an iron railing to create a public promenade.

The bad news from the commissioners was the cost. Six months after they warned generally that the estimates of the original engineers would be far exceeded, the commissioners put a new price tag on the work: $8,464,033, nearly $3.5 million more than the public had voted to allot in 1835. The cost would rise much higher still.

Taking the High Road?

There can scarcely be a doubt, that the work will stand the test of time,
and answer all the purposes for which it is designed.
—Henry Schenck Tanner, *Description of the*
Canals and Railroads of the United States

The years 1838 and 1839 determined the fortunes of the Croton project. Labor unrest, a withered economy, a fierce struggle over the Harlem crossing, and political upheaval threatened the work. Yet the water commissioners and their engineers remained focused on construction and at the end of the decade, with the start of construction on the Harlem bridge, the aqueduct was becoming a reality.

Winter of Some Discontent

Fortune shone on the project in the winter of 1838. The weather in January and for most of the rest of the season was mild; the ground was rarely frozen or snow-covered; excavation and tunneling continued at a faster pace than expected.[1]

The occasional deaths of laborers on other sections did little to dampen the enthusiasm of Sing Sing for the tunneling in town. On the evening of January 10, Young and Scott's workers broke through a hill, and the passage, 375 feet long, twelve feet across, and eight feet high, became an immediate attraction. "The tunnel was handsomely lighted," reported the

218

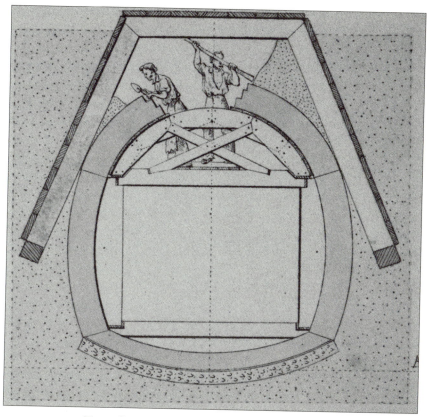

FIGURE 34. *Tunneling in earth*

Drawn by Croton draftsman Theophilus Schramke for his 1846 book on the aqueduct, the engraving illustrates the method of tunneling on the aqueduct. It is one of the few images of Croton work depicting laborers at work. (Jervis Public Library.)

Westchester Herald, "and a large number of our citizens in a body performed the subterranean trip each way." The tunneling had taken six months, with as many as twenty-five men working in shifts day and night. After the public viewing, the popular contractors set out a banquet at their Sing Sing lodgings.[2]

The Sing Sing tunnel had been blasted without injury but the casualty list lengthened elsewhere on the line. One Patrick Carr was killed by an explosion on a section down at Dobbs Ferry. An improperly extracted charge

shattered the life of a Ferrell section worker: "The unfortunate man was
. . . negligent of the precaution of keeping a sufficient quantity of water
in the hole, and when a part of the covering of the charge was removed,
a hissing noise was heard, and in the twinkling of an eye the explosion took
place."[3]

All was safe up at the dam, where Crandall and Van Zandt had arrived
with ten workers in early December. The entire section had been grubbed
and preparations were being made for construction of the dam's foundation, as well as the gatehouse for the intake gates for the aqueduct.[4]

On January 29, Fayette Tower spent his twenty-first birthday marveling
at the isolation of the Croton ("If the Canadians should cross into our
territory and plunder and destroy everything before their advancing to
this country the inhabitants here would not find it out soon enough
to retreat") and pondering his future. He was being "urged quite hard"
to join two acquaintances intending to become contractors in the spring.
"If it were not for getting aside from my profession I believe I would."
It was aggravating for him to see contractors "carry away their thousands,"
some clearing 25 percent profits, but a month later Tower rejected the
opportunity and glimpsed his fate: "I shall never make a fortune by
Engineering."[5]

No money would be made by anyone just yet at the Harlem crossing.
In early March, Jervis informed a would-be low bridge contractor that it
would be a while before any bidding.[6] The commissioners had made no
decisions on the crossing, and angry Westchesterites were organizing
their opposition to the low bridge, as well as existing obstructions downriver at Coles's Bridge and Macomb's Dam.

The Westchester ringleader this time was twenty-nine-year-old Lewis
Gouverneur Morris, an heir to the ancestral Morris lands on the Westchester side of the Harlem. At a meeting on March 3, 135 or so wealthy
Westchester landowners, including half a dozen Morrises, prepared a
memorial that young Lewis presented to the legislature. The memorial
argued that the Harlem was "an arm of the sea" that could not be crossed
in such a way as to harm its navigation. Unlike Van Wyck's effort the previous year against the entire concept of the Croton water supply, this
memorial acknowledged the city's implied right to bring water, nonetheless noting that the 1835 water law conferred no express right on the water

commissioners to cross the Harlem with the aqueduct. "As the manner of crossing the river is not designated in the act, they will not be permitted to look only at *what it will cost them*—but they must be governed by what will be *least injurious* to your memorialists." The less expensive low bridge on an embankment with a single central span would not do; only a high, arched bridge would preserve navigation rights, as well as a vision that "both shores of the Harlaem must become a city, with . . . immediate water communication with the city of New York." Incredibly or disingenuously, the landowners imagined Harlem becoming a separate, thriving city upriver from the metropolis consuming Manhattan from the south.

The memorial sought the removal of all obstructions on the Harlem, especially Macomb's Dam, built a quarter century earlier without a mandated drawbridge; the men also asked the legislature to specify how the aqueduct should cross the Harlem. The Westchesterites hired counsel to pursue their legal claims, sent a copy of their proceedings to the water commissioners, and arranged for publication of the memorial in county and city newspapers. This ensured a great bridge debate.[7]

The Whiggish *New York American* lined up for the high bridge, criticizing the commissioners, hailing fired high bridge planner Douglass, and questioning Jervis's abilities. The Democratic *Evening Post* backed the low bridge and Jervis, running a supportive letter from esteemed Fairmount engineer Frederick Graff: "The plan you have adopted in passing over Harlaem River with iron pipes, is, in my opinion, preferable to the high aqueduct; the manner you have planned the whole structure, together with the arrangement of the pipes cannot but succeed to give a copious supply of water."[8]

While the newspapers shaped public opinion over the shape of the bridge, the battle moved into the halls of state and local government. The Morris memorial came to an abrupt halt in the Assembly Committee on Grievances, which reported in early April that the low bridge would not interfere with navigation on the Harlem. As proposed by Jervis, the span of the low bridge would permit the passage of large steam boats and all but the highest masted sailing vessels, whose captains could hardly prefer the shallow, narrow Harlem to the deep water passage around Manhattan via the North (Hudson) and East Rivers.[9]

This early win at Albany for the low bridge came days after a humiliating session for Jervis before the Common Council's Committee on

Roads and Canals. Jervis was accused of scaring the water commissioners into the belief that a high bridge would settle and tumble into the river.
The hostile, Whig-dominated committee also suggested that Jervis was
simply afraid to risk a high bridge. Jervis was indignant at these charges;
he testified that he hadn't told the commissioners that the high bridge
couldn't be built, just that it would be much more expensive than the river
crossing needed to be.[10]

Any hopes of support from a change in the local government the
commissioners and Jervis might have gathered were dashed in the city elections in the second week of April. Whig Mayor Clark was reelected over
Isaac Varian (by only 519 votes out of 39,341 cast); the Whigs retained a
slender one-ward majority in the council.[11]

Not surprisingly, a majority of the road and canal committee reported
the following week that if the low bridge were built "the injury to the river
is permanent . . . and those who are to succeed us in after years, can only
express their unavailing regrets at the mistaken policy." But a minority report
issued two weeks after that derided the high bridge as "one of those wild
and visionary schemes that are often projected by speculators, for the purpose of increasing the value of their property at the expense of the public." Typically, the men of the Common Council had accomplished little
more than muddying the waters with conflicting opinions.[12]

The day after the minority report was filed, the commissioners tried
to press the council toward a decision. In a communication on May 8, the
commissioners again defended the low bridge and went so far as to suggest that it was Martineau's low bridge plan that voters had approved back
in 1835. At the same time, the commissioners conceded that if the council and the mayor wanted a high bridge built, the commissioners would
build it. But either way, the city ought to act fast. Whether high or low,
the crossing would be "a work of great magnitude, and its commencement
ought not to be delayed a moment more than what is absolutely necessary."[13] With that, the sharply divided council promptly dropped the
matter for the next two and a half months.

Financial decisions were rushing ahead much faster. At the end of
March, the legislature authorized the city to sell another $3 million in water
stock, at 6 percent interest, redeemable in twenty years. This was the
first increase in funds since the initial authorization of $2.5 million

arranged by Myndert Van Schaick back in 1834, when the project had been priced at $5 million. In accordance with the water commissioners new cost estimate of $8.5 million, the city was now authorized to spend $5.5 million.[14]

Chairman Allen, however, was not pleased. Less than $400,000 had actually been paid out by the end of 1837; by the end of 1838 total expenditures were just under $2 million. Allen rightly believed the city was mishandling the stock issues, forcing too much too soon onto the depressed market and further driving down its value. In 1837, the city had paid over $55,000 in interest and discounts on the bonds; in 1838, interest and discount payments rose to over $172,000. Allen was further outraged by the Whig-controlled council's new policies of paying water debt out of the water fund instead of new taxes, and borrowing from the fund to pay for unrelated improvements like street openings.[15]

More abhorrent to Allen was legislation sought by the city and passed in Albany in late March. In a provision of a broader law intended to raise city revenues, the legislature gave the city permission to use the Croton water stock fund to pay for all future *and past* pipe costs, including as much as $400,000 for the 13th Street distribution system. Even though plans were to tie the pipe into the Croton distribution system, the retroactive reimbursement to the city significantly reduced the money available to the commissioners. Allen condemned the arrangement as the price of Whig politics.[16]

The retroactive financing for distribution pipe opened the contentious issue of who had authority over the Croton distribution system: the state-appointed water commissioners or city government, which had been expressly excluded from Croton decision making. For the time being, the Democratic commissioners were content to let their authority end at the Murray Hill reservoir, even if the city was using Croton money to pay for the distribution system south of it.

The winter of 1838 remained uncommonly mild; by mid-March little snow remained on the ground. "Never, within our recollection," observed the *Westchester Herald*, "has the season of spring opened with a more promising aspect."[17]

The mild winter had failed to chill the anger over certain land takings, which now involved property in sections of the second division. Among

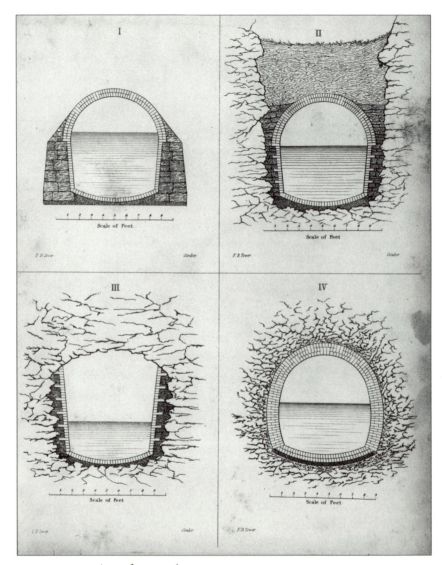

FIGURE 35. Aqueduct sections
Drawn by Fayette Tower for his 1843 book on the Croton Aqueduct, the engravings illustrate four methods of the aqueduct's construction: masonry in earth excavations, open cutting in rock, tunnel cutting in rock, and tunnel cutting in earth. (William Lee Frost; photo by Barry Rosenthal.)

other futile stands, in February, Justus Dearman threatened force against aqueduct workers to keep them from crossing his farm near the Jewell (now Barney) Brook viaduct work just above Dobbs Ferry. "Old Mr. Dearman," who had bought the farm for his retirement from the city twenty years earlier, desisted "after finding he was likely to get the worse of it." Still, the dispute with Dearman and other neighbors over the taking of their land was not settled for more than another year.[18]

For the most part, though, Westchester landowners had become reconciled to the aqueduct's passage. At the end of March, the commissioners advertised for bids on the remaining thirty-two sections in Westchester, comprising all of the third division and the six fourth division sections north of the Harlem.[19]

Labor Unrest

The 1838 building season brought the arrival of Horatio Allen. That Allen was willing to take a subordinate's role on Croton suggests just how important the Croton project was in American engineering. That Allen was a Whig and Jervis a Democrat suggests either how far the actual engineering was removed from politics, or how wise Jervis was in making it seem so. Allen was hired at an annual salary of $3,500. "It is hardly necessary for me to say," Jervis wrote the commissioners, "I consider him an able auxiliary in the department."[20] The first issue confronting Allen was a labor revolt.

The new season brought a slight increase in wages, from the five shilling winter wage back to the six shillings of the previous summer. As far as the contractors were concerned, the summer wage had been accepted by the workers "without the least anticipation" that more would be demanded.[21]

The contractors were wrong. In the first week of April, "some excitement took place" on sections of the first division north of Sing Sing. "A number of restless spirits among the laborers got up a *strike* as the phrase is, for higher wages," reported the *Westchester Herald*, "and instead of demanding in a proper way a higher wage for their labor of their employers, they clubbed together in large masses, and forced their fellow-laborers also to quit work." The turnout apparently began on the dangerous tunneling in section 15, where work had continued through the winter. Demanding as much as a dollar a day, "the malcontents" marched down to Sing Sing five hundred strong on April 5. The steadfast local magistrate, backed by armed citizens and contractors, arrested the ringleaders and induced the rest of the workers "to return to their quarters in the afternoon, without committing any serious outrages."

The *Herald* counseled peace: "We are assured the contractors in general are willing to raise the wages, but object to this mode of accomplishing it.—The wage ought to be raised,—for the winter pay would scarcely furnish [the workers] with food and clothing." Prosperity was ahead for everyone, the paper reasoned, so why battle over a few shillings?[22]

It was not until the following week, though, that Horatio Allen was able to report to Jervis that "all disturbance on the line has ceased," though not all the laborers had returned to work. For that, Allen had a suggestion: "The object is, I believe, to make the men feel the want of work, and then to re-employ them. I think it would be well to let it be known that men are in demand."[23]

Believing the revolt ended, Allen embarked on his first engineering duty, running levels above the dam site to confirm how much land the dam would overflow. Fayette Tower accompanied Allen, and was favorably impressed. "He is probably a man of more scientific acquirements than Mr. Jervis but less practical. In his travels he had devoted himself more particularly to objects connected to his profession, and he has amassed a great fund of information. . . . On the whole he is just such an Engineer as I should like to be." In the letter to his brother Charlemagne, Tower showed a mild jealousy of the independent means by which Allen had funded his years abroad, and signaled growing doubts about his own uncertain prospects. Still, Tower indicated he had decided to remain on the Croton project, drawing his modest, fixed salary.[24]

Tower returned from the surveying with mixed emotions for the changes planned. The dam would flood hundreds of cultivated acres: "many of the farmers have inherited the homesteads of the forefathers and are quietly enjoying their homes now, who will be obliged to flee to the hills from the rising waters." Despite his disdain for "Westchester people," Tower was unique among his professional contemporaries in acknowledging the local trauma.[25]

Despite Horatio Allen's generous labor policy, ill feeling remained. At the end of April, resentment turned to whiskey-fed rage. "What has been long feared from the unrestricted supply of liquor to the wretched workmen who love it on the Aqueduct, has at length transpired." The *Herald*, as well as the *Chronicle*, reported at length on "a most brutal and bloody attack" on a member of a prominent local family, and a separate "general fracas" that brought the first death and severe injuries by riot.[26]

In the first incident, Paul Lent, employed as a contractor's foreman, was beaten with clubs and left for dead near a stone quarry at nightfall by two or three laborers he had fired for their part in the strike; their replacements were "damned Corkonians," according to alleged assailant Michael Dunn. Incredibly, Lent regained consciousness, dragged himself into town, and identified Dunn and Edward O'Brien as his chief attackers.

The following morning, a fight on section 10 near Quaker Bridge between several "Corkonians" and "FarDowns" broadened into a liquored-up free-for-all involving hundreds of workers. Patrick Baxter, a second in the original fight, was killed in the "subsequent grand Waterloo contest, having his brains knocked out with a peck handle."

Suspects in both events were hauled off to jail for trial, but the *Chronicle* fingered a single culprit, "producing discords and mischief, and bringing ruin and destruction upon all around him.... His name is— *Whiskey*."

Resident engineer French was less troubled by the deadly violence on his division. He reported to Jervis that it was "nothing more than one of the usual Irish fighting frolics." "The workmen have become quiet," the *Chronicle* reported two weeks later, "the Corkonians and Far-Downs being fully satisfied that going to jail for breaking each others heads is but sorry amusement."[27]

Despite the riots, the remaining Westchester sections were put under contract in early May. The commissioners were happy to report that the "competition was spirited, and the prices lower" than expected. The twenty-six third division sections went for nearly $300,000 less than the precontracting estimate of just over $1.4 million. There were few serious engineering challenges on any of these sections (the Saw Mill River crossing involved a large but straightforward embankment and viaducts) and the depressed economy kept bids down. Jervis appointed his brother

William as resident engineer of the third division; Peter Hastie retained the more challenging fourth division. By summer, work was ongoing on all eighty-five sections in Westchester, from the dam down to the banks of the Harlem River. Section 86 was the river crossing, about which nothing had been decided.[28]

For the most part, the workers remained in line. Any inclination toward riot was dispatched at the end of May in court proceedings. Edward O'Brien and Michael Dunn were each sentenced to ten years in the state prison (at Sing Sing) for the attack on Lent, who by that time had recovered from his wounds. In separate proceedings, various rioters were sentenced to terms of up to six months in the county jail, and illegal liquor sellers were fined up to $80, a significant penalty.[29]

The only reported hindrance to work was the first of what would soon enough prove a regular and increasingly alarming occurrence in the steep and rocky terrain of the Croton Valley. After two days of heavy rain during the first week of June had swollen area streams, a "freshet" washed down the river, sweeping away a mill dam and causing considerable damage to aqueduct excavations.[30]

The only explosions along the line in June were those intentionally set. One carefully laid charge was reported to have saved the contractor some $500 in stone and labor costs: an immense rock was blasted from the path of the aqueduct "to the exact place and position where it was required to form the basement of a side or defence wall." Other blasts were less fortunate. A worker on a Ferrell section "was hit with a stone thrown by a blast some fifteen or twenty rods distant," fracturing his skull.[31]

On July 1, the workers received some compensation for the dangers they faced. Three months after the strike, the contractors suddenly increased the daily wage to a dollar a day, in some cases nine shillings. Whether the increase, which remained in effect through the fall, was a reward for labor peace, an inducement to promote it, or simply a reflection of the large demand for labor, is not clear. In any case, it represented a high water mark that, when later lowered, brought unprecedented revolt.[32]

The workers set off with their windfall to the city for the national holiday of their adopted land. "This afternoon I am seated alone in my office on the Croton," Fayette Tower wrote to his mother on July 3; "all around is quiet, the 'Pat-riots' are all leaving the work to join in the celebration tomorrow." Tower was marking his first anniversary on the Croton, content that "the star of my destiny was set in this country a year ago," and apologetic that he had no time to visit home: "an Engineer's work is never ended."[33]

The Commissioners Go Low across the Harlem

With the work unending in Westchester but stymied from the Harlem River south, the Common Council's attention was returned to the matter of the river crossing. A notorious figure in the city's water story helped the council along.

Richard Riker, the Manhattan Company apologist and recently retired longtime city recorder who had slowed the city's official response to cholera in 1832, was president of the Harlem River Canal Company. The company had been incorporated back in 1826 to cut a channel across the northernmost tip of Manhattan and thus bypass the least navigable stretch of the Harlem River. The company was also empowered to make other improvements farther south on the Harlem, all with the purpose of turning the river into a deep-water passage linking the Hudson with the East River and Long Island Sound. After some excavations in 1828, the company's charter lapsed in the early 1830s. But, with the formulation of plans to build the Harlem low bridge, Riker allied with other low bridge opponents and had the company's charter renewed by the legislature in the spring of 1838. Once again in the Harlem navigation business, Riker began lobbying the Common Council. He invited members on a summer steam boat cruise along the river's upper reaches and wined and dined them at a riverside resort. Denouncing "the suicidal policy of the Water Commissioners," Riker offered a toast: "The circumnavigation of the island of New York, derived from the God of Nature,—may it never be interfered with by any rude hand."[34]

The council did not all get drunk on Riker's rhetoric. In July, the assistants passed a resolution favoring a high bridge but also suggesting a popular vote to resolve the issue, while the aldermen passed resolutions declaring the Harlem crossing none of the council's business. The voting in both boards was not divided on party lines; both Whigs and Democrats were split on how to proceed. The full council never voted, and the debate once again moved to the newspapers.[35]

After a month of varied public opinion and continued council silence, the water commissioners took the initiative. On September 7, they advertised for bids on the low bridge, as well as for the Manhattan sections; they had earlier advertised for all the iron pipe needed from the bridge to the distributing reservoir. The *Evening Post* approved: "The Commissioners will now proceed to contract for the 'Low Bridge' across the Harlem river, according to the original plan. The whole, when finished, will be the most magnificent works in the United States."[36]

The commissioners' gambit inspired certain Harlem navigation proponents to prompt and radical action. The target was the river's most prominent existing obstruction, the wooden Macomb's Dam bridge a mile downriver from the proposed low bridge crossing. Emboldened by the opinions of counsel that force could rightfully be used to remove nuisances (i.e., the bridge without the required draw), Lewis Morris arranged an assault on the evening of September 14. Seeking to make a federal case of Harlem navigation, Morris loaded a chartered periauger, the *Nonpareil,* with out-of-state coal, and sailed up to the dam at high tide, demanding passage upriver to his dock. With no draw to raise, the bridge toll collector was unable to comply, so a crew of axe-wielding men on an escort flotilla of flat-bottom boats hacked a passage through the bridge for the *Nonpareil.* Though it bought Morris years of litigation (he eventually prevailed), the destruction of the dam removed one impediment to Harlem navigation and strengthened the high bridgers' case.[37]

Though he doubtless supported young Morris's aggressive tactics, old Richard Riker preferred less physical exertion. He and some fifty other canal company investors and Harlem-area landowners ran newspaper notices in the city and Westchester warning would-be contractors that they would take legal action "to prevent any and all persons obstructing the water at the natural channel" in any manner that would limit the passage of vessels.[38]

Despite the threatening notice, eleven bids for the low bridge contract came in by the end of October. Many of the bidders were familiar, including George Law, who submitted the low bid of $328,190. The high bid was more than double Law's, an indication of the many engineering and legal questions facing potential contractors. Law apparently retracted his bid, because the contract was awarded to the second-lowest bidder, a group of Pennsylvania men led by Lemuel Ellsworth and Hiram Mix; at $360,100, the winning bid was some $66,000 less than Jervis had estimated ten months earlier.

The competition for the major Manhattan work was even more intense. There were twenty-one bidders for section 91, the Manhattan Valley crossing, which went for $142,195. Section 94, the Clendening Valley crossing, went for just under $300,000, section 45 contractor Bishop & Campbell beating out Law and sixteen others. The York Hill receiving reservoir (section 96) was won on a bid of $565,748, making it the largest single Croton contract to date. The distributing reservoir contract (section 97) went to Thomson Price, who bested Law and eight others with a bid of $360,710.

Among the other winners on Manhattan was Thomas Carmichael, who had already completed his two upper Westchester sections. He and a partner won two low-priced but hotly contested conduit sections, including section 88, which had thirty-one bidders. Of ten bids for iron pipe, including three from English manufacturers, the winner was the familiar West Point Foundry, the company that had built pioneering steam locomotives for Jervis, Horatio Allen, and others at the beginning of the decade; for just under $100,000, the foundry would provide 2,750 tons of cast iron pipe, most thirty-six inches in diameter.

All told, the contracts from the Harlem to Murray Hill totaled over $2.2 million. Though the Harlem bridge contract would soon prove far from final, in eighteen months, Jervis and the commissioners had contracted the entire Croton Aqueduct.[39]

Awarding the low bridge contract brought renewed legal threats against the contractor by the high bridge faction, who served notice on the commissioners that a federal injunction would be sought. For the time being, though, the threat was moot; the building season was coming to a close and the commissioners had already informed the last group of contractors that incomplete land purchases on Manhattan would delay all work on those sections until the spring.[40]

Progress up the Line

At some remove from the disputes over the Harlem crossing, it had been a very productive year in Westchester. Earning their dollar a day wage, some three thousand laborers had sweated through the "ignited atmosphere" of an unusually hot and dry summer, without reported incident.[41]

After the slow start on the dam, Fayette Tower was on hand for the laying of its cornerstone on September 12: "all of us who were present felt quite enthusiastic tho we had no oration . . . or any thing of the kind to commemorate the occasion." Despite his sympathy for displaced farmers, Tower was certain the location below Garretson's Mill had been well chosen; in that summer's historic drought, the river was still flowing at twenty million gallons a day: "there will never be a want of water, tho many *would be* knowing ones predict such a thing." In general, Tower informed his brother, work was "getting on bravely," and he expected his five miles of the line to be finished by the end of the season, the entire first division but for the dam by the following year. In a personal aside, the engineer noted that two years of grueling labors had permanently diminished his endurance.[42]

Despite the gratifying progress of the work, Tower was tiring of the "monotonous course" of life in the "semi-civilization" of the Croton Valley, where some locals had been incredulous that a recent solar eclipse was predictable by calculations.[43] There was the occasional ball or soiree in the country society of Sing Sing, but even the visits of official New York were losing their charm.

A "grand day" had been anticipated at the end of September when Mayor Clark and the whole Common Council were due to arrive by steam boat, but "it rained most furiously all day" and many stayed home. As usual, the engineers served as guides on a tour that the weather conveniently served to shorten. "During the day we led them through our subterraneous passages, with torch in hand—and they plodded their way through seas of mud—the day was exceedingly unpleasant and their curiosity was soon satisfied." In the evening, Tower and the other engineers were invited to a "dinner . . . got up in grand style," presumably at public expense: "they brought wine and cooks from the city—We had roast pig, beef, oyster pies, partige [*sic*], wood cock &c," followed by pudding, wines and toasts and, "as if to drive away persons of good habits," cigars. "My companions & my self left the table, and their proceedings afterwards were enveloped in smoke."[44]

The smoke-filled rooms were soon to get smokier. In November, up and coming Whig William Seward won a rematch for governor over incum-

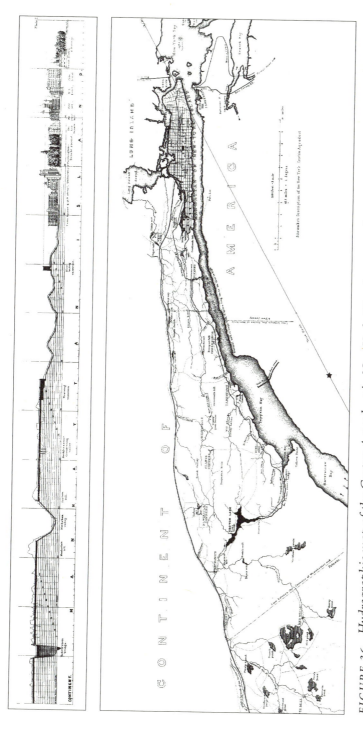

FIGURE 36. Hydrographic map of the Croton Aqueduct in New York, Westchester, and Putnam Counties

This detail of a map drawn by Theophilus Schramke for his book shows the aqueduct from source streams to Manhattan; the profile shows the aqueduct's elevations on Manhattan. (Linda Gilbert Cooper.)

bent William Marcy, who had appointed the Democratic water commissioners. Only a slender Democratic majority in the Senate protected them from replacement by Whigs.[45]

As the 1838 building season ended, Fayette Tower again found himself at a crossroads. He was friendly with the winners of the receiving reservoir contract, who had asked him to join them. "Here is a case," he wrote to his industrialist brother Charlemagne, "where my ambition comes into contact with a desire for a harty [*sic*] accumulation of money, or rather my ambition is all that wispers [*sic*] hesitation in my ears." He might earn twenty times his engineer's salary, but was reluctant to cash in. "If I prove constant in my exertions I shall be reasonably rewarded with success in my profession and I can always find enough to do, and I may depend upon a sure compensation. If I accept of this proposition I may for a year or two accumulate more money than to remain where I am." After a rare visit home for the holidays, Fayette was back on the Croton in January. "I am entirely alone here but am quite happy for I hear & see nothing of the troubles of the world."[46]

As Tower settled in for another Croton winter, the workers who remained engaged along the line saw their daily wages retreat from the treasured dollar to five or six shillings. If there were objections, they did not rise to open conflict.[47]

At year's end, the commissioners reported to the Common Council that just over eleven miles of aqueduct had been completed, roughly ten and a half miles during 1838.[48] In their relatively brief report, the commissioners did not bother to mention that only with constant oversight by the engineering corps had the work been adequately done.

Days before, Jervis had reported to the commissioners that workers had often laid masonry that appeared solid on the outside but had "numerous cavities on the interior," potentially catastrophic flaws detectable only by the "great vigilance" of inspectors. It had taken time to make contractors and workmen "understand the importance [and] practicability of complying with directions given."

Worse was work that may have been done to avoid detection. One contractor, whose men unbeknownst to him had laid a portion of conduit on a Sunday when engineers and masonry inspectors were off, was told by the resident engineer it would have to be redone in his presence. The contractor appealed to the commissioners, who referred the matter to Jervis; he backed his resident engineer. The work was redone and Jervis let the contractor know that his legal recourse was to his workers for wasting his materials.[49]

The State Says High across the Harlem

The year 1839 began with a blizzard of anti-Croton sentiment, in the form of a satirical broadside posted all over the city. "The Diaria of Freedom, or The Anti-hydrophobian Thunderbolt: A Weakly Bulletin, Published Every Half Hour, Or Oftener, As Occasion May Demand" reminded the citizenry of the Croton's slow and costly progress: "You have been taxed by the corporation to pay for the Croton Water Works! WE know it, and WE told you so five years ago."[50]

Such materials had little effect on chief engineer Jervis, who had a more worrisome problem at the end of the month. After a period of snow, hurricane-force winds, and temperatures below zero, a wind-driven rain set in on January 25. By the following day, much of Westchester had been devastated by flooding and wind damage. "Great injury was done to the Aqueduct in several places, by the rain, and washing down of the loose earth," reported the *Westchester Herald*. Several bridges over the upper reaches of the Croton were "carried away," swept down by the swollen river to the site of the ongoing dam work. In notes on "the freshet," the second in just over seven months, Jervis observed that the water had risen well above the height of the dam piers then under construction. Jervis did not record any specific damage to the dam, nor did he suggest that the dam as planned might not withstand future floods.[51]

Regardless of concerns with the dam, the focus of the project was now turning to the newly contracted sections on Manhattan. For the Clendening Valley crossing, a dedicated engineer was finally sprung from his "monotonous exile on the Croton." No more "Westchester people" for Fayette Tower. "I shall have charge of some very interesting work," he wrote to his mother in early March, "more so than any part of this great work—a great deal of mechanical work—splendid arches of masonry to support the Aqueduct." Tower's monthly pay was increased from $83.33 to $100. "I shall be drawn directly under the eye of our Chief and if I possess any merit it will be appreciated."[52]

The chief apparently believed that Tower possessed great merit. In the reorganization of the entire engineering department, first assistant Tower joined current fourth division first assistants James Renwick, Jr., and Edward Tracy, both of whom remained at $75 monthly salaries. The fourth division became the only one with three first assistants and no seconds but, if salary was any indication, the new man stood above the others.[53]

Tower may have taken some comfort in his choice to remain with the engineering department. Laborer wages were increased again to a dollar a day from April through October, cutting into the profits of contractors like his friends on the nearby York Hill reservoir. Yet, at the same time, financing for the entire project remained under threat by the continuing economic depression. Jervis wrote to Henry Anthony in March that conditions could "render the employment of the Engineer Department unnecessary."[54]

Tower arrived on Manhattan just as the Democrats were regaining local political control after two years. Isaac L. Varian defeated incumbent mayor Clark, and Democrats won twelve of the city's seventeen wards, causing Philip Hone to lament: "Violence, corruption, and immorality have prevailed. . . . The republic cannot stand."[55]

The power shift in the city did nothing to ward off the high bridge interests, who had abandoned legal threats for lobbying in Albany. With the building season approaching, Riker's canal company and the various Harlem-area landowners petitioned the Whig-controlled state Assembly. A year after a Democrat-controlled Assembly committee had reported in favor of a low bridge, the newly constituted full Assembly turned the tables, quickly and quietly passing a bill without full floor debate, calling for either a high bridge or a tunnel.

The commissioners, who learned of the bill from newspaper reports, were furious. Two of them, with Jervis in tow, rushed to Albany to prevail on the nominally Democratic Senate, but a committee had already reported the bill favorably. Out of courtesy, the commissioners were granted a hearing by the committee but the die was cast. The full Senate, feeling the Whig heat, passed the measure; on May 3, Governor Seward signed it. It was the shortest of laws—ninety words in one paragraph—but it required the commissioners to cross the Harlem on a bridge of arches at least eighty feet wide and with at least a one-hundred-foot clearance under them at high tide, or to dig a tunnel under the river bed.[56]

If the water commissioners thought that they had been had by political influence in Albany, their engineer privately felt differently. In a letter four months earlier to Potomac Aqueduct engineer John Abert, Jervis conceded that the high bridge might actually be necessary "to maintain our grade over the valley." Indeed, despite his public protestations about saving money, Jervis may have been looking forward to having the grander structure forced on him: "I cannot say by any means that I regret this— as you know Engineers are prone to gratify a taste for the magnificent when there is a good reason for the execution of prominent works."[57]

Their hands tied, the commissioners moved quickly. The act was passed on a Friday, a copy was delivered to them by counsel for high bridge interests on Monday, and on Tuesday the commissioners vacated the contract for the low bridge (on which no work had been done) and ordered Jervis to come up with suitable plans for a high bridge or a tunnel.[58]

Jervis already had plans for an arched bridge that was higher than the legislature had mandated. A tunnel would be a new challenge. There was no completed underwater tunnel anywhere in the world, and Jervis was well aware of the ongoing trouble building the first one that would eventually succeed. In London, the brilliant father and son engineers Marc and Isambard Brunel had been working on a twelve-hundred-foot passage under the Thames since 1825. Only after untold numbers of Irish sandhogs went blind, suffocated, or drowned (Isambard himself barely escaped one flood) was the tunnel finally nearing its 1841 completion, at four times the original cost estimate.[59]

Jervis spent May weighing the options, his rigid attention to business undaunted by what others would have considered personal tragedy. On May 9, his wife gave birth to a daughter, who died several hours later. Five days after that, exhausted from her own labors and perhaps despondent at the death of the baby, delicate Cynthia Jervis herself died. A month short of his fifth wedding anniversary, John Jervis was a childless widower. If he took any time to mourn his loss, it is not recorded.[60]

Jervis reported to the commissioners on June 1. A masonry tunnel carrying four thirty-six-inch pipes would cost $636,738, including a 50 percent addition for contingent expenses. The tunnel would require massive dredging, an immense cofferdam, and two large steam engines to pump it dry during construction. After completion of the tunnel (an estimated four years), it would require regular pumping to keep river salt water from entering the tunnel and corroding the iron pipes.

Jervis's redesigned high bridge would take five years to build and cost $836,623, including a standard 10 percent for contingencies. A bit less massive and $100,000 less expensive than the high crossing Jervis had planned a year and a half earlier, this design called for a bridge slightly below grade level, carried on fifteen arches: eight arches eighty feet wide and a hundred feet high across the river (the minimum required by law) and seven arches fifty feet wide over land (one on the steep Manhattan shore, six on the rising Westchester plain) leading to natural abutments. In dropping the arches to the legal minimum and the top of the bridge to 114 feet above tide and twelve feet below the grade of the aqueduct, Jervis abandoned masonry conduit in favor of a siphon of twin forty-eight-inch pipes for the water's passage over the bridge. As with the four smaller pipes of the tunnel siphon, the bridge siphon would deliver sixty million gallons of water a day. However, because Jervis imagined the city not needing that amount for another half-century, he recommended three-foot pipes initially, with provisions to replace them one at a time as needed with the larger pipes.

Despite the tunnel's significantly lower cost, the technological risks made Jervis favor the bridge, even though it too would be "attended with much difficulty in its execution." Because the rest of the aqueduct would be complete well before either the tunnel or the bridge, as a temporary measure, Jervis suggested precisely the sort of river obstruction the high bridge faction had defeated: an embankment across the river, carrying a single, twenty-two-inch pipe, which could be laid and later removed for only $50,000.[61]

Though they still believed a low bridge would be the cheapest, quickest, safest, and most permanent to build, the water commissioners promptly agreed with Jervis's preference to send the Croton over the Harlem instead of under it. On June 15, the commissioners advertised for bids on what was to be the Harlem High Bridge.[62]

In his private memoirs, Chairman Allen was hopeful that month: "The debt to be incurred by the city in accomplishing this great and magnificent [*sic*] work will be large, buth [*sic*] with proper and judicious management may be prevented from being burthensome." Jervis was more than ready. "It was natural," he wrote many years later, "that an engineer should incline to a work that would give prominence to professional character as a work of art."[63]

Fayette Tower was less taken with the prospect. "This will be the greatest work in the country—in fact it is too great and uncalled for," he wrote to a younger brother just before the bid advertisements appeared. The low bridge presented "decided advantages of economy and utility— yet the citizens of N. Y. have suffered the load of some 8 or 10 millions for construction of the Aqueduct to be increased by the addition of half a million just for Architectural beauty in a place where there is little necesity [*sic*] for it." The young idealist abhorred the influence on engineering of politics and money, by which "the designing few have accomplished their objects, before the people are awake to the consequences."[64]

A Record Year

Despite the intrusion of influence, engineer Tower remained dedicated. "Our great work goes on bravely," he told his brother. It had been a busy spring. The Croton labor gang was rising toward a record 4,206 men in June.[65] The great arch in Sing Sing, "the most astonishing specimen of art and ability of man" ever seen by the *Westchester Herald,* was nearing completion, as was the rest of the first division but for the dam. "Order and activity prevail on every section," the paper reported at the end of May.[66]

A week later, the paper was compelled to report that at least a hundred workers had breached the peace. On the last Sunday of May, riots broke out on sections just south of Sing Sing, with much damage to people and property. One worker was beaten nearly to death; several others severely injured, and the offices of contractors were broken into and robbed. Guns were fired. Only the slower fleeing rioters were arrested and taken off to jail. As always, the violence was blamed on the liquor-fired antipathies of Corkonians and Fardowns.[67]

Back on Manhattan that spring, the city continued to pave its way north. In May, the Common Council turned the office of Street Commissioner into a full department, with jurisdiction not only over road improvement and paving, but also wells and pumps, a marginalizing of the city's lamented natural waters. In June, assessments were made for filling in Sun Fish Pond, buried today beneath Park Avenue South at 32nd Street. For generations a favorite spot for fishing and muskratting by farm boys, by the 1830s, Peter Cooper's glue factory along its northern reaches had polluted the country pond.[68]

Life was changing in the Croton Valley as well. Two miles downriver from the dam construction was a wire mill, opened in 1831 and flourishing under English-born James Bailey and four sons. On Independence Day, the *Westchester Herald* made a tour of the extensive works. "Although the Croton Aqueduct, when completed, will deprive them of their supply of water, and consequently totally destroy their facilities, they are now augmenting their means of usefulness, in order to make the concern as profitable as possible." The paper counseled others to imitate the Baileys' "go-ahead spirit," subtle advice to anyone, like the Baileys, who were then negotiating the compensation due them for the impending loss of their business.[69]

As spring turned to summer, contractors once again re-instituted the dollar a day wage to the over four thousand laborers. The size of the Croton labor gang was astounding, many hundreds more than the total number of people in the service of city government, from the mayor to street sweepers.[70]

The level of activity proved too hot for the economic climate. On July 16, the water commissioners ordered the contractors into a slowdown. "At this time there is a great difficulty in obtaining funds," the resident engineers informed the contractors, who were told to pursue their work no faster than required by their contracts. The news was worse ten days later. "In consequence of the difficulty in raising funds," the contractors would until further notice be paid in $1,000 city bonds. Though the bonds were supposed to earn 6 percent interest payable every six months, contractors soon found that the bonds were being discounted at up to 8 percent. For the next eight months, the generally high margins obtained by the contractors were blotted by the city's red ink.[71]

Despite the prospect of diminishing returns, the water commissioners received thirteen bids for the High Bridge at the end of July. But uncertainty about the future induced the low bidder to decline the work, which brought the contract to the next lowest bidder, a group of four men, three of whom were contractors on numerous other sections. For just over $755,000 ($80,000 less than Jervis's estimate), the High Bridge contract was made with Timothy Ferrell, Samuel Roberts, Arnold Mason, and George Law. "They are worthy and enterprising men," offered the *Westchester Herald,* which had come to know them well, "and we wish them every success in their unparalleled undertaking." Success would come, but only after many engineering difficulties, a much higher cost, and more than double the four years specified in the contract. For Law, though, who had failed to win any Croton work after the Mill River sections, work on the High Bridge propelled him to his fortune and dubious fame.[72]

Fayette Tower, usually a candid commentator on momentous Croton events, was significantly distracted during the summer of 1839. On July 11, he married twenty-year-old Elizabeth Huntington Phelps of Baltimore. A highlight of the couple's weeklong "wedding excursion" was Philadelphia, featuring the engineer's obligatory pilgrimage to Fairmount, "the most delightful spot I have seen for a long time." Overwhelmed by the fountains, water jets, marble basins, and statuary, the newlyweds "exhausted all the words we could find to express our admiration and then felt it long in silence." On their return, Fayette and "Bessy" settled together in his lodgings at Bloomingdale near the Clendening Valley work. Glad to find that no deduction had been taken from his monthly pay, he and Bessy began a year of great happiness together; she redecorated their living quarters, corresponded frequently with her mother-in-law, and helped with her artistic husband's math: "she makes my calculations & I make pictures for her."[73]

Despite the summer's work slowdown, there were occasions for celebration, such as the placing of the keystone in the Sing Sing arch on a rainy Friday in mid-August. Incredibly, under the superintendence of resident engineer French and lead contractor Andrew Young, there had been no serious accidents or injuries on the often dangerous work. After a round of cheers at the construction site, the popular contractor gave a party for his crew, followed by a more select affair at his hotel lodgings, where "the mutual interchange of friendly feeling and courtesy took place between the contractors and villagers."[74]

Chief engineer Jervis was hardly one for parties, but he was well satisfied with the job done, after discovering less than half an inch of set-

FIGURE 37. *Sing Sing Arch*
Drawn by Fayette Tower for his Croton book, this engraving illustrates the enormous size of the arch that was the pride of Sing Sing and remains a tourist attraction. (William Lee Frost; photo by Barry Rosenthal.)

tling: "The work in this arch has no superior in comparison with other arches of this size."[75]

Such good feeling prevailed as well down at Sleepy Hollow, where George Law was making friends with an engaging older man who often happened by the Mill River arch work. In frequent, casual conversations at the site, they found each other "very intelligent and agreeable," a different sort of George Law from his later reputation. Law didn't learn the identity of his companion for some weeks, until a chance meeting on the Hudson River steamboat from New York to Tarrytown. While Law and his anonymous new friend spoke about the Croton work, the ship's bell rang out as they steamed past Washington Irving's estate at Sunnyside. Excusing himself, Law sought an explanation from the captain, who said that it was to alert Irving's coachman that his master was aboard and should be met at the Tarrytown landing. Expressing great admiration for the famous writer and a long-standing desire to meet him, Law asked the captain to point him out. Surprised, the captain indicated the man with whom Law had been speaking all the way up the river.[76] There is no indication of Law's response to Irving's little joke.

As the 1839 building season wound down, so did the workforce and wages. After historically heavy snows in mid-December ended construction in Westchester, only fourteen hundred laborers remained on the line, mostly in tunneling and excavations on Manhattan. Contractors cut the winter wage to the usual six shillings, believing it more "favorable to the laboring classes" than in previous winters because the depression had driven down the prices of consumer goods and the contractors were taking devalued bonds instead of cash payments from the city.[77]

Much had been accomplished during the year, and year-end reports by Jervis and the commissioners boasted of this. Fifty-four of ninety-seven sections, totaling nearly twenty-one miles, were complete; just over five miles of masonry conduit were finished in otherwise uncompleted sections. This left fourteen miles still under general construction, six and a half miles in Westchester, the rest on Manhattan. Only the grading along the line of Fifth Avenue for the pipes linking the reservoirs remained uncontracted.

In Westchester, the dam was over halfway done; many other major structures had been completed, including the Sing Sing crossing, all but one of 115 culverts (totaling over seventy-five hundred feet), twenty-three of an eventual thirty-three ventilators, one of an eventual six waste weirs, and seven of sixteen tunnels (twenty-five hundred of nearly seven thousand total feet).

Several of the simpler fourth division sections were nearly complete, but on the five major sections (Harlem bridge, Manhattan and Clendening Valleys, and the two reservoirs) less than a quarter of the $2.3 million worth of work had been done. Little had been done at the bridge, where preliminary investigations had pushed the anticipated cost over $880,000, well beyond the original contract price and Jervis's own estimate. When Jervis repeated his earlier suggestion that a temporary pipe cross the Harlem until the High Bridge was done, this time the commissioners approved it.

The commissioners reported that they had not concerned themselves with the distribution system below the Murray Hill reservoir. Despite the 1838 law that allowed the city to pay for distribution pipe out of Croton funds, the commissioners reiterated their position that water distribution was "the proper province of the [city government], and will be performed under their special supervision."

Just under $4 million had been disbursed (more than half of that in 1839), edging closer to the $5.5 million thus far authorized, but still far from what was now estimated to be a total cost of just under $9 million, nearly double original estimates. The commissioners felt compelled to dismiss the preconstruction estimates of Douglass and Martineau as "entirely delusive," but carefully blamed the unprecedented nature of the work, not their chosen engineer Jervis, for the rising cost.[78]

In a continuing depression, the $9 million project cast a lengthening shadow over New York. The city's population had increased relatively modestly in the second half of the 1830s, from 270,000 in 1835 to 312,000 in 1840, but at the same time, business activity had virtually stopped. After over eighteen hundred buildings were put up in 1836 (the year after the Great Fire), only 840 new buildings went up in 1837, 781 the next year, and just 674 in 1839. From 1836 to 1840, the assessed value of real estate in the city declined from nearly $234 million to $187 million and continued downward; personal property dropped from $76 million to $66 million and beyond. To cover these revenue losses, the average tax rate climbed from thirty-six cents to fifty-three cents per $100 and continued rising, although this did not stop the city debt from rising from $1 million in the 1830s to $9 million in 1840. The bulk of this new debt was the cost of building the Croton Aqueduct.[79]

The economics of the Croton project made the commissioners a choice target. The New York *Herald*, which had questioned the commissioners' competency back in 1836, launched a new offensive during the summer of 1839 to unseat them. No longer an upstart penny paper, James Bennett's journal was fast becoming the country's largest circulation daily, mixing aggressive news and financial coverage with its trademark scandal mongering. A spy for the paper "revealed" during the summer that the commissioners were monstrously mismanaging their affairs, building an aqueduct that must be defective because most of it was being hidden underground instead of marching toward the city on bold Roman arches. "Therefore," the paper urged in September, "let the rallying cry next election be—'the removal of the Water Commissioners!'"[80]

Bennett would get what he sought, but not exactly how he sought it. In the November state elections, the Whigs gained a Senate majority; with Governor Seward, they were free to replace the Democratic commissioners with Whigs. Though Stephen Allen expected his removal as soon as the new legislature was convened in January, New York City voters had elected Democrats to the Senate and Assembly, a political inconvenience for the Whigs that delayed immediate moves on the commissioners.[81]

Despite political and economic pressures, the commissioners' year-end report elicited high praise, even from the Whig press. The decision to go forward with the temporary Harlem crossing was judged by the *New York Whig* as of "inestimable advantage" in providing both water and income to service the debt sooner than otherwise expected. In a counterpoint to the *Herald*'s plaint about the lack of Roman grandeur, the *Whig* observed that the ventilators along the aqueduct route "rise up like pyramids." The paper pronounced the whole work "as durable as stone and water cement, in the hands of skilful workmen, can make it. The structure will endure for the ages."[82]

This sentiment was echoed in an authoritative book by Henry Schenck Tanner, a New York cartographer and statistical geographer well known for national atlases and travelers' gazetteers. The longest essay in his *Description of the Canals and Railroads of the United States*, written in early 1840, described in minute detail the partially completed Croton Aqueduct, "the true character and magnitude [of which] but few, even of the citizens of New York have an adequate conception." Having studied the most recent commissioners' report and many other materials, as well as conducted his own investigations, Tanner concluded: "there can scarcely be a doubt, that the work will stand the test of time, and answer all the purposes for which it is designed."

Incredibly, though, in writing the most precise, informed, and laudatory precompletion account of the work, Tanner thought it should have been built differently. Citing Westchester topography and reports back to Joseph Browne, the mapmaker was of the opinion that the Croton should have been tunneled into the Bronx River and an immensely cheaper fifteen-mile aqueduct built. Tanner's advocacy of the Bronx, when the Croton Aqueduct was by his own admission being brilliantly built, indicates the conceptual difficulty even discerning people still had with watering an American city from a distant river.[83]

ELEVEN

Filling the "Big Teapot"

Water! water! is the universal note which is sounded
through every part of the city.

—Philip Hone, *Diary*

The year 1840 proved decisive for the Croton project. Political upheaval, economic tensions, labor revolt, and continuing engineering challenges at the High Bridge threatened the endeavor by turns. Under the steady hand of chief engineer Jervis, the work advanced. Despite a confidence-shaking disaster at the dam early in 1841, Croton water flowed into New York the following year, with historic rejoicing.

The Whigs Take Control

The year 1840 would be a record spending year on the Croton, with the disbursement of $2.75 million. Just over $2.1 million would be paid for construction, the remainder in interest and deepening discounts on water bonds.[1] At the end of February, the commissioners sought bids for the last uncontracted work, grading Fifth Avenue for the pipes connecting the reservoirs; the contract was awarded at the end of March.[2]

The winter's main event involved the Manhattan Company. Negotiations for a transfer of its water system to the city had ended inconclusively three years earlier. Now, unsavory disclosures about its banking operations ended any hopes the company might redeem itself.

After the Panic of 1837, the federal government had begun withdrawing its large deposits at the bank, which in turn called in millions of dollars in loans to cash-poor and outraged customers. Seeking to correct the bank's historically irregular business practices, in January 1840, an earnest internal investigation concluded that the company should get out of the stock loan business and clean up its sloppy bookkeeping as well. In February, Bennett's *Herald* got wind of the company's self-analysis and published exposes of its banking and political intrigues: "The Manhattan Bank was first organized by Aaron Burr," the paper noted; "it does not, therefore, disgrace its venerable paternity."[3]

The bank sought to clear its reputation by agreeing to a public investigation led by Robert H. Morris, the crusading city recorder who had succeeded Richard Riker in 1838. The recorder, who since the formation of the Manhattan Company was the city's representative on the company board, was no longer appointed by the mayor but named in Albany; Democrat Morris now retained his office at the will of a Whig governor and Senate.

The *New York American* published Morris's report, which in sensational detail condemned the bank's practices, especially its long tradition of unsecured loans to company directors. Great crowds gathered outside the paper's offices as its March 18 issue went to press; many witnessed the bank's outgoing cashier, blamed for most of the bank's mismanagement, clubbing the bank's incoming reformist president.

Both the internal and public investigations confirmed the company's slight regard for its deteriorating water operations. It had added no iron pipe in years; its ancient log pipes were rotting away. As the company's overall worth had risen to nearly $5 million, its waterworks investment was less than $400,000, "without any income arising from it."[4]

The public revelations about the city's trickling Manhattan water were perhaps no more surprising than the momentous Croton news from Albany the day before. As Stephen Allen had expected since the November elections, Governor Seward finally dumped the water commissioners who had overseen the Croton project from its beginnings and replaced them with a slate of Whigs.

Allen was righteously outraged by "the most rancorous and malignant party that ever existed in this country," though he seemed to have forgotten how Myndert Van Schaick had chosen only Democrats in 1833. It was some consolation to Allen that Whig commissioner William Fox, who was asked to stay on, refused to do so.[5]

The five new commissioners were faithful party men, all but one new to water affairs. Samuel R. Childs and brass founder Benjamin Birdsall would not have much apparent effect on events. Zebedee Ring, Fox's replacement, owned the New York Screw Dock Company, elevator loading docks on the East River, and provided technical expertise. John D. Ward was a wealthy businessman for whom, of all the new commissioners, chief engineer Jervis would come to have the greatest respect.[6]

The fifth commissioner, selected as their chairman, was Samuel Stevens. After tilting at the Manhattan Company, mistakenly seeking the Bronx, and settling for the 13th Street system, old "Alderman Sam" finally got his chance to bring water to New York. Fortunately, most of the groundwork was already laid.

The new commissioners promptly sought to root out any "improper political influence" supposed to exist on the Croton, but were just as quickly disappointed. "They came into the office and called for information, especially as to the method of giving contracts," wrote Jervis, who laid open his detailed bidding records: "The new board spent considerable time in these examinations, and I did not learn that they discovered any wrong." Later, Jervis learned that the new commissioners had canvassed the contractors and the engineers but had found them "equally divided in politics." Jervis "was not surprised at the result. . . . I knew well there was no political favor exercised or in any way encouraged by the late board."[7]

A week after their ouster, the Democratic commissioners gave a final accounting of their accomplishments. Since their previous report three months earlier, nearly half a million more dollars had been spent, bringing the total to just under $4.4 million. The new commissioners, who would award the contract, received forty bids for the Fifth Avenue grading work. But for two pending lawsuits, "the laborious and perplexing attempts to negotiate with the landowners" were complete, and all of the land required for the works was in the city's possession. Work on the High Bridge was getting under way; a cofferdam was in place for the sinking of the first river pier, and workers had readied pilings for several land piers on the West-chester shore. Jervis had recently inspected the entire line and found little winter damage. There was nothing to prevent extensive operations during the approaching work season. Indeed, with nearly all the planning and contracting and much of the construction done, the outgoing com-missioners insinuated that their successors had only to pay bills and con-duct "a general supervision of the work."

The commissioners were most concerned that their "efficient and highly esteemed" but Democratic chief engineer would also be shown the door:

> The industry and ability with which he has conducted this great enter-prize, will carry his name to future time, let who will be charged with its completion. We cannot forbear expressing the hope, therefore, that our successors will avail themselves of the talents and acquired knowl-edge of Mr. Jervis, for the further prosecution of a work of so much importance to this city. The advantages of retaining his services, and also, of his present Assistants, must be obvious; as the information they possess . . . of the work . . . will be, in our opinion, of the first impor-tance to those who are to have supervision of its progress.[8]

Jervis's future would be decided with much handwringing later in the year, after the Whig commissioners assumed more than a "bill paying" role. First, though, they waited out a rebellion in the field.

The Croton War

The previous season had brought record numbers of Irish laborers to lands long settled by the Dutch and the English, arousing tensions sim-mering since the beginning of the work. Five days after the new com-missioners took office, they got an inkling of trouble from Joshua Purdy. In a bill demanding payment of $3,012 for specific damages to his prop-erty by aqueduct workers during the previous three years, Purdy registered his displeasure with the changes abroad in Westchester:

> In making this estimate of damage I have made it for damages actu-ally sustained and have not taken into consideration the inconvenience

FIGURE 38. *Mill River Crossing*
Shown in an engraving for the 1850 *Manual of the Common Council,* the aqueduct crossing in Sleepy Hollow was George Law's first Croton contract and, according to local resident Washington Irving, the scene of much spooking of Irish laborers. (General Research Division. The New York Public Library. Astor, Lenox and Tilden Foundations.)

trouble and anxiety of having between three & four hundred Irishmen upon my own farm and within a few rods of my dwelling house. . . . But I can assure you it is no pleasant thing to have [their] huts or shantees as they are called stuck up within a few rods of my dwelling and peopled with the lowest and most filthy of mankind, children nearly naked before your eyes, and that of your family.[9]

Anti-Irish sentiment flourished among the Westchester gentry that spring. On the same day the new commissioners were appointed, arch-Whig Washington Irving sent a letter to a New York editor about the Mill River crossing workers in Sleepy Hollow: "As the work is unfinished a Colony of Patlanders have been encamped about this place all winter, [forming] a kind of Patsylvania, in the midst of a 'wiltherness.'" As Irving told it, headless apparitions aroused by "strangers of an unknown tongue" had been harrying the Irish on their excursions past the haunted Dutch church to whiskey mills. "In a word, the whole wood has become such a scene of *spuking* and *diablerie,* that the paddys will not any longer venture out of their shantys at night, and a Whisky-shop, in a neighboring village, where they used to hold their evening gatherings, has been obliged to shut up, for want of custom." Irving warned that if the workers continued to be cut off from their whiskey they might "entirely abandon the Goblin regions of Sleepy Hollow, and the completion of the Croton Waterworks be seriously retarded."[10]

By the time Irving's letter was published in the April *Knickerbocker Magazine,* work had indeed stopped. But it was wage, not whiskey, deprivation that started "the Croton War" on Thursday, April 2.[11]

The continuing depression had compelled Croton contractors, paid for many months in devalued city bonds, to leave the six-shilling winter wage in place when the work season began on April 1. Early the next day, when it became known that the dollar a day wage of the previous two summers would not be forthcoming, some three hundred workers, armed with clubs, began a march south from Yonkers toward the Harlem.

Laborers who were content to work for the lower wage were beaten or driven off, as were masons, carpenters, and blacksmiths, their tools and carts scattered or destroyed and their horses turned loose. Commanding work boats hastily abandoned at the Harlem, a party of rioters crossed the river, upsetting work on upper Manhattan in a similar fashion, and returned to the Westchester plain with many more adherents.

There was no action taken to limit the rebellion. On Friday, the mob again crossed into Manhattan, drove off opponents, and fell back with greater numbers to Westchester. By Monday, a thousand strikers, as many workers as had been employed over the winter, were camped on the Westchester shore. The *Evening Post* reported threats by the rioters "to destroy [contractors'] lives and property, and . . . the works so far as they are constructed."

After pondering the options, Mayor Varian sent out three troops of cavalry; few could remember the last time the aging horsemen had been mustered. As the militia assembled Monday evening, even the *Evening Post* thought that perhaps the workers had spent their rebellious energy and were now simply enjoying a few more days off.

FIGURE 39. *"The Croton War"*
This banner cartoon and other such mocking coverage of the April 1840 Croton labor unrest in James Gordon Bennett's *Morning Herald* infuriated Croton con-tractors. (© Collection of The New-York Historical Society.)

"The dogs barked, the boys shouted, the men laughed, the ladies smiled, and the soldiers looked silly" to the mocking *Morning Herald* as the hundred-strong force led by the mayor rode north from the city Tuesday morning, past pockets of mostly amiable Irish resistance on the Manhattan line, until reaching a field overlooking the Harlem. The Rubicon was to be uncrossed; the forces saw no rioters. Wheeling their horses, the militia returned south, engaging idled but noncombative workers near the York Hill reservoir construction. Two would-be rabble-rousers named O'Brien and Dunn were chased down and arrested, but otherwise the cavalry returned safely to the city by evening, soothing their fresh saddle sores with champagne, brandy, crackers, and cheese at the mayor's house. "And so ended the 1st chapter of the bloodless Croton War," the *Herald* reported, under a banner cartoon of tipsy, stick-wielding Irishmen routing the cavalry on a field strewn only with a tumbled rider and a few dead pigs.

The Croton contractors were scandalized at the *Herald*'s mockery of what in fact remained a dangerous situation all along the line. "We are held up before the public as the most hardened oppressors," thirty-four contractors wrote in a long statement published in the offending *Herald* on April 15, "while sympathy and pity are extended to those who have outraged the most binding and sacred laws."

The contractors detailed the history of the wages they had paid over four years, pointing out that the same six-shilling wage had been paid in the first season when the economy was still relatively healthy. Dismissing the city militia as "wholly ineffectual," the contractors complained that the rebellion's ringleaders continued to keep willing workers off the line through "fears of punishment and death," while "threats of vengeance, the most violent and bloody, are thundered against us." The contractors delivered an ultimatum: "the continuation of the works under our charge must be suspended until our lives are safe in resuming its prosecution."[12]

Indeed, as John Jervis learned on the 16th from his brother William in Yonkers, the strike continued to shut down the entire third division. Specific threats of violence prevented teams from resuming work on section 68; the previous day, masons on section 70 were driven off, "some of them badly injured." The good news was that as many as ten leaders were rounded up: "I think this will awe the rest for a short time at least."[13]

Not from the city but in a Westchester posse the law finally had come riding "to put an end to . . . the organized band of ruffians which for two weeks has spread terror and despair throughout the region," ran a bulletin in the eminently responsible *New York Commercial Advertiser*. By the 18th, twenty ringleaders had been ushered to the county jail by Colonel Cogswell of West Farms, meriting "the gratitude of his country for periling his life in defence of our laws." The paper lamented "the tardy movements of the Mayor and city authorities." It was another week before work resumed unimpeded, at the same six-shilling wage.[14]

Tensions

While the contractors successfully held the line on wages, the Whig water commissioners signaled a new approach to economy. In a special report to the Whig-controlled Assembly in early April, the commissioners suggested that only one of the two planned basins for the York Hill receiving reservoir should be built; the intended 150 million gallon storage could not be needed "for a century to come, if ever required."[15]

There was more economizing ahead. In the coming months, the new commissioners sought to eliminate the minimal styling on the Murray Hill reservoir, scrap one of the three pipes linking the two reservoirs, replace the arched Clendening crossing with a solid wall, and replace the land-based arches of the High Bridge with solid walls. In reports to the commissioners from April to July, Jervis was forced to respond to these ideas, carefully arguing that the economies would be either minimal or a detriment to the finished product.[16]

The Whig commissioners avoided city government (Mayor Varian was re-elected in April and fellow Democrats won twelve of the city's seventeen wards) and used Albany to make their mark on the Croton project. When the legislature authorized another $3 million in water stock at the end of April, it included a provision that poisoned water politics.[17]

Two years earlier, the Whig-controlled Common Council had won the right from the Democrat-controlled legislature to pay for all water distribution costs out of Croton money. Now, the Whig-controlled legislature granted the water commissioners approval power over the city's distribution system spending.

On its face, the clause seemed simply to restore the commissioners' historic control over all Croton spending. Chairman Stevens interpreted the clause more broadly. Whereas the Democratic commissioners had been content to let the city build the distribution system, Stevens read the law as empowering him to do it.

The creator of the 13th Street system, Stevens relished the prospect of putting his name on the Croton pipe, especially as little had been laid in the past three years. A week after the law was passed, the Whig commissioners claimed pipe laying authority and informed the council that henceforth Croton engineers would supervise the city's pipe plans. Happy at first for expert guidance but concerned about how best to proceed, the council formed a special committee, chaired by new Democratic alderman Peter Cooper, the knowledgeable but deeply opinionated inventor and manufacturer.[18]

While Cooper deliberated, spring edged toward summer in familiar circumstances: the depression continued "with unabated severity"; a Croton worker was crushed in a cave-in and his death was ruled accidental; and John Jervis took a second wife and saw little of her. His forty-five year union with Eliza Coates, fifteen years his junior, would produce no children.[19] There was no honeymoon from work. As he fended off water commissioner economies, Jervis was most concerned that spring with figuring out how to make the High Bridge stand up.

Building Bridges and Laying Pipe

It long had been supposed that the bed of the Harlem River was solid rock. Instead, as with earlier surprises at the Croton dam and Sing Sing kill, the contractors found an assortment of bedrock, boulders, mud, and hard sand, an impossible foundation for the piers of the great bridge. Not only would workers have to get the boulders, some weighing six tons, out of the river to make room for the cofferdams, but they would also have to drive clusters of oak piles up to forty-five feet into sand to support five of the seven river piers (as well as five piers on the Westchester river plain).

The crucial question was knowing when the piles were deep enough. Jervis "had known a good many cases where bearing piles had been successfully used, but these were for much less weights, and I could not find any specific experiments that warranted full confidence of this bridge." So Jervis designed an experiment, conducted in late spring by Horatio Allen "with great care."

For what may have been the first full-scale tests of pile foundations in the United States, Allen built a hydraulic press that rammed test piles with a fourteen-hundred-pound hammer. A smaller ram gauged the pressure on the pile and a lever gauged its downward movement. The engineers discovered that the piles withstood three blows at a pressure of sixty tons without any perceptible movement, and yielded a bit at sixty-five tons but resumed their original position when the pressure was removed. Assured that clusters of piles would support the bridge's tremendous load, Jervis allowed work to resume under close supervision. It was slow going; by the end of 1840, the contractors had built only four cofferdams and managed to raise just two river piers above high water level.[20]

FIGURE 40. *High Bridge*

Drawn by Fayette Tower for his Croton book, this view looks south down the Harlem River, with the Manhattan highlands on the right; Tower's illustration predates the completion of the bridge by five years. A popular subject for scenic painters, the bridge is the only original aqueduct structure remaining on Manhattan, though its river arches were replaced with a single steel span in the 1930s. (William Lee Frost; photo by Barry Rosenthal.)

While Chief Engineer Jervis tested the limits of technology, Mayor Varian was testing the limits of power. Acting on the money saving ideas of the new water commissioners and against existing contracts, the Common Council voted to scrap the arches in the Clendening Valley crossing in favor of the cheaper solid wall. Varian argued that a wall would divide the future neighborhood (which was then farmland) and was beyond the authority of the council to order. At the end of June he said "No," the first veto by a New York mayor. A compromise was shortly reached: arches already being built from 98th to 100th Street would be completed; the wall would rise across 96th, 97th, and 101st Streets. The water commissioners were pleased to report eventual savings of $52,000.[21]

Peter Cooper's report came in at the end of June, with a recommendation that the city create a formal department to make pipe contracts and manage pipe laying. After Jervis and Horatio Allen handed in a pipe plan (based largely on Uzziah Wenman's 1835 scheme) in July, in August, the council created the Croton Aqueduct Department, the city's first modern water bureaucracy, with a supervising aqueduct commissioner, a superintending water purveyor, and a committee of Common Council members, featuring Cooper, with contracting and spending power.[22]

In the next weeks, the essential tensions between Democrats and Whigs, city and state, became clear. In September, the water commissioners challenged certain bills of the Aqueduct Department for paving, lead, stopcocks, and pipe. The department provided no explanations, and the council passed an ordinance cutting off water commissioner authority at the Murray Hill reservoir and directing the city comptroller to charge all of the department's expenses against the Croton water fund. In October, the commissioners reasserted their authority below the reservoir and took issue with the department's plans to use cast instead of remelted iron pipe; the comptroller replied with a documentary history showing that the commissioners had no say in matters below Murray Hill. Cooper pitched in with a report, backed by the city counsel, defending the department's expenditures.[23]

Chairman Stevens ignored the challenges to his authority. At the end of October, the water commissioners made three expensive contracts for over twelve hundred tons of pipe, most of it thirty-inch main from Philadelphia industrialist Samuel Vaughan Merrick, and another contract

FIGURE 41. Clendening Valley Crossing

Drawn by Fayette Tower for his Croton book, the engraving is notable for the foreground portrayal of tranquil farm life, suggesting the aqueduct's harmony with nature; an identical but unpublished ink drawing of the crossing done a year earlier shows the foreground as an empty land with broken fencing and sparse trees. (William Lee Frost; photo by Barry Rosenthal.)

for pipelaying from the Murray Hill reservoir down Fifth Avenue to 21st Street.[24] Countering Stevens's moves, the Common Council formed yet another special committee to investigate further.

While definitive action on these matters awaited, "pipelaying" took on a whole new meaning. Underlying the struggle for control of the Croton system south of its distributing reservoir was the hot political season leading up to the November elections. With the Whigs heavily favored to retain control of the governorship and state legislature, William Harrison was expected to unseat Democrat Martin Van Buren from the White House. In a play to blunt Whig ascendancy, city recorder Robert Morris chose October for investigations into the 1838 city voting that had elected William Seward governor.

The plot, as Morris discovered, was that leading city Whigs had hired one James B. Glentworth to go to Philadelphia, where he offered $30 to anyone who would come to New York to vote for Seward. In his communications from Philadelphia to the plotters in New York, Glentworth allegedly referred to the number of hired voters as so many yards of Philadelphia pipe destined for the Croton system. The accused Whigs countered that Glentworth had been sent merely to procure people who could identify Philadelphia pipelayers brought to vote in New York by the Democrats. Despite many sensational indictments, only Glentworth was eventually brought to trial, and ultimately the charges were dropped, after which he publicly confirmed the plot.

By then, the Whigs had gone on to smashing victories in the national and state elections. Shortly after the legislature convened at Albany in January, Seward removed Morris as city recorder, an act that clinched fame for the "Glentworth election frauds" and, via outraged Democratic newspapers, turned "pipelaying" into a byword for voting fraud and corrupt politics.[25]

Douglass Tells All

In the midst of the maneuvering over real and conjured pipe, politics induced a curtain call for David Douglass, four years after he had been ushered from the Croton stage. The idea of the Whig engineer's return to the project had percolated privately and in the press during the summer, before Douglass in early October, sent communications to Chairman Stevens and the commissioners generally, not overtly seeking his job back but angrily detailing the circumstances of his firing by Stephen Allen.[26]

Douglass claimed that as early as the summer of 1835 Allen had engaged in "confidential intercourse" with state Canal Commissioner Bouck at the Democratic presidential convention in Baltimore aimed at sacking Douglass. The aggrieved engineer also alleged that Bouck had initiated Allen's consultations with Jervis, who was given secret authority over Douglass's engineering corps requests. This scenario explained all of the complaints about Douglass's delays, the personal and physical attacks against him, the withholding of a large engineering corps, the questioning of expenses, and the commissioners' reluctance to visit the line and head off landowner opposition that delayed Douglass's work.

With political fervor running high in advance of the November elections, Stevens was in a tough spot: how to respond to allegations that secret politics had passed the Croton chief engineer's job from a Whig to a Democrat, a presumed tool of President Van Buren's Albany Regency. Unaware of Douglass's charges, Jervis glimpsed Stevens's anxiety from across their shared office:

> Mr. Stevens, with a significant sigh, remarked that it would be sad if, after spending so much money, the aqueduct should be a failure. I replied that it would be sad indeed; that I had no doubt of its success; ... that he must have faith, and if he did not think I was capable of conducting the work successfully it was his duty to engage an engineer on whom the commissioners could rely.[27]

Stevens wrote a brief reply to Douglass two days after receiving his materials, thanking him for the information with thinly masked relief that the engineer was seeking only vindication and not reappointment. Of Douglass's numerous allegations, Stevens acknowledged only that "the Engineer Corps was ample in its numbers and liberally compensated, after your departure." Stevens avoided the politics by confessing no particular knowledge of the circumstances prior to his tenure as a commissioner, and he tiptoed around Douglass's posterity in personal, not official, terms:

as a citizen of New York, I feel myself largely your debtor, for the original surveys and plans of the Croton Aqueduct, the main features of which as proposed by you are original; never having been before carried into execution in this or any country. And your name and your original Report to the late commissioners, will be handed down in a manner, in my judgement, highly honorable to yourself.

The publication of the Douglass and Stevens's communications in Whig newspapers at the end of October scandalized Jervis and Allen, who responded publicly. His reputation at stake, Jervis denied that he was "a political Engineer," claimed the old commissioners had never talked politics, and that he had never "sought to exercise any political influence" in any of his professional work."[28] Allen, with no job to protect and still bitter over his own overtly political dismissal earlier that year, denounced at great length all of Douglass's claims: "The true cause [of] his waking up, after a sleep of four years, must be plain . . . at a time of great political excitement, to create a political bias in his favor, and intended to operate upon the present commissioners, against his successor in the office of chief engineer."[29]

Jervis survived. In November, the Whigs won the national and state elections, but locally there was no clamoring for Jervis's head. Good notices of his ongoing engineering work appeared, even in the Whig press, and the commissioners retained him.[30]

Disaster and Distractions

Jervis was helped by gentle fall weather, allowing significant progress on Manhattan aqueduct work and especially the once troublesome dam, which by the end of the year was nearly finished. Water had risen behind the dam to form Croton Lake; the pent-up river flowed several feet deep over the dam's masonry lip. The embankment was not yet built to its full breadth and lacked its vertical protection wall. At the Bailey wire mill downriver, fifty workmen were still turning five tons of iron into wire on a good day, but those days were numbered. When the dam was complete, the business would shut down. The *Westchester Herald* trusted that ongoing negotiations with the appraisers would "award justice to the worthy and industrious" Baileys.[31]

As fall turned to winter, the Common Council special committee appointed in October reasserted the city's claims below the Murray Hill reservoir. In support of Aqueduct Department contracts for distribution pipe, the committee reported that the time was finally coming for the city to grasp its water destiny. If Department spending was controlled by the commissioners, the committee reasoned, then they held legislative control over the Common Council, effecting "at pleasure the credit of the city: they can continue or delay the great work of distributing the water of the aqueduct through the city, and bring the public authorities and the people into a state of subordination . . . utterly hostile to every principle of a representative government."[32]

The eloquence was lost on Chairman Stevens. He took the issue to the Whig state assistant vice chancellor who, after a hearing, granted an injunction against distribution pipe contracting by the city, which the Common Council promptly ignored. The city continued to lay pipe with Croton water funds and refused to pay commissioner bills, prompting a Stevens petition to the Whig legislature for a law delineating the rights and responsibilities of the commissioners below Murray Hill. That law would not be written until the following spring.[33]

As a deep freeze fell over commissioner-council relations in December, the fine fall weather gave way to wintry conditions in Westchester. Driven by a bitter northeast wind, snow drifted across the county in early December. Just before Christmas, another heavy snow fell. The Hudson down to Sing Sing, and Croton Cove where the Croton met the Hudson, were closed by ice. Another snowstorm before the new year was followed by record cold in the first week of January. Temperatures were well below zero at dawn on January 5.[34]

As the day progressed, though, the temperature began to rise dramatically and by nightfall heavy rain fell over the region. The thaw continued for several days and so did the rain. By the night of the 7th, a Thursday, eighteen inches of melting snow and three days of rain swelled Westchester's rivers and streams to bursting. Throughout the Croton Valley, alarmed residents prepared for the worst.[35]

Just after midnight on the 8th, the rising Croton wrenched Pines Bridge from its footings; it went crashing into the river, mingling with tributary stream bridges, small buildings, uprooted trees, thick and jagged ice floes, and other debris rushing inexorably toward the unfinished dam two and a half miles downriver. Two miles below the dam, James Bailey and his sons were trying desperately to protect their wire works. Since evening, the Baileys and dozens of their workers had been building levees to keep the menacing Croton out of their settlement on the river's western bank. At three in the morning, they retired, exhausted from their efforts, believing they had done all they could.

In the meantime, the Croton was swelling behind its artificial barrier. The frozen surface of the four-hundred-acre lake had broken up; the water had been rising at a foot an hour. In the darkness, laborers struggled to add a small dike to the top of the dam's incomplete embankment, but after midnight abandoned the effort. The water rose over the dike, spilling five feet above the embankment itself; the entire damworks was lost to sight below the roiled surface of the river.

At about two in the morning, as the remnants of Pines Bridge and other debris began pounding the embankment, a contractor's son, realizing that the dam was going to burst, sped south sounding alarm horns. Laborer Patrick Burke had already retired to his shanty just below the dam. It was later said that exhaustion and liquor had rendered him into a deep slumber from which he never awoke, despite the roar of water as the embankment finally collapsed at three in the morning.

The river smashed through Burke's shack and carried him away; the body was found the next day, half buried in a sandbank three miles downriver, stripped of all its clothing but for a pair of heavy boots and the tattered remains of corduroy pantaloons, the head and face bruised and disfigured. It was reported that one hand still clutched the bottle that had saved him from the awareness of his fate.

With Burke in its grasp, the flooding river rushed down the valley toward the Tompkins farm, which had prospered for sixty years. Believing his house safely back from the river, aged and infirm Solomon Tompkins had to be dragged from his bed by an alert son, who carried his father thirty feet uphill before a mass of ice and water crashed into the house and added its wreckage to the wall of destruction rolling south.

As the Baileys reached their quarters just after three, they could hear horns over the roar of the approaching flood. Old hand William Evans, a stout, sixty-eight-year-old Welshman known to all as "Uncle John," rushed in to warn his masters to open the sluices of the mill, but there was no time. Within moments, the water was upon them, and the entire settlement was engulfed in a frigid, raging sea. At the threshold of his house, family patriarch James Bailey, holding a box of gold coins, was met by his son John, who carried him through swirling, waist-deep water to high ground; the cashbox was lost in the effort. For others, the only path to safety was up trees. Among a dozen or so desperate people climbing for their lives were several Baileys, a young girl, and two mothers in soaked bedclothes clutching infants.

"Uncle John" Evans and another employee, Robert Smith, climbed a short cedar tree, which strained with their weight against the current. Their cries for help pierced the darkness until the feeble tree uprooted and flung the two men into the frenzied waters, their last desperate shrieks fading quickly in the ears of those who could do nothing to save them.

Some two hours after Evans and Smith were carried off, rescuers began forming rafts out of barn doors, snatching survivors from their perches. The last to come down, after five hours, were a mother and her infant, retrieved by a contractor's son.

By then, darkness had gone and the dawn revealed a landscape of mud and destruction. Every bridge and mill across the Croton for sixteen miles from its mouth was destroyed; the only structure remaining in the river was the masonry portion of the dam. Incredibly, only Burke, Evans, and Smith had lost their lives.

John Jervis and Samuel Stevens approached the disaster scene later that day. "On passing over the hill as the road entered the valley, the view was indeed sad and the aspect was severe in the extreme. . . . No one without such experience could imagine the severity with which this scene, with its attending circumstances, affected me." Jervis quickly gathered himself. From Sing Sing, he wrote a brief account for the Whig water commissioners, whose first semiannual report was due to be handed in to the Common Council on Monday. The engineer acknowledged some fault in the dam's design, with a tip to nature: "The embankment was gone, and it was manifest I had been in error in regard to the extent of waterway necessary for so great a flood. For three years I had seen no flood that gave me the suspicion of one of this magnitude."[36]

At least two floods during Jervis's tenure had suggested such a possibility, but this one was historic, "the largest freshet that has been witnessed in this part of the country for very many years," thought the *Hudson River Chronicle*. Indeed, the devastation had been unprecedented from Connecticut down to Delaware and the Lehigh Valley, where many lives were lost. Still, Jervis believed if the embankment had been completed to its full width and the protection wall carried up to its full height "the work might have proved adequate to the emergency."[37]

Damages to the works and private property ultimately totaled at least $673,000, all of it paid out of the city's Croton funds. The destruction of the Bailey mill changed their negotiating position with the appraisers. After years of litigation, they eventually collected $70,000.[38]

The Baileys and the Tompkins were not the only Croton mill put out of business. The Underhills of Quaker Bridge, near the mouth of the river, were forced to give up their half-century-old grist mill operation because the flood permanently wrecked navigation of the lower Croton, choking Croton Cove with rock, mud, and other debris. Periaugers could no longer sail upriver with wheat to be ground into flour at the Underhill mill.[39] It was no small irony that after great debate about the imagined navigation effect of the aqueduct's Harlem River crossing, in several hours, the burst dam ended real navigation on the Croton River.

The water commissioners put the best light on the flood as they could in their report to the Common Council. As Jervis had reported to them, only the dam had suffered. Despite the "unprecedented rain storm," aqueduct structures along the line had stood "remarkably well," culverts had amply discharged stream waters, and conduit embankments were mostly intact.[40]

Although the commissioners were content for the record to let nature shoulder the blame for the failure of the dam, they wondered privately whether their recent decision to retain the dam's engineer had been correct. Though Jervis had spent the past months cultivating good relations with his new bosses across their political divide, here was a real excuse to sack him. Jervis himself "did not then know how the board of commissioners might be influenced by this event." He gleaned impressions from occasional conversations with them but never raised the issue of his employment directly.[41] By the end of the month, it was apparent that his manner had convinced the commissioners to retain him.

Fayette Tower had confidently predicted Jervis's job security in a letter two weeks after the flood: "though his works did not prevail against the elements, I guess he came as near to it as any one. . . . There are many now who will say the plan was defective, but the same persons would not have discovered it before this disaster."[42]

Tower himself was greatly preoccupied that winter. In October he had taken a six-month leave to be with his cherished Bessy, sick with what turned out to be tuberculosis, from which she had "a small prospect of recovery." After she proved too ill for recuperative travel to Cuba or St. Croix, the couple took lodgings in the city, "pretty comfortable quarters" at 96 Orchard Street. Though another engineer had been assigned Tower's duties for the winter season, Jervis graciously put Tower on half-pay while he attended his wife's dying. By mid-January, the end was near: "Consumption has marked her for a victim and physicians may come armed with the Science of medicine but their exertions cannot wrest her from its grasp." The young engineer adopted the fatalism of his boss: "a higher hand rules—whose ways are past finding out." On January 31, Elizabeth died. "I feel that I am alone," the disconsolate Tower wrote to his mother.[43]

There was no consolation from the water commissioners. On New Year's Day, they had ended the half-pay that Tower had been counting on through the winter; Stevens had "complained of Mr. Jervis's arrangements as being too *liberal*."[44]

The petty economy practiced on Tower was a small part of the money-saving measures that the thrifty commissioners proudly outlined in their January report to the Common Council. Just under $6 million of the authorized $8.5 million had been spent through 1840 and savings were accomplished where possible. The commissioners' idea of building only one of the two basins for the York Hill reservoir was frustrated because work was too far along; instead, they announced a savings of $75,000 by not fully excavating the northern basin, the bottom of which would remain natural rock. They had saved another $10,000 by eliminating one of the three pipes between the York Hill and Murray Hill reservoirs.

But the most astounding suggestion of the Whig commissioners was to scrap the High Bridge. In rare but unacknowledged agreement with their predecessors, the commissioners questioned a million-dollar bridge whose "only duty" was to support two lines of three-foot pipe. Without exactly criticizing Jervis's abilities, the commissioners questioned the effort: "It is a fact not to be disguised that the erection of this bridge is not only a 'stupendous,' but is an *Herculean* task for our city to execute, and requires more engineering talent, inspection, and watchfulness than any other part, or we might almost say, all the other parts of the aqueduct work put together." The commissioners recommended that the Common Council seek a repeal of the act mandating the High Bridge and win approval for a bridge fifty feet high and wide enough to be used for a roadway.[45]

Far from insulted, Jervis saw this as vindication for the Democratic commissioners who had battled unsuccessfully for just such a low bridge. But times had changed. Jervis had settled on the professional value of building the big bridge and its piers were beginning to rise out of the Harlem.[46]

Content to let this last surprising flurry of low-bridge sentiment fade away, Jervis spent the final weeks of winter designing a new, historic dam. Clearly, he had not given the river enough space to spill over the dam; a significant widening of the weir was necessary. The problem was that the solid rock bed of the river extended only for the weir's ninety feet; beyond that, the riverbed was gravel. Jervis knew that the greatest long-term danger to a river dam was the effect of falling water on the stream bed below the dam: "Even a bed of solid rock has often been broken up and large masses taken out by the force of the falling water." Not knowing of any substantial dam that rested in part on a gravel foundation, Jervis recognized that he had to come up with a plan that eased the water's passage over the lip of the dam and gently down its lower side.

Pondering the limited options, Jervis "finally hit upon" an elegant first in American dam making: an S-shaped dam face with a small curve over the top of the dam and an elongated reverse curve along the lower face into a stilling basin downriver. Instead of the standard angled lip and linear slope along the downriver face of the dam, which created a great force of falling water at the base, Jervis's curving dam face, lined with courses of curved granite block, moved the water gently along the masonry, dissipating the river's destructive energy. In this way, Jervis could safely extend the width of the weir another 180 feet across the gravel portion

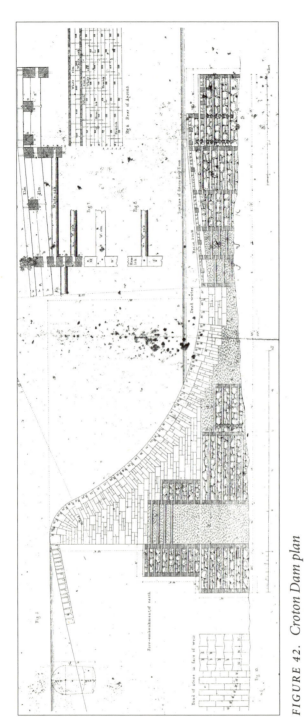

FIGURE 42. Croton Dam plan

This engraving from Schramke's book shows the Croton Dam as redesigned by John Jervis after the flood of 1841 damaged the partially completed original dam. The innovative S-shaped dam face and the stilling basin of the new structure became standard in American dam design. (William Lee Frost.)

of the riverbed, for a total overfall of 270 feet. The reverse curve and stilling basin, never used in the United States before, would become standard features of American dams.[47]

A new contracting group undertook the dam work in April, under obligation to have it substantially completed by fall.[48] In the meantime, Jervis suffered fallout from the dam's failure in the form of unsolicited opinions from self-styled experts. A visiting English engineer beseeched the commissioners with general ideas about the dam redesign that, under prompting from the Croton engineers, never rose to specifics. Complimentary allusions to the English engineer from Chairman Stevens were "rather too much" for Jervis, who told Stevens that the Englishman had a "total lack of engineering capacity." At the same time, another English engineer of uncertain hydraulic qualifications claimed the aqueduct would fail to deliver the promised amount of water. Though the fellow had impressed Governor Seward and the commissioners, Jervis exposed him with a trap, a set of specifications for a hypothetical aqueduct for which the engineer was asked to determine its flow. After a number of days, the engineer replied that the hypothetical aqueduct would supply no water, whereupon Jervis revealed the specifications were in fact real numbers for a French aqueduct that had supplied water quite adequately for many years. Jervis was deeply offended by the pretentious Englishmen, who "no doubt were of a class that supposed it was not possible anyone should know much of engineering in the woods of America."[49]

Finishing Touches

Whig political dreams were dealt a death blow in the spring of 1841. On April 4, President Harrison succumbed to pneumonia contracted at his inauguration a month earlier. Whigs attempted to soothe their loss with a spectacular New York funeral, at which a stunned Philip Hone was a pallbearer, but the great procession was abandoned after an hour in the face of a driving snowstorm. The snows continued up until the city elections. "Silk stocking" Whig voters stayed home and martyred Democrat Robert Morris, deposed as recorder by Governor Seward, swept into the mayor's office for the first of three terms. It was a "foul spot" on the city's honor, lamented Hone.[50]

Despite continuing Whig control in Albany, in May, the water commissioners lost their battle with the Common Council over Croton distribution. In a law authorizing a final $3.5 million in water stock, the city officially regained authority south of the Murray Hill reservoir, though the council was ordered to honor pipe contracts already made by the commissioners. The law did grant the commissioners formal permission, with the council's consent, to do no further excavation of the York Hill reservoir. A further provision of this last significant law before completion of the project allowed the city for the first time to levy direct taxes to cover the significant interest on the water bonds, whose value was still tumbling.[51]

Though the summer building season officially began in April, the spring snowstorms and subsequent high water in the Croton prevented any significant work on the new dam until mid-June. The weather was favorable through the summer, but flooding in October brought the river to a crest at the height of the unfinished dam. The rains caused the contractors to miss their deadline for completion of the first stage of the work, but Jervis was well satisfied with their energy and ability. In mid-December, the river rose higher than during the deadly flood of the previous winter, but the works held. "The Croton to-day is mad," Edmund French reported to Jervis the day before Christmas, but once again there was no damage. "This was a season of intense anxiety" for the chief engineer, who "watched the indications of rain very closely." Later Jervis acknowledged "the hand of Benign Providence who has so kindly tempered the storm, and saved us from material harm."[52]

Having earlier dispatched English pretenders, Jervis faced local academics during the summer and fall. In widely circulated comments, a math professor predicted "great disappointment" in the amount of water expected from the aqueduct; Jervis assured the anxious commissioners that it would furnish even more water than promised. A public lecture by a natural philosophy professor predicted "total failure" of the Manhattan Valley siphon. Again offering assurances that all would be well, Jervis expressed great annoyance at supposedly learned men who "impaired the confidence of the public and the water commissioners in the engineering of the works."[53]

Jervis did have the confidence of the richest man in America. The aqueduct's rising cost, a possible hike in property taxes, and the continuing economic decline caused panicked discussions of a real estate sell-off during 1841. One large property owner had the presence of mind to inquire first of John Astor, then nearly eighty years old. "We can hardly spend too much for a supply of good water," Astor calmly advised, and a sell-off was averted.[54]

Despite the uncertainties, New Yorkers with much to lose marveled at the aqueduct's approach. Buffeted by the depression, Philip Hone took a Sunday drive in late October to view the nearly complete reservoir at Murray Hill, scheduled for filling with great ceremony the next Fourth of July. With contractor Thomson Price as his guide, Hone took the measure of the "gigantic work," its massive granite walls, finely wrought Egyptian styling, and high promenade over as yet empty twin "Mediterranean seas." "The Philadelphians may boast of their Fairmount Works," Hone enthused, "but they are no more to be compared to this than the Schuylkill to the Hudson. I doubt whether there is a similar work in Europe of equal extent and magnificence with the Croton Aqueduct, its dams, bridges, tunnels and reservoirs."[55]

A few days later, Hone was less enthusiastic about the future. In the November state elections, Democrats regained control of the legislature, with a slim majority in the Senate and broad control of the Assembly, and Hone mourned the short-lived ascendancy of his party: "All the public improvements will be stopped and the wholesome laws passed by the Whigs repealed."[56] In just another twelve months, Canal Commissioner Bouck would be elected governor, leading to the reappointment of Stephen Allen and the other original water commissioners early in 1843.

In the meantime, the bottom fell out of Croton water bonds. With $12 million worth on the market, they hit a record low of 21 percent below par in December, a "ruinous rate," ex-Commissioner Allen trenchantly noted.[57]

Deliverance

The coming of 1842 marked the bottom of the depression begun, like the Croton Aqueduct, in the spring of 1837. "The business stringency continued this year," Charles Haswell recalled, "with securities much depressed, trade stagnant, and city real estate at the lowest point of salable value it

FIGURE 43. *Croton Dam view*
Drawn by Fayette Tower for his Croton book, this engraving illustrates the primitive surroundings of the historic dam. (William Lee Frost; photo by Barry Rosenthal.)

had reached for many years." Underscoring the city's withered prosperity, at the end of January the 13th Street reservoir was empty.[58]

Somehow the city persevered through its last unwatered months. Fayette Tower, preparing for a transfer to the city after completing his Clendening Valley work, expected that by June "we shall have finished the big '*Tea Pot*' with which we can fill the cups of the citizens of N.Y.," though he hoped "it may be neither *black* nor *green* tea."[59]

In April, the Democratic legislature passed a law giving the city full authority to manage the "Croton Water Works" and enforce by-laws and ordinances to protect them. Although the water commissioners and their engineers still oversaw remaining construction (primarily the High Bridge), the city's Croton Aqueduct Department would administer the operating works. Over the next few months, Uzziah Wenman became the department's first superintendent, and Horatio Allen shifted allegiances to become the department's first chief engineer. Allen would answer to the department's board, among whose five initial members was Myndert

Van Schaick, for the first time holding an official position in the water system he had envisioned ten years earlier.[60]

The spirits of fretful Chairman Stevens were raised in June, after two unique excursions. On June 8, the commissioners and engineers Jervis, Allen, and French began a three-day trip together, an "odd sort of journey" on foot, fully recorded by the press. The *Evening Post* reported that the party "entered the Aqueduct at its mouth at the Croton River and pursued the examination . . . under ground to Harlem river, a distance of thirty-three miles." The *Commercial Advertiser* reported chill and moist surroundings: "The temperature was found to be from 53 to 55 degrees. At the greatest depths . . . springs have frequently forced their way into the works. These, to some extent, it has been found more convenient to permit to flow into the work than to exclude." The walking tourists were said to be satisfied with the conduit and with the temporary Harlem pipe, which proved tight after a test filling.[61]

On the heels of that mostly dry run, the same travelers took a boat trip two weeks later, again amply documented by the press. At five in the morning on the 22nd, the gates at the dam were opened for the first time and a stream of Croton River water eighteen inches deep was let into the aqueduct. Four of the party climbed aboard the *Croton Maid,* a sixteen-foot wooden skiff designed for the occasion. While the rest of the commissioners and engineers followed above ground, the subterranean navigators floated south inside the aqueduct. Six hours later, they reached Sing Sing, a distance of eight miles. Here the water was drained from a waste weir until noon, when the journey resumed with a new crew toward the waste gates at Mill River, a five-mile run completed at three in the afternoon. At a quarter to four, the mariners set out on the ten-mile leg to Yonkers, where they arrived at ten-thirty in the evening. Again, the water was run off from a weir and the crew retired until dawn. The process was repeated for two more segments, until the last stop at the Harlem River, where three commissioners and Chief Engineer Jervis "emerged to the surface of the earth" at one in the afternoon. Stevens reported joyously that day to Mayor Morris that the average rate of flow during the cruise had been about forty-five minutes a mile, "a velocity greater, we are happy to say, than the calculations gave reason to expect." Everything tried during the excursion, from the dam gates to the waste weirs and the conduit had "been found

FIGURE 44. York Hill Reservoir, 1842

This lithograph by Nathaniel Currier shows the receiving reservoir's place in the empty high ground that today is Central Park's Great Lawn; the reservoir is now filled and buried beneath the lawn. (Eno Collection. Miriam and Ira D. Wallach Division of Art, Prints and Photographs. The New York Public Library. Astor, Lenox and Tilden Foundations.)

to answer most perfectly the objects of their construction." In short, the aqueduct worked, just as Jervis had promised it would.[62]

The following Monday afternoon, water was let across the Harlem, down upper Manhattan, and into the York Hill receiving reservoir. Governor Seward, Mayor Morris, the Common Council, and other officials joined twenty thousand citizens for a thirty-eight-gun salute as the water slowly spread across the bottom of the great pool. The correspondent for the notorious *New World* reported a "melancholy humbug" featuring just a "puddle of dirty water." Witty *Brother Jonathan* chuckled at the aquatic appearance of some water commissioners on the *Croton Maid* and the presentation of their "tub" to the fire department. "Croton Water is slowly flowing towards the city," young George Templeton Strong briefly noted in his now-famous diary, "which at last will stand a chance of being cleansed—if water *can* clean it."[63]

For engineer Fayette Tower, it was "a glorious day." He was introduced to many important people throughout the festivities, but an early visitor left the deepest impression:

> First in the morning John Jacob Astor came to see the work, seated in a very low carriage so that he could step out without difficulty, tho he has grown very infirm with age. I was introduced to him and took his hand. His head was bent forward beneath the weight of years and being introduced to one of the contractors for building the reservoir, he turned up one eye towards him and remarked "I think you ought to make *money* here." How characteristic of the man whose thoughts have turned to dollars.[64]

As planned for nearly a year, the water arrived with great fanfare at Murray Hill at sunrise on July 4. To the accompaniment of forty-five cannon, the Croton entered the twin basins, dirty at first from the wash of the pipes. The *Commercial Advertiser* reported that "the river had got up rather too early" for the mayor and other city officials who showed up later. Among the early risers was Fayette Tower, with his artful eye and pen: "At an hour when the morning guns had roused but few from their dreamy slumbers, and ere yet the rays of the sun had gilded the city's domes, I stood on the topmost wall of the reservoir and saw the first rush of the water as . . . [it]

FIGURE 45. *Murray Hill Reservoir, 1850*

This gouache by Augustus Fay, looking southwest, illustrates the undeveloped state in the mid-nineteenth century of what soon became the bustling intersection of Fifth Avenue and 42nd Street. The distributing reservoir was torn down in the 1890s to make way for the New York Public Library. (I. N. Phelps Stokes Collection. Miriam and Ira D. Wallach Division of Art, Prints and Photographs. The New York Public Library. Astor, Lenox and Tilden Foundations.)

entered the bottom and wandered about, as if each particle had consciousness." By day's end, twenty-five thousand New Yorkers had visited the reservoir, each offered "a glass of the water cooled with ice."[65]

Not by plan the water made a comic debut that day in the city proper, where both the 13th Street Reservoir and the Manhattan Company tank at Bleecker Street were dry. Concerned about fireworks danger, Mayor Morris asked at the morning ceremonies if the Croton could be let into the distribution mains to temporarily fill those reservoirs. With the commissioners' approval, the Murray Hill gates were raised, but the water failed to enter the mains because no ventilating pipes had yet been placed in them. Workers quickly made the attachments, and by late morning the Croton entered the city limits, proclaiming its presence in unsuspecting neighborhoods by "the roaring whistle" of escaping air. By afternoon, the 13th

Street Reservoir was brimming, and the water pressed south by evening to the Manhattan Company tank, housed in a three-story building. Here, reported the *Commercial Advertiser*, "Dame Croton cut a few antic capers, for not satisfied with filling this reservoir she made her overflow and *spill*. This was no pleasant affair and looked like satisfying an old grudge." Water spouted into neighboring houses from the windows of the building before axe-wielding firemen broke down the locked doors and stopcocks were finally closed: "Old Manhattan was greatly alarmed, and considered it an insult that the Croton had thus come to supply her customers; but two of a trade never agree."[66]

Completing the distribution system and attending to final construction details kept laborers and engineers busy for the rest of the summer. Fayette Tower "was so exceedingly engaged about the affairs of my *pet* the Croton Aqueduct, that I really thought of nothing else." There was still considerable finish work to be done on the reservoirs and the Croton Dam, work that Jervis estimated would not be completed until October.

The High Bridge remained a distant reality, its vertical progress only minimally visible above the surface of the Harlem. Seven cofferdams had been constructed but not all had been drained. Oak pile foundations had been put down for only four river piers (and five land piers); for the pier in the center of the river, workers bored through seventy feet of mud and soft sand before driving piles another thirty-five feet into a suitably firm foundation of hard sand and clay. Jervis estimated at least two more years to complete the bridge; it would take six.[67]

The public, meanwhile, took to its new reservoirs. York Hill was the summer's "fashionable place of resort," observed visitor Philip Hone who sampled the waters: "clear it is, and sweet and soft, for to be in the fashion I drank a tumbler of it and found it all these . . . a wholesome temperance beverage, well calculated to cool the palates and quench the thirst of the New Yorkers, and to diminish the losses of the fire insurance companies." Hone believed millions would take to the high promenade of the Murray Hill reservoir "for centuries after the present generation shall have passed away."[68] In fact, the Murray Hill reservoir would pass away before the end of Hone's century, but none contemplating its massive Egyptian presence in the summer of 1842 could imagine anything less than the permanence of the Pyramids.

FIGURE 46. Philip Hone, date unknown

Shown here in a portrait reproduced in the 1863 *Manual of the Common Council,* the ex-mayor and wealthy merchant kept a diary of his city's life in the second quarter of the nineteenth century, which included much commentary on the construction and celebration of the Croton Aqueduct. (General Research Division. New York Public Library. Astor, Lenox and Tilden Foundations.)

The promise of Croton water brought the advent of the Croton plumber. In early July, A. Brower was among the first to advertise his ability to supply lead pipes and brass faucets to any house desiring Croton water. Although the number of New York plumbers would grow from fewer than a dozen before Croton to some two hundred by midcentury, there was no boom in 1842. "Very small exertions are at present made by our citizens to introduce this water into their dwellings," the *Evening Post* reported in early August, after water was flowing beneath some neighborhoods. The hesitation was ascribed to uncertainties about cost. The city had not announced if the water was to be free to all by a general tax, or to building owners for a fee. If the latter, the paper foresaw Croton water used only by the rich, with no incentive for landlords to hook up: "The great mass of the people, who are tenants, will derive no benefits from it, and the health of the city will not be materially improved."[69]

But even the wealthy like George T. Strong hesitated to call the plumber that summer: "There's nothing new in town, except the Croton Water, which is all full of tadpoles and animalculae, and which moreover flows through an aqueduct which I hear was used as a necessary by all the Hibernian vagabonds who worked upon it. I shall drink no Croton for some time to come." Strong, likely drinking the best carted water money could buy, would significantly alter his Croton attitudes in the coming months.[70]

The city did not announce until late September that it would build Croton street hydrants, "from which water may be taken gratuitously by any who may wish." Private service would cost $10 a year for two-story houses and $12 for three-story houses. It was no wonder that the Croton plumber had time on his hands.[71]

Eager to commemorate the "vast importance" of the city's underappreciated bounty (and to seductively promote its use), the Common Council planned a celebration of historic proportions for October 14. The heralds were two great fountains, built during September in Union Square and the Park at City Hall.[72]

Typically, George Strong was an early detractor—"a circular basin with a squirt in the middle, and nothing more"—but public response was favorable when the Union Square fountain was tested on October 11. "It throws up a noble column of water to a height as great almost as the houses which surround the square," observed the *Evening Post.* "In the course of the afternoon, the column and surrounding jets were made to take different appearances, by enlarging or narrowing the apertures." By moonlight, "the effect of the fountain showering its spray on every side, was exceedingly fine."[73]

Tests of the larger City Hall fountain attracted growing crowds, among them a temporary New Yorker with the keenest Croton eye since Fayette Tower: "I shall never forget my sensations when I first looked upon the Fountains. My soul jumped, and clapped its hands, rejoicing in exceeding beauty. I am a novice, and easily made wild by the play of graceful forms; but those accustomed to the splendid displays of France and Italy, say the world offers nothing to equal the magnificence of the New-York *jets.*"[74]

The writer was Massachusetts-born Lydia Maria Child, perhaps best known today for the sleighing verse that starts "Over the river and through the wood." A popular writer of prose and poetry, Child had arrived in the city the previous year to edit an abolitionist weekly with her husband; her correspondence about life in New York for the *National Anti-Slavery Standard* and the *Boston Courier* became best-selling books.[75]

Child related the operational details of the Park fountain, with its central pipe and eighteen jets arrayed in a basin a hundred feet across. By shifting various plates and bars, the display took on myriad forms: the Maid of the Mist, the Croton Plume, the Vase, the Dome, the Bouquet, the Sheaf of Wheat, and the Weeping Willow: "As the sun shone on the sparkling drops, through mist and feathery foam, rainbows glimmered at the sides, as if they came to celebrate a marriage between the Spirits of Light and Water Nymphs." She found the Union Square fountain "scarcely less beautiful. It is a weeping willow of crystal drops; but one can see that it weeps for *joy.* Now it leaps and sports as gracefully as Undine in her wildest moods, and then sinks into the vase under a veil of woven pearls, like the undulating farewell courtesy of her fluid relations."[76]

The frolic of the fountain waters melted the resolve of George Strong. After observing the fountains at full strength, he wrote, "They're splendid, both . . . I hope they'll play permanently."[77] On October 12, Philip Hone recorded the transformation of his depressed city: "Nothing is talked of or thought of in New York but Croton water; fountains, aqueducts, hydrants, and hose attract our attention and impede our progress through the streets. . . . Water! water! is the universal note which is sounded

FIGURE 47. *Croton water celebration, 1842*

This anonymous lithograph was on the cover of the sheet music for the "Croton Ode," sung at the October 14, 1842, celebration. Compare this view of Broadway, City Hall Park, and Park Row with the 1830 John William Hill watercolor in Figure 23. (I. N. Phelps Stokes Collection. Miriam and Ira D. Wallach Division of Art, Prints and Photographs. The New York Public Library. Astor, Lenox and Tilden Foundations.)

through every part of the city, and infuses joy and exultation into the masses, even though they are somewhat out of spirits."[78]

The sun rose bright and strong on Friday, the 14th, for the "Croton Celebration." As cannon roared at the Battery, the fountains at City Hall and Union Square rushed to life, and church bells pealed throughout the city. From eight to ten in the morning, tens of thousands of marchers mustered around the Battery, forming into ten divisions of dozens of parts: military companies; government officials of assorted cities and states including the various water officials of New York; fire companies from New York and elsewhere; Croton contractors and workers; doctors, lawyers, learned and trade societies; ethnic societies; temperance societies; and, in the rear guard, "citizens and strangers." At ten, the marchers began "the largest procession ever known in the city," a seven-mile route up Broadway past Bowling Green, Wall Street, and City Hall Park to Union Square, then down the Bowery, and through various streets to the east side of the park, where there would be speeches. Buildings were adorned with flags, banners, and floral displays; people were adorned with commemorative silk badges and engraved medals commissioned for the celebration. From a Broadway rooftop, "the eye could see nothing beneath but the dense unbroken throng of people, with a column moving along the center." To George Strong, "all the population of the city, and of the surrounding country too . . . seemed to have precipitated itself bodily into Broadway."[79]

As many as a quarter million people were either marching or watching the procession, whose head reached the park at one-thirty in the afternoon as the tail was just making its first pass on the Broadway side. The city's volunteer firemen, it seemed to observers, had turned out in the largest numbers, as many as four thousand strong, followed by the temperance societies that won high marks for their display of a water hydrant chasing a rum cask and a banner with an inverted decanter reading "Right Side Up." In additions to its engineers, commissioners, contractors, and workers, the Croton was represented by one horse-drawn truck bearing an assortment of pipe, another with men working a machine for tapping water pipes, and a third with men simulating the hammering and laying of pipe.[80]

By four-thirty, under skies that had clouded over, as many celebrants as the area could hold were crowded around the park for speeches and song. Samuel Stevens officially delivered custody of the works to the Croton Aqueduct Department with a twenty-minute oration. He traced the city's quest for "pure and wholesome water" as far back as the Tea Water Pump, with nods to Christopher Colles, William Weston, and the Manhattan Company, on which he went easy: "Their pipes, though they furnished not pure and wholesome water, have nevertheless, in cases of fire, been frequently highly beneficial to the city." He moved quickly through the 1820s without mentioning Mayor Allen's efforts, before digressing a bit on the 13th Street system featuring, of course, Stevens's own efforts. For the origins of the Croton supply, Whig Stevens carefully named just about everyone involved except Democrat Myndert Van Schaick, the strongest claimant to the Croton idea and a member of the department to which Stevens was turning over control. Stevens described the "skill and science" of aqueduct planner David Douglass, and faintly praised the "performance of . . . duty" of John Jervis, who had "shown himself admirably calculated" to complete it.[81]

Some calculation had been required to keep the Croton contingent marching that day. By one account, the engineers and contractors had threatened to boycott the parade because Jervis had been accorded no more honor than to walk with them; Governor Seward had saved the day by having Jervis ride up front with him. Assigned a place merely with the city's ex-mayors, Stephen Allen had shown up early at the Battery to claim a seat in a leading carriage, "a more conspicuous situation than those who succeeded me in conducting the water."[82]

The president of the Croton Aqueduct Board, John H. Lawrence, obliged the crowd with a short acceptance speech, and just past five in the afternoon, two hundred members of the New-York Sacred Choral Society launched into the "Croton Ode," a sentimental seven-stanza verse commissioned by the city from poet-editor George Pope Morris, otherwise famous for "Woodman, Spare That Tree":

> Water leaps as if delighted,
> While her conquered foes retire!
> Pale contagion flies affrighted
> With the baffled demon Fire!
> . . .
> Round the Aqueducts of story
> As the mists of Lethé throng,
> Croton's waves, in all their glory,
> Troop in melody along.—
> Ever sparkling, bright and single,
> Will this rock-ribbed stream appear,
> When Posterity shall mingle
> Like the gathered waters here.

The gathered masses were not spared the opportunity to sing along, as a horse-drawn printing press rolled off lyric sheets along the parade route: "It operated like a nauseating dose upon every one in whose hands it fell." Upon the cessation of the choir, the crowd gave nine cheers and rapidly dispersed to an assortment of public balls and private parties. At ten in the evening, the heavens opened up. Just hours after the city's crowded celebration of water, the streets were abandoned to the rain.[83]

Philip Hone, who had been pleased to ride with the ex-mayors, turned homeward with sober civic pride: "not a drunken person was to be seen. The moral as well as the physical influence of water pervaded everything. . . . It was a day for a New Yorker to be proud of."[84] Bostonian Lydia Child was greatly moved: "Oh, who that has not been shut up in the great prison-cell of a city, and made to drink of its brackish springs, can estimate the blessings of the Croton Aqueduct? Clean, sweet, abundant water!"[85]

Ten years earlier, the agonizing cholera deaths of Mary, Margaret, and Jeremiah Fitzgerald had set the city on a course to the Croton. Now, as spectacular fountains poured out a distant river's bounty, generations of bad water began to fade into a misty memory of Old New York.

New York's Water
from Then to Now

Water is the only drink for a wise man.

—Henry David Thoreau, *Walden*

"If ever a man deserved a monument, it is he who first devised the plan of bringing Croton river into the city," gushed Lydia Child in 1844: "But it so happens, that his name is as uncertain as the birth-place of Homer. No matter. If his soul is as large as his deed, he will care little for the credit of it."[1] Child was wrong about this.

A brief obituary for Samuel Stevens the next January credited him with the introduction of Croton water. An infuriated and formerly discreet Myndert Van Schaick sent a long statement to the *Evening Post* revealing his essential role and discrediting Stevens, as well as reinstated water commission chairman Stephen Allen. Allen fired back with an account triumphing his own efforts, and the front-page battle raged for several months before both sides tired. In 1852, eighty-year-old Allen was killed in a steamboat explosion. At the opening of a billion gallon reservoir in Central Park ten years later, longtime Croton Aqueduct Department board member Van Schaick delivered a speech recounting his enterprise in the 1830s. This time, none contested it.[2]

It had taken a while for demand to meet that new reservoir's supply. Though the richest New Yorkers hooked up early (in the summer of

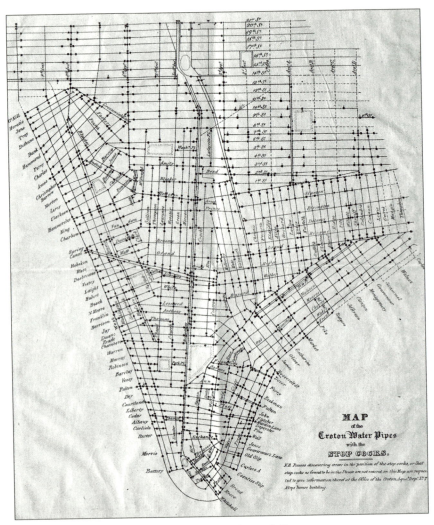

FIGURE 48. *Croton water pipe map, circa 1842*

This lithograph of the Croton distribution network illustrates the expansion of the city up to its limits at 21st Street. (© Collection of The New-York Historical Society.)

1843, young diarist George Strong was leading "an amphibious life" in his new bathtub), Croton had only six thousand paying customers and revenues of $100,000 in 1844, while total costs were rising above $13 million. Two years after it opened, Croton was primarily a *public* amenity of great fountains and thousands of fire and free street hydrants; most homeowners and landlords had little inclination to install costly service pipe.[3]

The city's last great fire, in the summer of 1845, killed thirty people and destroyed $6 million worth of property, but failed to change attitudes. Three years later, fewer than one in three New Yorkers had signed up for Croton; most continued to get water from free hydrants and remaining wells, and shared back alley privies, especially in the festering tenements of the poor.[4]

Business finally boomed for the Croton plumber after the completion of the High Bridge in 1848 boosted water pressure. The city suffered its second cholera epidemic the following year. Five thousand New Yorkers died in 1849, many more than in 1832 but a much smaller ratio of the total population, which had doubled to half a million. Croton gained new customers by the tens of thousands and water use quickly jumped to thirty-five million gallons a day, bringing the first, futile calls for strict regulation. The aqueduct was "a far nobler token for New York than even her steamships," thought Walt Whitman, editorializing in 1851 for a water supply for his adopted Brooklyn.[5]

With the beginnings of a sewer system in the 1850s, the Croton-supplied bathroom became a fixture in city dwellings. In 1857, Joseph Gayetty met a new demand, with the world's first toilet tissue; fifty cents bought five hundred manila hemp sheets of "Gayetty's Medicated Paper." At the same time, an age-old feature of New York life got a new name: the local cockroach *Blatella germanica* became known simply as "the Croton bug," supposedly introduced to the home through Croton pipe.[6]

In the mid-1870s, annual revenues of $1.5 million finally exceeded debt-fueled annual expenses. With the addition of two watershed reservoirs in Putnam County, Croton supplied over sixty million daily gallons. As Manhattan's population passed a million in the early 1880s, per capita daily use soared extravagantly to nearly a hundred gallons, the highest in the world and double what Philadelphians used. The demand on the aqueduct was so far beyond the designed maximum of 75 million gallons that water was leaking from the roof of the unpressurized conduit. Just forty

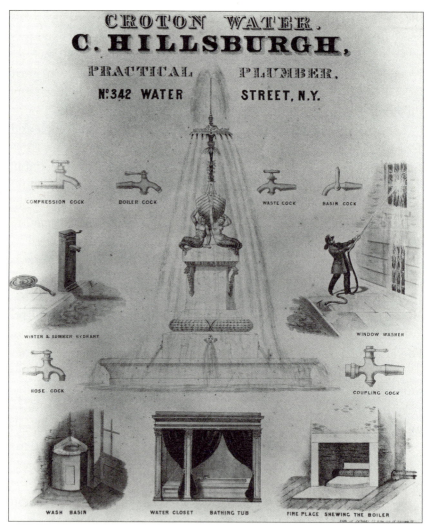

FIGURE 49. Plumber's advertisement, 1840s

This lithograph illustrates the great expectations aroused by the Croton for domestic comfort and public ornament. New York plumbers would not flourish, though, until after the city's second major cholera epidemic in 1849. (© Collection of The New-York Historical Society.)

years after it was built to supply New York for generations, John Jervis's Croton Aqueduct had reached the limits of its capacity.[7]

In 1885, the Bronx and Byram Rivers were finally harnessed, but only for annexed Westchester territory that became part of the city's Bronx borough. To service Manhattan, a massive new Croton aqueduct was completed in the early 1890s. Following a route farther inland than the original aqueduct, the water was tunneled through Westchester and three hundred feet below the Harlem in a twelve-foot round conduit, and down Manhattan in iron pipe to the Central Park Reservoir. On the lower Croton River, a 240-foot-high masonry dam was completed in 1905; then the world's tallest dam, it created a thirty-six-hundred-acre lake that submerged Jervis's historic dam three miles upriver. With the addition of nine more watershed reservoirs by 1911, the available daily supply of the Croton system reached over 400 million gallons.[8]

When mostly Manhattan New York expanded to its current five boroughs in 1898, its population instantly doubled to 3.5 million, on the way to a 1950s peak of 8 million. Even the twin Croton aqueducts could not meet these needs.

The Catskill Aqueduct, begun in 1907, placed in service in 1917, and extended in 1926, brought water from the Catskill Mountains over one hundred miles north of the city and west of the Hudson River. Featuring two watershed storage reservoirs that displaced thousands of resentful rural residents, and a tunnel eleven hundred feet beneath the Hudson, the Catskill Aqueduct was the largest municipal water supply in the world, delivering 555 million daily gallons. From 1937 to 1965, the city built the Delaware Aqueduct, drawing up to 800 million gallons a day from four reservoirs gathering Delaware River tributary waters west of the Catskills. The Catskill and Delaware systems, distributed from two Westchester reservoirs into city water tunnels opened in 1917 and 1936, now supply 90 percent of the city's 1.5-billion-gallon daily demand; the ongoing construction of an immense new distribution tunnel eventually will allow the first inspection and repair of the original tunnels.

The city still gets 10 percent of its water from the Croton watershed, via the new aqueduct alone. As the Catskill and Delaware systems came on line, the "Old Croton" gradually was cut back and stopped sending water to New York in 1955, just 113 years after it was opened to serve the city

for untold centuries. After supplying water to several Westchester communities for another ten years, the aqueduct was shut completely. Its northernmost section was reopened in 1989 to serve Ossining, the twentieth century name of Sing Sing.

Little evidence of the aqueduct remains in Manhattan. The Murray Hill reservoir was torn down in the late 1890s to make way for the New York Public Library. The York Hill reservoir was filled during the 1930s to become Central Park's Great Lawn. Both reservoirs had been bypassed by the Central Park Reservoir, itself taken out of active service during the 1990s in favor of suburban storage reservoirs. The street-blocking Clendening Valley crossing was replaced by underground pipes in the 1870s. Only the High Bridge remains, the city's oldest bridge but long stripped of its water function and its towering river arches; in conjunction with other improvements on the Harlem, a single steel span was installed in the 1930s to finally permit river navigation.

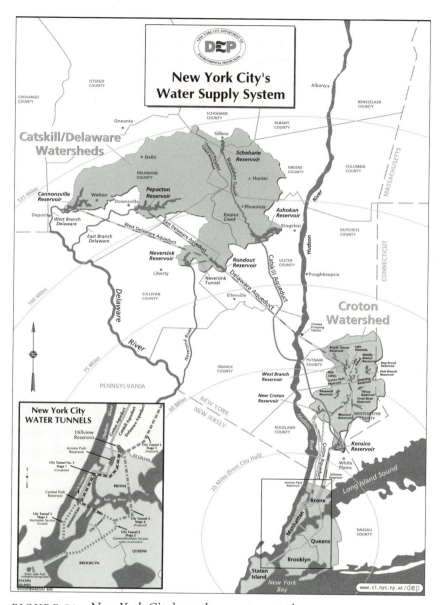

FIGURE 51.   *New York City's modern water supply*

This map shows the broad expansion of the city's water supply beyond the old Croton. (City of New York Department of Environmental Protection.)

In Westchester, nearly all the above-ground structures remain, though John Jervis's pioneering dam is preserved beneath Croton Lake, peeking out during severe droughts. The Sing Sing archwork is an attraction for tourists who can enter the emptied conduit through a waste weir. The stone ventilating towers mark the aqueduct's right of way that has become a twenty-six-mile trail park. The aqueduct itself was designated a national historic landmark in 1992.

Nothing of the city's oldest waterworks remain. The 13th Street works were sold off by the city during the 1840s and gradually torn down. The Manhattan Company works at Chambers Street, emptied soon after Croton was turned on, were demolished in the early 1900s, though a bank employee ceremoniously pumped water at the site every day until 1923 for fear of losing the company's precious state charter; in 1965, a national charter was written for what had become Chase Manhattan.

The Croton Aqueduct shaped many lives connected to its creation. John Jervis, who remained at his Croton post until completing the High Bridge, was consulting engineer on Boston's Cochituate water works and designed American railroads as far west as the Mississippi; he died at age eighty-nine. Horatio Allen ran the Novelty Iron Works until 1870, consulted on the Brooklyn Bridge and the Panama Canal, and died at age ninety-seven. Longtime assistant Edward Tracy succeeded Jervis as Croton chief engineer for five years beginning in 1848, and returned for another five years in the 1870s. Myndert Van Schaick remained a Croton Aqueduct Board member into his eighties and died in 1865. Fayette Tower published a book of illustrations of the aqueduct in 1843, married his late wife's sister, pursued various engineering and manufacturing work, and became mayor of Cumberland, Maryland, and a state legislator in the early 1850s. But his health had been permanently impaired by his early Croton labors, and Tower returned to his upstate New York hometown in 1857 and died there two weeks after his fortieth birthday.[9]

As it enters the twenty-first century, New York City has the world's oldest continuously running urban water supply. The city no longer seeks new sources of water but preserves and conserves its existing supplies, especially in the suburbanized Croton Valley. The Croton remains a bridge between the city's past and future: its first successful water quest that made the modern city possible.

ONE   "Give Us Cold Water"

1. Dudley Atkins, M.D., ed., *Reports of Hospital Physicians and Other Documents in Relation to the Epidemic Cholera of 1832* (New York: G. & C. & H. Carvill, 1832), 9–10; *The Cholera Gazette* (Philadelphia), Sept. 26, 1832.

2. Atkins, *Reports of Hospital Physicians,* 46–47.

3. Joseph Seavy, *A Treatise on the Asiatic Cholera* (New York: Elliott and Palmer, 1832), 8–9.

4. New York City, Department of Health, Borough of Manhattan, *Register of Deaths,* June 1832.

5. *Niles' Weekly Register,* June 23, 1832; Geoffrey Marks and William K. Beatty, *Epidemics* (New York: Charles Scribner's Sons, 1976), 194–96, 200; J. S. Chambers, *The Conquest of Cholera, America's Greatest Scourge* (New York: Macmillan, 1938), 19–20.

6. "The Memoirs of Stephen Allen (1787–1852), ed. with Introduction and Notes by John C. Travis, one of his Great-Grandsons, New York, 1927," typescript in New-York Historical Society, 137 (hereafter listed as Allen, "Memoirs"); Chambers, *Conquest of Cholera,* 27; Edward Warren, M.D., *Sketch of the Progress of the Malignant or Epidemic Cholera from Its Arrival in America* (Boston: Carter, Hendee & Co., 1832), 35–36; *The Albion,* July 14, 1832; *The Cholera Bulletin* (New York), July 30, 1832.

7. Marks and Beatty, *Epidemics,* 200.

8. Philip Hone, *The Diary of Philip Hone 1828–1851,* 2 vols., ed. Allan Nevins (New York: Dodd, Mead and Company, 1927), 1:66.

9. New York *Evening Post,* July 2, August 6, 1832; John Pintard, *Letters from John Pintard to his Daughter Eliza Pintard Davidson 1816–1833,* 4 vols. (New York: New-York Historical Society, 1941) 4:66, 74; *New York American,* July 7, 1832; John Casilear to Asher Durand, July 28, 1832, Asher Brown Durand Papers, New York Public Library.

10. Atkins, *Reports of Hospital Physicians,* 90.

11. *Cholera Bulletin,* July 6, August 13, 1832; Atkins, *Reports of Hospital Physicians,* 89, 149.

12. *Encyclopaedia Britannica,* 15th ed., "Anesthetic," "Drugs and Drug Action"; Marks and Beatty, *Epidemics,* 207; Norbert Hirschhorn and William B. Greenough III, "Cholera," *Scientific American,* 225 (August 1971):15; Charles King, *A Memoir of the Construction, Cost, and Capacity of the Croton Aqueduct, Compiled from Official Documents* (New York: Charles King, 1843), 59.

13. J. Mauran, T. H. Webb, S. B. Tobey, *Remarks on the Cholera* (Providence: W. Marshall and Co., 1832), 20; *New-York Commercial Advertiser,* July 2, 1832, *Cholera Bulletin,* July 9, 1832.

14. *Peter Kalm's Travels in North America: the America of 1750,* ed. Adolph B. Benson (New York: Dover, 1987 [1937]), 133; I. Finch, *Travels in the United States of America and Canada* (London: Longman, Rees, Orme, Brown, Green, and Longman, 1833), 35.

15. Frontinus, *The Stratagems and The Aqueducts of Ancient Rome,* trans. Clemens Herschel, rev. Charles E. Bennett (Cambridge, Mass.: Harvard University Press, 1925); J. G. Landels, *Engineering in the Ancient World* (Berkeley: University of California Press, 1978); *Encyclopaedia Britannica,* "Public Works."

16. Marc Reisner, *Cadillac Desert: The American West and its Disappearing Water,* rev. ed. (New York: Penguin Books, 1993), 15–103; Norris Hundley, Jr., *The Great Thirst: Californians and Water, 1770s–1990s* (Berkeley: University of California Press, 1992), 1–200; John Russell McCarthy, "Water: The Story of Bill Mulholland," *Los Angeles Saturday Night* (December 11, 1937): 31, as quoted in Margaret Leslie Davis, *Rivers in the Desert: William Mulholland and the Inventing of Los Angeles* (New York: HarperCollins, 1993), 26.

TWO   *Manahata Goes Dutch*

1. Robert Steven Grumet, *Native American Place Names in New York City* (New York: Museum of the City of New York, 1981), 23–24; I. N. Phelps Stokes, *The Iconography of Manhattan Island,* 6 vols. (New York: Arno Press, 1967 [1915]), 2:121–22; Henry Gannett, *The Origin of Certain Place Names in the United States* (Williamstown, Mass.: Corner House Publishers, 1978), repr. of U.S. Department of the Interior, *Bulletin of the United States Geological Survey,* No. 197, Series F, Geography, 32 (Washington, D.C.: GPO, 1902), 170.

2. Edward F. Grier, ed., *Walt Whitman: Notebooks and Unpublished Prose Manuscripts,* vol. 3 (New York: New York University Press, 1984), 1011.

3. Horace Traubel, *With Walt Whitman in Camden,* vol. 5, ed. Gertrude Traubel (Carbondale: Southern Illinois University Press, 1964), 470.

4. Horace Traubel, *With Walt Whitman in Camden,* vol. 6, ed. Gertrude Traubel and William White (Carbondale: Southern Illinois University Press, 1982), 56.

5. Walt Whitman, *Good-bye My Fancy* (Philadelphia: David McKay, 1891), 46.

6. Jacob Steendam, *Complaint of New Amsterdam in New Netherland to Her Mother, of Her Beginning, Growth and Present Condition* (Amsterdam, 1659), in Henry

Cruse Murphy, *Jacob Steendam, Noch Vaster: A Memoir of the First Poet of New Nether-land with His Poems Descriptive of the Colony* (The Hague: The Brothers Giunta D'Al-bani, 1861), 27; see *Dictionary of American Biography* (*DAB*), "Jacob Steendam"; Stokes, *Iconography,* 2:228–29; James D. Hart, *Oxford Companion to American Lit-erature,* 4th ed. (New York: Oxford University Press, 1965), "Jacob Steendam."

7. Daniel Denton, *A Brief Description of New-York: Formerly Called New Nether-lands* (New York: Columbia University Press, 1937 [1670]); Stokes, *Iconography,* 4:148–49; David Piertsz DeVries, "Voyage from Holland to America, A.D. 1632 to 1644," in New-York Historical Society, *Collections,* 2d ser. vol. 3, part 1 (New York: D. Appleton & Co., 1857); *Journal of Jasper Danckaerts 1679–1680,* ed. Bartlett Burleigh James and J. Franklin Jameson (New York: Barnes and Noble, 1959 [1913]).

8. John Kieran, *A Natural History of New York City* (Boston: Houghton Mifflin Company, 1959), 3–4; Michael Kammen, *Colonial New York* (1975; New York: Oxford University Press, 1996), 31; Henry M. Christman, ed., *Walt Whitman's New York* (New York: Macmillan, 1963), 24.

9. George Everett Hill and George E. Waring, Jr., "Old Wells and Water-Courses of the Island of Manhattan," in *Papers on Historic New York,* 2 series, 4 volumes (Port Washington, N.Y.: Ira J. Friedman, 1969 [1897]), 1:1: 204–5.

10. Stokes, *Iconography,* 4:92, 6:72; Frank L. Walton, *Tomahawks to Textiles: The Fabulous Story of Worth Street* (New York: Appleton-Century-Crofts, 1953), 1–31.

11. "Description of ye Towne of Mannadens in New Netherland, as it was in Sept. 1661," in J. Franklin Jameson, ed., *Narratives of New Netherland, 1609–1664* (New York: Charles Scribner's Sons, 1909), 421–23; A. J. McClane, "The Saturday of Marten Van Kleek," *Field & Stream,* 80, 10 (Feb. 1976): 138.

12. Stokes, *Iconography,* 2:246.

13. Edmund B. O'Callaghan, ed., *Documents Relative to the Colonial History of the State of New-York,* 15 vols. (Albany: Weed, Parsons, and Co., 1856–87), 14:16–17.

14. Ernest L. Abel, *Alcohol Wordlore and Folklore* (Buffalo: Prometheus Books, 1987), 46; *The Encyclopedia of New York City,* ed. Kenneth T. Jackson (New Haven: Yale University Press, 1995), "brewing and distilling."

15. Stokes, *Iconography,* 2:229–30; "Members of the City Council from 1653 to the Present Date," in *Manual of the Corporation of the City of New York, 1842–43,* ed. David Thomas Valentine (New York: Thomas Snowden, 1842), 147–237 (here-after, *Manual of the Common Council*).

16. Berthold Fernow, ed., *The Records of New Amsterdam from 1653 to 1674,* 7 vols. (New York: Knickerbocker Press, 1897), 1:31, 33.

17. Fernow, *Records of New Amsterdam,* 1:38, 7:187; Berthold Fernow, ed., *Minutes of the Orphanmasters of New Amsterdam, 1665 to 1663,* 2 vols. (New York: F. P. Harper, 1902–1907), 2:106.

18. Fernow, *Records of New Amsterdam,* 1:8, 16, 38, 5:5, 7:87.

19. Fernow, *Records of New Amsterdam,* 5:87.

20. Fernow, *Records of New Amsterdam,* 7:190.

21. O'Callaghan, *Documents,* 2:248; Stokes, *Iconography,* 4:97, 208; Hugh Morrison, *Early American Architecture* (New York: Dover, 1987), 105; *Narratives of New Netherland, 1609–1664,* 421–23.

22. O'Callaghan, *Documents,* 2:248–49.

23. O'Callaghan, *Documents,* 2:440–41.

24. O'Callaghan, *Documents,* 2:500.

THREE   *English Well-Being*

1. Stokes, *Iconography,* 4:262; *Journal of Jasper Danckaerts,* 46.

2. Fernow, *Records of New Amsterdam,* 6:279–80, 308.

3. Victor Hugo Paltsits, ed., *Minutes of the Executive Council of the Province of New York, Administration of Frances Lovelace, 1668–1673,* 2 vols. (Albany: State of New York, 1910), 1:163–64, 2:761–73; *Magazine of American History,* 16:234–35.

4. Kammen, *Colonial New York,* 91.

5. *Proceedings of the Common Council of the City of New York, 1674–1690* (New York: New York Printing Co., 1871), 51, 106.

6. *Proceedings of the Common Council, 1674–1690,* 438, 441–42, 449–51.

7. Hill and Waring, "Old Wells and Water-Courses," 200. In 1696, the responsibilities of well maintenance and assessments passed to the alderman and assistant alderman of each ward; *Minutes of the Common Council of the City of New York, 1675–1776,* 8 vols. (New York: Dodd, Mead, 1905), 1:427–28 (hereafter, *MCC, 1675–1776*).

8. Stokes, *Iconography,* 4:348; Leisler to the governor of Boston, 19 June 1689, in Edmund B. O'Callaghan, ed., *Documentary History of the State of New-York* (Albany: Weed, Parsons, and Co., 1849–1851, 4 vols.), 2:6; Stephen Van Cortlandt to Captain Nicholson, August 5, 1689, in O'Callaghan, *Documents,* 3:609; Leisler to Connecticut Governor Treat, in O'Callaghan, *Documentary History,* 2:20; Leisler to William and Mary, August 20, 1689, in O'Callaghan, *Documents,* 3:615.

9. Berthold Fernow, comp., *Calendar of Council Minutes, 1668–1783* (Harrison, N.Y.: Harbor Hill Books, 1987 [1902]), 94.

10. Wayne Andrews, "A Glance at New York in 1697: The Travel Diary of Dr. Benjamin Bullivant," *New-York Historical Society Quarterly,* 40, 1 (January 1956), 55–73.

11. O'Callaghan, *Documents,* 4:420.

12. *MCC, 1675–1776,* 2:103.

13. *MCC, 1675–1776,* 4:103.

14. *Records of New Amsterdam,* 6:273, 349; *Proceedings of the Common Council 1674–1690,* 33, 324, 404; *MCC, 1675–1776,* 1:224, 376, 377, 420, 2:57, 75, 144, 195–97, 3:12, 57, 4:103.

15. Paltsits, *Minutes of the Executive Council,* 1:191–93; John Duffy, *A History of Public Health in New York City 1625–1866* (New York: Russell Sage Foundation, 1968), 34.

16. *Mr. Charles Lodwick, his acct. of New Yorke, in a Letter to his Unkel, Mr. Francis Lodwicke, and Mr. Hooker, Members of ye Royal Society, dated from New York, May 20, 1692. Recd. Sept. 5,* A.D. *1692, and read before ye Royal Society, Nov. 26, 1713,* printed as "New York in 1692," New-York Historical Society, *Collections,* 2d ser. 1848(49), 2:245, 247.

17. *Peter Kalm's Travels,* 141.

18. *MCC, 1675–1776,* 2:203; O'Callaghan, *Documents,* 4:1004; Duffy, *History of Public Health in New York City,* 35–36.

19. Duffy, *History of Public Health in New York City,* 54, 58; *American Magazine & Historical Chronicle* (Boston), October, 1743.

20. Cadwallader Colden, "Observations on the Fever which prevailed in the City of New-York in 1741 and 2" (1743), in *The American Medical and Philosophical Register* (1811), 1:310–30.

21. *Journal of the Votes and Proceedings of the General Assembly of the Colony of New-York,* 2 vols. (New York: Hugh Gaine, 1774–1776), 2:7.

22. *MCC, 1675–1776,* 5:111–14. The swamp was at the center of the new Montgomerie Ward, created in 1731.

23. *MCC, 1675–1776,* 5:118–21.

24. Cadwallader Colden, "Account of the Climate and Diseases of New-York," in *American Medical & Philosophical Register* (1811), 1:308.

25. E. B. Greene and V. D. Harrington, *American Population before the Federal Census of 1790* (New York: Columbia University Press, 1932); Carl Bridenbaugh, *Cities in Revolt: Urban Life in America, 1743–1760* (New York: Knopf, 1955), 5.

26. Alexander Hamilton, *Itinerarium* (New York: Arno Press and the New York Times, 1971 [1907]), 107.

27. Hamilton, *Itinerarium,* 24.

28. *Peter Kalm's Travels,* 26, 133.

29. Stokes, *Iconography,* 4:612.

30. James Birket, *Some Cursory Remarks Made by James Birket in his voyage to North America 1750–1751* (Freeport, N.Y.: Books For Libraries Press, 1971 [1916]), 44.

31. Andrew Burnaby, *Travels Through the Middle Settlements in North America in the years 1759 and 1760 with observations on the state of the colonies* (New York: Augustus M. Kelley, 1970 [1775]), 112.

FOUR   *Tea Water and the Works That Weren't*

1. Thomas F. DeVoe, *The Market Book: A History of the Public Markets of the City of New York* (New York: Augustus M. Kelley, 1970 [1862]), 265–66.

2. Thomas J. Davis, ed., *The New York Conspiracy by Daniel Horsmanden* (Boston: Beacon Press, 1971), xi. The water poisoning rumors are mentioned in numerous modern texts (see Edwin Hoey, "Terror in New York—1741," *American Heritage* 25 (June 1974), 72–77; Kammen, *Colonial New York,* 286; Ferenc M.

Szasz, "The New York Slave Revolt of 1741: A Re-examination," *New York History,* 48 (July 1967), 215–30; Herbert Aptheker, *The Colonial Era* (New York, 1959), 44. Recorder Daniel Horsmanden, the contemporary compiler of the 1741 judicial records, makes no mention of the rumors.

3. Ira Rosenwaike, *Population History of New York City* (Syracuse, N.Y.: Syracuse University Press, 1972), 8; Carl Bridenbaugh, *Cities in the Wilderness: The First Century of Urban Life in America, 1625–1742* (New York: Alfred A. Knopf, 1968 [1938]), 409.

4. Davis, *New York Conspiracy,* 120, 138.

5. Davis, *New York Conspiracy,* 438.

6. Hoey, "Terror in New York," 77.

7. *MCC, 1675–1776,* 5:50.

8. Hamilton, *Itinerarium,* 107.

9. *Peter Kalm's Travels,* 133.

10. Stokes, *Iconography,* 4:398; New York City Wills, Liber 23, p. 533; New York City Deeds, Liber 55, 395, 396, Liber 65, 102, Liber 66, 454, Liber 68, 225, 227, Liber 169, 334, Liber 170, 7, in New York City Surrogates Court.

11. Birket, *Cursory Remarks,* 44; *MCC, 1675–1776,* 6:92, 268; *New York Mercury,* Jan. 25, 1768.

12. See Christopher Colles, *Proposal of Christopher Colles for Furnishing the City of New-York with a Constant Supply of Fresh Water* (New York: Hugh Gaine, 1774), broadside.

13. *The Colonial Laws of New York,* 5 vols. (Albany, 1896), chap. 719 (1741).

14. *Colonial Laws,* chap. 772 (1744), chap. 941 (1753), chap. 1104 (1759), chap. 1259 (1764), chap. 1445 (1770). Under the 1753 revision, overseers were appointed by the full Common Council, which was authorized to raise an annual tax of £120 (£200 in 1764) to cover the increasing costs of the well system.

15. *MCC, 1675–1776,* 5:109, 144, 212, 300, 419, 445, 466; 6:148, 261, 324, 330, 383; 7:140, 224; Arthur Everett Peterson and George William Edwards, *New York as an Eighteenth Century Municipality* (Port Washington, N.Y.: Ira J. Friedman, 1967 [1917]), 337–38.

16. *The Journal of Madam Knight,* ed. Malcom Freiberg (Boston: David R. Godine, 1972), 30–31; Hamilton, *Itinerarium,* 106, 108, 220, 224, 228.

17. Bridenbaugh, *Cities in Revolt,* 5, 157; Kammen, *Colonial New York,* 282; *New York Mercury,* July 20, 1767.

18. Bridenbaugh, *Cities in Revolt,* 256, 271; "Life in New York at the Close of the National Period," *National Magazine,* 19, 8–9 (Sept.-Oct. 1894), 446–47.

19. Frank Monaghan and Marvin Lowenthal, *This Was New York: The Nation's Capitol in 1789* (Garden City, N.Y.: Doubleday, Doran & Co., 1943), 24–26; "Life in New York," *National Magazine,* 446–47; Alice Morse Earle, "Old Colonial Drinks and Drinkers," *National Magazine* 16, 2 (June 1892): 154, 157.

20. Monaghan and Lowenthal, *This Was New York,* 25; *MCC, 1675–1776,* 8:211, 440 (similarly 7:213, 269, 394, 8:14, 15, 24, 26).

21. "Life in New York," *National Magazine,* 448.

22. Hamilton, *Itinerarium,* 102.

23. Colles, *Proposal.* A 1761 housing census by city surveyor Gerard Bancker counted 2,737 houses; an informal estimate by Jean de Crèvecoeur in his *Letters from an American Farmer* suggests 3,400 houses in 1776; see Stokes, *Iconography,* 4:716, 909.

24. John W. Francis, "Reminiscences of Christopher Colles," in *The Knickerbocker Gallery* (New York: S. Hueston, 1855), 197–208. The following sketch of Colles's early life is drawn from Richard Colles Johnson, "Notes on the Family of Colles," unpublished typescript (Petoskey, Michigan, 1956), and "Memoranda Regarding Christopher Colles (1739–1816), Prior to His Leaving Ireland for America; His Birth and Parentage," compiled by Richard Colles, handwritten, undated. Copies of both items were provided to the author by Richard Colles Johnson.

25. *Pennsylvania Chronicle,* Aug. 26, 1771; *Pennysylvania Packet,* Jan. 27, Mar. 28, 1772; *Pennsylvania Assembly Votes,* Jan. 28, Feb. 3, 1773; Neal FitzSimons, "Benchmarks in Civil Engineering," *Civil Engineering* (Sept. 1967), 72; Robert Thurston, *A History of the Growth of the Steam-Engine* (Ithaca, N.Y.: Cornell University Press, 1939), 243; Thompson Westcott, *Life of John Fitch, the Inventor of the Steam-boat,* (Philadelphia: J. B. Lippincott & Co., 1878), 153.

26. William Nelson, *Josiah Hornblower and the First Steam Engine in America* (Newark, N.J.: Daily Advertiser Printing House, 1883); Iren D. Neu, "Hudson Valley Extractive Industries Before 1815," in *Business Enterprise in Early New York,* ed. Joseph R. Frese, S. J. and Jacob Judd (Tarrytown, N.Y.: Sleepy Hollow Press, 1979), 133–65.

27. Westcott, *Life of John Fitch,* 155–56; American Philosophical Society, *Early Proceedings, 1744–1838* (Philadelphia: Press of McCalla & Stavely, 1884), 82–83.

28. *MCC, 1675–1776,* 8:26–27.

29. *Rivington's Gazetteer,* Apr. 28, 1774; Philip Ranlet, *The New York Loyalists* (Knoxville: University of Tennessee Press, 1986), 40; *MCC, 1675–1776,* 7:26–27.

30. John Nathan Kane, *Famous First Facts* (New York: H. W. Wilson Company, 1981), 698; Carl Bridenbaugh, *Cities in the Wilderness,* 62, 214; Nelson M. Blake, *Water for the Cities: A History of the Urban Water Supply Problem in the United States* (Syracuse, N.Y.: Syracuse University Press, 1956), 15.

31. *Famous First Facts,* 698; Blake, *Water for the Cities,* 15; Isaac Weld, Jr., *Travels through the States of North-America, and the Provinces of Upper and Lower Canada, during the Years, 1795, 1796, and 1797,* 2 vols. (London: John Stockdale, 1800), 2:363; "Welcome to the Historic Properties of Historic Bethlehem Incorporated," pamphlet, Historic Bethlehem, Inc. (n.d.); *The American City & County,* July 1976, 62.

32. Blake, *Water for the Cities,* 16.

33. Colles, *Proposal;* "Christopher Colles, Early Life by Commander Dudley Colles," n.d., typescript copy in NYPL; *Encyclopaedia Britannica,* "James Watt."

34. Peterson and Edwards, *New York as an Eighteenth Century Municipality*, 397, 403.

35. Undated Bancker survey in NYC Municipal Archives; Stokes, *Iconography*, 4:856 gives a date of June 14, 1774, based on a subsequent itemized account of various work from 1772–1775, in the NYC Comptroller's Office; *MCC 1675–1776*, 8:139.

36. *MCC, 1675–1776*, 8:41.

37. *New York Journal*, July 28, 1774; *New York Gazette and Weekly Mercury*, Aug. 1, 1774; Michel Guillaume Jean de Crèvecoeur, *Lettres d'un Cultivateur Américain, écrites à W. S., écuyer, depuis l'Année 1770, jusqu'à 1781*, 2 vols. (Paris, 1787), as excerpted and translated in *Magazine of American History* 2 (1878): 750. The translated section is erroneously titled "New York in 1772"; the reference to Colles's waterworks suggests a date of 1774 or 1775.

38. *MCC, 1675–1776*, 8:43, 47–48, 63–64; Bancker Plans, box 2, folder 2, manuscript division, NYPL.

39. Memorandum by Christopher Colles, in *Report of Manhattan Committee* (New York: John Furman, 1799), 17–18; Christopher Colles memorial "To the Honourable the Mayor, Aldermen and Common Council of the City of New York," undated but likely Oct. 27, 1784, in New York City Municipal Archives; "Proposals by Mr. C. Collis [*sic*] for Carrying Water through N. York in 1774," in 1798 Memorandum Book of John McComb, Jr., New-York Historical Society, Manuscript Division. The proposal puts the well itself at £165 and a wall around it at £54 if built of brick or just over £79 if built of stone; the actual construction is unknown.

40. The 4,000 six-pence notes were never printed, lowering the initial outlay to £2400; see Eric P. Newman, *The Early Paper Money of America* (Racine, Wisc.: Whitman, 1967), 210; Eric P. Newman, "The Continental Dollar of 1776 Meets its Maker," *Numismatist*, 72 (Aug. 1959): 914–26; Stokes, *Iconography*, 4:865; *Journal of Lieutenant Isaac Bangs, April 1 to July 29, 1776*, ed. Edwards Bangs (New York: Arno Press, 1968 [1890]), 25; *MCC, 1675–1776*, 8:48–49, 59.

41. *New York Mercury & Weekly Gazette*, Sep. 5, 1774; *MCC, 1675–1776*, 8:62–63; *The Irish Times* (Dublin), Nov. 2, 1992, 12; *Allibone's Critical Dictionary of English Literature* (Detroit: Gale Research, 1965 [1858–1871]), s.v. "Isaac Mann." The original contract is in the NYC Municipal Archives.

42. McComb 1798 Memorandum Book.

43. The McComb 1798 Memorandum Book prices the embankment at £1049:12, the coping wall at £173:5 and the reservoir wall at £576 for stone or £679:4:8 for brick; the construction material chosen for the wall is unknown; Colles memorial to Common Council, Oct. 27, 1784.

44. *New York Journal*, Aug. 20, 1767; Stokes, *Iconography*, 5:1276; *New York Mercury*, Feb. 22, 1773.

45. *Rivington's New-York Gazetteer*, Feb. 16, 1775; see also Thurston, *History and Growth of the Steam Engine*, 243.

46. McComb 1798 Memorandum Book; *Report of Manhattan Committee,* 18.

47. McComb 1798 Memorandum Book.

48. MCC, *1676–1775,* 8:67, 78; *London Chronicle,* June 13–15, 1775; *New York Mercury,* May 15, 1775.

49. *MCC, 1675–1776,* 8:100, 121, 131; see *MCC, 1784–1831,* Index, for various claims; *New York Journal and Daily Patriotic Register,* July 15, 1788; Augustine Costello, *Our Firemen: A History of the New York Fire Departments* (New York: Knickerbocker Press, 1997 [1887]), 54.

50. O'Callaghan, *Documents,* 8:667; "Occupation of New York City by the British: Extracts from the Diary of the Moravian Congregation," *Pennsylvania Magazine of History and Biography,* 1, 2 (1877): 134; *MCC, 1675–1776,* 8:127; *New York Mercury,* Feb. 19, 1776; Henry C. Van Schaack, *The Life of Peter Van Schaack* (New York: D. Appleton, 1842), 53.

51. *New York Mercury,* Mar. 4, 11, 1776.

52. *Report of Manhattan Committee,* 18.

53. *Journal of Lieutenant Isaac Bangs,* 24.

54. Two months later, Bangs found himself at the abandoned Schuyler copper mines where, from "the incombustible Matter" remaining, he judged the ruined Hornblower engine "greatly superiour in Magnitude" to the engine in New York; *Journal of Lieutenant Isaac Bangs,* 47.

55. *MCC, 1675–1776,* 8:139; *MCC, 1784–1831,* 1:175, 380.

56. Rosenwaike, *Population History of New York City,* 14–15.

57. American Scenic and Historic Preservation Society, *Annual Report,* 1917, 22: 454; John Colles to William Colles, Oct. 22, 1778, letter in possession of Richard Colles Johnson.

58. Colles memorial to Common Council, Oct. 27, 1784.

59. *MCC, 1784–1831,* 2:423, 515.

60. James Thacher, *A Military Journal During the American Revolutionary War, from 1775 to 1783* (Boston: Richardson & Lord, 1823), 92.

61. William Dunlap, *A History of the American Theatre,* 2 vols. (London: R. Bentley, 1833), 2:84.

FIVE   New City, Old Trouble

1. "Journal of an Irishman in New York at the Close of the American Revolution," ed. Victor H. Paltsits, *Bulletin of the New York Public Library,* 27 (Nov. 1923): 892–93; Baroness Fredericke Riedesel, *Letters and Journals Relating to the War of the American Revolution, and the Capture of the German Troops at Saratoga* (New York: New York Times, 1968 [1867]), 173; Stokes, *Iconography,* 5:1060, 1100, 1132.

2. Stokes, *Iconography,* 5:1110; "Journal of Lt. John Charles Philip von Krafft," New-York Historical Society, *Collections* (1882), 167–69.

3. *The Journal of Nicholas Cresswell, 1774–1777* (New York: L. MacVeagh, Dial Press, 1924), 244–45; Stokes, *Iconography,* 5:1106, 1130.

4. *New York Mercury,* Feb. 13, 1775; Stokes, *Iconography,* 4:874; Peterson and Edwards, *New York as an Eighteenth Century Municipality,* 247.

5. *New York Mercury,* Jan. 5, 1777; DeVoe, *Market Book,* 170, 289; Stokes, *Iconography,* 1:326, 5:1060.

6. Rosenwaike, *Population History of New York City,* 15.

7. *Royal Gazette,* July 1, 1780, Mar. 31, 1781.

8. *New York Packet,* Jan. 22, 1784 (and regularly thereafter through Mar. 11).

9. Stokes, *Iconography,* 5:1185; *MCC, 1784–1831,* 1:11; *New York Packet,* Mar. 11, 1784.

10. *Pennsylvania Packet,* July 20, 1784, in DeVoe, *Market Book,* 267.

11. *New York Packet,* Aug. 19, 1784.

12. See William Alexander Duer, *New-York as It Was, during the Latter Part of the Last Century* (New York: Stanford and Swords, 1849), 13.

13. *New York Packet,* Oct. 25, 1784.

14. *New York Journal,* Aug. 25, 1785.

15. *MCC, 1784–1831,* 1:64, 96, 107, 160, 187, 195, 239, 244, 247, 272, 298, 332, 340–41, 344–45, 363, 366, 380, 485.

16. Stokes, *Iconography,* 5:1200; *MCC, 1784–1831,* 1:129; Edward Hagaman Hall, *Water for New York City* (Saugerties, N.Y.: Hope Farm Press, 1993 [1917]), 41–42; *DAB,* "Samuel Ogden."

17. "Emory & Newton Plan for Water works, 30 May 1785," handwritten memorial in New York City Municipal Archives. The proposal is addressed to the Common Council, but there is no indication that the council formally considered it. Little is known about Emory. Newton was an architect in the 1780s; in 1803, he was head carpenter for the building of the current City Hall, the cornerstone of which bears his name. See John A. Kouwenhoven, *The Columbia Historical Portrait of New York* (Garden City, N.Y.: Doubleday & Company, 1953), 91; Stokes, *Iconography,* 5:1404, plate 59a.

18. *MCC, 1784–1831,* 1:194.

19. *MCC, 1784–1831,* 1:197, 198–200; *New York Journal,* Feb. 23, 1786; also *New York Packet,* Feb. 20, 1786, *New York Gazetteer or Daily Evening Post,* Mar. 3, 1786.

20. *Daily Advertiser,* Feb. 21, 1786. The correspondence is signed "A.B.," the initials of Aaron Burr but also a then-common device to preserve anonymity.

21. *MCC, 1784–1831,* 1:213–14.

22. *New York Packet,* Jan. 29, 1788; see also *Daily Advertiser,* Jan. 28, Mar. 12, 20, 1788. *MCC, 1784–1831,* 1:354–55.

23. *MCC, 1784–1831,* 1:426; James Thomas Flexner, *Steamboats Come True* (Boston: Little, Brown and Company, 1978 [1944]), 67–213; *DAB,* "James Rumsey."

24. *New York Journal,* Feb. 9, 1793; *Daily Advertiser,* Feb. 24, 1794.

25. *Minerva,* Dec. 6, 1796.

26. *Report of the Manhattan Committee,* 33.

27. Devoe, *Market Book,* 204–5; Stokes, *Iconography,* 5:1336; *MCC, 1784–1831,* 2:325.

28. *Henry Wansey and His American Journal 1794,* ed. David John Jeremy (Philadelphia: American Philosophical Society, 1970), 137.

29. *Moreau de St. Méry's American Journey 1793–1798,* trans. and ed. Kenneth Roberts and Anna Roberts. (Garden City, N.Y.: Doubleday & Co., 1947), 147.

30. François Alexandre Frédéric, duc de La Rochefoucauld-Liancourt, *Travels through the United States of North America, the Country of the Iroquois, and Upper Canada in the Years 1795, 1796, and 1797; with an Authentic Account of Lower Canada,* 2 vols. (London: R. Phillips, 1799), in Stokes, *Iconography,* 5:1344.

31. William Winterbotham, *An Historical, Geographical, Commercial, and Philosophical View of the American United States, and of the European Settlements in America and the West-Indies,* 4 vols. (New York: Tiebout and O'Brien, for J. Reed, 1796), 2:319.

32. Liancourt, *Travels,* in Stokes, *Iconography,* 5:1344; Thomas Cooper, *Some Information Respecting America* (New York: Augustus M. Kelley, 1969 [1794]), 11, 49; *Henry Wansey and His American Journal,* 75; "Talleyrand in America as a Financial Promoter, 1794–1796," unpublished letters and memoirs, trans. and ed. Hans Huth and Wilma J. Pugh, in American Historical Association, *Annual Report* (1841), 2:94–95; John Bernard, *Retrospections of America 1797–1811,* ed. Bayle Bernard (Bronx: Benjamin Blom, 1969 [1887]), 50.

33. "A New & Accurate Plan of the City of New York in the State of New York in North America," Benjamin Taylor and John Roberts, 1797, in *Manual of the Common Council* (1853), 324; *MCC, 1784–1831,* 2:65; *New York Directory,* 1794.

34. Duffy, *History of Public Health in New York City,* 78–79, 177–78; *Encyclopedia of NYC,* "police"; *Struggles through Life, Exemplified in the Various Travels and Adventures in Europe, Asia, Africa, and America of Lieut. John Harriott,* 2 vols. (London: Longman, Hurst, Rees & Orme, 1808), 2:60.

35. Duffy, *History of Public Health in New York City,* 82.

36. *Laws of New York* (1787), chap. 59.

37. *MCC, 1784–1831,* 2:561, 568.

38. *MCC, 1784–1831,* 1:701–2.

39. Sidney Pomerantz, *New York: An American City 1783–1803* (New York: Columbia University Press, 1938), 279. Prices were often reckoned in pounds or dollars throughout the 1790s in New York, where £1 equaled about $2.50; see John J. McCusker, *How Much Is That in Real Money? A Historical Price Index for Use as a Deflator of Money Values in the Economy of the United States* (Worchester, Mass.: American Antiquarian Society, 1992), 333.

40. *MCC, 1784–1831,* 1:682, 750, 2:18, 160. Among Stevens's prominent sons was Samuel Stevens, who would take an active role in the city's water search several decades later.

41. *MCC, 1784–1831,* 2:63, 135, 137, 212, 225, 231–32, 250, 254, 307, 314; *American Minerva,* Feb. 21, 1796; Stokes, *Iconography,* 5:1330.

42. *Diary,* Feb. 4, 1797.

43. *Minerva,* Mar. 9, 1797; also, *New York Journal,* Mar. 11, 1797; *Daily Advertiser,* Mar. 18, 1797; *New York Gazette & General Advertiser,* Mar. 18, 1797; *Diary,* Mar. 22, 1797.

44. Irene D. Neu, "Hudson Valley Extractive Industries Before 1815," 157; Flexner, *Steamboats Come True,* 263.

45. In 1785, Colles published, promoted, and did initial surveys for the first plan to link the Hudson with the Great Lakes, via improvements of the Mohawk River; a nonstarter then, it is considered the idea that led to the Erie Canal. In 1789, Colles published "A Survey of the Roads of the United States of America," the first roadmaps of the new nation; the "roadbook" found few subscribers. Numerous other inspirations followed, with similar results. Christopher Colles, *A Survey of the Roads of the United States of America,* ed. Walter W. Ristow (Cambridge, Mass.: Belknap Press, 1961); Greville Bathe, *An Engineer's Miscellany* (Philadelphia: Press of Patterson & White Company, 1938); Henry O'Reilly, "Material for Telegraph History, II. Christopher Colles and the First Proposal for a Telegraphy System in the United States," *The Historical Magazine,* 5 (April 1869): 262–69.

46. *MCC, 1784–1831,* 2:347.

47. *MCC, 1784–1831,* 2:356–57.

48. *MCC, 1784–1831,* 2:352, 356.

49. *MCC, 1784–1831,* 2:420, 423, 515, 621, 622.

50. *New York Gazette & General Advertiser,* Mar. 2, 1798.

51. Stokes, *Iconography,* 5:1282.

52. See J. H. Powell, *Bring Out Your Dead: The Great Plague of Yellow Fever in Philadelphia in 1793* (New York: Time Life Books, 1965 [1949]).

53. *MCC, 1784–1831,* 2:38, 47, 48, 49, 51, 53, 58, 61.

54. Duffy, *History of Public Health in New York City,* 104; Stokes, *Iconography,* 5:1324; Richard Bayley, *An Account of the Epidemic Fever which Prevailed in the City of New-York, during the Summer and Fall of 1795* (New York: T. and J. Swords, 1796); Valentine Seaman, *An Account of the Epidemic Yellow Fever as it Appeared in the City of New-York in the Year 1795* (New York: Hopkins, Webb & Co., 1796); DeVoe, *Market Book,* 373; "Diary of Dr. Alexander Anderson, 1793–1799," in *Medical Repository* (1798), 1:315–25; Blake, *Water for the Cities,* 7.

55. Duffy, *History of Public Health in New York City,* 105.

56. *Laws of New York* (1797), chap. 16; (1798), chap. 65; see Duffy, *History of Public Health in New York City,* 131–34.

57. Duffy, *History of Public Health in New York City,* 130–33; *MCC, 1784–1831,* 2:428, 460–64. Bayley (1745–1801) was the father of Elizabeth Ann Bayley Seton, known as Mother Seton, who in 1975 became the first native-born American canonized by the Roman Catholic Church.

58. Stokes, *Iconography,* 5:1356; *Keepers of the Revolution: New Yorkers at Work in the Early Republic,* ed. Paul A. Gilge and Howard B. Rock (Ithaca, N.Y.: Cornell University Press, 1992), 76. After the introduction of cut nails, Thorburn turned to the seed business, issuing the first American seed catalog in 1812. Scottish novelist John Galt told the seedsman's life story in *Lawrie Todd* (1830), the pen name Thorburn adopted for numerous of his subsequent writings. See *DAB,* "Grant Thorburn"; *Encyclopedia of NYC,* "Scots."

59. Smith to Dr. Mason Fitch Cogswell, Sep. 2, 1798, in Stokes, *Iconography,* 5:1355.

60. Stokes, *Iconography,* 5:1356–157.

61. *MCC, 1784–1831,* 2:467–69, 473, 476, 483.

62. Devoe, *Market Book,* 208–9; *DAB,* "Alexander Anderson"; Hone, *Diary,* 2:854; *Spectator,* Sept. 22, 29, 1798.

63. Duffy, *History of Public Health in New York City,* 107–9.

64. *Commercial Advertiser,* Aug. 28, Sept. 1, 1798; *New York Gazette & General Advertiser,* Aug. 24, 1798.

65. *Commercial Advertiser,* Sept. 5, 1798.

66. *Proceedings of the Corporation of New-York, on Supplying the City with Pure and Wholesome Water, with a Memoir of Joseph Browne, M. D. on the Same Subject* (New York: John Furman, 1799), 9–29.

67. Joseph Browne, *Treatise on the Yellow Fever; Shewing its Origin, Cure and Prevention* (New York: Thomas Greenleaf, 1798).

68. The Saw Mill River originates in springs and a small lake around the highlands of today's Chappaqua, flowing south for twenty miles through Hawthorne and Elmsford before emptying into the Hudson at Yonkers, where that city's namesake Adriaen Van Der Donck established a saw mill in the mid-1600s; see Richard M. Lederer, *The Place Names of Westchester County, New York* (Harrison, N.Y.: Harbor Hill Books, 1978), 127, 160.

69. The landmark bridge, built before the Revolution by local farmer John Williams, is long gone, but the neighborhood in today's northern Bronx retains the name Williamsbridge; see J. Thomas Scharf, *History of Westchester County,* 2 vols. (Camden, Maine: Picton Press, 1992 [1886]), 1:323.

70. The other commissioners were Ebenezer Stevens, Robert Watts, Jr., and James Morris (no relation to Lewis Morris). Stokes, *Iconography,* 4:846, 5:1264, 6:32; *Daily Advertiser,* Oct. 12, 1792; *MCC, 1784–1831,* 2:20.

71. Coles's Bridge, twenty-four feet wide and equipped with a lock for the passage of shallow draft boats, was replaced by the first city-owned Third Avenue Bridge in 1867, itself replaced in 1898 by the current bridge. Coles, alderman of the moneyed First and Second Wards from 1797–1802, laid the Manhattan and Westchester roads leading to the bridge. "Coles's Boston Road," as it came to be known, took four miles off the existing route to Boston via King's Bridge at the northern tip of Manhattan. Dixon Ryan Fox, *The Decline of Aristocracy in the Politics of New York, 1801–1840,* ed. Robert V. Remini (New York: Harper & Row, 1965 [1919]), 18; *MCC,*

1784–1831, 2:48; *Laws of New York* (1795), chap. 31; *Daily Advertiser*, May 2, 1794, Jan. 26, 1795; *Minerva*, Nov. 4, 1796; *Encyclopedia of NYC*, "bridges"; Stokes, *Iconography*, 3:926.

72. Milton Lomask, *Aaron Burr: The Years from Princeton to Vice President, 1756–1805* (New York: Farrar Straus Giroux, 1979), 81, 197; Herbert S. Parmet and Marie B. Hecht, *Aaron Burr: Portrait of an Ambitious Man* (New York: Macmillan, 1967), 66–67. The often sickly Theodosia died in 1794, undiagnosed and uncured by the various prescriptions of Joseph Browne and Philadelphia's renowned Benjamin Rush.

SIX   Aaron's Water

1. *MCC, 1784–1831*, 2:483, 484.

2. Weston was in the United States from 1793–1800, commanding high fees for his work on the Schuykill and Susquehanna Canal (1793), Middlesex Canal (1794), the Great Falls lock canal on the Potomac (1795), and the Mohawk River canals (1796–1797). *DAB*, "William Weston."

3. *MCC, 1784–1831*, 2:487, 489.

4. *MCC, 1784–1831*, 2:490. Burr's U.S. Senate term had ended in January 1797; he was elected to the state Assembly the following April, and re-elected for a second and final term a year later. The three-month legislative sessions began the January following the April elections. The following account of the founding of the Manhattan Company draws heavily on the excellent analysis by Beatrice G. Reubens, "Burr, Hamilton and the Manhattan Company, Parts I and II," *Political Science Quarterly*, 72 (1957): 578–607 and 73 (1958): 100–125. Other significant materials are cited individually.

5. Mary-Jo Kline, ed., *Political Correspondence and Public Papers of Aaron Burr*, 2 vols. (Princeton, N.J.: Princeton University Press, 1983), 1:400.

6. See *Commercial Advertiser*, Jan. 18, 1799; *Daily Advertiser*, Jan. 24, 30, 1799; *New York Gazette & General Advertiser*, Feb. 18, 1799.

7. *MCC, 1784–1831*, 2:485–86; *New York Gazette & General Advertiser*, May 1, 1799.

8. *MCC, 1784–1831*, 2:514–15. Later in the same session, the council dispatched Colles log contractor Isaac Mann's recently pressed claim, suggesting he try a lawsuit.

9. *MCC, 1784–1831*, 2:517–21.

10. *Encyclopedia of NYC*, "government and politics"; Milton M. Klein, "From Community to Status: The Development of the Legal Profession in Colonial New York," *Business Enterprise in Early New York*, ed. Joseph R. Frese, S.J., and Jacob Judd (Tarrytown, N.Y.: Sleepy Hollow Press, 1979), 185.

11. A 1783 Bank of North America stock certificate, the oldest known American certificate, made out to "John Carter," was sold at auction in 1995 for a world record $33,000; the bank, the first chartered by Congress in 1781 to help fund the Continental Army, survives as CoreState; see "America's Oldest Stock Certificate Draws Highest Price Ever at Auction," press release, R. M. Smythe & Co., auction firm, Jan. 31, 1995; *Famous First Facts*, 93.

12. *A Season in New York 1801: Letters of Harriet and Maria Trumbull*, ed. Helen M. Morgan (Pittsburgh: University of Pittsburgh Press, 1969), 53n; Barbara A. Chernow, "Robert Morris and Alexander Hamilton: Two Financiers in New York," in *Business Enterprise in Early New York*, 87–88, 90, 94–95; see *Richmond Times Dispatch*, May 19, 1996, G-1.

13. *Report of William Weston, Esquire, on the Practicability of Introducing the Water of the River Bronx into the City of New-York* (New York: John Furman, 1799).

14. *Famous First Facts*, "Water Purification"; see M. N. Baker, *The Quest for Pure Water* (New York: American Water Works Association, 1949), 125–31; *Encyclopaedia Britannica*, "water purification."

15. *MCC, 1784–1831*, 2:527, 537.

16. *MCC, 1784–1831*, 2:494–509; *Laws of New York* (1799), chap. 70; Duffy, *History of Public Health in New York City*, 135–37, 180–81.

17. New York Assembly, *Journal*, 22d Sess., 261. Fairlie was a two-time Assemblyman (1798–1799, 1808–1809), and a Manhattan Company director from 1803–1823; Kline, *Political Correspondence*, 374, n.6; Gregory S. Hunter, *The Manhattan Company: Managing a Multi-unit Corporation in New York, 1799–1842* (New York: Garland Publishing, 1989), 301–2.

18. New York Assembly, *Journal*, 22d Sess., 261–63.

19. Blake, *Water for the Cities*, 50–51.

20. See Pomerantz, *New York: An American City*, 184.

21. Matthew L. Davis, *Memoirs of Aaron Burr*, 2 vols. (New York: Harper & Brothers, 1837), 1:411, 413–14; *DAB*, "Samuel Jones"; Pomerantz, *New York*, 188; Fox, *Decline of Aristocracy*, 12; *New York Times*, Dec. 18, 1988, sec. 12, 29.

22. Davis, *Aaron Burr*, 414; Fox, *Decline of Aristocracy*, 32; *DAB*, "Stephen Van Renssalaer," "Ambrose Spencer."

23. Davis, *Aaron Burr*, 414; Pomerantz, *New York*, 188–89.

24. The Council of Revision's powers were defined in 1778; it was abolished under the state's new constitution in 1821, after rejecting so many proposed laws that it was seen as a de facto super legislature, and replaced with limited veto power for the governor. See Stokes, *Iconography*, 3:515–16, 5:1063.

25. *Encyclopedia of NYC, DAB*, "John Jay."

26. *Encyclopedia NYC, DAB*, "Egbert Benson"; Fox, *Decline of Aristocracy*, 16.

27. *DAB,* "John Lansing"; see Estelle Fox Kleiger, *The Trial of Levi Weeks or The Manhattan Well Mystery* (Chicago: Academy, 1989).

28. "Minutes of the Meeting of the Council of Revision of New York State, re: Bill Incorporating the Manhattan Company, as Extracted by Archibald Campbell, Deputy Secretary of State, April 29, 1836," handwritten item in Chase Archives, Record Group #1; also printed in Davis, *Aaron Burr,* 1:415–16. See also A. B. Street, *The Council of Revision of the State of New York: Its History* (Albany: W. Gould, 1859), 423–25, which gives Lansing's argument that corporations serving private advantage should have limits on their activities.

29. Davis, *Aaron Burr,* 416; Reubens, *Political Science Quarterly,* 72:606; *Laws of New York* (1799), chap. 84.

30. *MCC, 1784–1831,* 2:534–35.

31. Manhattan Company, Minute Book No. 1 (1799–1808), 1 (hereafter, MC Minutes); and Record Group Number 1, Records of the Manhattan Company, both in Chase Manhattan Archives, New York; see also *New York Journal,* May 22, 1799.

32. Stevens to Livingston, Apr. 12, 1799, Robert R. Livingston Papers, New-York Historical Society.

33. Ibid.

34. MC Minutes, 1:7–10; *New York Journal,* May 1, 1799. The board also named Burr stepson John Bartow Prevost company secretary.

35. *Commercial Advertiser,* Apr. 19, 1799.

36. *Report of the Manhattan Committee,* 29–37. Eight months later, Ring's niece was found drowned in a Manhattan Company well, spawning the trial and acquittal of her suitor Levi Weeks, whose lawyers were Burr, Hamilton, and Livingston, and whose brother Ezra was a Manhattan Company log contractor. After his acquittal, Weeks became a successful architect in New Orleans. See Kleiger, *Trial of Levi Weeks.*

37. Colles, *Survey of the Roads,* 82–83; *Famous First Facts,* "Canal"; Gorton Carruth, *The Encyclopedia of American Facts and Dates* (New York: Harper & Row, 1987), 113.

38. *Burr Papers,* reel 13, Dec. 9, 1786, New-York Historical Society. The resolution of the damage claims against one Andrew Moody, totaling £189, is unclear.

39. *Report of the Manhattan Committee,* 17–23.

40. *Report of the Manhattan Committee,* 12–17.

41. Irene D. Neu, "Hudson Valley Extractive Industries Before 1815," 157; Flexner, *Steamboats Come True,* 263.

42. Neu, "Hudson Valley Extractive Industries Before 1815," 157; Chernow, "Robert Morris and Alexander Hamilton: Two Financiers in New York," 95; Flexner, *Steamboats Come True,* 262–67; Blake, *Water for the Cities,* 32; *Report of the Manhattan Committee,* 11–12.

43. *Report of the Manhattan Committee,* 24–29.

44. See *New York Gazette & General Advertiser,* May 1, 1799.

45. MC Minutes, 1:13–14; *Report of the Manhattan Committee,* 3–10.

46. MC Minutes, 1:13, 15–16, 23.

47. MC Minutes, 1:18, 19. Laight's position was filled on May 27 by wealthy merchant Henry A. Coster, who remained a director until December 1801; see MC Minutes, 1:25, 97. Another wealthy Coster, John G., would serve as a director from 1810–1832 and 1834–1839, and as company president from 1825–1829; see Hunter, *Manhattan Company,* 300; Stokes, *Iconography,* 3:775; Charles H. Haswell, *Reminiscences of New York by an Octogenarian, 1816 to 1860* (New York: Harper and Brothers, 1896), 413.

48. *Commercial Advertiser,* May 22, 1799; MC Minutes, 1:27, 40–43.

49. *New York Journal,* May 8, 1799; MC Minutes, 1:26–27, 29–30; *New York Spectator,* June 12, 1799.

50. MC Minutes, 1:28, 30–31. The position had been advertised in the *New York Journal,* June 7, 1799.

51. Hunter, *Manhattan Company,* 88; Blake, *Water for the Cities,* 33, 38–40, 58; Livingston to Osgood, Coles, and Stevens, Sept. 2, 1799, Robert R. Livingston Papers, New-York Historical Society.

52. *DAB, Encyclopaedia Britannica,* "Oliver Evans." In 1803, Benjamin Latrobe reported that only five engines were at work in the United States; see Stephen F. Ginsberg, "The History of Fire Protection in New York City, 1800–1842," diss., New York University, 1968, 326.

53. MC Minutes 1:31–32, 121–27, 2:144–46, 155–57; *Encyclopedia of NYC,* "metal founding and metal working"; Richard B. Stott, *Workers in the Metropolis: Class, Ethnicity, and Youth in Antebellum New York City* (Ithaca, N.Y.: Cornell University Press, 1990), 43; Hunter, *Manhattan Company,* 109, 309. McQueen served in the Common Council from 1816 to 1823.

54. Browne to Burr, July 7, 1799, Burr Papers, New-York Historical Society. In this letter, Browne provides operational details of McQueen's horse pumps.

55. See Edward H. Winant, "The Hydraulics Revolution: Science and Technical Design of Urban Water Supply in the Enlightenment," diss., West Virginia University, 1996, 1–151.

56. Browne to Burr, July 7, 1799, Burr Papers, New-York Historical Society.

57. Duffy, *History of Public Health in New York City,* 109–10; *MCC, 1784–1831,* 2:563, 571.

58. *MCC, 1784–1831,* 2:552, 561; MC Minutes, 1:48. The tank was eventually enclosed in a three-story building and demolished in the 1910s; see Hall, *Water for New York City,* 49; "Bank of Manhattan and Its Water Tank," *New York Times Illustrated Magazine,* April 2, 1899; *New York Times,* July 9, 1914.

59. Stokes, *Iconography,* 5:1370.

60. Burr to Robert L. Livingston, Sept. 20, 1799, Burr Papers, New-York Historical Society.

61. *New York Journal,* Nov. 16, 1799.

62. Manhattan Company, Waterworks Journal, August 27, 1799–March 10, 1821 (hereafter, MC Water Works Journal), June 30, July 8, 1800, in Chase Manhattan Archives, New York.

63. *New York Gazette & General Advertiser,* June 11, 1800; see MC Water Works Journal, Dec. 9, 23, 31, 1799, June 20, July 4, Sept. 30, 1800; MC Minutes 1:86, 88.

64. *New York Journal,* June 22, 1799; MC Minutes, 1:62, 63, 66, 72–73.

65. MC Water Works Journal, Jan. 21, Sept. 30, Dec. 31, 1800.

66. *MCC, 1784–1831,* 2:625; MC Water Works Journal, June 16, July 4, Aug. 12, 26, 1800; MC Minutes, 1:101. Mangin later designed and built the first St. Patrick's Cathedral on Mott Street, where the Fitzgeralds were buried in 1832.

67. No plans exist of the reservoir, which was torn down along with the iron tank in the 1910s long after their active use; see Kenneth Holcomb Dunshee, *As You Pass By* (New York: Hastings House, 1952), 180–81; MC Minutes 1:123–25.

68. MC Water Works Journal, June 20, July 4, Sept. 30, 1800; MC Minutes, 1:123–25, 137–38.

69. *MCC, 1784–1831,* 3:6, 29, 248, 286, 326, 345, 355–56, 400; MC Minutes, 1:95–96, 130–31; Reubens, *Political Science Quarterly,* 73:105–6.

70. *MCC, 1784–1831,* 3:123–24, 132, 333–34; MC Minutes, 1:131–32, 137–38.

71. MC Minutes 1:148–49.

72. MC Minutes 1:93–94, 102, 120–27; MC Water Works Journal, Mar. 7, 1803. Walter Bowne and John R. Livingston were elected to the company board in December 1801. Livingston, the second of an eventual three Livingstons to serve on the board, remained for only two years; Bowne served until 1817 and went on to become mayor from 1829 to1833.

73. MC Minutes, 1:105–6, 109–11 (this entry, dated Sept. 23, 1802, includes the previously unrecorded minutes of July 17, 1800, pertaining to the original loan); Reubens, *Political Science Quarterly,* 73:119.

74. MC Minutes, 1:100.

75. MC Minutes 1:123–25; Rosenwaike, *Population History of New York City,* 18.

76. *Daily Advertiser,* Oct. 31, 1803; *Columbian Centinel,* Nov. 5, 1803; New York *Evening Post,* July 11, 1803; *New York Gazette & General Advertiser,* July 21, 1803; New York *Evening Post,* July 26, 27, 1803.

77. Burr arranged for Browne's March 1805 appointment by Jefferson as secretary of the Louisiana Territory, from which Burr and assorted cohorts for the next several years launched an enigmatic separatist "conspiracy"; see Kline, *Political Correspondence,* 911, 918–19. Burr removed to Europe (1808–1812), but Browne apparently remained in the west. In an 1816 letter to "uncle Burr," Browne's son indicates that his father had died about five years earlier, and describes the family's resulting poverty in St. Louis; see Joseph Browne, Jr., to Burr, Dec. 15, 1816, *Burr Papers,* reel 7:1066, New-York Historical Society.

78. MC Minutes, 1:140–41.

SEVEN   Fools of Gotham

1. *Brewer's Dictionary of Phrase and Fable,* Centenary Edition, revised by Ivor H. Evans (New York: Harper & Row, 1970), "Gotham. Wise men of Gotham"; *Encyclopaedia Britannica,* "Wise Men of Gotham"; *The Merriam-Webster New Book of Word Histories* (Springfield, Mass.: Merriam-Webster, 1991), "knickerbocker"; *Encyclopedia of NYC,* "Gotham"; "Gotham," *New Yorker* (Aug. 7, 1965): 19–20; Edward Robb Ellis, *The Epic of New York City: A Narrative History* (New York: Old Town Books, 1966), 203; *The Oxford Book of Royal Anecdotes,* ed. Elizabeth Longford (New York: Oxford University Press, 1989), 86–91.

2. *The Macmillan Book of Proverbs, Maxims and Famous Phrases,* ed., Burton Stevenson (New York: Macmillan Publishing Company, 1976), "Gotham"; *The Travellers' Dictionary of Quotation: Who Said What, About Where?* ed. Peter Yapp (New York: Routledge, 1988), 289.

3. Bartlett Jere Whiting, *Early American Proverbs and Proverbial Phrases* (Cambridge, Mass.: Belknap Press, 1977), 184; William Safire, "On Language," *New York Times,* July 30, 1995: 6:14.

4. *Washington Irving: History, Tales and Sketches* (New York: Library of America, 1983), 69, 85, 220, 307–12; see also 240, 244, 250, 350, 351, 359.

5. Rosenwaike, *Population History of New York City,* 16.

6. The following description of Philadelphia's early water supply is drawn from Moreau de St. Mery, *American Journey,* 262; Blake, *Water for the Cities,* 18–43, 78–99; B. Henry Latrobe, *View of the Practicability and Means of Supplying the City of Philadelphia with Wholesome Water in a Letter to John Miller, Esquire, December 29, 1798* (Philadelphia: Zachariah Poulson, Jr., 1799); "The Fairmount Waterworks," Philadelphia Museum of Art, *Bulletin,* 84, 360, 361 (Summer 1988): 1–48; "The Philadelphia Water Department: An Historical Perspective," pamphlet (n.p., n.d.); *Report of the Committee for the Introduction of Wholesome Water into the City of Philadelphia,* Oct. 12, 1801 (Philadelphia: Z. Poulson, 1801). Other references are individually cited below.

7. Edward Miller, *Report on the Malignant Disease, which prevailed in the City of New York, in the Autumn of 1805: Addressed to the Governor of the State of New-York* (n.p., n.d.), 92; John Melish, *Travels in the United States of America, in the Years 1806 & 1807, and 1809, 1810, & 1811; Including an Account of Passages Betwixt America and Britain, and Travels through Various Parts of Great Britain, Ireland, and Upper Canada,* 2 vols. (Philadelphia: Thomas & George Palmer, 1812), 1:61, 157–58.

8. Blake, *Water for the Cities,* 41.

9. John M. Duncan, *Travels Through Part of the United States and Canada in 1818 and 1819,* 2 vols. (New York: W. B. Gilley, 1823), 1:192.

10. "The Fairmount Waterworks," 5; *Famous First Facts,* 328–29. Philadelphia's discarded wood pipe was not consigned to the great sawdust heap of history; neighboring Burlington, New Jersey, bought much of the pipe, which remained in

use until the 1880s; "History of Plumbing in America," *Plumbing & Mechanical Magazine,* July 1987 (at www.theplumber.com).

11. Frances Trollope, *Domestic Manners of the Americans* (Barre, Mass.: Imprint Society, 1969 [1832]), 206.

12. Tyrone Power, *Impressions of America During the Years 1833, 1834, and 1835* (New York: Benjamin Blom, 1971 [1836]), 75–76; Captain Frederick Marryat, *A Diary in America, with remarks on Its Institutions* (Bloomington: Indiana University Press, 1960 [1839]), 172–73, 174; Thomas Ewbank, *A Descriptive and Historical Account of Hydraulic and Other Machines for Raising Water, Ancient and Modern: With Observations of Various Subjects Connected with the Mechanic Arts: Including the Progressive Development of the Steam Engine* (New York: Appleton & Co., 1842), 301; Charles Dickens, *American Notes for General Circulation* (Boston: James R. Osgood, 1871 [1842]), 282. Also see J. E. Alexander, *Transatlantic Sketches,* 2 vols. (London: Richard Bentley, 1833) 2:262; Alexander Bölöi Farkas, *Journey in North America,* trans. Theodore and Helen Bendek Schoenman (Philadelphia: American Philosophical Society, 1977 [1834]), 213–14.

13. "Extracts from the Report of the Commissioners Appointed By His Majesty to Inquire into the State of the Supply of Water in the Metropolis, dated 21st April, 1828," *Facts Relative to the Impurity and Insalubrity of the Water Supplied from the Thames,* pamphlet, (London: Page and Sons, 1928), 2. See also Sydney Smith to Lady Grey, November 19, 1834, in *The Travellers' Dictionary of Quotation,* ed. Peter Yapp (London and New York: Routledge, 1988), 311.

14. Loammi Baldwin, *Report on the Subject of Introducing Pure Water into the City of Boston* (Boston: J. H. Eastburn, 1834); L. M. Sargent to Eliphalet Williams, Feb. 21, 1838, printed letter in bound pamphlet volume, NYPL; Blake, *Water for the Cities,* 172–218.

15. Blake, *Water for the Cities,* 69–77, 219–47.

16. Blake, *Water for the Cities,* 265–66.

17. King, *Memoir,* 79–81. For anecdotal accounts, see Trollope, *Domestic Manners,* 31, and Marryat, *Diary,* 259–63.

18. King, *Memoir,* 81–82; Marryat, *Diary,* 89.

19. New York *Evening Post,* Jan. 26, 1808.

20. "An Act Supplementary to the Act, Entitled 'An Act for Supplying the City of New-York with Pure and Wholesome Water,' Mar. 25, 1808," in *The Act of Incorporation of the Manhattan Company Passed April 2, 1799* (New York: Grattan's Office, 1830), 9–12; *Laws of New York* (1808), chap. 83. A scholar, educator, philanthropist, and future governor and national politician, Clinton served nine terms as mayor and five terms as state senator during his tenure from 1803 to 1812 as a leading director of the Manhattan Company, which held nearly $9,000 worth of his notes; see *DAB, Encyclopedia of NYC,* "De Witt Clinton"; Blake, *Water for the Cities,* 104; Reubens, *Political Science Quarterly,* 73:120; Hunter, *Manhattan Company,* 56–57, 299.

21. MC Minutes 1:106; *MCC, 1784–1831,* 3:107, 111, 132, 181, 255, 583–84.

22. *MCC, 1784–1831,* 4:614, 7:718; *L'Oracle and Daily Advertiser,* Aug. 26, 1808; *New York Gazette & General Advertiser,* Aug. 26, 1808.

23. *American Citizen,* Oct. 15, 1806; *New York Magazine* (June 1790): 341–43, April 1795: 256; John W. Francis, *Old New York: Or Reminiscences of the Past Sixty Years* (New York: W. J. Widdleton, 1865) 23–24; Kieran, *Natural History of New York City,* 247–49; Report by John Fellows to the President and Directors of the Manhattan Company, June 7, 1810, Manhattan Company Records, New-York Historical Society; *MCC, 1784–1831,* 6:188.

24. *Commercial Advertiser,* May 9, 1809

25. MC Minutes, 2:74–75.

26. *Commercial Advertiser,* May 22, 31, 1809, Oct. 28, 1812; *Public Advertiser,* June 16, 1809; MC Minutes, 2:48–50, 144–46, 155–57, 167–68; New York *Evening Post,* Sept. 19, 1820; Hunter, *Manhattan Company,* 110–18.

27. Hunter, *Manhattan Company,* 126–27.

28. New York *Evening Post,* Apr. 19, 1824.

29. Digest of Patents, 1790–1839, Mar. 24, 1825; Hunter, *Manhattan Company,* 129; Blake, *Water for the Cities,* 119–22; New York *Evening Post,* Mar. 28, 1825; *Commercial Advertiser,* June 3, 1825.

30. *Commercial Advertiser,* June 5, 1828; Hone Diary, June 7, 1828, manuscript in New-York Historical Society; Hunter, *Manhattan Company,* 129–30; Blake, *Water for the Cities,* 163.

31. New York *Evening Post,* Feb. 18, 1831; Haswell, *Reminiscences,* 337.

32. *New York Evening Journal,* undated clipping in Stephen Allen Scrap Book, New-York Historical Society; the paper was published from 1829 to 1832.

33. Edward Miller, *Report on the Malignant Disease,* 45–75, 97.

34. New York *Evening Post,* Aug. 24, 1805, Feb. 10, 1806; *New-York Herald,* Aug. 28, 1805; *American Citizen,* May 19, 1806; Stokes, *Iconography,* 5:1415, 1429, 1441, 1447, 1452, 1463; *Encyclopedia of NYC,* 308; *MCC, 1784–1831,* 3:253, 280, 341.

35. *Manual of the Common Council* (1864), 847–56.

36. *MCC, 1784–1831,* 5:411, 631, 689–90, 733–34, 753, 795. In 1809 inflation-adjusted dollars, the city's 1774 investment of £1,050 would equal $4,000; if all thirty lots had been sold at $1,200 apiece, the city would have realized a profit of $32,000; see McCusker, *How Much Is That in Real Money?* 325–26.

37. *MCC, 1784–1831,* 6:66, 75, 109, 142, 300, 625, 660, 7:168–69; Stokes, *Iconography,* 5:1538.

38. *Laws of New York* (1812), chap. 212; Thomas Poppleton journal, ms, New York Public Library. For their services, Poppleton was paid $1,330.64, Whitney $315, and Fulton $153.

39. *The Columbian,* Nov. 25, 1818; Stokes, *Iconography,* 3:560–62, 5:1571, 1587, 1590, 1591.

40. Stokes, *Iconography,* 1:472.

41. Stokes, *Iconography,* 5:1532; Paul E. Cohen and Robert T. Augustyn, *Manhattan in Maps, 1527–1995* (New York: Rizzoli, 1997), 103.

42. Stokes, *Iconography,* 1:472.

43. Stokes, *Iconography,* 5:1449. A 1798 watercolor of St. Paul's shows the pump in a commanding location in Broadway; a sepia painting, done between 1809 and 1813, shows the pump relocated to the curb; Stokes, *Iconography,* 1: plate 68b, 3: plate 81a.

44. *MCC, 1784–1831,* 5:181, 232–33, 433.

45. Hunter, *Manhattan Company,* 104–5; Duffy, *History of Public Health in New York City,* 170; Joan H. Geismar, "Where is Night Soil? Thoughts on an Urban Privy," *Historical Archaeology* 27, 2 (1993): 57; *MCC, 1784–1831,* 3:189–91, 352, 459.

46. Duffy, *History of Public Health in New York City,* 209; Bayrd Still, *Mirror for Gotham* (New York: New York University Press, 1956), 97.

47. *Encylopedia of NYC,* "seltzer"; *MCC, 1784–1831,* 6:528, 537, 551, 11:2, 167.

48. James Stuart, *Three Years in North America.* 2 vols. (Edinburgh: R. Cadell, 1833), 1:32; *Encyclopedia of NYC,* "seltzer"; *Famous First Facts,* "soda water machine manufacturer."

49. *Oxford Companion to American Literature,* "Samuel Woodworth"; Augustine E. Costello, *Our Firemen,* 308. The Woodworth poem appears in numerous contemporary anthologies, including J. Gilchrist Lawson, *The World's Best Loved Poems* (New York: Harper & Row, 1955 [1927]), *The Best Loved Poems of the American People, Selected by Hazel Felleman* (Garden City, N.Y.: Garden City Publishing Company, 1975 [1936]), *The Family Album of Favorite Poems,* ed. P. Edward Ernest (New York: Grosset & Dunlap, 1959), Richard Jackson, *Popular Songs of 19th Century America: Complete Original Sheet Music for 64 Songs* (New York: Dover, 1976), and *Anthology of American Poetry,* ed. George Gesner (New York: Avenal Books, 1983).

50. The parody appears in *The Best Loved Poems of the American People, The Family Album of Favorite Poems,* and *The World's Best Loved Poems.*

51. Grant Thorburn, *Fifty Years' Reminiscences of New-York, or, Flowers from the Garden of Laurie Todd, Being a Collection of Fugitive Pieces which Appeared in the Newspapers and Periodicals of the Day* (New York: D. Fanshaw, 1845), 212–15.

52. *Manual of the Common Council* (1864), 847–56; Costello, *Our Firemen,* 304–5; Haswell, *Reminiscences,* 36.

53. *New York Evening Journal,* clipping in Stephen Allen Scrap Book, New-York Historical Society.

54. Ginsberg, "History of Fire Protection," 164–71, 344; *Encyclopedia of NYC,* "firefighting."

55. Costello, *Our Firemen,* 311, 314; *MCC, 1784–1831,* 6:631–32, 9:220, 254; *Laws of New York* (1817), chap. 25.

56. Rosenwaike, *Population History,* 36.

57. *MCC, 1784–1831,* 3:594–95, 597, 606, 622, 626; Stokes, *Iconography,* 5:1427–428.

58. *MCC, 1784–1831,* 8:464–65; *Manual of the Common Council* (1854), 217.

59. *MCC, 1784–1831,* 10:503, 11:15–16; *Manual of the Common Council* (1854), 217; *Encyclopedia of NYC,* "Macombs Dam," "Macombs Dam Bridge"; Hunter, *Manhattan Company,* 119.

60. *Messages from the Governor Comprising Executive Communications to the Legislature, and Other Papers Relating to the Legislature, from the Origins of the First Colonial Assembly to 1906,* 11 vols., ed. Charles Z. Lincoln (Albany: J. B. Lyon Co., 1909), 2:1017.

61. On March 5, 1821, Allen became the city's last mayor named by the state Council of Appointment; under changes in the state constitution made in November 1821, he subsequently was elected by the Common Council for two more terms.

62. Edward Pessen, "The Wealthiest New Yorkers of the Jacksonian Era: A New List," *New York Historical Society Quarterly,* 54, 2 (April 1970): 156; *Encyclopedia of NYC,* "Stephen Allen"; Allen, "Memoirs," introduction; Moses Yale Beach, *Wealth and Biography of the Wealthy Citizens of New York City, Comprising an Alphabetical Arrangement of Persons Estimated to be Worth $100,000 and Upwards . . . ,* 6th ed. (New York: The Sun Office, 1845).

63. *MCC, 1784–1831,* 12:168–69, 175; *DAB,* "Canvass White"; *Famous First Facts,* "Cement"; *The Reminiscences of John B. Jervis, Engineer of the Old Croton,* ed. Neal FitzSimons (Syracuse, N.Y.: Syracuse University Press, 1971), 33, 37.

64. *MCC, 1784–1831,* 12:309–11.

65. *MCC, 1784–1831,* 12:311.

66. Duffy, *History of Public Health in New York City,* 119.

67. *MCC, 1784–1831,* 12:560; Allen, "Memoirs," 98.

68. *MCC, 1784–1831,* 12:766–71.

69. Blake, *Water for the Cities,* 110–11.

70. *Laws of New York* (1823), chap. 90; Blake, *Water for the Cities,* 111.

71. *Reminiscences of John B. Jervis,* 63; *MCC, 1784–1831,* 13:658, 364; Edward Wegmann, *The Water-Supply of the City of New York, 1658–1895* (New York: J. Wiley & Sons, 1896), 14–15; Stokes, *Iconography,* 5:1635, 1636.

72. White's and Wright's reports of Jan. 28, 1824 are printed in "Report of Committee on Fire and Water," New York City Board of Aldermen, *Documents,* Dec. 28, 1831, 17–40, 41–44, resp. (hereafter, Bd. Ald., *Docs.*).

73. Blake, *Water for the Cities,* 111–12; Bender, *New York Intellect,* 84–85; Stokes, *Iconography,* 5:1637; New York *Evening Post,* Aug. 7, 1824.

74. Blake, *Water for the Cities,* 112.

75. Blake, *Water for the Cities,* 112–15.

76. *MCC, 1784–1831,* 14:288, 326–27, 351; New York *Evening Post,* Mar. 15, 1825.

77. *Laws of New York* (1825), chap. 46; New York *Evening Post,* Mar. 28, 1825.

78. *New York Mirror,* 2:370; New York *Evening Post,* Apr. 18, 20, June 20, 1825.

79. New York *Evening Post,* Nov. 26, 1825.

80. New York *Evening Post,* Nov. 28, 29, Dec. 2, 1825. Capitalized at $1 million in 1818, the Franklin Bank suspended payments ten years later; Stokes, *Iconography,* 5:1597, 1677; Haswell, *Reminiscences,* 193.

81. New York *Evening Post,* Dec. 14, 16, 22, 29, 30, 1825, Jan. 9, 19, 21, 26, 27, Feb. 3, 1826.

82. White's Jan. 9, 1826 report, with supporting notes from Wright, is printed in "Report of Committee on Fire and Water," Bd. Ald., *Docs.,* Dec. 28, 1831, 53–61; also see New York *Evening Post,* Jan. 18, 19, 23, 28, 1826.

83. New York *Evening Post,* Jan. 9, 28, 1826; Blake, *Water for the Cities,* 117.

84. New York *Evening Post,* Jan. 9, 27, 1826; Blake, *Water for the Cities,* 118.

85. Blake, *Water for the Cities,* 118.

86. New York *Evening Post,* July 15, 1826; *Manual of the Common Council* (1854), 218; Wegmann, *Water-Supply,* 15.

87. *Laws of New York* (1826), chap. 290; New York *Evening Post,* Sept. 13, 1826; Costello, *Our Firemen,* 310; Stokes, *Iconography,* 3:551–53, 6:524; Pessen, "Wealthiest New Yorkers"; Beach, *Wealth and Biography* (1845); *Encyclopedia of NYC, DAB, Encyclopaedia Britannica,* "James Renwick"; *Encyclopedia of NYC,* "Phelps, Dodge."

88. Stokes, *Iconography,* 3:636

89. Haswell, *Reminiscences,* 217; *Manual of the Common Council* (1854), 218.

90. Stokes, *Iconography,* 5:1669; Haswell, *Reminiscences,* 158–59. The well was on Jacob Street, originally called Leather Street when the swamp was first filled. One of the last major tanners at the site, Jacob Lorillard was among the city's wealthiest citizens in the late 1820s, as were his older brothers Peter and George, who had several decades earlier moved the family snuff factory from Manhattan to a mill on the Bronx River; the Lorillards became the nation's largest manufacturer of snuff and tobacco, the company surviving today as the cigarette division of Loews Corporation. See Stokes, *Iconography,* 3:1003, 1004; *Encyclopedia of NYC,* "P. Lorillard and Company"; Pessen, "Wealthiest New Yorkers," 155; Hone, *Diary,* 343.

91. Beach, *Wealth and Biography* (1845); Ginsberg, "History of Fire Protection," 340; Blake, *Water for the Cities,* 122.

92. *MCC, 1784–1831,* 17:561. Bowne was busied with mayoral duties and Peter Cooper left the Manhattan glue business for his Canton Iron Works near Baltimore, where he built the *Tom Thumb,* America's first steam locomotive; *Famous First Facts,* 356, 357; *Encyclopedia of NYC, DAB,* "Peter Cooper."

93. *MCC, 1784–1831,* 17:722–24; "Semi-Annual Report of the Water Commissioners, August 8, 1842," New York City Board of Aldermen, *Document no. 9* (1842), 86–87 (hereafter, Bd. Ald., *Doc.*). Though its source was never specified, the 13th Street system likely drew its water from the network of underground springs that are the font of the long-buried Minetta Water, flowing from the nearby high ground at Union Square through Greenwich Village to the Hudson.

94. *MCC, 1784–1831,* 18:25, 50–51, 112, 191, 212, 352–53.

95. *MCC, 1784–1831,* 18:357, 394, 465–66.

96. *MCC, 1784–1831,* 18:674–76; New York *Evening Post,* Apr. 20, 1830; Costello, *Our Firemen,* 313; Haswell, *Reminiscences,* 285.

97. *MCC, 1784–1831,* 19:664, 715–16; Rosenberg, "History of Fire Protection," 348–49; New York City Board of Aldermen, *Proceedings,* 1:18 (hereafter, Bd. Ald., *Procs.*). In April 1830, the legislature significantly revised the city charter that had been in place since 1731. Starting in 1831, annual city elections were switched from early November to the second week in April, and the Common Council was split into a Board of Aldermen and a Board of Assistant Aldermen, with each electing a president from among its members. The mayor, still annually elected by the council, was severed from it, gaining a veto power that Board majorities could override. Council committees were supposed to give way to separate bureaucratic departments, but the committee system remained in place well into the next decade. Together with an 1833 amendment to the state constitution that provided for the annual election of mayors by popular vote beginning the following year, this was the system of city government that operated until the middle of the century. See *Encyclopedia of NYC,* "charter"; Stokes, *Iconography,* 5:1691, 1723.

98. Bd. Ald., *Procs.,* 1:112–15.

99. Bd. Ald., *Doc. 37* (1833), 411–16; New-York Historical Society, *Bulletin* (October 1917), 70; Hall, *Water for New York City,* 51–52; U[zziah] Wenman, *The Firemen's Guide* (New York: P. Desobry, 1834).

100. *The Family Magazine or Monthly Abstract of General Knowledge* (1839): 6:117; *Manual of the Common Council* (1853), 134.

101. Finch, *Travels in the United States and Canada,* 35. The date of Finch's New York City impressions is unclear; Stokes places the comments in 1832 but textual references suggest the later 1820s.

EIGHT   *Catching the Croton Bug*

1. Irving to King, Aug. 9, 1832, *Works of Washington Irving,* 40 vols. (New York: G. P. Putnam & Co., 1910), 24:713.

2. *MCC, 1784–1831,* 18:604, 19:89; New York *Evening Post,* June 17, 1830. Among the special committee members were aldermen and future water commissioners Benjamin M. Brown and Thomas Woodruff and assistant alderman Henry Arcularius, whose uncle Philip had helped Aaron Burr launch the Manhattan Company.

3. "The People vs. The President and Directors of the Manhattan Company," in John L. Wendell, comp., *Reports of Cases Argued and Determined in the Supreme Court of Judicature and in the Court for the Correction of Errors of the State of New-York* (Albany, 1829–1842), 9:351–94; Hunter, *Manhattan Company,* 61–65, 198–201.

4. New York *Evening Post,* Feb. 15, 18, Mar. 1, 4, 1831; *MCC, 1784–1831,* 19:519–23.

5. A New York Temperance Society was organized in 1828, three years after a national organization was founded in Boston; by 1833, five thousand such groups, claiming well over a million members, had sprung up around the country. Stanley Wade Baron, *Brewed in America: A History of Beer and Ale in the United States* (Boston: Little, Brown and Company, 1962), 191 passim; Abel, *Alcohol Wordlore and Folklore,* 137–39; *Brewer's Dictionary of Phrase and Fable,* Centenary Edition, "Teetotal"; John Russell Bartlett, *The Dictionary of Americanisms* (New York: Crescent Books, 1989 [1849]), "TEE-TOTAL."

6. An 1816 graduate of the College of Physicians and Surgeons, Townsend was a prominent early member of the Lyceum, founded in 1817 by his famous professor, Samuel Latham Mitchill; see Simon Baatz, *Knowledge, Culture, and Science in the Metropolis: The New York Academy of Sciences, 1817–1970* (New York: New York Academy of Sciences, 1990); Bender, *New York Intellect,* 53, 69–72; *Encyclopedia of NYC,* "New York Academy of Sciences."

7. *Communication from the Committee of the Lyceum of Natural History of the City of New-York to an Enquiry from Mr. Townsend on the Source, Quality and Purity of the Water on this Island, February 22, 1831* (New York, 1831).

8. See Report of Col. De Witt Clinton, in Bd. Ald., *Doc. 61* (1832), 209–10.

9. Blake, *Water for the Cities,* 128.

10. Bd. Ald., *Procs.,* 1:50–51; New York *Evening Post,* May 25, 1831.

11. New York *Evening Post,* July 5, 1831. John Adams and Thomas Jefferson both died on July 4, 1826.

12. Bd. Ald., *Docs.,* Dec. 28, 1831, 1.

13. Bd. Ald., *Procs.,* 2:84; New York City Board of Assistant Aldermen, *Proceedings,* 1: 325 (hereafter, Bd. Assts., *Procs.*); James B. Murray, *The Origin of the Croton Aqueduct in the City of New York* (New York: Charles W. Baker, 1857), 9; "A Relation of the Measures which were Adopted for the Purpose of Supplying the City of New York with the Water of the Croton River. By Myndert Van Schaick. February 26, 1845. To Aldermen James Palmer, Charles Henry Hall, James B. Murray, Henry Meigs, Assistant Alderman Peter S. Titus, and the other friends of the Croton River project in the Common Council of 1832–3," in New York *Evening Post,* Mar. 18, 1845 (hereafter referred to by newspaper and date).

14. New York *Evening Post,* Apr. 14, May 19, 1845; Murray, *Origin of the Croton Aqueduct,* 9; Blake, *Water for the Cities,* 130.

15. New York *Evening Post,* Mar. 18, 1845.

16. Jerome B. Holgate, *American Genealogy* (New York: George P. Putnam, 1851), 143–47; Bender, *New York Intellect,* 90–95; William Dunlap, *A History of the Rise and Progress of the Arts of Design in the United States,* 2 vols. (Boston: C. E. Goodspeed & Co., 1918, 3 vols. [1834]), 3: 270–80; Stokes, *Iconography,* 3: 703; New York *Evening Post,* Mar. 18, 1845.

17. Hone, *Diary,* 122; New York *Evening Post,* Mar. 18, 1845.

18. New York *Evening Post,* Mar. 18, 1845.

19. Bd. Ald., *Procs.,* 3:248.

20. New York *Evening Post,* Mar. 18, May 19, 1845; Bd. Ald., *Procs.,* 3:267–68; Wright to Dewey, Oct. 29, 1832, in Bd. Ald., *Doc. 61* (1832), 251–52.

21. New York *Evening Post,* Mar. 18, 1845.

22. Wendell, *Reports of Cases,* 9:351–94; Hunter, *Manhattan Company,* 65–67; Blake, *Water for the Cities,* 135.

23. Jackson to Nicholas Philip Trist, U.S. Consul at Havana, Nov. 17, [1833], ms letter, New-York Historical Society.

24. For examples of Clinton's early private work, see Edwin Ferry Johnson, *Review of the Report for a Great Western Railway: Addressed to the Author of the Project, in May, 1829 . . .* (New York: W. D. Starr, 1831); De Witt Clinton, *Correspondence on the Importance & Practicability of a Rail Road, from New York to New Orleans . . .* (New York: Vanderpool and Cole, 1830); Eleazar Lord Papers, New-York Historical Society. For Clinton's federal government work, see United States War Department, *Survey of Connecticut River* (Washington, D.C., 1831); United States Army Corps of Topographical Engineers, *Letter from the Secretary of War transmitting a survey of a route for a railroad from the portage summit of the Ohio Canal to the Hudson River,* in 22d Cong., 1st sess. House doc. no. 133. On cholera, see John James Abert to Clinton, July 18, 1832, in Clinton Letter Book 1830–1832, New-York Historical Society.

25. Van Schaick had been introduced to Clinton in Washington by Cadwallader D. Colden expressly for the purpose of gaining Clinton's appointment, which was secured by Van Schaick through his friend Martin Van Buren, New York Democratic power broker and Jackson's Secretary of State. New York *Evening Post,* Mar. 18, 1845.

26. New York *Evening Post,* Mar. 18, 1845.

27. New York *Evening Post,* May 19, 1845; Murray, *Origin of the Croton Aqueduct,* 13. Aldermen Hall, Palmer, and Meigs were instrumental in pushing Van Schaick's nomination; New York *Evening Post,* Mar. 18, 1845.

28. Dewey and Serrell report to Wright, Nov. 29, 1832, in Bd. Ald., *Doc. 61* (1832), 253–59.

29. New York *Evening Post,* Mar. 18, 1845; "The Origin of the Croton Aqueduct and the New Grand Reservoir," by Myndert Van Schaick, Jan. 1, 1863, in Bd. Ald., *Doc.* (1863), 126–27; Murray, *Origin of the Croton Aqueduct,* 12–13.

30. Dewey and Serrell report, Bd. Ald., *Doc. 61* (1832), 253–59.

31. Clinton report to Fire and Water Committee, Dec. 22, 1832, in Bd. Ald., *Doc. 61* (1832), 192–250.

32. Stokes, *Iconography,* 3:848–49; Timothy J. Gilfoyle, *City of Eros: New York City, Prostitution, and the Commercialization of Sex, 1790–1920* (New York: W. W. Norton & Company, 1992), 70; Kline, *Political Correspondence,* 2:1218; *Encyclopedia of NYC,* "Elizabeth Jumel," "Stephen Jumel"; Judi Culbertson and Tom Randall,

Permanent New Yorkers: A Biographical Guide to the Cemeteries of New York (Chelsea, Vt.: Chelsea Green Publishing Co., 1987), 33.

33. A volunteer from his teens, Wenman rose to chief fire engineer in 1828; his bravery was especially in evidence at City Hotel fires in 1829 and 1833. His "Firemen's Guide," a map detailing the city's five fire districts, dozens of street hydrants, forty public cisterns, fifty-nine engine houses, and the 13th Street Reservoir system, was posted for many years in the firehouses of New York. See Costello, *Our Firemen*, 84, 89, 216–17, 392–93; Dunshee, *As You Pass By*, 123, endpiece (map reproduction).

34. Among the specific annual figures gathered by Clinton were $157,000 in property losses from fire, $50,000 in fire insurance premiums, $18,000 for maintaining the fire department, $110,000 in street cleaning costs, $18,000 for pump maintenance, $250,000 for carted spring water, $50,000 for water from various sources for shipping, and a meager $10,000 in Manhattan Company water fees.

35. New York *Evening Post*, Mar. 18, May 19, 1845.

36. New York *Evening Post*, Jan. 2, 1834.

37. Bd. Assts., *Procs.*, 2:232; Bd. Ald., *Doc. 10* (1833), 1–2.

38. New York *Evening Post*, Mar. 18, 1845.

39. Ibid.

40. "Report of the Celebration Held on the Completion of the New Reservoir, August 19, 1862," in Bd. Ald., *Docs.* (1863), 128; New York *Evening Post*, Mar. 18, May 19, 1845.

41. New York *Evening Post*, Apr. 14, May 13, 19, 1845; Bd. Ald., *Doc. 10* (1833), 3–6. Also see New York *Evening Post*, Dec. 24, 1832.

42. Bd. Ald. *Procs.*, 4:94; Bd. Assts., *Procs.*, 2:282.

43. New York *Evening Post*, Mar. 18, 1845; *Laws of New York* (1833), chap. 26.

44. Blake, *Water for the Cities*, 136; New York *Evening Post*, Mar. 18, May 3, 19, 1845; Murray, *Origin of the Croton Aqueduct*, 14–15; *Manual of the Common Council* (1865), 400; Costello, *Our Firemen*, 471–72; Pessen, "Wealthiest New Yorkers of the Jacksonian Era," 156, 165; Ginsberg, "History of Fire Protection," 40ff; Beach, *Wealth and Biography*, 5th ed. (1845), 12th ed. (1855); William Thompson Bonner, *New York, The World's Metropolis, 1623–4–1923–4* (New York: R. L. Polk & Co., 1924), 713; Scharf, *History of Westchester County*, 1:844–46; William Armstrong, *Aristocracy of New York: Who They Are and What They Were; being a Social and Business History of the City for many Years* (New York, 1848); Walton, *Tomahawks to Textiles*, 109–10; Haswell, *Reminiscences*, 222.

45. Allen, "Memoirs," 141; Blake, *Water for the Cities*, 121; New York *Evening Post*, May 10, 1845.

46. Allen, "Memoirs," 141; New York *Evening Post*, Apr. 14, 1845; also see New York *Commercial Advertiser*, Mar. 19, 1833.

47. John L. Sullivan, *An Address to the Mayor, the Aldermen, and the Inhabitants of New York Supplemental to Col. Clinton's Report on Water* (New York: Clayton &

Van Norden, 1833), 24. Also see Levi Disbrow & J. L. Sullivan, *Proposition for Ward Companies, to Supply the City of New-York with Rock Water, &c.* (New York, 1832). The son of patriot James S. Sullivan, John Langdon Sullivan worked on various canals and served on the federal Board of Internal Improvements until the 1820s; after proposing in 1830 to water New York with an aqueduct under the Hudson from New Jersey's Passaic River, he abandoned canaling, obtained a medical degree from Yale, and took up homeopathic medicine, apparently while bankrolling Levi Disbrow's deep wells. See J. L. Sullivan, *A Description of a Sub-Marine Aqueduct, to Supply New-York with Water from New-Jersey* (New York, 1830); *Reminiscences of John B. Jervis,* 66–71; Henry S. Tanner, *A Description of the Canals and Railroads of the United States* (New York: Augustus M. Kelley, 1970 [1840]), 158; *Appleton's Cyclopedia of American Biography* (Detroit: Gale Research, 1968 [1888]); New York *Commercial Advertiser,* Mar. 20, Sept. 7, 1833.

48. White to the Water Commissioners, New York, Oct. 30, 1833, in "Report of the Commissioners . . . Relative to Supplying the City of New-York with Pure and Wholesome Water," November 12, 1833, in Bd. Ald., *Doc. 36* (1833), 380; *DAB,* "Canvass White."

49. The following biographical sketch is drawn from Douglass entries in the *DAB; National Cyclopaedia of American Biography* (New York: James White & Co., 1897); *Appleton's Cyclopaedia of American Biography;* "Background Note," David Bates Douglass Papers, William L. Clements Library, University of Michigan; Larry D. Lankton, "The 'Practicable' Engineer: John B. Jervis and the Old Croton Aqueduct," in Public Works Historical Society, *Essays in Public Works History,* 5 (1977): 3–4, 8–9. A notable Douglass grandson was astronomer and archaeologist Andrew Ellicott Douglass, who coined the term and established the principals of dendochronology, the dating of events by analysis of tree rings; see *Encyclopaedia Britannica,* "Andrew Ellicott Douglass."

50. New York *Evening Post,* Jan. 10, 1837. Dedicated in 1837, the building was demolished in 1894, when the undergraduate school was relocated for a period to the Bronx.

51. Bd. Ald., *Doc. 11* (1834). Cartwright became prominent in Sing Sing, organizing area silver and copper mining operations, founding the local Episcopal congregation, laying out Van Cortlandt estate lands into lots that became today's North Tarrytown, and serving three terms as Sing Sing village president. Scharf, *History of Westchester County,* 2:287, 323–24, 333, 343.

52. Bd. Ald., *Doc. 36* (1833), 381, 408.

53. The Douglass report appears in Bd. Ald., *Doc. 36* (1833), 381–408.

54. Hone, *Diary,* 98. Eliza Jumel died in 1865, her mortal remains entombed beside the Astor family vault in Trinity Cemetery, a few blocks from her city home. Kline, *Political Correspondence,* 2:1218; *Encyclopedia of NYC,* "Elizabeth Jumel"; Culbertson and Randall, *Permanent New Yorkers,* 33; Gore Vidal, *Burr: A Novel* (New York: Random House, 1974), 189; Lomask, *Burr,* xii.

55. The Commissioners' report appears in Bd. Ald., *Doc. 36* (1833), 357–79.

56. Bd. Ald., *Doc. 48* (1833), 495–500.

57. Bd. Ald., *Doc. 45* (1833), 449–52; Bd. Ald., *Procs.,* 6:42.

58. The committee asked to be discharged from further consideration of the matter; in February, a special joint committee was appointed to take up the negotiations, but no action immediately was forthcoming. Bd. Ald., *Doc. 49* (1833); Blake, *Water for the Cities,* 144. The next few council sessions featured John Sullivan's renewed Disbrow well pitches, which were referred to the fire and water committee; Bd. Ald., *Procs.,* 6:76; Bd. Ald., *Doc. 50* (1833); Blake, *Water for the Cities,* 137.

59. *Westchester Herald,* Feb. 4, 1834. Born in the county to an English-born father, Roscoe (1800–1877) worked in publishing in New York City before purchasing the *Herald,* which he ran with great success until a disastrous fire in 1856 shut its doors; see Scharf, *History of Westchester County,* 2:352–53.

60. *Westchester Herald,* Jan. 1, 1834.

61. Bd. Ald., *Procs.,* 6:140–41; see New York *Evening Post,* Mar. 18, 1845.

62. The mayoral contest brought out many wealthy and older citizens opposed to the Democrats, who labeled their Whig opponents the "Silk Stocking" party, the first use of the term that continues to be applied to voting districts in today's Upper East Side. See Haswell, *Reminiscences,* 289.

63. New York *Evening Post,* Mar. 18, 1845; "Report of the Celebration," in Bd. Ald., *Docs.* (1863), 130.

64. "Report of the Celebration," in Bd. Ald., *Docs.* (1863), 130–31.

65. New York *Evening Post,* Mar. 18, 1845.

66. *Westchester Herald,* Apr. 29, 1834; "Report of the Celebration," in Bd. Ald., *Docs.* (1863), 130; *Laws of New York (1834),* chap. 256; New York *Evening Post,* Mar. 18, Apr. 14, 1845.

67. Report of the Water Commissioners, Feb. 16, 1835, in Bd. Ald., *Doc. 44* (1835) 44, 325, 330, 332; Bd. Ald., *Procs.,* 7:151; Duffy, *History of Public Health in New York City,* 288, 443; Stokes, *Iconography,* 5:1727; Blake, *Water for the Cities,* 140, 227.

68. *The New-York Mirror,* Aug. 2, 9, 16, 1834. Founded in 1823 by Samuel Woodworth, the *Mirror* had been edited by Morris since its second year. In 1844–1845, after Morris's retirement, the paper's notorious literary critic, Edgar Allan Poe, launched plagiarism attacks on Longfellow. After several title changes, the journal shut down in 1860. See *Oxford Companion to American Literature,* "New-York Mirror."

69. During the 1830s, Stein also built waterworks for Lynchburg and Richmond, Virginia, Cincinnati, and New Orleans, where he directed a private company's improvements on the inadequate Latrobe-engineered public works. "The History of the Nashville Water System," www.nashville.org/ws/w_history.html; King, *Memoir,* 82; Blake, *Water for the Cities,* 260, 266.

70. Bd. Ald., *Procs.,* 6:81, 86; Bd. Ald., *Doc. 54* (1833), *Doc. 57* (1834), *Doc. 109* (1834); Bd. Ald., *Doc. 44* (1835), 325–29; also *Westchester Herald,* May 13, 1834.

71. Bd. Ald., *Doc. 44* (1835), 329-30; *Reminiscences of John B. Jervis,* 54.

72. Bd. Ald, *Doc. 44* (1835), 341, 356.

73. The Commissioners' report and appended documents appear in Bd. Ald., *Doc. 44* (1835), 323–525.

74. "Report of the Committee on Fire and Water, to whom was referred the Report of the Commissioners ... March 4, 1835," Bd. Ald., *Doc. 45* (1835), 517–24; Bd. Ald., *Procs.,* 8:272, 282; New York *Evening Post,* Mar. 20, 1835; New York *Commercial Advertiser,* Mar. 21, 1835; *New York Gazette & General Advertiser,* Mar. 27, 1835.

75. J. L. Sullivan, *Exposition of the Errors in the Calculation of the Board of the Water Commissioners* ... (New York: George P. Scott & Co., 1835); M[oses] Hale, *Spring Water Versus River Water, for Supplying the City of New-York, Containing a Compendious Examination of the Internal Supplies, the Method, and the Actual Expense of Obtaining Them* ... (New York: Marsh & Harrison, 1835); see *New-York Daily Advertiser,* Apr. 11, 1835. The Whiggish paper, continuing the *New-York Courier* (1815–1817) and continued by the *New York Express* (1836–1864), is not to be confused with the earlier Democratic-Republican *Daily Advertiser* (1787–1806).

76. New York *Evening Post,* Mar. 17, 20, 1835; New York *Commercial Advertiser,* Mar. 21, 1835; *Evening Star,* Apr. 13, 1835.

77. Blake, *Water for the Cities,* 142.

78. Hone, *Diary,* 155; New York *Commercial Advertiser, New York Gazette & General Advertiser, New-York Daily Advertiser,* Apr. 16, 1835.

79. *New-York Daily Advertiser,* Apr. 14, 1835; New York *Commercial Advertiser,* Apr. 15, 1835; New York *Evening Post,* Mar. 18, 1845.

80. New York *American,* Apr. 16, 1835; see generally the *Evening Star,* New York *Commercial Advertiser, New-York Daily Advertiser, Morning Courier and New-York Enquirer, New York Gazette & General Advertiser,* and New York *Sun* for Apr. 14–16, 1835.

81. *Evening Star,* Apr. 17, 1835; New York *Commercial Advertiser,* Apr. 28, 1835. A year later, Lawrence was elected against nominal Whig opposition for a third and final term, while the Whigs gained exactly half of the Common Council.

82. New York *Commercial Advertiser,* Apr. 17, 1835; New York *Evening Post,* Apr. 23, 1835.

83. See Eric Homberger, *The Historical Atlas of New York City* (New York: Henry Holt and Company, 1994), 80–81; *Manual of the Common Council* (1854), 220–21; Robert Ernst, *Immigrant Life in New York City 1825–1863* (Syracuse, N.Y.: Syracuse University Press, 1994 [1949]), 191.

84. New York *Commercial Advertiser,* Apr. 21, 28, 1835; *Morning Courier and New-York Enquirer,* Apr. 23, 1835; New York City Common Council, *Proceedings of the Boards of Aldermen and Assistant Aldermen, and Approved by the Mayor,* 2:401–3 (hereafter, *Procs., Approved by the Mayor*); Blake, *Water for the Cities,* 142.

85. "Communication from the Water Commissioners," Bd. Ald., *Doc. 12* (1836).

86. *New York Times and Evening Star,* Oct. 30, 1840.

87. "Communication from the Water Commissioners," Bd. Ald., *Doc. 12* (1836).

88. *New York Times and Evening Star,* Oct. 30, 1840; "Communication from the Water Commissioners," Bd. Ald., *Doc. 12* (1836), 63.

89. "Description of Outer Bounds or Property Line to be Followed in Making the Survey of Lands for the New York City Reservoir," from survey by George W. Cartwright, David Bates Douglass Papers, The Archives, Warren Hunting Smith Library, Hobart and William Smith Colleges, Geneva, N.Y., in Tema Harnik, "Temperament, Temperance and Tolerance: An Appraisal of Conflicts Over Land Values and Laborers Along the Line of the Croton Aqueduct," *The Old Croton Aqueduct: Rural Resources Meet Urban Needs* (Yonkers, N.Y.: The Hudson River Museum of Westchester, 1992), 34; also see "Water Commissioners' Semi-Annual Report," in Bd. Ald., *Doc. 25* (1838), 269–70.

90. See Lederer, *Place Names of Westchester County,* passim; "Communication from the Water Commissioners," Bd. Ald., *Doc. 12* (1836).

91. Allen, "Memoirs," 156.

92. Hone, *Diary,* 185–86. The following discussion of the fire and its effects is drawn from Hone, *Diary,* 185–93; Stephen F. Ginsberg, "The History of Fire Protection in New York City," 174–203; and Augustine Costello, *Our Firemen,* 270–302; New York *Evening Post,* Dec. 17, 1835.

93. Commissioned a decade earlier by the city's leading merchants and finally sculpted out of Carrara marble by English-born (Robert) Ball Hughes, the Hamilton statue was the first marble statue carved in the United States and the subject of much admiration; *DAB,* "Robert Ball Hughes"; *Encyclopedia of NYC,* "sculpture"; New York *Commercial Advertiser,* Apr. 20, 1835.

94. Stokes, *Iconography,* 5:1259, 1269, 1735.

95. *New-York Daily Advertiser,* Apr. 14, 1835; Hone, *Diary,* 186.

96. Hone, *Diary,* 190; Christine Chapman Robbins, *David Hosack: Citizen of New York* (Philadelphia: American Philosophical Society, 1964), 186.

97. *New York Times and Evening Star,* Oct. 30, 1840.

98. *Morning Courier and New York Enquirer,* Nov. 12, 1840.

99. *New York Times and Evening Star,* Oct. 30, 1840.

100. See Harnik, "Temperament, Temperance and Tolerance," 35.

101. Bd. Ald., *Doc. 89* (1836).

102. *New York Times and Evening Star,* Oct. 30, 1840. Allen disputed many of Douglass's public claims; *Morning Courier and New-York Enquirer,* Nov. 12, 1840. *Reminiscences of John B. Jervis,* 123; Larkin, *John B. Jervis,* 66.

103. *New York Times and Evening Star,* Oct. 30, 1840; Bd. Ald., *Doc. 12* (1836), 64.

104. *Reminiscences of John B. Jervis,* 120; F. Daniel Larkin, "Preliminary Plans for the Old Croton Aqueduct and the Structure of Its Engineering Department," *The Old Croton Aqueduct,* 20–21.

105. Bd. Ald., *Doc. 12* (1836); *Laws of New York* (1836), chap. 468.

106. *Westchester Herald,* June 14, 1836.

107. *New York Times and Evening Star,* Oct. 30, 1840; *Morning Courier and New-York Enquirer,* Nov. 12, 1840; Bd. Ald., *Doc. 12* (1836), 64–65.

108. *New York Times and Evening Star,* Oct. 30, 1840.

109. *Westchester Herald,* Aug. 2, 1836.

110. Bd. Ald., *Doc. 12* (1836); Bd. Assts., *Doc. 24* (1837).

111. Stokes, *Iconography,* 5:1741, 1742.

112. Bd. Ald., *Doc. 12* (1836), 65. Although Douglass dated the resolution and reply as July 19 and 22, Allen gave July 23 and 26; *New York Times and Evening Star,* Oct. 30, 1840; *Morning Courier and New-York Enquirer,* Nov. 12, 1840.

113. *Morning Courier and New-York Enquirer,* Nov. 12, 1840.

114. Ibid.

115. Allen, "Memoirs," 157–59; *Morning Courier and New-York Enquirer,* Nov. 12, 1840.

NINE   The Work Begins

1. New York *Herald,* Oct. 14, 1836. Founded a year earlier by James Gordon Bennett, the ostensibly nonpartisan penny paper's motto was "not to instruct but to startle"; see *Encyclopaedia Britannica,* "James Gordon Bennett."

2. Stephen Allen, "New York Water Works—Narrative," ms in New-York Historical Society, book 1.

3. The following biographical sketch is drawn from *Reminiscences of John B. Jervis,* 1–118; F. Larkin, *John B. Jervis,* 3–60; Larry D. Lankton, "Manhattan Life Line: Engineering the Old Croton Aqueduct, 1833–1842," diss., University of Pennsylvania, 1977, 69–75; Winant, "The Hydraulics Revolution," 196–202.

4. On the West Point Foundry Association, see Stokes, *Iconography,* 5: 1599, 1684, 1688, 1697.

5. *New York Times and Evening Star,* Oct. 30, 1840; *Morning Courier and New-York Enquirer,* Nov. 3, 12, 1840; *Reminiscences of John B. Jervis,* 21n, 126n, 166; Lankton, "Manhattan Life Line," 66–68; Timothy Brewster Jervis to John Jervis, Jan. 27, Feb. 16, Mar. 25, 1836, Jervis Papers.

6. New York *Evening Post,* Mar. 18, Apr. 14, May 3, 10, 13, 19, 22, 1845; *Reminiscences of John B. Jervis,* 43n, 119–20. In 1836, the annual salary of the mayor was $3,000, the recorder and street commissioner $2,500; see Stokes, *Iconography,* 5:1615; *Manual of the Common Council,* 1843–1844. Douglass assistant engineers Edmund French and Henry Anthony were earning $125 and $100 per month, respectively; "Schedule of Pay," Sept. 1836, Jervis Papers. Many years later, Jervis asserted that he had decided as early as 1825 that the Croton would be "the true source" of New York's water; see *Reminiscences of John B. Jervis,* 164–66.

7. *Reminiscences of John B. Jervis,* 120, 121; Lankton, "Manhattan Life Line," 81; "Report to the Board of Water Commissioners," Dec. 31, 1836, Jervis Papers.

8. *Reminiscences of John B. Jervis,* 170, 171.

9. "Memo for Commissioners Meeting," Nov. 12, 1836, Jervis Papers; Jervis to Anthony, Nov. 10, 1836, Jervis to French, Nov. 10, 1836, quoted in Lankton, "Manhattan Life Line," 80–81; see also Larkin, *John B. Jervis,* 67. Douglass's September payroll included five assistant engineers, two draftsmen, two levelers, seven rodmen, and five axemen; see "Schedule of Pay," Sept. 1836, Jervis Papers.

10. Jervis to Allen, Nov. 4, 1836, Jervis Papers; "Resolutions of the Water Commissioners for Regulation of the Engineers Department," Nov. 19, 1836, Jervis Papers.

11. Lankton, "Manhattan Life Line," 78.

12. MC Minutes, 6:11–13 (March 7–17, 1833); Hunter, *Manhattan Company,* 137–39; Blake, *Water for the Cities,* 145.

13. *Reminiscences of John B. Jervis,* 122.

14. Among the other engineering volumes then owned by Jervis were Olinthus Gregory, *Mathematics for Practical Men* (London, 1825), Thomas Tredgold, *Tracts on Hydraulics* (London: J. Taylor, 1826), and the 1832 edition of the *Edinburgh Encyclopedia;* Lankton, "Manhattan Life Line," 95–96; *Reminiscences of John B. Jervis,* 40n, 130–31; Emory Kemp, "The Engineering Design and Hydraulic Concepts for the Croton Aqueduct," *The Old Croton Aqueduct,* 27; "Calculations of Discharges of Pipes," no date, Jervis Papers; also see Winant, "The Hydraulics Revolution," 206–20.

15. T[homas] J. Carmichael to Jervis, Dec. 21, 1836, Jervis Papers; Lankton, "Manhattan Life Line," 83–84, 273.

16. Of five other Douglass hires reemployed by Jervis, two were especially notable. Douglass leveler Marlborough Churchill, like Douglass a West Point graduate, rose to first assistant engineer under Jervis, and later became a leading educator and industrialist in Sing Sing; see Scharf, *History of Westchester County,* 1:542, 2:338, 344, 351, 359; Lankton, "Manhattan Life Line," 272; Churchill to Jervis, Apr. 27, July 24, 1837, Jervis Papers. Douglass rodman M. O. Davidson (whose precocious poet sisters Lucretia and Margaret died tragically and famously in their teens) rose to first assistant, married a lineal descendant of Miles Standish, and became a prominent engineer of railroads, bridges, and mines; see Scharf, *History of Westchester County,* 1:835–36, 838; *DAB,* "Lucretia Maria and Margaret Miller Davidson"; Davidson to Jervis, Jan. 12, 1839, Mar. 7, 1840, Jervis Papers.

17. New York *Evening Post,* Dec. 19, 1836; *Manual of the Common Council, 1842–43;* see also *New York Commercial Advertiser,* May 1, 1840.

18. Bd. Ald., *Doc. 84* (1836).

19. "Report to the Water Commissioners," Dec. 23, 1836, Jervis Papers; *Reminiscences of John B. Jervis,* 123, 124, 169; Lankton, "Manhattan Life Line," 91–98. In another report, Jervis detailed how the aqueduct would be carried along hillsides and across valleys, though he did not yet specify the major valley crossings at Sing Sing, Mill River, the Harlem, and Manhattan Valley; "Report to the Water Commissioners," Dec. 27, 1836, Jervis Papers.

20. "Report to the Water Commissioners," Jan. 31, 1837, Jervis Papers; "Water Commissioners' Semi-Annual Report," Jan. 1 to June 30, 1837, in Bd. Ald., *Doc. 14* (1837).

21. The appraisers were Judge William Jay, a son of late U.S. Chief Justice John Jay; lawyer, politician, and leader of the Westchester bar William Nelson; and Abraham Miller. See *Reminiscences of John B. Jervis,* 124; Scharf, *History of Westchester County,* 1:486, 487, 528, 543; Harnik, "Temperament, Temperance and Tolerance," 34. Harvey oversaw the remodeling of neighbor Washington Irving's old Dutch cottage, renamed "Sunnyside," in 1835; see Scharf, *History of Westchester County,* 2:234–36.

22. "Water Commissioners' Report," in Bd. Assts., *Doc. 24* (1837).

23. *Reminiscences of John B. Jervis,* 124.

24. "Report—Water Course & Croton Dam," Feb. 13, 1837, Jervis Papers; John B. Jervis, *Description of the Croton Aqueduct* (New York: Slamm and Guion, 1842), 5, 14–18, 30; "Water Commissioners' Semi-Annual Report," in Bd. Ald., *Doc. 14* (1837); Larkin, *John B. Jervis,* 69.

25. The plan also called for a small arch in the northern wall for passage of an existing road that crossed the kill at an angle on a low wooden bridge. "Report on Sing Sing Aqueduct Bridge, Feb. 8, 1837," Jervis Papers; Samuel Smiles, *Selections from the Lives of the Engineers* (Cambridge, Mass.: MIT Press, 1966), 330–31.

26. "Notice for letting contracts for Croton Aqueduct," Feb. 28, 1837, Jervis Papers; "Water Commissioners' Semi-Annual Report," in Bd. Ald., *Doc. 14* (1837); "Water Commissioners' Semi-Annual Report," in Bd. Ald., *Doc. 10* (1839), 140.

27. *Westchester Herald,* Mar. 7, 14, 1837; Blake, *Water for the Cities,* 148.

28. Hone, *Diary,* 253; Allen, "Memoirs," 155, 191.

29. New York *Evening Post,* May 11, June 6, 1837; Benjamin Jervis to John Jervis, Sept. 8, 1837, Jervis Papers. Whigs won control of the state Assembly in November but it was the Senate and governor who appointed the water commissioners.

30. "Aggregate Results of Proposals for Croton Aqueduct," Apr. 1837, "Results of Letting," Apr. 26, 1837, Jervis Papers; *Reminiscences of John B. Jervis,* 124; Hone, *Diary,* 262–63; Jervis, *Description of the Croton Aqueduct,* 29; see "Water Commissioners' Semi-Annual Report," in Bd. Ald., *Doc. 14* (1837).

31. The resident engineers were hired at annual salaries of $1,500 to $1,800, first assistants from $900 to $1,200, and second assistants at $600. "Water Commissioners' Semi-Annual Report," in Bd. Ald., *Doc. 14* (1837); Larkin, *John B. Jervis,* 68, 167n; Lankton, "The 'Practicable' Engineer," 23–24; Lankton, "Manhattan Life Line," 79; Larkin, "Preliminary Plans for the Old Croton Aqueduct," 24; *Reminiscences of John B. Jervis,* 124, 125; T. J. Carmichael to Jervis, May 6, 13, 1837, Jervis Papers; also see Hastie to Jervis, Nov. 20, Dec. 2, 26, 1836, Jervis Papers. Tracy would succeed Jervis as the Croton's chief engineer from 1848 to 1852, and serve again from 1870 to his death in 1875.

32. "Articles of Agreement," Mar. 1837, Jervis Papers.

33. Stott, *Workers in the Metropolis*, 143–44.

34. *Laws of New York* (1837), chap. 328. Another law formally allowed the discontinuation of planned streets in the anticipated locations of the Manhattan reservoirs; *Laws of New York* (1837), chap. 274.

35. *Westchester Herald*, May 23, 1837.

36. "Monthly Report," June 30, 1837, Jervis Papers. "Shanty" may be derived from the Irish *sean tig*, a house in disrepair; see John Ciardi, *A Browser's Dictionary* (New York: Harper & Row, 1980), 352; also, Mitford M. Mathews, *Dictionary of Americanisms on Historical Principles* (Chicago: University of Chicago, 1951), "shanty."

37. "Statement of Croton Water Works Contractors," in New York *Morning Herald*, Apr. 15, 1840; Stott, *Workers in the Metropolis*, 60, 285.

38. See Ernst, *Immigrant Life in New York City*, 105; Sister Mary Borromeo Brown, *The History of the Sisters of Providence of Saint Mary-of-the-Woods* (New York: Benziger Brothers, 1949), 314–15; David Burr (Indiana Canal Commissioner) to Gov. Noah Noble, Dec. 30, 1835, as quoted in "The Wabash & Erie Canal Through Huntington County, Indiana," at www.centralnet.net/jjosh/work; Mathews, *Dictionary of Americanisms*, "Corkonian."

39. "Water Commissioners' Semi-Annual Report," in Bd. Ald., *Doc. 14* (1837).

40. Blake, *Water for the Cities*, 150; Harnik, "Temperament, Temperance and Tolerance," 39.

41. "Water Commissioners' Semi-Annual Report," in Bd. Ald., *Doc. 55* (1838), 349–50; "Report in Relation to Clark, Yates & Co.," Aug. 31, 1837, "Resolution of Water Commissioners Calling for New Plan of Dam," Sept. 12, 1837, "Notice of Letting of Croton Dam," Oct. 3, 1837, "Abstracts of Proposals for Section #1," Nov. 6, 1837, Jervis Papers; also see Lankton, "Manhattan Life Line," 146–51.

42. "Monthly Report," July 31, 1837, "Monthly Report, Aug. 31, 1837, "Report in Relation to Claims of Young & Scott," Oct. 13, 1837, Jervis Papers; Smiles, *Selections from Lives of the Engineers*, 237–46; *Reminiscences of John B. Jervis*, 128–29.

43. *Reminiscences of John B. Jervis*, 126; Fayette Bartholemew Tower to mother, Apr. 13, 1838, Tower Letters, private collection of Helen Tower Wilson; William H. Brown, *The History of the First Steam Locomotives in America* (New York: D. Appleton and Company, 1871), chap. 1; see "Notes," Horatio Allen Papers, Hagley Museum and Library, Greenville, Delaware.

44. FBT to CT, Jan. 27, 1834, Tower Letters. After losing his father's inheritance on early business failures, Charlemagne Tower (1809–1889) became a millionaire industrialist in Philadelphia; his same-named son was a prominent financier and diplomat; see Hal Bridges, *Iron Millionaire: The Life of Charlemagne Tower* (Philadelphia: University of Pennsylvania Press, 1952); *DAB*.

45. FBT to CT, Oct. 10, 1834, Tower letters.

46. FBT to CT, July 5, 1835, Tower Letters. On his brief Chenango employment, Tower seems not to have made the acquaintance of chief engineer Jervis.

47. FBT to mother, July 31, 1836, Tower Letters. (Tower was not much taken with Harlem, where prices were high and morals low: "Every house, almost, is a resort for horse-jockeys & sporting characters from the city"; Tanner, *Canals and Railroads,* 73–74.)

48. FBT to mother, Sept. 12, 1836, Tower Letters.

49. FBT to mother, Jan. 29, Apr. 17, 1837, Tower Letters; FBT to Jervis, July 13, 1837, Jervis Papers.

50. FBT to mother, Aug. 20, 1837, Tower Letters.

51. *Westchester Herald,* Sept. 5, 1837.

52. *Westchester Spy,* Aug. 30, 1837. White Plains's first newspaper was published from 1830 to 1847; see Scharf, *History of Westchester County,* 1:738.

53. Stott, *Workers in the Metropolis,* 155–61.

54. T. J. Carmichael to Jervis, Dec. 21, 1836, Jervis Papers; "Water Commissioners' Semi-Annual Report," in Bd. Ald., *Doc. 55* (1838), 355–56.

55. "Number of men employed at Croton Aqueduct," July 28, 1837, Jervis Papers; Scharf, *History of Westchester County,* 2:72, 346; Thomas C. Cornell, *The Beginnings of the Roman Catholic Church in Yonkers* (Yonkers: The *Gazette* Press, 1883). After Cummiskey's departure, regular Catholic services did not resume in Sing Sing and Yonkers until the mid-1840s.

56. Nathaniel Bartlett Sylvester, *History of the Connecticut Valley in Massachusetts,* 2 vols. (Philadelphia: Louis H. Everts, 1879) 2:938; also see unnamed newspaper clipping, dated July 28, 1968, in "Croton Dam, Book 2," looseleaf binder, Croton Historical Society.

57. "Names of Contractors and results of letting," Sept. 5, 1837, Jervis Papers.

58. Junius Henri Browne, *The Great Metropolis: A Mirror of New York* (Hartford: American Publishing Company, 1869), 642–44; a shorter but curiously similar profile appears in Matthew Hale Smith, *Sunshine and Shadow in New York* (Hartford: J. B. Burr, 1869), 421–22; also see *A Sketch of Events in the Life of George Law* (New York: J. C. Derby, 1855); *DAB; National Cyclopedia of Biography; Who Was Who in America, Historical Volume 1607–1896.*

59. "Report on Crossing Mill River Valley," June 5, 1837, Jervis Papers.

60. "Names of Contractors and Results of Letting," Sept. 5, 1837, Jervis Papers.

61. Stokes, *Iconography,* 5:1749. Jervis later corresponded with Abert about the Harlem River crossing. Larkin, *John B. Jervis,* 69; Tanner, *Canals and Railroads,* 158–59.

62. FBT to mother, Nov. 5, 1837, Tower Letters.

63. *Hudson River Chronicle,* Nov. 14, 1837. This was the fourth issue of Wells's weekly, which he edited until Governor Seward appointed him county surrogate in 1840. "He wrote with force and facility," observed Westchester historian J. Thomas Scharf, "but his impetuous nature led him often into mistakes which a more prudent journalist might have avoided." Scharf, *History of Westchester County,* 1:544, 627–28, 652, 2:354.

64. New York *Evening Post,* Dec. 2, 1837; "Statement of Croton Water Works Contractors," New York *Morning Herald,* Apr. 15, 1840.

65. *Hudson River Chronicle,* Dec. 19, 1837.

66. Bd. Ald., *Doc. 55* (1838), 345–445, which includes: "Water Commissioners' Semi-Annual Report, Jan. 2, 1838" (345–381), "Opinion of Counsel. . . ." (383–88), "Report of the Chief Engineer in Relation to the Plan for Crossing Harlem River, Dec. 12, 1837" (389–406), "Report in relation to the Location of the Line of the Croton Aqueduct, from Harlaem River to the Reservoirs. . . , Dec. 27, 1837" (407–35), plus various drawings and tabular statements. Relative to the following discussion, also see Jervis, *Description of the Croton Aqueduct,* 22–28; Tanner, *Canals and Railroads,* 66–67; Profile of lower part of Croton Aqueduct, Jervis Library; "Specifications for Construction of Foundation for Iron Pipe across Manhattan Valley," "Specifications for Constructing Aqueduct Bridge across Clendinning Valley," "Specifications for Receiving Reservoir at York Hill," "Specifications for Building a Reservoir on Murray Hill," Sept. 1838, Jervis Papers.

67. Because much had been invested in the original decision on the Schenectady bridges, Jervis's recommendation was eventually ignored. Larkin, *John B. Jervis,* 56–60; David Jacobs and Anthony E. Neville, *Bridges, Canals & Tunnels* (New York: American Heritage Publishing Company, 1968), 15; Tanner, *Canals and Railroads,* 52–53; Louis Leonard Tucker, ed., *A Knickerbocker Tour of New York State, 1822* (Albany: New York State Library, 1968), 95, 130 n.96; *Reminiscences of John B. Jervis,* 113.

68. The six-piered Schuylkill railroad viaduct, opened in 1834, was 984 feet long, thirty-eight feet high, and built of wood. Tanner, *Canals and Railroads,* 114, 116.

TEN   *Taking the High Road?*

1. *Westchester Herald,* Jan. 16, 1838; FBT to mother, Jan. 29, 1838, Tower Letters.

2. *Westchester Herald,* Jan. 16, 1838; *Hudson River Chronicle,* Jan. 16, 1838.

3. *Westchester Herald,* Jan. 16, 1838; *Hudson River Chronicle,* Jan. 16, 1838.

4. *Hudson River Chronicle,* Jan. 16, 1838; Jervis to Van Zandt & Crandall, Jan. 16, 1838, Jervis Papers.

5. FBT to mother, Jan. 29, Mar. 3, 1838, Tower Letters.

6. Blake, *Water for the Cities,* 152.

7. Scharf, *History of Westchester County,* 1:797, 798, 828; *Hudson River Chronicle,* Mar. 27, 1838. Ironically, Lewis Gouverneur Morris's late uncle Lewis Morris had won state permission in 1790 for the bridge that John Coles later built, the first obstruction of the lower Harlem.

8. *New York American,* Mar. 9, 15, 1838; New York *Evening Post,* Mar. 13, 29, 1838. Also see *Journal of Commerce,* Mar. 12, 1838; Larkin, *John B. Jervis,* 73–74.

9. Blake, *Water for the Cities,* 154.

10. Larkin, *John B. Jervis,* 74; Lankton, "Manhattan Life Line," 221; Blake, *Water for the Cities,* 154.

11. Richard Riker, running as a Conservative, won nearly four hundred votes; *Encyclopedia of NYC,* "mayoralty"; Stokes, *Iconography,* 5:1752.

12. Committee on Roads and Canals, "Report on Carrying the Aqueduct across the Harlaem River, April 23, 1838," in Bd. Ald., *Doc. 88* (1838); Committee on Roads and Canals, "Minority Report on Carrying the Aqueduct across the Harlaem River, May 7, 1838," in Bd. Ald., *Doc. 99* (1838).

13. "Communication from the Water Commissioners to the Common Council, May 8, 1838," in Bd. Ald., *Doc. 2* (1838).

14. *Laws of New York* (1838), chap. 127.

15. Allen, "Memoirs," 191; "Water Commissioners' Semi-Annual Report," in Bd. Ald., *Doc. 55* (1838), 346; "Expenditures for the New York City Water Supply from 1829 to 1881," in "The New York Water Supply," Water Supply Pamphlets, 1830–1920, bound volume, Engineering Societies Library, New York; similar construction but lower debt figures are found in New York City Board of Water Supply, *Water Supply of New York City 1832–1922, Financial Review* (New York, 1924), statement 2, Engineering Societies Library. Avoiding the depressed domestic market, the city managed to unload $1.2 million worth of water bonds in Europe between 1838 and 1840; Bd. Assts., *Procs.,* 15:366–68.

16. *Laws of New York* (1838), chap. 107; Allen, "Memoirs," 191. Allen's pipe cost figure of $400,000 seems exaggerated; the highest official estimate of all costs related to the 13th Street system before 1835 is $267,700 (see "Aggregate Cost to the City and to Property," in "The New York Water Supply").

17. *Westchester Herald,* Mar. 13, 1838.

18. H. T. Anthony to Jervis, Feb. 20, 1838, as quoted in Harnik, "Temperament, Temperance and Tolerance," 37; H. T. Anthony to Jervis, Jan. 14, 1839, Jervis Papers. The farm was finally sold in 1848, laid out as the village of Dearman in 1850, and renamed Irvington by the residents in 1854; see Scharf, *History of Westchester County,* 190; Lederer, *Place Names of Westchester County,* 39, 73.

19. "Water Commissioners' Semi-Annual Report," in Bd. Ald., *Doc. 5* (1838), 49–50.

20. Larkin, *John B. Jervis,* 166, n.42; see also 169, n.23.

21. "Statement of Croton Water Works Contractors," in New York *Morning Herald,* Apr. 15, 1840.

22. *Westchester Herald,* Apr. 10, 1838; "Water Commissioners' Semi-Annual Report," in Bd. Ald., *Doc. 5* (1838).

23. Horatio Allen to Jervis, Apr. 10, 1838, Jervis Papers.

24. Larkin, *John B. Jervis,* 166, n.42; FBT to CT, Apr. 13, 1838, Tower Letters.

25. FBT to CT, Apr. 13, 1838, Tower Letters.

26. *Westchester Herald,* May 1, 1838; also see *Hudson River Chronicle,* May 1, 1838. The following material draws from both accounts.

27. French to Jervis, Apr. 25, 1838, Jervis Papers; *Hudson River Chronicle,* May 15, 1838.

28. "Water Commissioners' Semi-Annual Report," Bd. Ald., *Doc 5* (1838), 49–50; *Reminiscences of John B. Jervis,* 126; "Report," Dec. 27, 1837, "List of Contractors," May 7, 1838, "Statement of Progress," June 25, 1839, Jervis Papers.

29. *Hudson River Chronicle,* June 5, 1838; *Westchester Herald,* June 5, 1838.

30. *Westchester Herald,* June 12, 1838.

31. *Hudson River Chronicle,* June 19, 26, 1838.

32. "Statement of Contractors," New York *Morning Herald,* Apr. 15, 1840.

33. FBT to mother, July 3, 1838, Tower Letters.

34. Stokes, *Iconography,* 5:1657, 1676; *Encyclopedia of NYC,* "Harlem River Ship Canal [U.S. Ship Canal]"; *Laws of New York* (1838), chap. 311; Blake, *Water for the Cities,* 154.

35. Blake, *Water for the Cities,* 155; Larkin, *John B. Jervis,* 74; Lankton, "Manhattan Life Line," 223.

36. New York *Evening Post,* Aug. 9, 15, 16, 25, Sept. 7, 1838.

37. Morris's legal advice proved correct, though the matter never left the state courts. William Renwick, who had succeeded bankrupt Robert Macomb as owner of the dam and bridge twenty years earlier, sued Morris for damages; Morris prevailed at trial and on appeal, and the Court of Errors (then New York's highest court) affirmed in 1844: "The Harlem River is an arm of the sea and a public navigable river; it was a *public nuisance* to obstruct the navigation thereof without authority of law." The dam was never repaired, but the bridge, with a new draw for masted vessels, survived until 1858, when a new turntable bridge was ordered by the legislature; it was another forty years before the present steel bridge was completed. *Renwick vs. Morris,* 7 Hill 575; Scharf, *History of Westchester County,* 1:797–99; *Encyclopedia of NYC,* "Macombs Dam," "Macombs Dam Bridge"; Stokes, *Iconography,* 3:706, 926.

38. Stokes, *Iconography,* 3:706. The notice ran in September and October issues of the New York *Evening Post* and the *Westchester Herald.*

39. "Abstract of Propositions," Oct. 23, 1838, "List of Contractors," Oct. 27, 1838, "Form of Contract for Cast Iron Pipes," Dec. 1838, Jervis Papers; Stokes, *Iconography,* 5:1754; also, *Reminiscences of John B. Jervis,* 126. The West Point Foundry moved its shops fifty miles up the Hudson from the city to Cold Spring, New York, in 1839; see John Matthew to Jervis, Aug. 27, 1842, Jervis Papers.

40. "Water Commissioners' Semi-Annual Report," in Bd. Ald., *Doc. 25* (1838); reference to October 22, 1838, notice is in "Report on Section 86 Contract," July 25, 1839, Jervis Papers.

41. *Westchester Herald,* July 24, 1838; FBT to CT, Sept. 12, 1838, Tower Letters.

42. FBT to CT, Sept. 12, 1838, Tower Letters. The 20 million gallons is Tower's figure; actual gaugings that summer by Horatio Allen indicated over 27 million gallons, much closer to the 30 million gallon worst-drought estimate of Albert Stein. "Water Commissioners' Semi-Annual Report," in Bd. Ald., *Doc. 25* (1838), 246.

43. FBT to mother, Sept. 30, 1838, Tower Letters.

44. FBT to CT, Sept. 30, 1838, Tower Letters.

45. Seward became New York's first non-Democratic governor since Federalist John Jay at the turn of the century. The Whigs also won broad control of the state Assembly.

46. FBT to CT, Nov. 15, 1838; FBT to mother, Jan. 28, 1839, Tower Letters.

47. "Statement of Contractors," New York *Morning Herald,* Apr. 15, 1840.

48. "Water Commissioners' Semi-Annual Report," in Bd. Ald., *Doc. 25* (1838).

49. "General Report," Dec. 26, 1838, Jervis Papers; Lankton, "Manhattan Life Line," 157.

50. "The Diaria of freedom . . . ," broadside (New York, 1839)

51. *Westchester Herald,* Jan. 29, 1839; "Area of the freshet at Croton Dam in Winter 1839," Jervis Papers.

52. FBT to mother, Mar. 7, 1839, Tower Letters.

53. "Report of Tour of Line; and of New Organization of Engineer Corps," Mar. 8, 1839, Jervis Papers.

54. "Statement of Contractors," New York *Morning Herald,* Apr. 15, 1840; Blake, *Water for the Cities,* 151.

55. Stokes, *Iconography,* 5:1757; *Encyclopedia of NYC,* "mayoralty"; Hone, *Diary,* 388.

56. "Water Commissioners' Semi-Annual Report," in Bd. Ald., *Doc. 10* (1839), 118–21; *Reminiscences of John B. Jervis,* 127; *Laws of New York* (1839), chap. 318.

57. Lankton, "Manhattan Life Line," 225; Larkin, *John B. Jervis,* 75; Blake, *Water for the Cities,* 157.

58. "Water Commissioners' Semi-Annual Report," in Bd. Ald., *Doc. 10* (1839), 121–23; *Reminiscences of John B. Jervis,* 127; "Statement of the Progress of Work on the 4th Division of the Croton Aqueduct, up to 25th June 1839," Jervis Papers. Ellsworth & Mix did pursue a settlement for the breaking of its contract; see "Report on Section 86 contract," July 25, 1839, Jervis Papers.

59. "Report of the Chief Engineer on Plans for Crossing Harlaem River, June 1, 1839," in Bd. Ald., *Doc. 10* (1839), 151–52. See James Dugan, *The Great Iron Ship* (New York: Harper & Brothers, 1953), 27–29. The Wapping-Rotherhithe (or Thames) Tunnel was a success; the trains of the East London Railway still run through it.

60. Larkin, *John B. Jervis,* 104; *Reminiscences of John B. Jervis,* 8.

61. "Report of the Chief Engineer on Plans for Crossing Harlaem River, June 1, 1839," in Bd. Ald., *Doc. 10* (1839), 143–58.

62. "Water Commissioners' Semi-Annual Report," in Bd. Ald., *Doc. 10* (1839), 123–27; also see "Resolution of Board of Water Commissioners," June 8, 1839, "Notice for Harlem Aqueduct Bridge," June 1839, "Specifications on Constructing an Aqueduct Bridge across the Harlem River," July 1839, Jervis Papers; Jervis, *Description of the Croton Aqueduct,* 19–22; *Reminiscences of John B. Jervis,* 127; Larkin, *John B. Jervis,* 75–76.

63. Allen, "Memoirs," 165; *Reminiscences of John B. Jervis,* 143.

64. FBT to Julius Tower, June 12, 1839, Tower Letters.

65. From January to May, the labor gang had risen from 2,382 to 3,358; after the peak in June, only 3,328 were employed by late July, and the number continued to drop as sections were completed. "Water Commissioner's Semi-Annual Report," in Bd. Ald., *Doc. 10* (1839), 135; "Report of the Chief Engineer on the progress of the work on the Croton Aqueduct," Dec. 24, 1839, in Bd. Ald., *Doc. 42* (1840), 469.

66. *Westchester Herald,* May 21, 1839.

67. *Westchester Herald,* June 4, 1839.

68. Stokes, *Iconography,* 5:1758; Dunshee, *As You Pass By,* 230–31; Haswell, *Reminiscences,* 15.

69. Scharf, *History of Westchester County,* 2:469; *Westchester Herald,* July 9, 1839.

70. Edward K. Spann, *The New Metropolis: New York City, 1840–1857* (New York: Columbia University Press, 1980) 46–47.

71. "Circular to Resident Engineers," July 16, 1839, Jervis Papers. The slowdown compelled first assistant engineer J. J. Zabriskie, then employed on the second division, to quit the project; Zabriskie to Jervis, July 17, 1839, Jervis Papers; "Circular to Resident Engineers in Relation to Payment in Corporation Bonds," July 26, 1839, Jervis Papers; "Statement of the Croton Water Work Contractors," in New York *Morning Herald,* Apr. 15, 1840.

72. *Reminiscences of John B. Jervis,* 128; *Westchester Herald,* Aug. 6, 1839; Blake, *Water for the Cities,* 156; Larkin, *John B. Jervis,* 76. Ferrell dropped out of the work in 1840; see "Estimated Cost of 4th Division and of Work Remaining," Dec. 23, 1840, Jervis Papers.

73. FBT to mother, July 2, 1839, Tower Letters; Helen Tower Wilson, telephone conversation with author, Dec. 18, 1997 (Mrs. Wilson is the great-great-granddaughter of Fayette and second wife Ann Regina Phelps, Elizabeth's sister). The wedding ceremony was at the famous Troy Female Seminary, founded by Elizabeth's in-law Emma Willard; FBT to mother, Aug. 1, 1839, FBT to CT, Aug. 30, 1839, FBT to mother, Jan. 29, 1840, Tower Letters.

74. *Westchester Herald,* Aug. 20, 1839.

75. *Reminiscences of John B. Jervis,* 128–29.

76. Scharf, *History of Westchester County,* 2:307.

77. *Westchester Herald,* Dec. 17, 24, 1839, Feb. 18, 1840; "Statement of Contractors," in New York *Morning Herald,* Apr. 15, 1840; "Water Commissioners' Supplemental Report," in Bd. Ald., *Doc. 65* (1840).

78. "Water Commissioners' Semi-Annual Report," and "Report of the Chief Engineer . . . ," in Bd. Ald., *Doc. 42* (1840); "Estimate of Work Remaining to be Done on 4th Division," Dec. 23, 1839, "Abstract Shewing the Estimated Value of Work Done . . . from December 25th 1839 to the 20th of March 1840," Jervis Papers; Jervis, *Description of the Croton Aqueduct,* 12–14; *Reminiscences of John B. Jervis,* 129–30.

79. *Manual of the Common Council, 1842–43,* 104–5, 254; Stokes, *Iconography,* 5:1761, 1762; Spann, *New Metropolis,* 429.

80. New York *Morning Herald,* July 18, Sept. 4, 1839 (the paper's name changed from the *Herald* to the *Morning Herald* in 1837, and to the *New York Herald* in September 1840).

81. Allen, "Memoirs," 168–69. Among the Whig losers in the city was Senate hopeful Philip Hone; Hone, *Diary,* 431.

82. Undated item from *New York Whig,* reprinted in *Westchester Herald,* Feb. 18, 1840.

83. Tanner, *Canals and Railroads,* 59–70; *DAB,* "Henry Schenck Tanner."

ELEVEN   Filling the "Big Teapot"

1. "Expenditures for the New York Water Supply from 1829 to 1881," in "The New York Water Supply." A very similar construction figure, but lower debt service number appears in the 1924 Board of Water Supply financial review.

2. The work was to be completed by mid-October 1841. "Water Commissioners' Supplemental Report," in Bd. Ald., *Doc. 65* (1840).

3. New York *Morning Herald,* Feb. 12, 1840.

4. Hunter, *Manhattan Company,* 139n, 209–20; Hone, *Diary,* 467; New York *Morning Herald,* Feb. 12, 1840; *Report of the Commissioners Appointed to Investigate the Condition of the Manhattan Company . . . March 14, 1840* (New York, 1840); *New York American,* Mar. 18, 1840.

5. Allen, "Memoirs," 170.

6. Stott, *Workers in the Metropolis,* 42; Haswell, *Reminiscences,* 232; Bonner, *New York, The World's Metropolis,* 628; Beach, *Wealth and Biography,* 6th ed. (1845); *Reminiscences of John B. Jervis,* 142, 157.

7. *Reminiscences of John B. Jervis,* 155–56.

8. "Water Commissioners' Supplemental Report," in Bd. Ald., *Doc. 65* (1840).

9. Joshua Purdy to Water Commissioners, Mar. 21, 1840, Jervis Papers. Jervis discounted Purdy's claims; Jervis to Water Commissioners, July 9, 1840, Jervis Papers.

10. *The Complete Works of Washington Irving,* gen ed. Richard Dilworth Rust (Boston: Twayne, 1982), 25:48–49.

11. The following account is derived principally from the New York *Evening Post,* Apr. 6, 7, 23, 1840, and the New York *Morning Herald,* Apr. 13, 1840.

12. "Statement of the Croton Water Work Contractors," in New York *Morning Herald,* Apr. 15, 1840.

13. William Jervis to JBJ, Apr. 16, 1840, Jervis Papers.

14. *New York Commercial Advertiser,* Apr. 19, 1840; *Westchester Herald,* Apr. 28, 1840.

15. Blake, *Water for the Cities,* 158–59.

16. "Report on the Receiving Reservoir," Apr. 28, 1840, "Report on Clendening Bridges," May 26, 1840, Jervis to Water Commissioners, June 8, July 28, 1840, "Resolution," June 30, July 10, 23, Jervis Papers.

17. *Laws of New York* (1840), chap. 175.

18. Bd. Ald., *Doc. 59* (1840); Bd. Ald., *Doc. 72* (1840); Blake, *Water for the Cities,* 161. Cooper had served as an assistant alderman from 1828 to 1831.

19. Hone, *Diary,* 485; *Westchester Herald,* June 16, 1840; Larkin, *John B. Jervis,* 104; *Reminiscences of John B. Jervis,* 8.

20. *Reminiscences of John B. Jervis,* 143–47; Horatio Allen to Water Commissioners, June 9, 1840, Jervis Papers; "Water Commissioners' Semi-Annual Report, March 20 to Dec. 31, 1840," in Bd. Ald., *Doc. 39* (1841), 516, 550–52; Lankton, "Manhattan Life Line," 241–45.

21. New York *Evening Post,* July 1, 1840; "Resolution," July 21, Aug. 11, 1840, Jervis Papers; "Water Commissioners' Semi-Annual Report," in Bd. Ald., *Doc. 39* (1841), 518–21. The contractor was eventually reimbursed $4,500 for materials and lost income. "Water Commissioners' Semi-Annual Report," in Bd. Ald., *Doc. 55* (1842), 370.

22. Jervis to Water Commissioners, July 20, 1840, Jervis Papers; Blake, *Water for the Cities,* 160, 161.

23. "Communications of the Comptroller, the Water Commissioners, and the Croton Aqueduct Committee, &c. on the subject of the ordinance to amend the ordinance to instruct the water commissioners . . . ," in Bd. Assts., *Doc. 70* (1840); "Water Commissioners' Semi-Annual Report," in Bd. Ald., *Doc. 39* (1841), 526–29.

24. *Laws of New York* (1841), chap. 306; *DAB,* "Samuel Vaughan Merrick."

25. Stokes, *Iconography,* 5:1754; Hone, *Diary,* 505; Haswell, *Reminiscences,* 379–80; New York *Evening Post,* Jan. 18, 1841; John Russell Bartlett, *The Dictionary of Americanisms* (New York: Crescent Books, 1987 [1849]), "pipe-laying"; *Webster's Revised Unabridged Dictionary of the English Language* (Springfield, Mass.: G. & C. Merriam Company, 1913), "pipelayer," "pipelaying"; *The New Shorter Oxford English Dictionary,* ed. Lesley Brown (New York: Oxford University Press, 1993), "pipe-lay," "pipe-layer."

26. *New York American,* July 18, 1840. Douglass's communications, dated Oct. 10, 1840, were subsequently published in the *Morning Courier and New-York Enquirer,* Oct. 28, 1840, and the *New York Times and Evening Star,* Oct. 30, 1840.

27. *Reminiscences of John B. Jervis,* 167.

28. *Morning Courier and New-York Enquirer,* Nov. 3, 1840.

29. *Morning Courier and New-York Enquirer,* Nov. 12, 1840.

30. See, for example, *New Yorker,* 10, 1 (Sept. 19, 1840).

31. *Westchester Herald,* Oct. 20, Dec. 8, 1840; Jervis, *Description of the Croton Aqueduct,* 14–15.

32. "Report of the Majority of the Special Committee, on the Subject of the Ordinance Creating the Aqueduct Department, &c. and to Amend the Ordinance to Instruct the Water Commissioners," in Bd. Ald., *Doc. 32* (1840).

33. "Water Commissioners' Semi-Annual Report," in Bd. Ald., *Doc. 39* (1841), 526–31; *New York Commercial Advertiser,* Mar. 15, 1841.

34. *Westchester Herald,* Dec. 8, 22, 29, 1840; *New York Commercial Advertiser,* Jan. 11, 1841.

35. The following account is based on: *Hudson River Chronicle,* Jan. 12, 1841; *New York Commercial Advertiser,* Jan. 11, 1841; *New York Herald,* Jan. 9, 11, 12, 1841; "Water Commissioners' Semi-Annual Report," in Bd. Ald., *Doc. 39* (1841), 532–36, 553–54; Scharf, *History of Westchester County,* 2:462–63, 469; Alvah P. French, *History of Westchester County, New York,* 5 vols. (New York: Lewis Historical Publishing Co., 1925), 1:347–48; Renoda Hoffman, "The Night the Dam Broke," *Westchester Historian,* 44, 4 (Fall 1968): 87–89.

36. *Reminiscences of John B. Jervis,* 133.

37. *Hudson River Chronicle,* Jan. 12, 1841; *New York Commercial Advertiser,* Jan. 11, 1841; Jervis, *Description of the Croton Aqueduct,* 16.

38. Scharf, *History of Westchester County,* 2:469.

39. Roger Panetta, "The Croton Aqueduct and Suburbanization of Westchester," *The Old Croton Aqueduct,* 44–46.

40. "Water Commissioners' Semi-Annual Report," in Bd. Ald., *Doc. 39* (1841), 535–36, 553–54.

41. *Reminiscences of John B. Jervis,* 134.

42. Tower had become something of a philosopher about engineering disasters: "Experience is a pretty good school and Engineers can avail themselves of its advantages, and the beauty of it is—those who employ them pay the expense of those experiments." FBT to CT, Jan. 21, 1841, Tower Letters.

43. FBT to Julius Tower, Oct. 19, 1840, FBT to CT, Jan. 21, 1841, FBT to mother, Feb. 3, 1841, Tower Letters.

44. FBT to CT, Jan. 21, 1841, Tower Letters.

45. "Water Commissioners' Semi-Annual Report," in Bd. Ald., *Doc. 39* (1841), 518–26.

46. *Reminiscences of John B. Jervis,* 159.

47. *Reminiscences of John B. Jervis,* 10–11, 134–35; Jervis, *Description of the Croton Aqueduct,* 16–17; Winant, "The Hydraulics Revolution," 245–49.

48. "Contract and Specifications for Extending the Masonry and Rebuilding the Embankment of the Croton Dam," 1841, Jervis Papers. Expert stonemason James Delaney returned from projects in Massachusetts for the dam rebuilding; Sylvester, *History of the Connecticut Valley in Massachusetts,* 2:938.

49. *Reminiscences of John B. Jervis,* 139–42.

50. Hone, *Diary,* 540.

51. *Laws of New York (1841),* chap. 306. In 1841 $2.6 million was spent, including roughly half a million dollars on bond interest and discounts; see "Expenditures for the New York Water Supply from 1829 to 1881," in "The New York Water Supply"; "Water Supply of New York City 1832–1922"; *Manual of the Common Council, 1842–43,* 48.

52. *Reminiscences of John B. Jervis,* 138, Jervis, *Description of the Croton Aqueduct,* 17; Edmund French to JBJ, Oct. 30, Dec. 17, 24, 1841, Jervis Papers.

53. *Reminiscences of John B. Jervis,* 131–32, 151–52.

54. Ibid., 151–52.

55. Hone, *Diary,* 570–71.

56. Hone, *Diary,* 572.

57. Allen, "Memoirs," 191.

58. Haswell, *Reminiscences,* 381; *New York Commercial Advertiser,* Jan. 29, 1842.

59. FBT to mother, Dec. 29, 1841, Tower Letters.

60. *Laws of New York (1842),* chap. 225. Allen's appointment deeply annoyed Jervis, who had been considered for the position. Allen later publicly explained that he would not have sought the job if Jervis had wanted it but knew that Jervis would not have taken it. Privately, Jervis questioned the motives of his subordinate, who, Jervis believed, was well aware of Jervis's concern that Allen's new title was too similar to his own; see Larkin, *John B. Jervis,* 80; *Manual of the Common Council, 1842–43.* In any case, Allen held the office only briefly before joining the great Novelty Iron Works for the next thirty years. Established in 1830 along the East River, Novelty grew into the region's largest employer by midcentury, with nearly a thousand workers, a sprawling five-acre factory, and a million dollars in annual business. Stott, *Workers in the Metropolis,* 31, 43–45, 47–48, 126–27, 200; *Encyclopedia of NYC,* "Novelty Ironworks"; Robert Greenhalgh Albion, *The Rise of New York Port* (New York: Charles Scribner's Sons, 1970 [1939]), 149–50; Spann, *New Metropolis,* 405.

61. "Water Commissioners' Semi-Annual Report," in Bd. Ald., *Doc. 9* (1842), 81; New York *Evening Post,* June 13, 1842; *New York Commercial Advertiser,* June 14, 1842.

62. *New York Commercial Advertiser,* June 24, 1842. When the water depth in the aqueduct was subsequently raised to four feet, the velocity increased to two miles per hour, some 15 percent greater than expected and a significant vindication for Jervis. "Water Commissioners' Semi-Annual Report," in Bd. Ald., *Doc. 9* (1842), 81–82; "Report on the General State of the Work on the Croton Aqueduct," in Bd. Ald., *Doc. 9* (1842), 99–100.

63. *New World,* 5:16 (July 2, 1842); *Brother Jonathan,* 2:10 (July 2, 1842); "Water Commissioners' Semi-Annual Report," in Bd. Ald., *Doc. 9* (1842), 82–83; *The Diary of George Templeton Strong,* ed. Allan Nevins and Milton Halsey Thomas, 4 vols. (New York: Macmillan, 1952), 1:184. Also see *New York Commercial Advertiser,* June 28, 1842; New York *Evening Post,* June 28, 29, 1842; Hone, *Diary,* 608–9.

64. FBT to "brother," June 28, 1842, Tower Letters.

65. *New York Commercial Advertiser,* July 5, 1842; FBT to Helen M. Phelps, July 5, 1842, as quoted in Lankton, "Manhattan Life Line," 254–55.

66. *New York Commercial Advertiser,* July 5, 1842.

67. FBT to CT, July 14, 1842, Tower Letters; Jervis, *Description of the Croton Aqueduct,* 19–22, 29. The single twenty-two-inch line resting on the cofferdam embankment was soon replaced by a thirty-six-inch pipe.

68. Hone, *Diary,* 609–10 (July 12, 1842).

69. New York *Evening Post,* July 8, Aug. 12, 1842; Stott, *Workers in the Metropolis,* 65, 198; Stokes, *Iconography,* 5:1776.

70. Strong, *Diary,* 1:184.

71. New York *Evening Post,* Sept. 28, 1842.

72. Stokes, *Iconography,* 5:1777.

73. Strong, *Diary,* 1:186; New York *Evening Post,* Oct. 12, 1842; also see *New York Commercial Advertiser,* Oct. 3, 1842.

74. Lydia Maria Francis Child, *Letters from New-York* (New York: Charles S. Francis & Co., 1843), 200–201.

75. See entries in *DAB, Famous American Women, Oxford Companion to American Literature;* also *Encyclopedia of NYC,* "popular fiction."

76. Child, *Letters from New-York,* 200–201; also see *New York Herald,* Oct. 13, 1842.

77. Strong, *Diary,* 1:188.

78. Hone, *Diary,* 624 (Oct. 12, 1842).

79. *New York Commercial Advertiser,* Oct. 15, 1842; Strong, *Diary,* 1:188–89; also see *The Ladies Companion* (November 1842): 52.

80. New York *Evening Post,* Oct. 15, 1842.

81. *New York Commercial Advertiser,* Oct. 15, 1842.

82. *New York Weekly Plebeian,* Oct. 15, 1842; Allen, "Memoirs," 200–201.

83. *New World,* Oct. 22, 1842; *New York Herald,* Oct. 15, 1842.

84. Hone, *Diary,* 625.

85. Child, *Letters from New-York,* 200.

EPILOGUE   *New York's Water from Then to Now*

1. Child, *Letters from New-York,* 30–31, 168–69.

2. *American Agriculturalist,* 4, 1 (January 1845): 15; New York *Evening Post,* Mar. 18, Apr. 14, May 3, 10, 13, 19, 1845; "Report of the Celebration," in Bd. Ald., *Docs.* (1863), 124–35.

3. Strong, *Diary,* 1:203–4, 210, 226; New York *Evening Post,* June 26, Dec. 14, 1844; "Report of Croton Aqueduct Board on Paying off the Water Debt," in Bd. Ald., *Doc. 58* (Dec. 27, 1842).

4. Strong, *Diary,* 1:265; also Hone, *Diary,* 740–44; Stokes, *Iconography,* 5:1792; *Encyclopedia of NYC,* "firefighting"; Spann, *New Metropolis,* 120.

5. Twenty-five hundred New Yorkers died from cholera in 1854 and only eleven hundred in 1866 during the next and last global cholera epidemic to have a significant effect on New York. Duffy, *History of Public Health in New York City,* 290, 441–46, 588; Croton Aqueduct Board, *Annual Reports,* 1852, 1853.

6. Under the direction of the Croton Aqueduct Department, the first hundred miles of sewers were laid from 1849 to 1854; *Manual of the Common Council* (1854), 226. *Famous First Facts,* 449; Mathews, *Dictionary of Americanisms,* "Croton."

7. Croton Aqueduct Department, 2d quarterly report, 1876; *The American Year-Book and National Register for 1869* (Hartford, 1869), 518; "The New York Water Supply"; Lankton, "Manhattan Life Line," 263–65; also see James Dabney McCabe, *A Comprehensive View of Our Country and Its Resources* (Philadelphia: Hubbard Brothers, 1876), 1171; Stokes, *Iconography,* 5:1976; Blake, *Water for the Cities,* 277.

8. Robin Marx and Eric A. Goldstein, *A Guide to New York City's Reservoirs and Their Watersheds* (Natural Resources Defense Council, 1993) 24–60; Stokes, *Iconography,* 5:1978, 1980–81, 2002, 2005, 2011; Blake, *Water for the Cities,* 277.

9. On Tower, see Peter Hastie to John Jervis, Dec. 3, 1842, FBT to Jervis, Oct. 13, 1845, Jervis Papers; F. B. Tower, *Illustrations of the Croton Aqueduct* (New York and London: Wiley and Putnam, 1843); "Pure and Wholesome Water, Fayette B. Tower and the Croton Aqueduct," exhibit, Museum of the City of New York, October 1942, biographical materials; *New-York Historical Society's Dictionary of Artists in America, 1564–1860,* ed. George C. Groce and David H. Wallace (New Haven: Yale University Press, 1957); Helen Tower Wilson to author, Dec. 18, 1997.

Index